ArtScroll Mishnah Series®

משנה

A rabbinic commentary to the Six Orders of the Mishnah

Rabbi Nosson Scherman / Rabbi Meir Zlotowitz

General Editors

A PROJECT OF THE

Mesorah Heritage Foundation

ששה סדרי משנה

THE COMMENTARY HAS BEEN NAMED **YAD AVRAHAM**
AS AN EVERLASTING MEMORIAL AND SOURCE OF MERIT
FOR THE *NESHAMAH* OF
אברהם יוסף ע"ה בן הר"ר אליעזר הכהן גליק נ"י
AVRAHAM YOSEF GLICK ע"ה
WHOSE LIFE WAS CUT SHORT ON 3 TEVES, 5735

Published by
Mesorah Publications, ltd

the mishnah

ARTSCROLL MISHNAH SERIES / A NEW TRANSLATION WITH A COMMENTARY **YAD AVRAHAM** ANTHOLOGIZED FROM TALMUDIC SOURCES AND CLASSIC COMMENTATORS.

INCLUDES THE COMPLETE HEBREW TEXT OF THE COMMENTARY OF **RAV OVADIAH BERTINORO**

FIRST EDITION
First Impression . . . May 1987
Second Impression . . . February 1992
Third Impression . . . November 2001
REVISED EDITION
First Impression . . . January 2008
Second Impression . . . June 2010

Published and Distributed by
MESORAH PUBLICATIONS, Ltd.
4401 Second Avenue
Brooklyn, New York 11232

Distributed in Europe by
LEHMANNS
Unit E, Viking Business Park
Rolling Mill Road
Jarrow, Tyne & Wear NE32 3DP
England

Distributed in Australia & New Zealand by
GOLDS WORLD OF JUDAICA
3-13 William Street
Balaclava, Melbourne 3183
Victoria Australia

Distributed in Israel by
SIFRIATI / A. GITLER — BOOKS
6 Hayarkon Street
Bnei Brak 51127

Distributed in South Africa by
KOLLEL BOOKSHOP
Ivy Common 105 William Road
Norwood 2192, Johannesburg, South Africa

THE ARTSCROLL MISHNAH SERIES®
SEDER NEZIKIN Vol. II(a); *SANHEDRIN*

ISBN 10: 0-89906-295-4
ISBN 13: 978-0-89906-295-2

Typography by Compuscribe at ArtScroll Studios, Ltd.
4401 Second Avenue / Brooklyn, NY 11232 / (718) 921-9000

Printed in the United States of America by Noble Book Press Corp.
Bound by Sefercraft Inc., Quality Bookbinders, Brooklyn, N.Y.

Seder Nezikin Vol. II(a):
מסכת סנהדרין
Tractate Sanhedrin

Translation and anthologized commentary by
Rabbi Matis Roberts

Edited by
Rabbi Yehezkel Danziger

The Publishers are grateful to
YAD AVRAHAM INSTITUTE
and the
MESORAH HERITAGE FOUNDATION
for their efforts in the publication of the
ARTSCROLL MISHNAH SERIES

This volume is dedicated
to the memory of

סימא בת ר׳ שמעון ע״ה

Sima Rabinowitz

נפטרה ד׳ אייר, תשמ״ז

Devoted mother, wife and sister.
Living modestly and quietly,
she was appreciated by her friends
and relatives for her sensitivity
and concern for the feelings and needs of others.

תהא נפשה צרורה בצרור החיים

The Zweig and Steinmetz families

PATRONS OF THE MISHNAH

With generosity, vision, and devotion to the perpetuation of Torah study, the following patrons have dedicated individual volumes of the Mishnah.

SEDER ZERAIM

BERACHOS:

In memory of

ר׳ אברהם יוסף ז״ל ב״ר אליעזר הכהן ודבורה נ״י

Avraham Yosef Glick ז״ל

PEAH:

In memory of

הגאון הרב ר׳ אהרן ב״ר מאיר יעקב זצ״ל

Rabbi Aron Zlotowitz זצ״ל

והרבנית פרומא בת ר׳ חיים צבי ע״ה

Rebbetzin Fruma Zlotowitz ע״ה

DEMAI:

Chesky and Sheindy Paneth and family

In memory of their parents

ר׳ אברהם מרדכי בן ר׳ שרגא פייוועל ז״ל – Avrohom Mordechai Mendlowitz ז״ל

ר׳ יעקב חיים בן ר׳ יחזקאל ז״ל – Yaakov Chaim Paneth ז״ל

and in memory of his brother

ר׳ משולם בן ר׳ יעקב חיים ז״ל – Meshulam Paneth ז״ל

Moshe and Esther Beinhorn and family

In memory of their grandparents

ר׳ ישראל מרדכי ב״ר חיים צבי הי״ד וזוג׳ פעסיל ב״ר משה הי״ד

ר׳ משה ב״ר שלום יוסף הי״ד וזוג׳ איידיל ב״ר יהודה אריה ע״ה

ר׳ יחיאל מיכל ב״ר אברהם זאב הי״ד וזוג׳ שיינדל ב״ר יוסף הי״ד

ר׳ יצחק ב״ר משה הי״ד וזוג׳ לאה גיטל ב״ר חיים עזרא הי״ד

KILAYIM:

Mr. and Mrs. Louis Glick

In memory of

יעקב מאיר חיים בן אפרים אליעזר הכהן ז״ל – Jerome Schottenstein ז״ל

SHEVIIS:

In memory of

ר׳ אריה לייב בן שמואל יוסף ז״ל

Aryeh Leib Pluchenik ז״ל

TERUMOS:

Benzi and Esther Dunner

In memory of their grandparents

ר׳ אורי יהודה ב״ר אברהם אריה ז״ל וזוג׳ מרת רבקה בת שרה ע״ה

PATRONS OF THE MISHNAH

MAASROS, MAASER SHENI:

Barry and Sipora Buls and Family

In memory of our parents

אברהם בן מרדכי ז״ל   חיה שיינדל בת חיים צבי ע״ה

Abraham and Jeanette Buls ע״ה

אלטר חיים משולם בן יעקב ז״ל   אסתר בת ראובן ע״ה

Meshulam and Esther Kluger ע״ה

and in memory of our grandparents

מרדכי בן אברהם יצחק ז״ל וזוג׳ רבקה בת אברהם ע״ה – בולס

חיים צבי בן דוד ז״ל וזוג׳ פיגא בת יצחק ע״ה – מאשקאוויטש

יעקב ז״ל הי״ד וזוג׳ טאבא ע״ה הי״ד – קלוגר

ראובן ז״ל הי״ד וזוג׳ פיגא בת יחזקאל נתן ע״ה הי״ד – שעכטר-בירנבוים

CHALLAH, ORLAH, BIKKURIM:

Yossi and Linda Segel   Danny and Shani Segel   and families

In memory of their father

ר׳ ברוך בן ר׳ יוסף הלוי ז״ל – Baruch Segel ז״ל

Chesky and Sheindy Paneth and family

In memory of their parents

ר׳ אברהם מרדכי בן ר׳ שרגא פייוועל ז״ל – Avrohom Mordechai Mendlowitz ז״ל

ר׳ יעקב חיים בן ר׳ יחזקאל ז״ל – Yaakov Chaim Paneth ז״ל

and in memory of his brother

ר׳ משולם בן ר׳ יעקב חיים ז״ל – Meshulam Paneth ז״ל

Moshe and Esther Beinhorn and family

In memory of their uncle

ר׳ אברהם זאב בן ר׳ יחיאל מיכל ז״ל – Avrohom Beinhorn ז״ל

SEDER MOED

SHABBOS:

Mr. and Mrs. Philip Amin

Mr. and Mrs. Lee R. Furman

In memory of their son and brother

קלמן בן ר׳ פסח ז״ל – Kalman Amin ז״ל

ERUVIN:

Mr. and Mrs. Lawrence M. Rosenberg

In honor of their parents

ר׳ גרשון בן ר׳ יהודה ומרת שרה שיינא בת דוב בערל עמו״ש

Judge and Mrs. Gustave Rosenberg עמו״ש

and in memory of their brother and sister

אברהם דוד ודבורה חאשא חוה בני ר׳ גרשון

PATRONS OF THE MISHNAH

BEITZAH:

Mr. and Mrs. Herman Wouk

In memory of their בכור and ילד שעשועים

אברהם יצחק ע"ה בן חיים אביעזר זעליג נ"י

PESACHIM:

Mr. and Mrs. Leonard A. Kestenbaum

In memory of their father ר' דוד ב"ר אליהו זצ"ל – David Kestenbaum זצ"ל

SHEKALIM:

In memory of **ר' יוסף דוד ב"ר משה גאלדוואַרם זללה"ה**

ROSH HASHANAH, YOMA, SUCCAH:

ר' יוסף שמעון בן חיים ע"ה – 1st Lt. Joseph Simon Bravin ע"ה

TAANIS, MEGILLAH, MOED KATAN, CHAGIGAH:

In memory of

מו"ר הרה"ג ר' גדליה הלוי שארר זצ"ל

HaGaon HaRav Gedalia Halevi Schorr זצ"ל

SEDER NASHIM

YEVAMOS:

David and Rochelle Hirsch

In memory of their father Mr. Henry Hirsch ז"ל

KESUBOS:

In memory of

מרת בילא בת ר' צבי מאיר ע"ה – Mrs. Bertha Steinmetz ע"ה

NEDARIM:

The Knoll Family (Israel and Venezuela)

In memory of their parents

ר' צבי הירש בן ר' שרגא פייוול ע"ה

ומרת פעסיא דבורה בת ר' יעקב דוד ע"ה

NAZIR:

In memory of

יוטא ע"ה בת ר' יקותיאל יהודה לאי"ט – Yitty Leibel ע"ה

SOTAH:

In honor of the

Fifth Avenue Synagogue

GITTIN, KIDDUSHIN:

Bruce and Ruth Rappaport

In memory of his parents

ר' יששכר ב"ר יעקב ז"ל

ומרת בלומא שושנה בת ר' ברוך ע"ה

PATRONS OF THE MISHNAH

SEDER NEZIKIN

BAVA KAMMA:

In memory of

הרב שמעון ב״ר נחמיה הלוי ז״ל

Rabbi Shimon Zweig ז״ל

BAVA METZIA:

The Steinmetz family

In memory of their parents

ר׳ שמעון ב״ר שאול יהודה ז״ל

וזוגתו בילא בת ר׳ צבי מאיר ע״ה

BAVA BASRA:

In memory of

ר׳ יצחק מאיר ב״ר משה ז״ל – Mr. Irving Bunim ז״ל

SANHEDRIN:

The Zweig and Steinmetz families

In memory of

סימא בת ר׳ שמעון ע״ה – Sima Rabinowitz ע״ה

MAKKOS, SHEVUOS:

In memory of

יהושע יצחק ז״ל בן אברהם מאיר נ״י – Joshua Waitman ז״ל

EDUYOS:

Mr. and Mrs. Woli and
Chaja Stern (Saõ Paulo, Brazil)

In honor of their children

Jacques and Ariane Stern   Jaime and Ariela Landau

Michael and Annete Kierszenbaum

AVODAH ZARAH, HORAYOS:

In memory of our Rebbe

מור״ר שרגא פייבל בן ר׳ משה זצ״ל

Reb Shraga Feivel Mendlowitz זצ״ל

AVOS:

Mr. Louis Glick   **Mr. and Mrs. Sidney Glick**

Mr. and Mrs. Mortimer Sklarin

In memory of their beloved mother

מרת רבקה בת ר׳ משה גליק ע״ה – Mrs. Regina Glick ע״ה

Mr. Louis Glick   **Shimon and Mina Glick and family**

Shimon and Esti Pluchenik and family

In memory of their beloved wife, mother and grandmother

מרת דבורה בת ר׳ שמעון גליק ע״ה – Mrs. Doris Glick ע״ה

PATRONS OF THE MISHNAH

SEDER KODASHIM

ZEVACHIM:

Mr. and Mrs. Richard Hirsch

In memory of their son

הילד אליעזר ז"ל בן יהודה זליג שיחי' — Lawrence A. Hirsch ז"ל

MENACHOS:

In memory of

שמעון בן משה עמוס ז"ל – Simon Amos ז"ל

CHULLIN:

The Steinmetz and Barouch families

In memory of

רבקה עטיה בת ר' שמעון ע"ה — Ruth Barouch ע"ה

BECHOROS:

Yad Avraham Institute

In honor of

Bruce and Ruth Rappaport

ARACHIN:

In memory of

גילה מסעודה ע"ה בת ר' יעקב נ"י

Gillah Amoch ע"ה

דפנה ע"ה בת ר' יעקב נ"י

Amy Amoch ע"ה

KEREISOS:

In memory of

ר' דוד ז"ל בן ר' שמעון נ"י – David Litman ז"ל

TEMURAH, MEILAH:

Baruch and Susie Singer and Yitzchak Ahron

Rabbi Eli Hersh and Rivky Singer

Rabbi Nussie and Ruchy Singer

Yossie and Surie Singer

Sruly Singer and Leah

In honor of

Rebbetzin Bluma Singer שתחי'

In memory of

הרה"ג ר' יצחק אהרן בן הרה"ג ר' אליהו זינגער זצ"ל

נפ' י"ג טבת תשס"א

הרה"ג ר' אליהו בן הרה"ג ר' שמעון זינגער זצ"ל

וזוגתו הרבנית רייזל בת הרה"ח ר' יששכר דוב ע"ה

הרה"צ ר' ישראל אריה ליב האלפערן בן הרה"צ ר' ברוך מסאקאליוואקא זצ"ל

וזוגתו הרבנית שבע בת הרה"ג ר' אריה ליבוש ע"ה

PATRONS OF THE MISHNAH

TAMID, MIDDOS, KINNIM:

Hashi and Miriam Herzka **Moishe and Channie Stern**
Avi and Freidi Waldman **Benzi and Esti Dunner**
Dovid and Didi Stern **Avrumi and Esti Stern**
In honor of our dear parents
William and Shoshana Stern שיחי'
London, England

SEDER TOHOROS

KEILIM I-II:

Leslie and Shira Westreich
Adam and Dayna – Joshua **Rayna and Dina**
In memory of
ז"ל אריה לייב ב"ר יהושע ז"ל – Larry Westreich
and in memory of our parents and grandparents
הרב יהושע בן מו"ר הרב הגאון יוסף יאסקא ז"ל
גיטל בת זאב וואלף ע"ה

OHOLOS:

In memory of
הרב יהושע בן מו"ר הרב הגאון יוסף יאסקא ז"ל
Rabbi Yehoshua Westreich ז"ל
and
ע"ה גיטל בת זאב וואלף ע"ה – Gerda Westreich

NEGAIM:

Moshe and Esther Beinhorn and family
In memory of
יוסף דוד ז"ל בן יצחק אייזיק
Yosef Dovid Beinhorn ז"ל

PARAH:

Moshe and Esther Beinhorn and family
In memory of their uncles and aunts
אברהם צבי, חוה, רחל, חיים עזרא, אריה לייביש,
ישראל ברוך, שמואל דוד, ומשה הי"ד, והילד שלמה ע"ה
children of
יצחק בן משה שטיינבערגער ז"ל וזוג' לאה גיטל בת חיים עזרא ע"ה הי"ד

Chesky and Sheindy Paneth and family
In memory of their grandparents
הרב יחזקאל ב"ר יעקב חיים פאנעטה ז"ל הי"ד וזוג' רחל לאה בת ר' אשר לעמל ע"ה
הרב חיים יהודה ב"ר משולם ווייס ז"ל וזוג' שרה רחל בת ר' נתן קארפל ע"ה
הרב שרגא פייוועל ב"ר משה מענדלאוויטץ זצ"ל וזוג' בלומא רחל בת ר' שמעון הלוי ע"ה
ר' ישכר בעריש ב"ר אברהם הלוי לאמפערט ז"ל וזוג' גיטל פערל בת ר' בצלאל ע"ה

PATRONS OF THE MISHNAH

MIKVAOS:

Mr. and Mrs. Louis Glick

In memory of his father

ר׳ אברהם יוסף בן ר׳ יהושע העשיל הכהן ז״ל

Abraham Joseph Glick ז״ל

NIDDAH:

Moshe and Esther Beinhorn and family

In memory of his beloved mother

טילא בת ר׳ יצחק ע״ה

Mrs. Tilli Beinhorn ע״ה

נפ׳ כ״ו טבת תשס״ח

MACHSHIRIN, ZAVIM:

David and Joan Tepper and family

In memory of their parents

ר׳ מנחם מענדל ב״ר יעקב ז״ל ומרת מינדל בת ר׳ אריה ליב ע״ה

Milton and Minnie Tepper ז״ל

ר׳ ראובן ב״ר נחמיה ז״ל ומרת עטיל בת ר׳ ישראל נתן נטע ע״ה

Rubin and Etta Gralla ז״ל

TEVUL YOM, YADAYIM, UKTZIN:

Barry and Tova Kohn and family

In memory of their beloved brother

הרב מנחם מנדל בן ר׳ יוסף יצחק אייזיק זצ״ל

HaRav Menachem Kohn זצ״ל

נפ׳ כ״ז מנחם אב תשס״ו

And in memory of their fathers, and grandfathers

ר׳ יוסף יצחק אייזיק ב״ר בן ציון ז״ל, נפ׳ י׳ שבט תשנ״ח — Josef Kohn ז״ל

ר׳ בנימין אלכסנדר ב״ר דוד ז״ל, נפ׳ ל׳ שבט תשס״א — Benjamin Wiederman ז״ל

and יבל״ח in honor of their mothers and grandmothers שתחי׳ לאוי״ט

Helene Kohn   Sylvia Wiederman

הדרן עלך ששה סדרי משנה

הסכמה

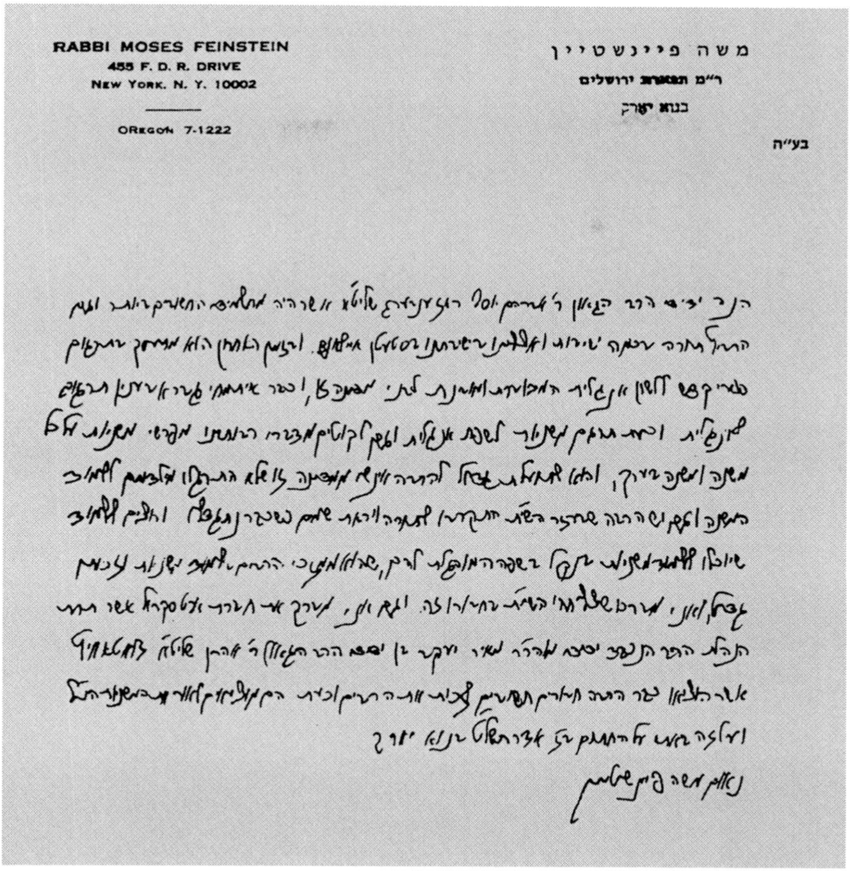
RABBI MOSES FEINSTEIN
455 F. D. R. DRIVE
NEW YORK, N. Y. 10002
OREGON 7-1222

משה פיינשטיין
ר״מ תפארת ירושלים
בנוא יארק

בע״ה

הנה ידידי הרב הגאון ר׳ אברהם יוסף ראזענבערג שליט״א אשר היה מתלמידי החשובים ביותר וגם הרביץ תורה בכמה ישיבות ואצלינו בישיבתנו בסטעטן איילאנד, ובזמן האחרון הוא מתעסק בתרגום ספרי קדש ללשון אנגלית המדוברת ומובנת לבני מדינה זו, וכבר איתמחי גברא בענין תרגום לאנגלית וכעת תרגם משניות לשפת אנגלית וגם לקוטים מדברי רבותינו מפרשי משניות על כל משנה ומשנה בערך, והוא לתועלת גדול להרבה אינשי ממדינה זו שלא התרגלו מילדותם ללמוד המשנה וגם יש הרבה שבעזר השי״ת התקרבו לתורה ויראת שמים כשכבר נתגדלו ורוצים ללמוד שיוכלו ללמוד משניות בנקל בשפה המורגלת להם, שהוא ממזכי הרבים בלמוד משניות וזכותו גדול. ואני מברכו שיצליחהו השי״ת בחבורו זה. וגם אני מברך את חברת ארטסקרול אשר תחת הנהלת הרב הנכבד ידידי מוהר״ר מאיר יעקב בן ידידי הרב הגאון ר׳ אהרן שליט״א זלאטאוויץ אשר הוציאו כבר הרבה חבורים חשובים לזכות את הרבים וכעת הם מוציאים לאור את המשניות הנ״ל.

ועל זה באתי על החתום בז׳ אדר תשל״ט בנוא יארק.

נאום משה פיינשטיין

מכתב ברכה

יעקב קמנצקי

RABBI J. KAMENECKI

38 SADDLE RIVER ROAD

MONSEY, NEW YORK 10952

בע"ה

יום ה' ערב חג השבועות תשל"ס, פה מאנסי.

כבוד הרבני איש החסד שוע ונדיב מוקיר רבנן מר אלעזר נ"י גליק שלו' וברכת כל טוב.

מה מאד שמחתי בהודעי כי כבודו רכש לעצמו הזכות שייקרא ע"ש בנו המנוח הפירוש מבואר על כל ששת סדרי משנה ע"י "ארטסקראל" והנה חברה זו יצאה לה מוניטין בפירושה על תנ"ך, והנה נקוה שכשם שהצליחה בתורה שבכתב כן תצליח בתורה שבע"פ. ובהיות שאותיות "משנה" הן כאותיות "נשמה" לפיכך טוב עשה בכוונתו לעשות זאת לעילוי נשמת בנו המנוח אברהם יוסף ע"ה, ומאד מתאים השם "יד אברהם" לזה הפירוש, כדמצינו במקרא (ש"ב י"ח) כי אמר אין לי בן בעבור הזכיר שמי וגו'. ואין לך דבר גדול מזה להפיץ ידיעת תורה שבע"פ בקרב אחינו שאינם רגילים בלשון הקדש. וד' הטוב יהי' בעזרו ויוכל לברך על המוגמר. ויראה רוב נחת מכל אשר אתו כנפש מברכו.

יעקב קמנצקי

מכתב ברכה

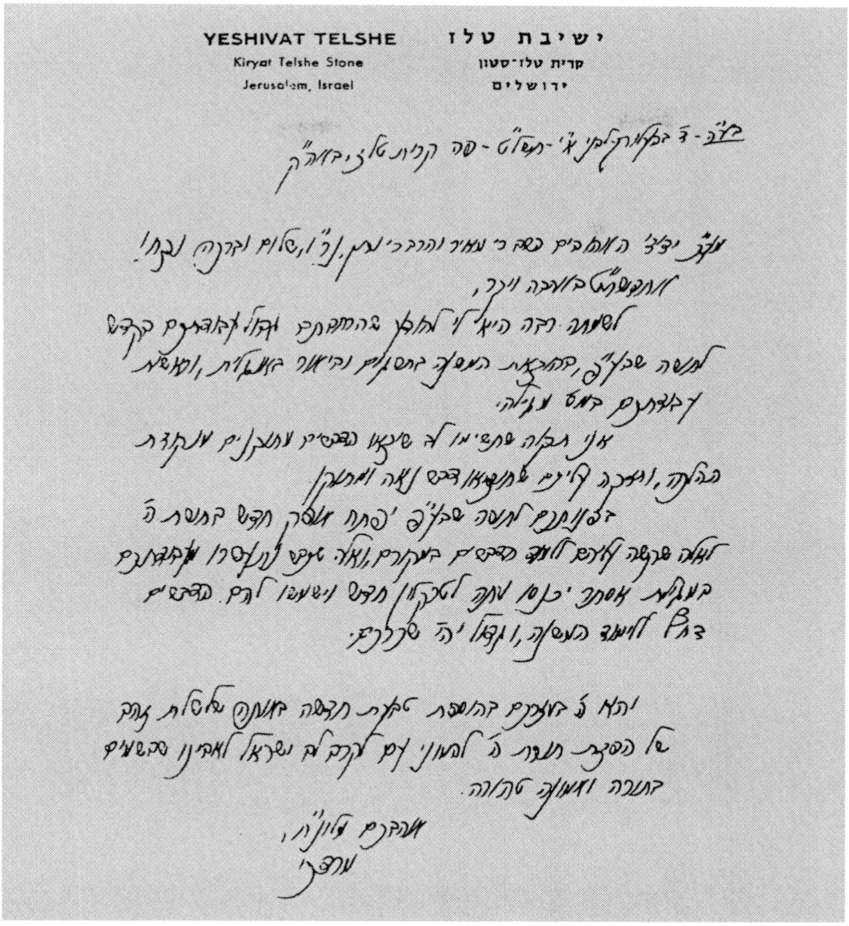

ישיבת טלז
קרית טלז־סטון
ירושלים

YESHIVAT TELSHE
Kiryat Telshe Stone
Jerusalem, Israel

בע״ה – ד׳ בהעלותך – לבני א״י – תשל״ט – פה קרית טלז, באה״ק

מע״כ ידידי האהובים הרב ר׳ מאיר והרב ר׳ נתן, נר״ו, שלום וברכה נצח!

אחדשה״ט באהבה ויקר,

לשמחה רבה היא לי להודע שהרחבתם גבול עבודתכם בקדש לתורה שבע״פ, בהוצאת המשנה בתרגום וביאור באנגלית, וראשית עבודתכם במס׳ מגילה.

אני תקוה שתשימו לב שיצאו הדברים מתוקנים מנקודת ההלכה, וחזקה עליכם שתוציאו דבר נאה ומתוקן.

בפנותכם לתורה שבע״פ יפתח אופק חדש בתורת ה׳ לאלה שקשה עליהם ללמוד הדברים במקורם, ואלה שכבר נתעשרו מעבודתכם במגילת אסתר יכנסו עתה לטרקלין חדש וישמשו להם הדברים דחף ללימוד המשנה, וגדול יהי׳ שכרכם.

יהא ה׳ בעזרכם בהוספת טבעת חדשה באותה שלשלת זהב של הפצת תורת ה׳ להמוני עם לקרב לב ישראל לאבינו שבשמים בתורה ואמונה טהורה.

אוהבכם מלונ״ח,
מרדכי

מכתב ברכה

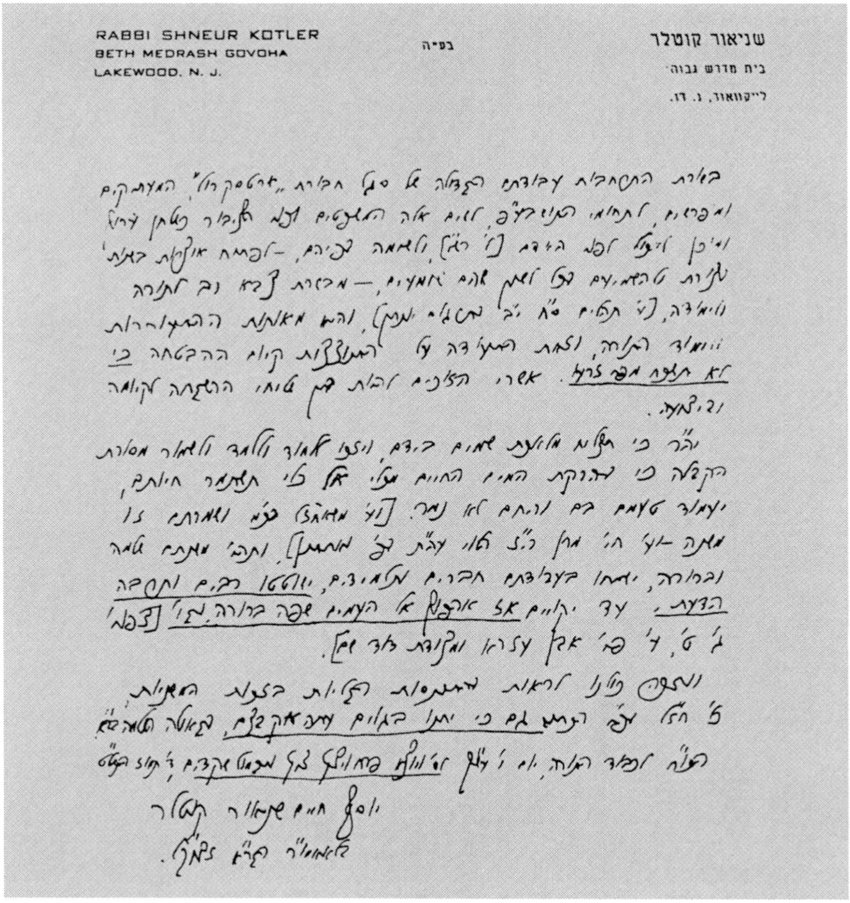
RABBI SHNEUR KOTLER
BETH MEDRASH GOVOHA
LAKEWOOD, N. J.

בע״ה

שניאור קוטלר
בית מדרש גבוה
לייקוואוד, נ. דז.

בשורת התרחבות עבודתם הגדולה של סגל חבורת ,,ארטסקרול״, המעתיקים ומפרשים, לתחומי התושבע״פ, לשים אלה המשפטים לפני הציבור כשלחן ערוך ומוכן לאכול לפני האדם [ל׳ רש״י], ולשימה בפיהם – לפתוח אוצרות בשנות בצורת ולהשמיעם בכל לשון שהם שומעים – מבשרת צבא רב לתורה ולימודה [ע׳ תהלים ס״ח י״ב בתרגום יונתן], והיא מאותות ההתעוררות ללימוד התורה, וזאת התעודה על התנוצצות קיום ההבטחה ,,כי לא תשכח מפי זרעו״. אשרי הזוכים להיות בין שלוחי ההשגחה לקיומה וביצועה.

יהי״ר כי תצליח מלאכת שמים בידם, ויזכו ללמוד וללמד ולשמור מסורת הקבלה כי בהרקת המים החיים מכלי אל כלי תשתמר חיותם, יעמוד טעמם בם וריחם לא נמר. [וע׳ משאחז״ל בכ״מ ושמרתם זו משנה – וע׳ חי׳ מרן רי״ז הלוי עה״ת בפ׳ ואתחנן]. ותהי׳ משנתם שלמה וברורה, ישמחו בעבודתם חברים ותלמידים, ,,ישוטטו רבים ותרבה הדעת״, עד יקויים ,,אז אהפוך אל העמים שפה ברורה וגו׳ ״ [צפני׳ ג׳ ט׳, ע׳ פי׳ אבן עזרא ומצודת דוד שם].

ונזכה כולנו לראות בהתכנסות הגליות בזכות המשניות, כל׳ חז״ל עפ״י הכתוב ,,גם כי יתנו בגוים עתה אקבצם״, בגאולה השלמה בב״א.

הכו״ח לכבוד התורה, יום ו׳ עש״ק לס׳ ,,ויוצא פרח ויצץ ציץ ויגמול שקדים״, ד׳ תמוז התשל״ט

יוסף חיים שניאור קוטלר
בלאאמו״ר הגר״א זצוק״ל

מכתב ברכה

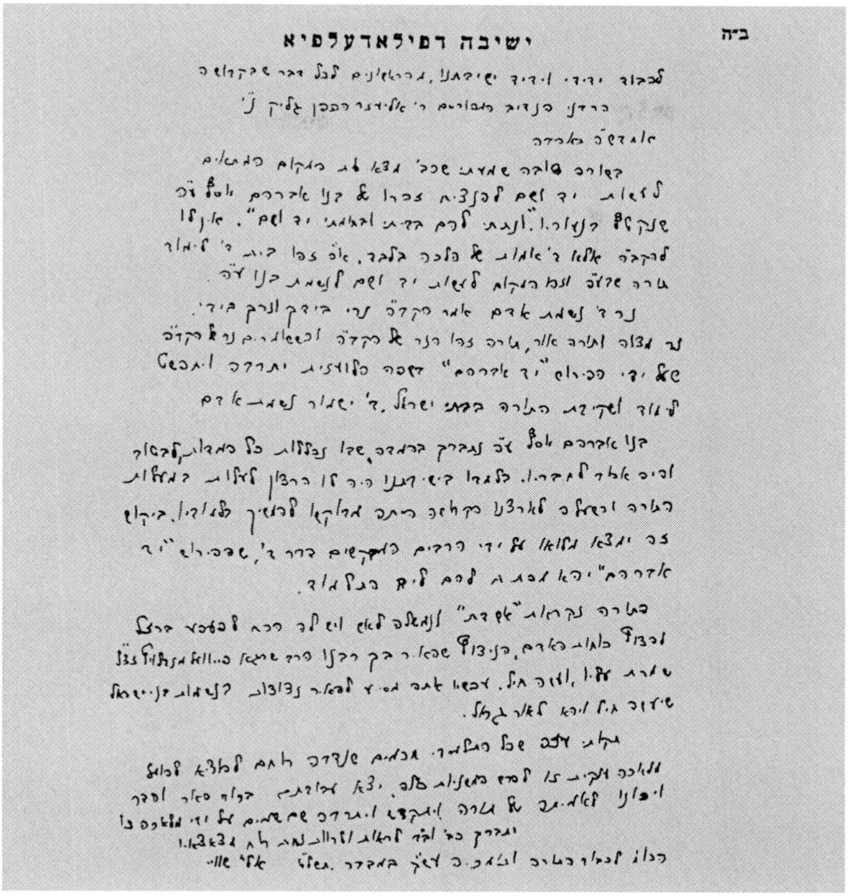
ב״ה
ישיבה דפילאדעלפיא

ב״ה
לכבוד ידידי וידיד ישיבתנו, מהראשונים לכל דבר שבקדושה
הרבני הנדיב המפורסם ר׳ אליעזר הכהן גליק נ״י
אחדש״ה באהבה

בשורה טובה שמעתי שכב׳ מצא את המקום המתאים לעשות יד ושם להנציח זכרו של בנו **אברהם יוסף ע״ה** שנקטף בנעוריו. ,,ונתתי להם בביתי ובחומתי יד ושם״. אין לו להקב״ה אלא ד׳ אמות של הלכה בלבד. א״כ זהו בית ד׳ לימוד תורה שבע״פ וזהו המקום לעשות יד ושם לנשמת בנו ע״ה.

נר ד׳ נשמת אדם אמר הקב״ה נרי בידך ונרך בידי. נר מצוה ותורה אור, תורה זהו הנר של הקב״ה וכששומרים נר של הקב״ה שעל ידי הפירוש ,,**יד אברהם**״ בשפה הלועזית יתרבה ויתפשט לימוד ושקידת התורה בבתי ישראל. ד׳ ישמור נשמת אדם.

בנו אברהם יוסף ע״ה נתברך בהמדה שבו נכללות כל המדות, לב טוב והיה אהוב לחבריו. בלמדו בישיבתנו היה לו הרצון לעלות במעלות התורה וכשעלה לארצנו הקדושה היתה מבוקשו להמשיך בלמודיו. ביקוש זה ימצא מלואו על ידי הרבים המבקשים דבר ד׳, שהפירוש ,,**יד אברהם**״ יהא מפתח להם לים התלמוד.

התורה נקראת ,,אש דת״ ונמשלה לאש ויש לה הכח לפעפע ברזל לקצוץ כוחות האדם, הניצוץ שהאיר בך רבנו הרב שרגא פייוועל מנדלויץ זצ״ל שמרת עליו, ועשה חיל. עכשיו אתה מסייע להאיר נצוצות בנשמות בני ישראל שיעשה חיל ויהא לאור גדול.

תקותי עזה שכל התלמידי חכמים שנדבה רוחם להוציא לפועל מלאכה ענקית זו לפרש המשניות כולה, יצא עבודתם ברוב פאר והדר ויכונו לאמיתה של תורה ויתקדש ויתרבה שם שמים על ידי מלאכה זו.

יתברך כב׳ וב״ב לראות ולרוות נחת רוח מצאצאיו.
הכו״ח לכבוד התורה ותומכיה עש״ק במדבר תשל״ט

אלי׳ שוויי

מכתב ברכה

דוד קאהן

ביהמ"ד גבול יעבץ
ברוקלין, נוא יארק

בס"ד כ"ה למטמונים תשל"ט

כבוד רחימא דנפשאי, עושה ומעשה
ר' אלעזר הכהן גליק נטריה רחמנא ופרקיה

שמוע שמעתי שכבר תקעת כפיך לתמוך במפעל האדיר של חברת ארטסקרול — הידוע בכל קצווי תבל ע"י עבודתה הכבירה בהפצת תורה — לתרגם ולבאר ששה סדרי משנה באנגלית. כוונתך להנציח זכר בנך הנחמד אברהם יוסף ז"ל שנקטף באבו בזמן שעלה לארץ הקודש בתקופת התרוממות הנפש ושאיפה לקדושה, ולמטרה זו יכונה הפירוש בשם „**יד אברהם**"; וגם האיר ה' רוחך לגרום עילוי לנשמתו הטהורה שעי"ז יתרבה לימוד התורה שניתנה בשבעים לשון, על ידי כלי מפואר זה.

מכיון שהנני מכיר היטיב שני הצדדים, אוכל לומר לדבק טוב, והנני תקוה שיצליח המפעל הלזה לתת יד ושם וזכות לנשמת אברהם יוסף ז"ל. חזקה על חברת ארטסקרול שתוציא דבר נאה מתוקן ומתקבל מתחת ידה להגדיל תורה ולהאדירה.

והנני מברך אותך שתמצא נוחם לנפשך, שהאבא זוכה לברא, ותשבע נחת — אתה עם רעיתך תחיה — מכל צאצאיכם היקרים אכי"ר

ידידך עז
דוד קאהן

Preface

אָמַר ר׳ יוֹחָנָן: לֹא כָּרַת הקב״ה בְּרִית עִם יִשְׂרָאֵל אֶלָּא עַל־תּוֹרָה שֶׁבְּעַל
פֶּה שֶׁנֶּאֱמַר: ,,כִּי עַל־פִּי הַדְּבָרִים הָאֵלֶּה כָּרַתִּי אִתְּךָ בְּרִית . . .״
R' Yochanan said: The Holy One, Blessed is He, sealed a covenant with Israel only because of the Oral Torah, as it is said [Exodus 34:27]: For according to these words have I sealed a covenant with you . . . (Gittin 60b).

With gratitude to Hashem Yisbarach *we present the Jewish public with* Sanhedrin, *the fourth tractate of* Seder Nezikin. *Following the successful completion of* Moed *and* Nashim, *work is proceeding not only on the rest of* Nezikin *but on the other three other* sedarim *as well. All of this is thanks to the vision and commitment of* MR. AND MRS. LOUIS GLICK. *In their quiet, self-effacing way, they have been a major force for the propagation of Torah knowledge and the enhancement of Jewish life for a generation. The commentary to the mishnayos bears the name* YAD AVRAHAM, *in memory of their son* AVRAHAM YOSEF GLICK ע״ה. *An appreciation of the* niftar *will appear in Tractate Berachos. May this dissemination of the Mishnah in his memory be a source of merit for his soul.* תנצב״ה.

By dedicating the ArtScroll Mishnah Series, the Glicks have added a new dimension to their tradition of service. The many study groups in synagogues, schools, and offices throughout the English-speaking world are the most eloquent testimony to the fact that thousands of people thirst for Torah learning presented in a challenging, comprehensive, and comprehensible manner.

We are proud and grateful that such venerable luminaries as MARON HAGAON HARAV YAAKOV KAMINETZKI זצ״ל *and* להבל״ח MARAN HAGAON HARAV MORDECHAI GIFTER שליט״א *have declared that this series should be translated into Hebrew.* Baruch Hashem, *it has stimulated readers to echo the words of King David:* גַּל־עֵינַי וְאַבִּיטָה נִפְלָאוֹת מִתּוֹרָתֶךָ, *Uncover my eyes that I may see wonders of Your Torah* (*Psalms* 119:18).

May we inject two words of caution:

First, although the Mishnah, by definition, is a compendium of laws, the final halachah does not necessarily follow the Mishnah. The development of halachah proceeds through the Gemara, commentators, codifiers, responsa, and the acknowledged poskim. *Even when our commentary cites the*

Shulchan Aruch, *the intention is to sharpen the reader's understanding of the Mishnah, but not to be a basis for actual practice. In short, this work is meant as a first step in the study of our recorded Oral Law — no more.*

Second, as we have stressed in our other books, the ArtScroll commentary is not meant as a substitute for the study of the sources. While this commentary, like others in the various series, will be immensely useful even to accomplished scholars and will often bring to light ideas and sources they may have overlooked, we strongly urge those who can, to study the classic sefarim *in the original. It has been said that every droplet of ink coming from* Rashi's *pen is worthy of seven days' contemplation. Despite the exceptional caliber of our authors, none of us pretends to replace the study of the greatest minds in Jewish history.*

The author of this volume, RABBI MATIS ROBERTS, *currently serving as* mashgiach ruchni *of Yeshiva Shaar HaTorah of Kew Gardens, N.Y., is familiar to ArtScroll Mishnah readers from his fine work on tractates* Gittin, Kiddushin *and* Bava Basra. *His manuscript was edited by* RABBI YEHEZKEL DANZIGER, *whose work is well known from earlier volumes of the Mishnah Series.*

We are also grateful to the staff of Mesorah Publications: RABBI HERSH GOLDWURM, *whose encyclopedic knowledge is always available;* REB ELI KROEN, *whose very fine graphics production of this volume carries on the tradition of* REB SHEA BRANDER, *who remains a leader in bringing beauty of presentation to Torah literature;* RABBI AVIE GOLD, RABBI SHIMON GOLDING, SHMUEL KLAVER, YOSAIF TIMINSKY, YEHUDAH NEUGARTEN, LEA FREIER, MRS. ESTHER FEIERSTEIN, MRS. SIMIE KORN, MENUCHA MARCUS, SARA ADLER, MRS. FAYGIE WEINBAUM, MRS. JUDI DICK, *and* ESTIE ZLOTOWITZ.

Finally, our gratitude goes to RABBI DAVID FEINSTEIN שליט״א *and* RABBI DAVID COHEN שליט״א, *whose concern, interest, and guidance throughout the history of the ArtScroll Series have been essential to its success.*

Rabbi Nosson Scherman / Rabbi Meir Zlotowitz

ז׳ אייר תשמ״ז / *May 6, 1987*
Brooklyn, New York

◆§ Note to revised edition

We would like to acknowledge the contribution of the following individuals who worked on this revised edition, each in their own area of expertise: Rabbi Moshe Rosenblum, Rabbi Yechezkel Sochaczewski, Rabbi Yitzchok Herzberg, Mrs. Faygie Weinbaum, Mrs. Chumie Lipschitz, Miss Sara Rivka Spira, and Miss Sury Reinhold.

מסכת סנהדרין
Tractate Sanhedrin

Translation and anthologized commentary by
Rabbi Matis Roberts

Edited by
Rabbi Yehezkel Danziger

General Introduction to Sanhedrin

שֹׁפְטִים וְשֹׁטְרִים תִּתֶּן-לְךָ בְּכָל-שְׁעָרֶיךָ אֲשֶׁר ה׳ אֱלֹהֶיךָ נֹתֵן לְךָ לִשְׁבָטֶיךָ
וְשָׁפְטוּ אֶת-הָעָם מִשְׁפַּט-צֶדֶק. (דברים טז:יח)

Judges and enforcers you shall appoint for yourself in all your gates which H*ASHEM your God is giving you according to your tribes; and they shall judge the people a righteous judgment.* (*Deut.* 16:18)

The Jewish people are commanded by the Torah to set up a system of courts to judge the people according to Torah law. This system includes courts of three judges, those of twenty-three, and a high court of seventy-one judges, each with its own distinct level of jurisdiction (see chapter one). The authority of these courts extends to all facets of Jewish law, both civil and religious. It is prohibited for a Jew to turn to a secular or gentile court, unless he first attempts to take his case to a *beis din* — a court of Jewish law — and the opposing party refuses to go (*Gittin* 88b; *Rambam, Hil. Sanhedrin* 26:7). One who defies this principle is considered as if he blasphemed and attacked the Torah (*Rambam* ibid.).

In order to fully appreciate this idea — as well as to understand many of the concepts of this tractate — it is necessary to be aware of the following principles of Torah law and jurisprudence. The dichotomy between civil and religious matters common to most societies is non-existent in Torah law. This difference in perspective leads to differences in law in two major respects: Firstly, every facet of Jewish life is governed by laws stated either in the written Torah or in the Oral Law taught by God to Moshe at Sinai and transmitted down through the ages by the Torah sages of each generation. Thus, even pecuniary laws are based on principles and rules dictated by God, into which we may have no clear logical insight. For example, an owner is liable for the damages caused by his animal as it walks. Nevertheless, if the damage is inflicted by stones shooting out from under the animal's feet, the halachah decrees that he is liable for only half the damages (*Bava Kamma* 2:1). Secondly, even issues generally relegated to the realm of ethics and philosophy are defined with the same type of legal reasoning employed in civil law. For example, the seemingly ethical question of when one is required to give up his life for the sake of Judaism is defined in legal terms rather than philosophical ones (see *Gem.* 74a; *Rambam, Hil. Yesodei HaTorah* ch. 5).

It is thus apparent that the responsibilities of the Torah's judiciary as arbiters of both civil and religious law are very great. The men who fill these positions, therefore, must be highly erudite and must possess exemplary character and great acumen. Accordingly, many laws exist regarding the nature and

qualifications of those who may be chosen as members of the judiciary (see *Rambam, Hil. Sanhedrin* ch. 2). The appointment of Jewish judges was overseen by the High Court itself, which sent agents throughout the land to seek out men fit to fill this role (*Gem.* 88b; *Rambam* loc. cit. 8).

Consistent with the inextricable bond between the Jewish people and the Land of Israel, the rule governing the structure of the judiciary, as well as a great deal of the authority granted to it, is applicable only in Eretz Yisrael (see *Rambam, Hil. Sanhedrin* 1:2; 5:9). This is because much of the authority of the courts is rooted in the institution of *semichah* — a form of ordination (see comm. to 1:3) which existed only in Eretz Yisrael and which lapsed even there by the end of the fourth century C.E. under the pressure of relentless persecution. The mishnayos in this tractate, however, which predate this period by several centuries, generally assume the existence of these factors.

In approaching this tractate it is worthwhile noting several features of the judicial process. A *beis din* consists of a group of judges who try and decide all cases; no jury exists in Jewish law. When there is disagreement among the judges, majority rule prevails (se 1:6). Once the decision has been made, it is presented unanimously; no minority opinions are recorded when the verdict is issued. It is even prohibited for one of the dissenting judges to express his view privately to the litigants (3:7). Once a decision has been reached it is implemented immediately, even in cases of capital punishment (6:1). However, an abundance of precautionary measures are included in the process to prevent miscarriages of justice (see chs. 5,6). In fact, a court that meted out capital punishment once in seven years — and according to another view once in seventy years — was referred to as a destructive court (*Makkos* 1:10).

Another noteworthy point is that the courts have the authority to impose extra-legal measures — even capital punishment — if they perceive a compelling need to do so for the benefit of society (*Gem.* 46a; see 6:4).

One of the primary issues dealt with in this tractate is that of testimony, which is also rooted in Divinely ordained precepts. In order for a person to be liable for any punitive measures, his action must be attested to by two witnesses (*Duet.* 19:15) who not only observed the deed but also warned him in advance of its prohibition and punishment (see *Gem.* 8b). The method of questioning witnesses to establish their veracity is discussed at length in this tractate in chapters 3 and 5. Once the testimony of witnesses has been accepted by the court it can no longer be retracted; even if they admit to having perjured themselves, they are not believed and their original testimony stands (*Gem.* 44). There are many qualifications for the witnesses testifying in a Jewish court; these too are dealt with in this tractate (ch. 3).

At this juncture, a brief description of the way the courts deal with conflicting testimony is of major importance. If the testimony of witnesses is contradicted by other witnesses, and it cannot be ascertained which are telling the truth, neither testimony can be used.[1] However, there is one method

1. There is discussion among the authorities as to whether such a situation is viewed as if neither testimony is extant or whether both remain in force but are considered inconclusive because of the contradiction. Since the testimony of two witnesses outweighs almost any other proof presented in a court of Jewish law, this discussion has many repercussions in regard to the validity of other forms of evidence in the face of these conflicting testimonies (see *Teshuvos R' Akiva Eiger* 136).

whereby witnesses can refute the testimony of others so that the words of the earlier ones are totally rejected by the court. This happens when the second pair testifies that at the time the alleged deed took place the first pair were in a different location than that of the purported deed to which they attested. In such a case, the word of the second pair is fully accepted and the original testimony is discarded as false (*Makkos* 1:4). In addition, if the subject of the original testimony had been sentenced to be punished but the sentence had not yet been carried out, or he had been obligated monetarily by the court on the basis of the now discredited testimony, the discredited witnesses must suffer the same penalty which they sought to impose upon their victim (*Deut.* 19:19; *Makkos* 4:6; 5b). This process of refutation is referred to as *hazamah* — from the words of the Torah (ibid.): *And you shall do to him as he plotted* [כַּאֲשֶׁר זָמַם] *to do to his fellow man.*

פרק ראשון

Chapter One

The Torah commands us to appoint judges for every city in the Land of Israel, as stated (*Deut.* 16:18): *Judges and officers you shall appoint for yourselves in all your gates.* There are three levels of courts: courts of three judges, which may rule on monetary matters; courts of twenty-three judges, which have jurisdiction over capital offenses; and the High Court — the Great Sanhedrin — which has jurisdiction over certain specific issues enumerated in this chapter.

By Torah law, the courts must consist of סְמוּכִים, *duly ordained judges* (*Rambam, Hil. Sanhedrin* 4:1; see commentary to mishnah 3, s.v. סמיכת זקנים). This ordination is known as *semichah.* However, *semichah* can be granted only in Eretz Yisrael, not outside[1] the Land (ibid. 6). Accordingly, the courts outside Eretz Yisrael were not staffed by judges with *semichah.* The only basis for the authority of courts in the diaspora and their Rabbinic judges who are not ordained is that they are considered to be acting as the agents of those judges in Eretz Yisrael who decreed that courts must be established in other lands as well. Nevertheless, the authority granted the diaspora courts was only over monetary matters, and even then only for collecting debts but not to mete out fines (ibid. 5:8).

1. Although Rabbinic ordination is granted even today, and is colloquially known as *semichah,* this is not the ordination required by Torah law for judicial authority but only a lesser authority which applies even outside Eretz Yisrael. The classical *semichah* no longer exists, even in Eretz Yisrael (see *Rambam, Hil, Sanhedrin* 4:11).

[א] **דִּינֵי** מָמוֹנוֹת בִּשְׁלֹשָׁה; גְּזֵלוֹת וַחֲבָלוֹת בִּשְׁלֹשָׁה; נֶזֶק וַחֲצִי נֶזֶק,

ר׳ עובדיה מברטנורא

פרק ראשון – דיני ממונות. (א) דיני ממונות. דהיינו הודאות והלואות: **בשלשה.** הדיוטות, ולא אצרכוהו רבנן לשלשה מומחין שלא תנעל דלת בפני לוין, שמא יכפור הלוה ולא ימצא מומחין לכופו לדין, אלא או יחיד מומחה או שלשה הדיוטות. אבל גזילות וחבלות בשלשה מומחין, דאלהים כתיב בפרשת שומרים בואלה המשפטים (שמות כב, ז–ח) שלש פעמים, ומינה ילפינן שלשה מומחין: **נזק.** אדם או שור המועד שהזיקו דמשלמים נזק שלם: **חצי נזק.** שור תם שהזיק. ואף על גב דהיינו חבלות, איידי דבעי למיתני תשלומי כפל ותשלומי ארבעה וחמשה שאינו משלם כמו מה שהזיק שמשלם יותר, תנא נמי חצי נזק שאינו משלם כמו שהזיק שהרי משלם פחות, ואיידי דתנא חצי נזק תנא נמי נזק:

יד אברהם

1

דִּינֵי מָמוֹנוֹת — *Monetary cases*

Since the mishnah proceeds to list separately various types of monetary litigations which require only three-judge panels, it is clear that the term *monetary cases* is being used to refer to certain specific types of monetary claims. The *Gemara* (3a) explains that it refers to cases of admissions — i.e., claims based on one party's admission before witnesses that he owes money to the other (*Rashi* to 2b) — and to litigations concerning loans (*Rav; Rashi*). Also included in this category are cases concerning *kesubos* (marriage contracts), inheritances, and gifts (*Tos.* 3a, s.v. שלא תנעל).

בִּשְׁלֹשָׁה; — *[are judged] by three;*

In discussing the case of a watchman who claims that the object with which he was entrusted was stolen from him, the Torah (*Ex.* 22:6-8) uses the word אֱלֹהִים — meaning in this instance judges[1] — three times. From this we learn that a court must contain at least three judges to try monetary cases (*Rav* from *Gem.* 31b).

In this instance, it is not necessary that the members of the court be duly ordained judges. Although the requirement for three judges is derived from the repeated use of the word אֱלֹהִים — which denotes ordained judges — the Rabbis allowed these cases to be brought before non-ordained judges to provide easier recourse to lenders. This was done so that people should not refrain from lending money out of concern for their inability to collect readily because of the difficulty of coming before a court of ordained judges (*Rav* from *Gem.* 3a).

There is another view in the *Gemara* that the use of non-ordained judges for monetary cases is permitted by Torah law, and only in the cases cited below are three

1. The Torah states (*Deut.* 1:17): כִּי הַמִּשְׁפָּט לֵאלֹהִים הוּא, *for justice is to God.* Since the appellation אֱלֹהִים is used in reference to God's justice, it is used by extension to refer to human courts which carry out God's justice as defined by the Torah (*Torah Temimah* to *Ex.* ad loc. 102).

1
1 1. **M**onetary cases [are judged] by three; [cases of] theft and bodily injury [are judged] by three; [claims for] full damages and half damages,

ordained judges required. Some commentators rule in accordance with this latter view (*R' Chananel*).

In those cases in which any three men are valid, a single judge who is a מוּמְחֶה לָרַבִּים — an accomplished and acknowledged Torah scholar who is expert at deriving legal conclusions from the Torah (*Rav, Rambam,* commentary to 3:1) — may preside over the case on his own (*Rav* from *Gem.* 5a).

גְּזֵלוֹת — *[cases of] theft*

This refers to one who steals from the possession of another or who denies having received an object which the latter claims to have given him for safekeeping (*Rashi*).

וַחֲבָלוֹת בִּשְׁלֹשָׁה; — *and bodily injury [are judged] by three;*

One who injures another is obligated in five types of compensation, as described in *Bava Kamma* 8:1 (*Rashi*).

In contrast to the previous category of monetary litigations, these cases must be tried by three ordained judges, as derived from the verse cited above (*Rav* from *Gem.* 3a). For this reason, the mishnah separates them into two distinct categories, despite the fact that thefts and injuries are also included in the general category of monetary cases (*Gem.* 3a).

Some contend that regular cases of theft were included in the ordinance allowing any three people to judge. The mishnah is discussing a situation in which theft was accompanied by bodily injury. Since this is not a common event, the Rabbis did not deem it necessary to waive, for this type of case, the requirement for three ordained judges (*Tos.* to 3a, based on *Bava Kamma* 84b).

Others distinguish between Eretz Yisrael and the diaspora in regard to this issue. In Eretz Yisrael, where ordained judges were available [at the time of the mishnah], the Rabbis waived the requirement for such judges only for cases of loans, as explained above. The *Gemara's* statement (*Bava Kamma* 84b) that judges who are not ordained may preside over cases such as those concerning thefts because they are considered agents of the ordained judges in Eretz Yisrael refers only to judges in the diaspora, where such measures were deemed necessary because there were no properly ordained judges available (*Rashi* to 13b, s.v. למידין דיני קנסות). Accordingly, the mishnah, which was written in Eretz Yisrael, allows such judges only for loans (*Tos. R' Akiva*).

נֶזֶק — *[claims for] full damages*

This covers most damage claims, such as a man who damaged the property of another or the animal of one which damaged the property of another (*Rav*).

וַחֲצִי נֶזֶק, — *and half damages,*

[If an ox gores another animal (or person) it is considered an unexpected act, and the Torah requires the owner to pay for only half the damage. Once the animal has done this three times, the owner is considered forewarned and any further damages must be recompensed in full (see *Bava Kamma* 1:4).]

תַּשְׁלוּמֵי כֶפֶל, וְתַשְׁלוּמֵי אַרְבָּעָה וַחֲמִשָּׁה,
בִּשְׁלֹשָׁה; הָאוֹנֵס, וְהַמְפַתֶּה, וְהַמּוֹצִיא שֵׁם רַע
בִּשְׁלֹשָׁה; דִּבְרֵי רַבִּי מֵאִיר. וַחֲכָמִים אוֹמְרִים:
מוֹצִיא שֵׁם רַע בְּעֶשְׂרִים וּשְׁלֹשָׁה, מִפְּנֵי שֶׁיֵּשׁ בּוֹ
דִּינֵי נְפָשׁוֹת.

ר' עובדיה מברטנורא

וּמוֹצִיא שֵׁם רַע. לֹא מָצָאתִי לְבִתְּךָ בְּתוּלִים וְעָנְשׁוּ אוֹתוֹ מֵאָה כֶסֶף (דברים כב, יט) **דִּינֵי
נְפָשׁוֹת.** דְּאִם אֱמֶת הָיָה הַדָּבָר וְחָנְתָה תַּחְתָּיו וּסְקָלוּהָ, וְדִינֵי נְפָשׁוֹת בְּעֶשְׂרִים וּשְׁלֹשָׁה כִּדְלַקְמָן
(מִשְׁנָה ז). וַהֲלָכָה כַחֲכָמִים:

יד אברהם

These cases could really have been
included in the category of injuries.
However, since the *Tanna* intended to
list the subsequent cases of extra
penalty payments [i.e., payments
required in excess of the actual
damages], he also cites the case of
half-payment, which is another
situation in which payment is not
equal to the damage. Once he listed
separately the case of half-payment
for damages, he also specified that of
full payment to complete the balance
(*Rav* from *Gem.* 3a).

תַּשְׁלוּמֵי כֶפֶל, — *twofold compensation,*

One who surreptitiously steals
from another [in contrast to a robber
who takes something by force] must
return the stolen object or repay him
for it and pay an additional penalty
equal to the value of the stolen object
(*Ex.* 22:3). Thus, he pays double the
amount of the theft.

וְתַשְׁלוּמֵי אַרְבָּעָה וַחֲמִשָּׁה, — *and fourfold or fivefold compensation,*

The Torah levies a special penalty
on one who steals a sheep or an ox and
slaughters or sells it. He must pay
fivefold for the ox and fourfold for
the sheep (*Ex.* 21:37).

בִּשְׁלֹשָׁה; — *[are judged] by three;*

All of these cases must be tried by
courts consisting of three ordained
judges (*Gem.* 8a).

הָאוֹנֵס, וְהַמְפַתֶּה, — *[claims against] a
rapist, a seducer,*

One who rapes or seduces an
unmarried girl must pay a fine of fifty
silver shekels (see *Ex.* 22:15-16; *Deut.*
22:28-29; *Kesubos* 3:4).

וְהַמּוֹצִיא שֵׁם רַע — *and a defamer*

[Jewish marriage consists of two
steps, *erusin* (betrothal) and *nisuin*
(full marriage). Although the man
and woman do not live together until
after the second stage, the laws of
adultery take effect with the first.
Today these two stages are generally
performed together at the wedding;
however, in former times an interval
of as much as a year separated the two
(see General Introduction to ArtScroll
Kiddushin).] If a man claimed that his
wife was guilty of infidelity during
their betrothal and brought witnesses
to that effect, but the witnesses were
discredited (see below), he is fined a
sum of one hundred silver shekels
which he must pay her (*Deut.* 22:13-
19). The mishnah here refers to the

1
1 twofold compensation, and fourfold or fivefold compensation, [are judged] by three; [claims against] a rapist, a seducer, and a defamer [are judged] by three; [these are] the words of R' Meir. However, the Sages say: [Claims against] a defamer are [judged] by twenty-three, because they involve a capital charge.

YAD AVRAHAM

trial of the husband for defaming his wife unjustly.]

בִּשְׁלֹשָׁה; דִּבְרֵי רַבִּי מֵאִיר. — *[are judged) by three; [these are] the words of R' Meir.*

[Claims against a rapist, seducer, and defamer require three ordained judges. However, with the exception of the last case, there is no dispute in the matter. Only the ruling concerning the defamer is the opinion of R' Meir alone.)

R' Meir considers the trial of a defamer to be primarily a monetary issue, regarding the fine of one hundred shekels. Although this case could conceivably lead to a capital issue — if the husband should manage to vindicate himself by bringing other witnesses to prove his wife's infidelity (since infidelity is punishable by death) — Meir is not concerned about this, since if additional judges will be necessary to try that aspect of the case, they can be added to the court afterward (*Rambam Comm.* from *Gem.* 8a).

וַחֲכָמִים אוֹמְרִים: מוֹצִיא שֵׁם רָע בְּעֶשְׂרִים וּשְׁלֹשָׁה, מִפְּנֵי שֶׁיֵּשׁ בּוֹ דִינֵי נְפָשׁוֹת. — *However, the Sages say: [Claims against] a defamer are [judged] by twenty-three, because they involve a capital charge.*

They contend that if this leads to a capital charge and new judges must be added, it will look as if the original judges were incompetent to judge the case. Therefore, they require twenty-three judges from the outset (*Tos.* 8a from *Gem.* ibid.).

There is much discussion among the commentators as to the precise nature of the witnesses' discreditation. Some explain that this refers to a case in which the witnesses contradicted each other when being interviewed by the court, thereby invalidating their testimony. Since we have no evidence that their statement is false, the Sages are concerned that it may indeed be true and that the husband may find other witnesses to testify to that effect. However, if they were contradicted by other witnesses (הַכְחָשָׁה) or totally discredited by other witnesses who testified that these were elsewhere at the time of the alleged act of adultery (הֲזָמָה), we would not be concerned that the charge may ultimately be proven true, and even the Sages would agree that three judges would suffice to try the defamation case (*Rabbeinu Tam* cited by *Tos.* 8a; see *Ran, Maharam; Rabbeinu Yonah*).

Others contend that if their testimony was not conclusively proven false, but merely discredited by their contradicting each other on certain details of their testimony, or by being contradicted by other witnesses, the husband would not have to pay the fine of one hundred shekels, since his claim has not been disproven but merely left unsubstantiated (*Rashi* to 8b,

מַכּוֹת בִּשְׁלֹשָׁה. מִשּׁוּם רַבִּי יִשְׁמָעֵאל אָמְרוּ: בְּעֶשְׂרִים וּשְׁלֹשָׁה. עִבּוּר הַחֹדֶשׁ

ר׳ עובדיה מברטנורא

(ב) **מכות.** מלקות ארבעים: **בשלשה.** דכתיב (דברים כה, א) ונגשו אל המשפט ושפטום, שנים, ואין בית דין שקול, מוסיפין עליהם עוד אחד, הרי כאן שלשה: **רבי ישמעאל אומר בעשרים ושלשה.** אתיא רשע רשע, כתיב הכא (שם) והרשיעו את הרשע, וכתיב התם (במדבר לה, לא) אשר הוא רשע למות, מה להלן בעשרים ושלשה אף כאן בעשרים ושלשה: **עבור החדש.** קדוש החדש, ואיידי דבעי למתני עבור שנה תנא נמי עבור החדש:

יד אברהם

witnesses. Therefore, twenty-three judges are required (*Ran;* cf. *Meiri*).

Rashi interprets this case of the mishnah to be dealing not with the defamation trial of a husband whose claim has been discredited, but with the initial charge in which the husband comes to court with a claim that his wife was not a virgin at the time of *nisuin* and therefore should not be eligible to receive the payment for her *kesubah* (see *Kesubos* and *Rashi* and *Tosafos* there; see also ibid. 12a). The Sages, however, are concerned that his claim in court may generate publicity which will cause witnesses to come forward and testify that she committed adultery during the *erusin* period, thus creating a need for twenty-three judges. Therefore, they require the full court from the beginning. R' Meir, however, is not concerned with this possibility as long as the husband himself did not bring such witnesses when he filed his claim (cf. *Ran; Meiri*).

The *Gemara* (8a-9b) offers several other interpretations of the dispute as well.

s.v. ובמקום; *Ramban* cited by *Ran*). Therefore, the mishnah cannot be referring to such a case [since there would be nothing to try] but must refer to one in which the girl's father brought witnesses who testified that those of the husband were someplace else at the time they claim to have seen the infidelity. Under Torah law, this suffices to prove them false. However, the father clearly states that his intention in bringing these witnesses is only to collect the fine from the husband, not to punish the witnesses for testifying falsely. R' Meir maintains that this distinction is legitimate, and we may therefore try the monetary case with three judges. The witnesses can be tried on a capital charge afterward by twenty-three for their false testimony. [This is according to the law of הֲזָמָה, *hazamah,* in which witnesses who are proven false in the manner described above receive whatever punishment they tried to bring upon the subject of their testimony (*Deut.* 19:19). Since their false testimony would have resulted in the wife being executed for adultery, they in turn suffer that penalty for testifying falsely about her.] The Sages, however, contend that the two aspects of the case are indivisible, and any judgment of the truth of this second testimony is automatically pertinent to the capital charge against the husband's

2.

מַכּוֹת בִּשְׁלֹשָׁה. — *[Cases of] lashes [are judged] by three.*

The punishment of thirty-nine lashes which is dictated by the Torah for certain transgressions is decided by a court of three ordained judges (*Rambam, Sanhedrin* 5:7; *Meiri*). This is derived from that which the Torah

1 2. [Cases of] lashes [are judged] by three. In the
2 name of R' Yishmael they said: By twenty-three. The intercalating of the month is

states concerning this punishment (*Deut.* 25:1): *And they shall judge them* — indicating that more than one judge is required. Since a court requires an odd number of judges to allow for a majority decision, the minimum amount of judges must be three (*Rav* from *Gem.* 10a).

מִשּׁוּם רַבִּי יִשְׁמָעֵאל אָמְרוּ: בְּעֶשְׂרִים וּשְׁלֹשָׁה. — *In the name of R' Yishmael they said: By twenty-three.*

The Torah uses the term רָשָׁע, *evildoer*, both in regard to one who is to be punished with lashes (*Deut.* 5:2) and one who is to be put to death (*Num.* 35:32). From this R' Yishmael derives that just as the latter must be judged by twenty-three judges (see mishnah 4), so must the former (*Rav* from *Gem.* ad loc.).

The *Gemara* cites another explanation, that flogging is viewed as a substitute for capital punishment — since he transgressed the command of his Creator and is thus fit to be put to death (*Rashi* ibid.) — and is therefore subject to the same rules (see *Likkutim* on this mishnah, *Yachin U'Boaz* ed.).

עִבּוּר הַחֹדֶשׁ — *The intercalating of the month*

The lunar month lasts precisely twenty-nine days, twelve hours, and 793 *chalakim*.[1] Since the Torah requires that the calendar be arranged so that the months consist of full days, it is necessary to make some months twenty-nine days and some thirty.

According to Torah law, this is to be adjusted on a monthly basis, based on the testimony of witnesses regarding the sighting of the New Moon. If the court accepts testimony that the moon was sighted on the evening of the thirtieth, the following day — the thirtieth day — is declared *Rosh Chodesh* (New Moon), i.e., the first day of the next month. If the new moon was not sighted, or no acceptable testimony came forth, the thirty-first day after the previous new moon automatically begins the next month (*Meiri* from *Gem.* 10b; *Rambam, Hil. Kiddush HaChodesh* 2:8).

Accordingly, actual intercalation, in which the month is extended to thirty days by pushing *Rosh Chodesh* off to the thirty-first, is effected automatically and does not require the involvement of the courts. The mishnah must therefore be understood to refer to the declaration of *Rosh Chodesh* when the month is not extended. This declaration is made by the courts on the thirtieth day after the previous new moon — that day which, if circumstances dictate, is designated for the day of intercalation. Thus, the mishnah should be understood as saying: [*The declaration on the day of the*] *intercalating of the month* ... (*Gem.* 10b).[2]

1. In the Talmudic system, the hour is divided into 1080 parts, called *chalakim*. Each *chelek* is therefore equal to 3 ⅓ seconds. 792 *chalakim* comes to 44 minutes.

2. There are actually two other opinions as to when declaration of the New Moon is necessary and when it occurs automatically, and the *Gemara* provides a different explanation of the mishnah in accordance with each of these views. The commentary

סנהדרין
א/ב

בִּשְׁלֹשָׁה; עִבּוּר הַשָּׁנָה בִּשְׁלֹשָׁה; דִּבְרֵי רַבִּי מֵאִיר. רַבָּן שִׁמְעוֹן בֶּן גַּמְלִיאֵל אוֹמֵר: בִּשְׁלֹשָׁה מַתְחִילִין, וּבַחֲמִשָּׁה נוֹשְׂאִין וְנוֹתְנִין, וְגוֹמְרִין

ר' עובדיה מברטנורא

בשלשה מתחילין. לראות אם יש להושיב בית דין על כך, אם אחד מהשלשה אומר לריך בית דין ליֵשב ולעיין אם לריכה שנה לעבר מפני התקופה והאביב והפירות, ושנים אומרים

יד אברהם

This arrangement for maintaining the calendar was used until the year 4119 after Creation (359 C.E.), when circumstances rendered it necessary to establish a permanent calendar (see ArtScroll commentary to *Rosh Hashanah* 1:3 and *History of the Jewish People* vol.II, pp. 190-191).

;בִּשְׁלֹשָׁה — *is by three;*

The Torah charges the courts with the obligation to sanctify the day of the new moon by declaring *Rosh Chodesh* (*Ex.* 12:2; *Rosh Hashanah* 24a, *Rambam*, loc. cit. 1:7). From the fact that Moses was commanded to include Aaron in his performance of this *mitzvah*, the *Gemara* (*Rosh Hashanah* 25b) derives that one ordained judge is not sufficient. Since an odd number of judges is always necessary, as explained above, we derive from this that three judges are required (see *Tos. Yom Tov*).

Rambam (*Hil. Kiddush HaChodesh* 5:1) states that only the High Court, or another court of ordained judges designated by the High Court in Eretz Yisrael, is authorized to intercalate the month or year (see below). Thus, once conditions in Eretz Yisrael deteriorated to the point where it became apparent that the Sanhedrin would have to cease functioning, a permanent calendar was instituted (ibid. 5:3). [This was done by Hillel II in the year 359 C.E. See ArtScroll *History of the Jewish People* vol.II, pp.190-191.]

Ramban (*Sefer HaMitzvos* Positive Precept 153) contends that any court of three duly ordained judges is acceptable although whenever there is a Sanhedrin, such action is deferred to them.

.עִבּוּר הַשָּׁנָה בִּשְׁלֹשָׁה; דִּבְרֵי רַבִּי מֵאִיר — *the intercalating of the year is by three; [these are] the words of R' Meir.*

The solar year, upon which the seasons are based, exceeds the twelve-month cycle of the lunar calendar by approximately eleven days. Thus, if

has followed the opinion which is accepted as the halachah.

Rav explains the word *intercalation* to mean the sanctification of the New Moon, and adds that the mishnah uses the term עִבּוּר חֹדֶשׁ — intercalation of the month — only because it parallels the terminology of the following case, which deals with the actual intercalation of the leap year. However, as *Tos. Yom Tov* notes, this explanation is offered by the *Gemara* only according to one of the conflicting opinions, which interprets the mishnah to refer to the deliberations concerning whether or not to extend the month another day.

[Nevertheless, it is conceivable that once the *Gemara* offered this interpretation, *Rav* considered it to be a viable explanation for the difficult wording of the mishnah according to our view as well, even though the *Gemara* did not deem it necessary to offer this explanation until it cited the conflicting view.]

1 by three; the intercalating of the year is by three;
2 [these are] the words of R' Meir. Rabban Shimon ben Gamliel says: It is begun with three, discussed by five, and concluded by seven. If

YAD AVRAHAM

no adjustments are made to the lunar calendar upon which the Jewish calendar is based, there would be no coordination whatsoever between the two. The months of the lunar year would arrive eleven days earlier each year (relative to the solar calendar). In the course of time this would result in the months and the holidays falling out during different seasons of the solar year. The Torah, however, commands the Jewish people to *guard the month of the spring* (*Deut.* 16:1) — i.e., to make sure that the month of Nissan, described elsewhere (*Ex.* 13:18) as the month of spring, actually falls out during that season. Similarly, the Torah refers to *Succos* as taking place at the turn of the year (ibid. v. 22), which means at the end of the growing season. It is thus evident that calendar manipulations must be made in order to correlate the lunar calendar with the seasons of the solar year. Since it is only permitted to add full months to the year, not extra days [aside from the extension of a month for one day as described above] (*Megillah* 5a), the occasional enactment of a leap year, with a thirteenth month added to it, is necessary. Until the permanent calendar was established (see above), this was left in the hands of the courts, who ordained the leap year whenever they saw the necessity of doing so.

Aside from the primary astronomical purpose of coordinating the year with the seasons, they also would add an extra month if the produce of that year was delayed in ripening and the month of Nissan would thereby not include the advent of actual אָבִיב, *spring*, which refers literally to the ripening of the produce. Similarly, if it was evident that the trees were behind schedule in producing their fruits, and they would thus not be ripe in time for *Shavuos* — to which the Torah refers as the day of the first fruits (*Num.* 28:26) — a leap year would be declared (*Gem.* 11b, as explained by *Rashi;* cf. *Ran* to 11a; *Meiri* to mishnah; *Rambam, Hil. Kiddush HaChodesh* 4:2,3). The *Gemara* (11a) also cites additional factors which are considered legitimate causes to extend the year.

The *Gemara* states that the year is extended only if two of the three causes cited above are pertinent — whereas any of the other reasons for intercalation is in itself sufficient (*Gem.* 11a; *Tos.* ibid.). However, *Rambam* maintains that the correlation of Nissan with spring is sufficient reason in itself to adjust the calendar (*Kiddush HaChodesh* 4:2), and only when the month of Tishrei alone is affected does the *Gemara* require another factor as well (*Likkutei Halachos* to 11b). Others dispute this view, and contend that two reasons are always necessary (*Rama*, gloss to *Rambam*, ad loc.).

Once the fixed calendar was established, it was divided into nineteen-year cycles, of which the third, sixth, eighth, eleventh, fourteenth, seventeenth, and nineteenth years are designated as leap years (see *Meiri*).

רַבָּן שִׁמְעוֹן בֶּן גַּמְלִיאֵל אוֹמֵר: בִּשְׁלֹשָׁה מַתְחִילִין, וּבַחֲמִשָּׁה נוֹשְׂאִין וְנוֹתְנִין, וְגוֹמְרִין בְּשִׁבְעָה. — *Rabban Shimon ben Gamliel says: It is begun with three, discussed by five, and concluded by seven.*

בְּשִׁבְעָה. וְאִם גָּמְרוּ בִשְׁלֹשָׁה מְעֻבֶּרֶת.

[ג] **סְמִיכַת** זְקֵנִים וַעֲרִיפַת עֶגְלָה בִּשְׁלֹשָׁה;

ר׳ עובדיה מברטנורא

אין צריך, שאין כאן ספק דודאי אינה צריכה עבור, בטל יחיד במעוטו, שנים אומרים לישב ואחד אומר שלא לישב, הולכין אחר השנים, ומוסיפין עוד שנים אחרים שישאו ויתנו בדבר, והרי כאן חמשה. שנים אומרים צריך לעבר ושלשה אומרים אין צריך, בטלו שנים במעוטן, שנים אומרים אינה צריכה ושלשה אומרים צריכה, הולכים אחר הרוב, ומוסיפין עוד שנים שיהיו שבעה ומעברין אותה. ובגמרא (י, ב) מפרש, דהני שלשה חמשה ושבעה כנגד ברכת כהנים, שיש בפסוק ראשון שלש תיבות, ובשני חמשה, ובשלישי שבעה. והלכה כרבן שמעון בן גמליאל: (ג) **סמיכת זקנים.** על ראש פר העלם דבר של צבור. ויש במשמעות הדברים גם מנויי הדיין, שהגדול הסומך צריך שיצרף עמו שנים כשרוצה לסמוך חכם כדי שיקרא רבי וידון דיני קנסות, ולשון סמיכה משום דכתיב (במדבר כז, כג) ויסמוך את ידיו עליו, ולאו דבעי מסמך ידיה עליה אלא בשמא קרו ליה רבי. ואין סמיכה בחוצה לארץ, אלא צריך שהסומך והנסמך יהיו כולן בארץ ישראל, ואז יהיה לו רשות לדון דיני קנסות ואפילו בחוץ לארץ, לפי שסנהדרין נוהגת בין בארץ בין בחוץ לארץ אחר שנסמכו בארץ. וכתב רמב״ם שנראה לו שבזמן הזה שאין לנו סמוך איש מפי איש עד משה רבינו, אם היו מסכימים כל החכמים שבארץ ישראל לסמוך יחיד או רבים, הרי אלו סמוכים ויכולים לדון דיני קנסות ויש להן לסמוך לאחרים. והדבר צריך הכרע: **ועריפת העגלה בשלשה.** דכתיב (ויקרא ד, טו) זקני

יד אברהם

The head of the High Court[1] gathers seven of its members to consider the possibility of intercalating (*Meiri, Rambam, Kiddush HaChodesh* from *Gem.* 11a). At first, three of them weigh the issue. If only one considers it necessary to give it serious consideration, but the other two do not, the matter is dropped. If two of them deem it necessary, another two judges are added and the matter is pursued further. If three of those five decide that it is unnecessary to intercalate, the year remains unchanged. If three feel a leap year is called for, another two judges are added and the seven declare a leap year (*Rav* from *Gem.* 10b). *Rambam* (*Kiddush HaChodesh* 4:10) states that after the sixth and seventh judges are added the matter is weighed yet again before the leap year is declared.

The *Gemara* (ibid.) explains that these numbers were chosen because they parallel the verses of the Kohanic blessing (*Num.* 6:22ff) of which the first verse contains three words, the second five, and the third seven. The power of blessing is thereby invoked to help insure the success of the intercalation in arranging that the seasons take place in the proper time (*Tos. Yom Tov*).

The *Gemara* discusses only those situations in which there was disagreement among the judges as to the necessity of declaring a leap year. If all agreed that it was necessary, there are those who maintain that no further discussion was required and the leap year would be declared immediately (*Yad Ramah;* cf. *Meiri*). Others contend that the same process is

1. The wisest member of the High Court is appointed head of the court and thus fills the role of *Nasi* in place of Moshe [who headed the original Sanhedrin] (*Rambam, Hil. Sanhedrin* 1:3).

1
3

they concluded with three it is valid.

3. The *semichah* of the elders and the decapitation of the calf are by three;

required whether or not there is dispute (*Rabbeinu Yonah*).

וְאִם גָּמְרוּ בִשְׁלֹשָׁה מְעֻבֶּרֶת. — *If they concluded with three it is valid.*

If three judges decided the issue on their own and declared the leap year, it is valid, as long as the head of the Sanhedrin concurs (*Meiri* from *Gem.* 11a; *Rambam, Kiddush HaChodesh* 4:10).

Another interpretation of this phrase of the mishnah is that if the three judges who began deliberations all agreed that it was necessary, they may declare the leap year without further discussion (*Yad Ramah;* see above).

3.

סְמִיכַת זְקֵנִים — *The semichah of the elders*

Semichah is a rite, required in the service of most animal sacrifices, in which the owner of the offering places both his hands on top of the animal's head and leans on it with all his weight, and confesses to God the sin for which he is bringing the offering.

Generally, this rite is reserved for sacrifices brought on behalf of an individual. However, there are two public offerings which require it. One is the *Azazel* goat which is sent out to its death on *Yom Kippur* (see *Yoma* Ch. 6). The *semichah* in this instance is performed by the *Kohen Gadol* (on behalf of the entire people). The other is the פַּר הֶעְלֵם דָּבָר, the bull brought for certain types of sins performed by the majority of the congregation due to a mistaken decision rendered by the Sanhedrin.[1] The Torah mandates (*Lev.* 4:14) that in this case a special offering is brought by the High Court [instead of individual offerings on the part of all who transgressed). This offering requires *semichah,* which is performed by the members of the Sanhedrin, as specified in the Torah (ibid. v. 15) (*Meiri*).

As explained in the *Gemara* (13b), the term *semichah* has another connotation as well, viz., ordination to serve as Rabbinic judge, to be entitled "Rabbi," and to be able to mete out monetary fines (see preface to chapter). This term is used because the Torah (*Num.* 27:23), in describing how Moses granted his authority to Joshua, states, *And he leaned his hands on him.* Although no actual laying of hands is required for this conferral of authority, the term *semichah* is nevertheless used to describe it (*Rav*). For *semichah* of this sort to be valid, it must be granted by three judges, at least one of whom has received *semichah* ordination from the line stretching back to the *semichah* of Moses (*Rambam, Hil. Sanhedrin* 4:1-3).

וַעֲרִיפַת עֶגְלָה — *and the decapitation of the calf*

If the body of a murder victim is discovered outside a city in Eretz Yisrael and it is not known who killed

1. These are sins for which one is liable to *kares* (Divinely decreed premature death) for a deliberate violation and a sin-offering for an inadvertent violation; several other qualifications apply as well — see *Horayos* Ch. 1.

דִּבְרֵי רַבִּי שִׁמְעוֹן. וְרַבִּי יְהוּדָה אוֹמֵר: בַּחֲמִשָּׁה. הַחֲלִיצָה וְהַמֵּאוּנִין,

ר׳ עובדיה מברטנורא

העדה, מעוט זקני שנים, ואין בית דין שקול, הוסיף עליהם עוד אחד הרי שלשה: **רבי יהודה אומר בחמשה.** וסמכו, שנים, זקני, שנים, ואין בית דין שקול, הוסיף עליהם עוד אחד, הרי חמשה. והלכה כרבי יהודה: **מצות חליצה בשלשה.** דכתיב (דברים כה, ט) ונגשה יבמתו אליו לעיני הזקנים, זקנים, שנים, ואין בית דין שקול, הוסיף עליהם עוד אחד, הרי שלשה. ושנים אחרים שמוסיפין אינו אלא לפרסומי מילתא: **מיאונין.** קטנה יתומה שהשיאוה אמה ואחיה לדעתה ויוצאה במיאון שממאנת בבעלה, צריך שיהיה בשלשה. וביבמות (קז, ב) מוכח דמיאון בפני שנים מספיק:

יד אברהם

him, the Torah mandates that the town nearest to where the body was found must take a calf which was never worked and bring it down to a valley of unworked ground, where it is decapitated (*Deut.* 21:1-4).

The mishnah refers here to the process of measuring the distance between the corpse and the surrounding towns to determine which is closest and thus responsible to bring the calf and decapitate it. The decapitation was not performed by members of the Sanhedrin but by the court of the town which was closest, as stated explicitly in the Biblical passage (*Meiri; Tos.* to 14a).

בִּשְׁלֹשָׁה; דִּבְרֵי רַבִּי שִׁמְעוֹן. — *are by three; [these are) the words of R' Shimon.*

Both the *semichah* of the bull brought for a mistaken ruling of the High Court and the measurement for the purposes of the decapitated calf require three judges of the Sanhedrin.

R' Shimon is of the opinion that three judges from the Sanhedrin must perform the rite of *semichah* because the Torah states (*Lev.* 4:15): *The elders of the congregation shall lean,* using the plural. Since the plural indicates at least two judges, and since a court cannot consist of an even number of judges, we may derive that three elders are required (*Gem.* 13b).[1]

Similarly, the measurement of the distance between the corpse and nearby towns to determine which is closest must be done by members of the Sanhedrin, as stated in that passage (v. 2): *And your elders and your judges shall go out and they shall measure,* etc. Since the verse uses the plural at least two are indicated, and since a court must always consist of an odd number of judges, we derive that three are required (*Rav* from *Gem.* 14a; *Tos.* ibid.).[2]

1. Although an odd number of judges is required only to insure that any vote will result in a majority decision, the requirement for three judges is pertinent to the *semichah* of the bull as well. It is possible that the bull will develop a blemish, necessitating a ruling as to whether or not it is of the sort which disqualifies the bull from being an offering, and thereby necessitating a majority decision in case of a dispute (*Yad Ramah* to 14a).

2. In this case, too, the need for a majority decision may arise, since there are different opinions as to the precise spot from which the corpse is measured (*Yad Ramah* to 14a).

1 [these are] the words of R′ Shimon. R′ Yehudah,
3 however, says: By five. *Chalitzah* and refusal

YAD AVRAHAM

וְרַבִּי יְהוּדָה אוֹמֵר: בַּחֲמִשָּׁה. — *R′ Yehudah, however, says: By five.*

R′ Yehudah maintains that in both these instances five judges are required. In the case of *semichah* the verse states (*Lev.* 4:15): וְסָמְכוּ זִקְנֵי הָעֵדָה אֶת יְדֵיהֶם עַל רֹאשׁ הַפָּר, *And the elders of the congregation shall lay their hands on the head of the bull.* He understands the word וְסָמְכוּ, *And they shall lay,* to denote a second plural, thereby indicating that yet another two judges are required (*Gem.* 13a).

Similarly, in regard to the calf, R′ Yehudah interprets the words *your elders and your judges* to teach that two sets of two are necessary, plus a fifth to make an odd number (*Gem.* 14a from *Sotah* 9:1).

The halachah follows the view of R′ Shimon concerning *semichah* (*Rambam, Hil. Maaseh HaKorbanos* 3:6, *Hil. Sanhedrin* 4:3), and the view of R′ Yehudah in regard to the decapitation of the calf (ibid. 5:5). This is based on *Yerushalmi,* which decides in this manner (*Meiri*).

הַחֲלִיצָה — *Chalitzah*

If a man dies without children, the Torah declares it a *mitzvah* for his brother to marry his widow. This marriage is known as *yibum* (levirate marriage). Pending this, the widow is forbidden to marry anyone else. If the brother should refuse to fulfill the *mitzvah* of *yibum,* he must release her from her *yibum*-bond by performing the alternate rite of *chalitzah,* in which she removes his shoe before the court and spits before him and declares, *So should be done to the man who will not build his brother's house* (*Deut.* 25:5-10).

In describing this procedure, the Torah states (v.9): *And his yevamah (widow) shall approach him in the presence of the elders* — thereby indicating that at least two judges are required. Since a court must comprise an odd number of judges [because a ruling on the validity of the *chalitzah* may be required, thereby necessitating a majority decision], three judges are necessary (*Rav* from *Yevamos* 101a).

וְהַמֵּאוּנִין — *and refusal,*

The Torah grants the father of a girl who is a minor the authority to marry her off (see *Kiddushin* 2:1). If a girl has no father, the Rabbis enacted that her mother or brothers can do so. However, since a marriage effected by her mother or brothers is only Rabbinic in nature, when she comes of age she has the right to refuse the marriage and thereby retroactively negate it (see *Yevamos* Ch. 13). This refusal must be done before a court of three judges, since the Rabbis, whenever possible, modeled their ordinances after the precedents of the Torah (*Rashi*).[1]

1. This statement is very difficult to understand, since a divorce from a marriage which is valid by Torah law does not require the participation of the court and can be done merely in the presence of two witnesses (*Tos. R′ Akiva*). It is possible, however, that *Rashi* is referring to the law of *chalitzah,* in which the refusal of the *yavam* to marry the *yevamah* creates the necessity for the negation of their bond by the process of *chalitzah;* for this a court of three is

סנהדרין א/ג

בִּשְׁלשָׁה. נֶטַע רְבָעִי וּמַעֲשֵׂר שֵׁנִי שֶׁאֵין דָּמָיו יְדוּעִין, בִּשְׁלשָׁה. הַהֶקְדֵּשׁוֹת בִּשְׁלשָׁה; הָעֲרָכִין הַמִּטַּלְטְלִין בִּשְׁלשָׁה. רַבִּי יְהוּדָה אוֹמֵר:

ר׳ עובדיה מברטנורא

נטע רבעי. אם בא לחללו על המעות, [וכן] מעשר שני, ואין דמיהן ידועים, כגון פירות והרקיבו שאין להם שער ידוע: **וההקדשות.** הבא לפדותן צריך שלשה לשומן: **הערכין המטלטלין.** הרי שאמר ערך פלוני עלי, ואין לו מעות ליתן כפי הדמים הקצובים בפרשה, ובא ליתן מטלטלין, צריך שלשה לשום אותן מטלטלים:

יד אברהם

בִּשְׁלשָׁה. — *are before three.*

[Both *chalitzah* and refusal require a court of three judges, as explained above.]

In these cases, the judges need not be ordained (*Yevamos* ibid.), but if at all possible they should at least be sufficiently knowledgeable to be able to dictate the *chalitzah* formula to the *yevamah* (*Yevamos* 101a; *Even HaEzer* 169:1; *Beis Shmuel* 3). Although three judges are sufficient, it is preferable that the court consist of five judges to facilitate greater publicity (*Yevamos* 101b; *Even HaEzer* 169:3).

In regard to refusal, the *Gemara* (*Yevamos* 107b) cites the opinion of R' Yose ben R' Yehudah and R' Eliezer ben R' Shimon that two judges are sufficient, and rules that the halachah follows that opinion (*Rav*).

נֶטַע רְבָעִי — *The fourth-year fruit*

The fruit produced by a tree in Eretz Yisrael the first three years after it has been planted (or transplanted) is prohibited by Torah law. This is known as *orlah*. In the fourth year, the fruit is consecrated in the same manner as *maaser sheni* (the second tithe, see below) and it must be eaten in Jerusalem or be redeemed, with the money then spent in Jerusalem on food (*Lev.* 19:23, 24; *Rashi* ad loc.).

וּמַעֲשֵׂר שֵׁנִי — *and the maaser sheni*

On the first, second, fourth, and fifth years of the seven-year *Shemittah* cycle, a second *maaser* (tithe) must be taken — in addition to the first *maaser* which is given to a *Levi*. The *maaser sheni* (second tithe) must be taken to Jerusalem and eaten there or redeemed for money, with the money being taken to Jerusalem and used there for food (*Deut.* 14:22-26).

שֶׁאֵין דָּמָיו יְדוּעִין, בִּשְׁלשָׁה. — *whose value (lit., that its value) is unknown are [judged] by three.*

I.e., if one decides to redeem them and their value is not apparent, it must be assessed by a court of three (*Rav*). The *Gemara* (14b) cites the mishnah in *Maaser Sheni* 4:2 which

necessary, as stated above (*Rashash*). [Alternatively, the requirement for the participation of a court may be necessary as a fundamental component of the ordinance, since the retroactive annulment of a marriage is not something which can be left without Rabbinic supervision. *Rashi* means only to explain why the court must include *three* judges. To this he cites the precedent of those matters which require the participation of a court by Torah law.]

1 are before three. The fourth-year fruit and the
3 *maaser sheni* whose value is unknown are [judged] by three. [Redemption] of articles of *hekdesh* is [judged] by three. Assessments of movable objects is by three. R' Yehudah says:

gives as examples of this wine which has begun to sour (*Rav* ibid.) and fruit which has spoiled. These have no clear-cut price because the extent of the damage must be carefully assessed in each case to determine their remaining value (*Tif. Yis.* ibid.).

The laws of *maaser sheni* are derived from those of *hekdesh* (consecrated objects, see below) to require three, since they are discussed in the same passage (*Lev.* 27:31), and the laws of the fourth-year fruit are derived from those of *maaser sheni* (*Ran* to 14b).

As the *Gemara* explains, the assessment is not made by judges but by three buyers (*Gem.* 14b) — i.e., three merchants who are experts in assessing its value (*Rashi*).

Others interpret this to refer to people who are interested in buying this produce, with the assessment following the highest bid (see *Tos.*). Some suggest that both factors are required (*Rabbeinu Yonah*).

The mishnah's reference to fruit *whose* [lit., *its*) *value is unknown* applies only to the case of *maaser sheni* produce. [This is evident from the fact that the word דָּמָיו, literally, *its value*, is used in the singular.] In the case of fourth-year fruit, however, all fruit must be assessed by three. Since the owner is very anxious to eat these fruits [having already waited three years], his judgment in assessing them fairly is not considered reliable (*Tos.* 14b; cf. *Rama; Rash* to *Maaser Sheni* 5:2).

Others maintain that this phrase refers to both cases (*Rashi; Meiri*). Indeed, according to some versions, the mishnah reads שֶׁאֵין דְּמֵיהֶם יְדוּעִין, *that their value is unknown* (see *Rashi; Rabbeinu Yonah*).

הַהֶקְדֵּשׁוֹת בִּשְׁלֹשָׁה; — *[Redemption] of articles of hekdesh is [judged] by three;*

One who wishes to redeem an object of *hekdesh* [something consecrated for Temple use] must have its value assessed by a court of three (*Rav*). This is derived from the Torah's triple mention (*Lev.* 27:11,12) of the *Kohen*, who is described as the one to assess the animal which is being redeemed (*Gem.* 14b; see *Yad Ramah*).

הָעֲרָכִין הַמִּטַּלְטְלִין בִּשְׁלֹשָׁה; — *assessments of movable objects is by three.*

The Torah (*Lev.* Ch. 27) sets standard values for men and women of different ages in regard to one who vows to donate his worth to the Temple. If someone made such a vow, but he has no money with which to fulfill it, and he wishes to donate movable objects instead, the value of those objects must be assessed by a court of three (*Rav* from *Gem.* 15a). This is derived logically: Just as the assessment of an object for its redemption from the possession of the Temple requires three since a lone assessor may err, so too does that of an object being donated to the Temple to fulfill an obligation (*Gem.* ibid.).

אֶחָד מֵהֶן כֹּהֵן. וְהַקַּרְקָעוֹת תִּשְׁעָה וְכֹהֵן, וְאָדָם כַּיּוֹצֵא בָהֶן.

[ד] **דִּינֵי** נְפָשׁוֹת בְּעֶשְׂרִים וּשְׁלֹשָׁה. הָרוֹבֵעַ וְהַנִּרְבָּע בְּעֶשְׂרִים וּשְׁלֹשָׁה, שֶׁנֶּאֱמַר: ,,וְהָרַגְתָּ אֶת־הָאִשָּׁה וְאֶת־הַבְּהֵמָה״, וְאוֹמֵר: ,,וְאֶת־הַבְּהֵמָה תַּהֲרֹגוּ״. שׁוֹר הַנִּסְקָל בְּעֶשְׂרִים וּשְׁלֹשָׁה,

ר׳ עובדיה מברטנורא

אחד מהן כהן. דבערכין כהן כתיב (ויקרא כז, יב) כערכך הכהן: **והקרקעות.** ואם אין לו מטלטלין ובא ליתן קרקע, צריך שישומו עשרה אנשים ואחד מהן כהן אותה קרקע שיהיה כפי הערך שיש עליו ליתן: **ואדם כיוצא בהן.** ואם אמר דמי פלוני עלי, שמין אותו כמה הוא יפה לימכר בשוק ונותן דמיו, צריך גם כן שיהיו עשרה ואחד מהן כהן בשומא זו: **(ד) והרגת את האשה ואת הבהמה.** היינו רובע, ואתקש לאשה, מה אשה בעשרים ושלשה אף בהמה בעשרים ושלשה. ואומר (ויקרא כ, טו) ואת הבהמה תהרוגו, בנרבע כתיב. למדנו רובע ונרבע:

יד אברהם

רַבִּי יְהוּדָה אוֹמֵר: אֶחָד מֵהֶן כֹּהֵן. — *R' Yehudah says: One of them [must be] a Kohen.*

As stated in the Torah (*Lev.* 27:12): *As the Kohen shall assess for you* (*Rav* from *Gem.* 15a). The same reasoning would apply to the previous case of the redemption of objects from *hekdesh* (*Tos. Yom Tov*).

It is not clear why the first *Tanna* does not accept this reasoning (*Gem.* ibid.). Nevertheless, the halachah follows that view (*Likkutei Halachos* from *Rambam, Hil. Arachin* 8:2).

וְהַקַּרְקָעוֹת — *That of real property*

I.e., if he had no movable objects and offered land for the fulfillment of his vow (*Rav; Rambam Comm.*).

Others explain this to refer to one who wishes to redeem real estate belonging to the Temple treasury (*Rashi;* see *Tos. Yom Tov*).

תִּשְׁעָה וְכֹהֵן, — *is by nine and a Kohen,*

The Torah mentions the word *Kohen* ten times in the passage concerning *arachin* (donations of personal worth) and redemption of Temple property, thereby indicating that ten people must be involved in the assessment. Having mentioned the fact that it must be done by a *Kohen* once, it was unnecessary to constantly repeat it. It is therefore understood that these extra mentions of *Kohen* come in fact to teach that a *Kohen* is not necessary for the additional assessors. Since there are nine redundant references to a *Kohen,* nine of the ten assessors need not be *Kohanim* and only one must (*Gem.* 15a).

The question is raised why an eleventh is not required in order to create a court with an odd number of judges (*Tos. Megillah* 23b, s.v. עשרה; *Arachin* 19b, s.v. או דלמא). Some explain that the decision of the ten who assess the property must be unanimous; majority rule does not apply in this case. Therefore, there is no reason to require an odd number (*Turei Even* to *Megillah* ad loc.).

וְאָדָם כַּיּוֹצֵא בָהֶן. — *and likewise for a human being.*

1
4
One of them [must be] a *Kohen*. That of real property is by nine and a *Kohen*, and likewise for a human being.

4. Capital cases are [judged] by twenty-three. The [animal] which commits an act of bestiality or is its recipient [is judged] by twenty-three, as it says: *And you shall kill the woman and the animal*, and it says: *And the animal you shall kill.* An ox which is to be stoned [is judged] by twenty-three,

YAD AVRAHAM

If someone vowed to donate to the Temple the actual market value of a certain person [i.e., the price he would fetch if sold as a slave], the assessment must also be done by a group of ten, with one of them a *Kohen* (*Rav* from *Gem.* loc. cit.). This is because such value is determined in regard to the slave market, and a slave is legally treated as real estate, not movable property, in regard to many laws of the Torah (*Gem.* ibid.).

4.

דִּינֵי נְפָשׁוֹת בְּעֶשְׂרִים וּשְׁלֹשָׁה. — *Capital cases are [judged) by twenty-three.*

This refers to any case involving the possibility of the death penalty in whatever form (*Meiri*). The requirement of a court of twenty-three is derived from Scripture, as explained in mishnah 6.

הָרוֹבֵעַ וְהַנִּרְבָּע, — *The [animal] which commits an act of bestiality or is its recipient*

I.e., the male animal which has intimate relations with a woman or the animal which was the recipient of such relations from a man (*Rashi* 2a) is executed, as is its human partner.

בְּעֶשְׂרִים וּשְׁלֹשָׁה, שֶׁנֶּאֱמַר: ,,וְהָרַגְתָּ אֶת־הָאִשָּׁה וְאֶת־הַבְּהֵמָה״, — *[is judged] by twenty-three, as it says* (*Lev.* 20:16): *"And you shall kill the woman and the animal,"*

This is the verse which delineates the punishment for a woman who had relations with an animal. By including the two in one condemnation, the Torah teaches that just as the woman's death sentence requires a court of twenty- three judges (as stated above), so too does that of the animal (*Rav*).

וְאוֹמֵר: ,,וְאֶת־הַבְּהֵמָה תַּהֲרֹגוּ״. — *and it says* (*ibid.* v. 15): *"And the animal you shall kill."*

This is stated in reference to an animal on which a man committed an act of bestiality. We derive the need for twenty-three from the similarity to the case cited above (*Rav;* cf. *Tos. Yom Tov*).

שׁוֹר הַנִּסְקָל בְּעֶשְׂרִים וּשְׁלֹשָׁה, — *An ox which is to be stoned [is judged] by twenty-three,*

I.e., an ox that killed a human being, which is put to death by stoning, must be judged and condemned by a court of twenty-three (*Tif. Yis.*).

שֶׁנֶּאֱמַר: „הַשּׁוֹר יִסָּקֵל וְגַם בְּעָלָיו יוּמָת״ — כְּמִיתַת הַבְּעָלִים כָּךְ מִיתַת הַשּׁוֹר.

הַזְּאֵב, וְהָאֲרִי, הַדֹּב, וְהַנָּמֵר, וְהַבַּרְדְּלָס, וְהַנָּחָשׁ מִיתָתָן בְּעֶשְׂרִים וּשְׁלֹשָׁה. רַבִּי אֱלִיעֶזֶר אוֹמֵר: כָּל הַקּוֹדֵם לְהָרְגָן זָכָה. רַבִּי עֲקִיבָא אוֹמֵר: מִיתָתָן בְּעֶשְׂרִים וּשְׁלֹשָׁה.

ר׳ עובדיה מברטנורא

כמיתת הבעלים. כלומר כמו שהיה הבעל נדון בעשרים ושלשה אם היה חייב מיתה: **כל הקודם להורגן זכה.** כשהמיתו את האדם, ואין צריך להביאם לבית דין: **רבי עקיבא אומר וכו׳.** בגמרא (טו, ב) מפרש דאיכא בין תנא קמא לרבי עקיבא, נחש. דלתנא קמא נחש מיתתו בעשרים ושלשה, ולרבי עקיבא הזאב הארי והדוב והנמר והברדלס מיתתן בעשרים ושלשה, אבל נחש הקודם להרגו זכה, שסלק המזיק מן העולם. והלכה כרבי עקיבא:

יד אברהם

— שֶׁנֶּאֱמַר: „הַשּׁוֹר יִסָּקֵל וְגַם בְּעָלָיו יוּמָת״ — *as it says (Ex. 21:29): "The ox shall be stoned and also its owner shall be put to death"* —

This cannot be taken literally to mean that the owner of the ox is executed for the killing committed by his animal, because the Torah states elsewhere (*Num.* 35:21): *The one who struck the blow shall be put to death, he is a murderer,* which indicates that one is punished with the death penalty only for a murder which he himself perpetrates, not for the actions of his animal. The verse must therefore be interpreted in the following manner (*Gem.* 15b).

כְּמִיתַת הַבְּעָלִים כָּךְ מִיתַת הַשּׁוֹר. — *in the same manner as the owner [is put to] death, the ox is [put to] death.*

I.e., just as the death sentence of the owner requires a court of twenty-three, so does that of the ox (*Rav* from *Gem.* 15a).

הַזְּאֵב, וְהָאֲרִי, הַדֹּב, וְהַנָּמֵר, וְהַבַּרְדְּלָס, וְהַנָּחָשׁ — *The wolf, the lion, the bear, the leopard, the bardelas, and the snake*

Our translation of נָמֵר as leopard follows *Rashi* to *Jeremiah* 13:23; see also *Radak* in *Shorashim.*

There is much controversy concerning the identity of the bardelas. *Rashi* (*Gem.* 15b) identifies it as a skunk. *Tosafos* dispute this, since it is listed among those animals which are likely to kill people. They suggest that it refers to a type of snake. *Aruch* renders it a leopardess, which is fiercer than its male counterpart. Other commentators identify it as cheetah, and some, as the hyena (*Kafich*). See *Aruch HaShalem.*

מִיתָתָן בְּעֶשְׂרִים וּשְׁלֹשָׁה. — *are sentenced to death* (lit., *their death is*) *by twenty-three.*

1 as it says: *The ox shall be stoned and also its owner*
4 *shall be put to death* — in the same manner as the owner [is put to] death, the ox is [put to] death.

The wolf, the lion, the bear, the leopard, the *bardelas*, and the snake are sentenced to death by twenty-three. R' Eliezer says: Whoever is first to kill them acquires merit. R' Akiva says: Their death is by twenty-three.

YAD AVRAHAM

This is based on the *Gemara's* (*Bava Kamma* 54b) conclusion that the Torah's reference to a murderous ox is only by way of example, and the ruling stated applies to all animals (*Rashi;* cf. *Tos. Yom Tov*). However, this applies only to an animal which has an owner. If it is wild, everyone agrees with the opinion of R' Eliezer (below) that anyone may kill it (*Likkutei Halachos* from *Rambam, Sanhedrin* 5:2; see also *Rashi* to 15b, s.v. יש להם תרבות).

רַבִּי אֱלִיעֶזֶר אוֹמֵר: כָּל הַקּוֹדֵם לְהָרְגָן זָכָה. — *R' Eliezer says: Whoever is first to kill them acquires merit.*

I.e., they do not need to be judged and condemned by a court — rather, they may be killed on sight by anyone. However, this is only if they killed a human being (*Rav* from *Gem.* ibid.). Otherwise, since they are someone's property, they may not be killed, because in general they are capable of being tamed. However, if one of them kills, it indicates that it is not capable of being tamed. Thus, it may not be kept and it is therefore not protected by due process (*Rashi* ad loc.).

Others contend that this explanation is not valid because R' Eliezer maintains his position even in regard to domesticated animals. Rather, he disputes the basic assumption of the other view and contends that other animals are not compared to the ox to be protected by due process (*Yad Ramah*).

רַבִּי עֲקִיבָא אוֹמֵר: מִיתָתָן בְּעֶשְׂרִים וּשְׁלֹשָׁה. — *R' Akiva says: Their death is by twenty-three.*

Although he seems to be saying the same thing as the first *Tanna*, the *Gemara* concludes that they disagree in regard to a snake, which R' Akiva contends may be put to death by anyone (*Rav*).

The halachah follows the opinion of the first *Tanna* in regard to all the other animals (*Rambam, Sanhedrin* 5:2). Concerning the snake, some maintain that the halachah follows the view of R' Eliezer and R' Akiva (*Rav, Rambam,* loc. cit.), whereas others contend that the view of the *Tanna Kamma* prevails here as well (*Ravad*, ad loc.).

5.

The mishnah now lists those matters which require the authority of the High Court — the Great Sanhedrin — of seventy-one judges.

סנהדרין [ה] **אֵין** דָּנִין לֹא אֶת הַשֵּׁבֶט, וְלֹא אֶת נְבִיא הַשֶּׁקֶר, וְלֹא אֶת כֹּהֵן גָּדוֹל, אֶלָּא עַל פִּי בֵית דִּין שֶׁל שִׁבְעִים וְאֶחָד. וְאֵין מוֹצִיאִין לְמִלְחֶמֶת הָרְשׁוּת אֶלָּא עַל פִּי בֵית דִּין שֶׁל שִׁבְעִים וְאֶחָד. אֵין מוֹסִיפִין עַל הָעִיר וְעַל הָעֲזָרוֹת

א/ה

ר׳ עובדיה מברטנורא

(ה) **את השבט.** רובו של שבט שעבדו עבודה זרה במזיד אין דנין אלא בבית דין של שבעים ואחד, דכתיב (דברים יז, ה) והוצאת את האיש ההוא או את האשה ההיא אל שעריך, איש ואשה אתה מוציא אל שעריך, ואי אתה מוציא את השבט אל שעריך אלא בבית דין הגדול: **ולא את נביא השקר.** גמר דבר דבר מזקן ממרא, כתיב הכא (שם יח, כ) אשר יזיד לדבר דבר, וכתיב בזקן ממרא (שם יז, ח) כי יפלא ממך דבר, מה זקן ממרא בבית דין הגדול דכתיב (שם) וקמת ועלית, אף נביא שקר בבית דין הגדול: **ולא את כהן גדול.** דאמר קרא (שמות יח, כב) את הדבר הגדול יביאו אליך, דבריו של גדול יביאו אליך, ומשה במקום שבעים [ואחד] קאי: **ואין מוציאין למלחמת הרשות.** כל מלחמה חוץ ממלחמת שבעה עממין ומלחמת עמלק קרויה מלחמת הרשות:

יד אברהם

אֵין דָּנִין לֹא אֶת הַשֵּׁבֶט, — *A tribe ... may not be judged* (lit., *we do not try a tribe*)

This refers to the trial of a complete tribe, or the majority of one, for the crime of idolatry (*Rav; Rashi*).

The necessity of having a High Court to try a tribe is derived from the verse (*Deut.* 17:5): *And you shall take out that man or that woman, who did this evil thing, to your gates* [i.e., to the court of the town, which in ancient times met at the town gate] ... *and stone them with stones until they die.* The *Gemara* (16a) infers: A man or a woman [i.e., an individual] is taken out to your gates [i.e., local court of twenty-three], but not a tribe, which requires the High Court (*Rav*). Since the general rule is that the majority of any body is treated like the whole, the majority of a tribe is also included in this ruling (*Maharsha.*).

וְלֹא אֶת נְבִיא הַשֶּׁקֶר, — *a false prophet,*

I.e., one who declares in the name of God a prophecy which he never received, whose punishment is death by strangulation [see below, 11:1] (*Meiri*). The fact that he spoke falsely is determined by the fact that his prediction does not come true (*Deut.* 18:21-22).

Such a person is judged by the Great Sanhedrin because he is compared exegetically to a זָקֵן מַמְרֵא, *rebellious sage* — a qualified judge who refused to abide by a decision of the High Court. Should he continue to rule in conflict with their ruling, he is executed (see below, 11:2). Just as the designation of *rebellious sage* applies only to one who rejects the majority decision of the Great Sanhedrin, not any other, so does the authority to judge a false prophet (*Rav* from *Gem.* 16a).

The rebellious sage himself, however, is judged by a court of twenty-three. The tradition comparing him to a false prophet is only in regard to the rebellion itself, not the trial of the rebellious sage (*Gem.* 16a).

וְלֹא אֶת כֹּהֵן גָּדוֹל, — *and a Kohen Gadol,*

A *Kohen Gadol* (High Priest) may be tried only before the court of seventy-one judges. This is derived

1
5

5. **A** tribe, a false prophet, and a *Kohen Gadol*, may not be judged except before the court of seventy-one. A discretionary war may not be waged without the approval of the court of seventy-one. Additions to the city and to the courtyards may be made

YAD AVRAHAM

from that which the Torah records Yisro as saying to Moses (*Ex.* 18:22): כָּל־הַדָּבָר הַגָּדֹל יָבִיאוּ אֵלֶיךָ, *every great matter they shall bring to you,* which the *Gemara* (16a) interprets to mean that matters concerning the גָּדוֹל, *great* — i.e., the *Kohen Gadol* — they shall bring to you.[1] Since Moses stood in place of the High Court — because he judged by direct communication with the Almighty (*Rashi* to 16b, s.v. דאוקי הסנהדראות) — we derive from this that the High Court is required for trying a *Kohen Gadol* (*Rav*). This applies, however, only to capital cases; in monetary matters a *Kohen Gadol* is judged in the same manner as anyone else (*Gem.* 16a).

אֶלָּא עַל פִּי בֵית דִּין שֶׁל שִׁבְעִים וְאֶחָד. — *except before the court of seventy-one.*

[These last three may be tried only before the High Court — the Great Sanhedrin — which consisted of seventy-one judges.)

וְאֵין מוֹצִיאִין לְמִלְחֶמֶת הָרְשׁוּת אֶלָּא עַל פִּי בֵית דִּין שֶׁל שִׁבְעִים וְאֶחָד. — *A discretionary war may not be waged without the approval of the court of seventy-one.*

This refers to any war besides those waged against the seven nations which inhabited Eretz Yisrael prior to the Jewish conquest, wars against Amalek (*Rav; Rambam Comm.*), and defensive wars to repel an attacker (*Meiri*). [See *Sotah* 8:7.]

This is derived from the wars waged by King David, who consulted with the Sanhedrin before initiating them. The source for this is the verse (*I Chron.* 27:34), which states: *And after Achitophel, Binayahu ben Yehoyada and Evyasar, and Yoav, the general of the army.* Binayahu was the head of the Sanhedrin as may be seen from another verse there (18:17), and it is evident that he consulted with them before waging war (*Rav* from *Gem.* 16b).

אֵין מוֹסִיפִין עַל הָעִיר — *Additions to the city ... may be made* (lit., *they do not add to the city*)

I.e., the city of Jerusalem, which has a greater degree of sanctity than the rest of the Land of Israel (*Rav*). [This added sanctity has a practical effect — it allows for *offerings of lesser holiness* and *maaser sheni*, second tithe, to be eaten throughout the city (*Keilim* 1:8). Thus, expanding the city's limits is not merely a civic concern but a religious one as well. For this reason, in Temple times such expansion had to be accompanied by a formal ritual of sanctification — see *Shevuos* 2:2.]

וְעַל הָעֲזָרוֹת — *and to the courtyards*

I.e., the courtyards to the Temple, which enjoy an even higher level of sanctity [see *Keilim* 1:8] (*Rav*).

1. Although this was the advice of Yisro (Jethro), not the commandment of God, the Torah relates (ibid. v. 24): *And Moses heeded the voice of his father-in-law and fulfilled all that he had said, which he certainly did only with Divine approval.*

אֶלָּא עַל פִּי בֵית דִּין שֶׁל שִׁבְעִים וְאֶחָד. אֵין עוֹשִׂין סַנְהֶדְרִיּוֹת לַשְּׁבָטִים אֶלָּא עַל פִּי בֵית דִּין שֶׁל שִׁבְעִים וְאֶחָד. אֵין עוֹשִׂין עִיר הַנִּדַּחַת אֶלָּא עַל פִּי בֵית דִּין שֶׁל שִׁבְעִים וְאֶחָד. וְאֵין עוֹשִׂין עִיר הַנִּדַּחַת בַּסְּפָר, וְלֹא שָׁלֹשׁ, אֲבָל עוֹשִׂין אַחַת אוֹ שְׁתַּיִם.

─────────── ר' עובדיה מברטנורא ───────────

אלא בבית דין של שבעים ואחד. דכתיב בדוד (דברי הימים-א כז, לד) ואחרי אחיתופל בניהו בן יהוידע, אחיתופל זה יועץ, בניהו בן יהוידע זה סנהדרין, שהיה מופלא שבכולן וכולן נגררים אחריו: **על העיר.** ירושלים, שקדושתה גדולה מקדושת שאר ארץ ישראל: **והעזרות.** קדושתן גדולה מקדושת ירושלים. ואי אפשר לחדש קדושה אלא בבית דין של שבעים ואחד, דאמר קרא (שמות כה, ט) ככל אשר אני מראה אותך וגו' וכן תעשו, לדורות, מה משכן קדוש על פי משה שהוא שהוא במקום סנדרי גדולה, אף לדורות תוספת עיר ועזרות על פי סנדרי גדולה: **ואין עושין סנדראות לשבטים.** כדאשכחן במשה דאוקי סנדראות ומשה במקום שבעים ואחד קאי: **אין עושין עיר הנדחת בו'.** דכתיב (דברים יז, ה) והוצאת את האיש ההוא [או את האשה ההיא], איש ואשה אתה מוציא אל שעריך, לבית דין שבעיריך, ואי אתה מוציא את כל העיר אל שעריך, אלא לשער המיוחד: **בספר.** עיר המבדלת בין ארץ ישראל לארץ העמים, דכתיב (דברים יג, יד) מקרבך, ולא מן הספר. וטעמא דקרא, שמא ישמעו עכו"ס ויבואו ויחריבו ארץ ישראל, לפיכך אין מניחין הטיר של עולם כמשפט עיר הנדחת, אבל הורגין את יושביה בלבד: **ולא שלשה.** עיירות. עיר הנדחת, בבית דין אחד, ובמקום אחד, כלומר קרובים זו לזו. אבל בשנים ושלשה מקומות עושים:

─────────── יד אברהם ───────────

אֶלָּא עַל פִּי בֵית דִּין שֶׁל שִׁבְעִים וְאֶחָד —
only with the court of seventy-one.

In regard to the construction of the Tabernacle, God said to Moshe (*Ex.* 25:9): *Like everything that I show you ... so shall you do*, which is understood to mean *so shall you do for all generations.* Just as the Tabernacle was sanctified by Moshe, who was the equivalent of the High Court, so must all future sanctifications be done by that court (*Rav* from *Gem.* 16b).

In addition to the Sanhedrin, it is necessary to consult with the king, a prophet, and with the *Urim VeTumim*[1] before adding to the city or the courtyards (*Shevuos* 2:2)

אֵין עוֹשִׂין סַנְהֶדְרִיּוֹת לַשְּׁבָטִים אֶלָּא עַל פִּי בֵית דִּין שֶׁל שִׁבְעִים וְאֶחָד — *Sanhedrins for the tribes may be appointed only by the court of seventy-one.*

The courts of twenty-three, which were required for every town (see mishnah 6), were appointed by the High Court (*Rashi*). This, too, is derived from Moses' appointment of these courts in the desert (*Rav* from *Gem.* 16b).

אֵין עוֹשִׂין עִיר הַנִּדַּחַת אֶלָּא עַל פִּי בֵית דִּין שֶׁל שִׁבְעִים וְאֶחָד. — *An apostate town can be so designated only by the court of seventy-one.*

If an entire town is found guilty of

1. This was a parchment which was enfolded in the garments of the *Kohen Gadol* through which Divine guidance was miraculously communicated (see ArtScroll *Yoma* p. 141).

1 only with the court of seventy-one. Sanhedrins for
5 the tribes may be appointed only by the court of seventy-one. An apostate town can be so designated only by the court of seventy-one. They cannot designate an apostate town on the border, nor three, but they may so designate one or two.

YAD AVRAHAM

idolatry, the town is burnt to the ground and all its inhabitants are put to death (*Deut.* 13:16,17; see below, 10:4-6). Their trial must take place before the court of seventy-one in order for this punishment to be imposed.

This is derived from the same source as the law concerning an entire tribe (see above, s.v. אין דנין לא את השבט). Only an individual can be tried by a court of twenty-three, not an entire town (*Rav* from *Gem.* 16b).

וְאֵין עוֹשִׂין עִיר הַנִּדַּחַת בַּסְּפָר, — *They cannot designate an apostate town on the border,*

A town on the border between Eretz Yisrael and another country may not be sentenced as an apostate town, even if its inhabitants deserve it. This is derived from the Torah's use of the word מִקִּרְבֶּךָ, *from your midst* (ibid. v. 14), to describe the mass defection (*Rav* from *Gem.* 16b). The *Gemara* (ibid.) offers an additional insight into this distinction; a razed town on the border would be an invitation to an enemy to invade (ibid.; see *Tos. Yom Tov*).

וְלֹא שָׁלֹשׁ, — *nor three,*

Nor may they designate three cities as apostate towns in any part of the country, as derived from the words (ibid. v.13), *in one of your cities* (*Gem.* 16b).

The precise limitation imposed by this principle is the subject of two disputes in the *Gemara* — one relating to time and the other to place. One view holds this rule to apply only to one High Court — but once it is replaced by another, they may designate another apostate town; while another view contends that even subsequent Sanhedrins may not add to the total of two towns. Secondly, some maintain that this ruling applies only to three cities within one province, whereas others contend that it pertains to the entire Land of Israel.

Rambam (*Hil. Avodas Kochavim* 4:4) rules that one court cannot designate three apostate towns in one province. *Ravad* (ibid.), however, rules that the limitation pertains even to more than one court and extends to the entire land (see *Kesef Mishneh* ad loc.).

אֲבָל עוֹשִׂין אַחַת אוֹ שְׁתַּיִם — *but they may so designate one or two.*

Although the Torah says *one*, it also uses the plural form of the word town, thereby indicating that two towns may also be condemned but not three (*Gem.* 16b).

The mishnah adds this seemingly redundant phrase to indicate that even if the two towns are neighbors and are thus comparable to a single town, they are nevertheless viewed as two separate towns, thus precluding the condemnation of a third (*Tos. Yom Tov*).

סנהדרין [ו] **סַנְהֶדְרִי** גְדוֹלָה הָיְתָה שֶׁל שִׁבְעִים וְאֶחָד,
א/ו וּקְטַנָּה שֶׁל עֶשְׂרִים וּשְׁלֹשָׁה.
וּמִנַּיִן לַגְּדוֹלָה שֶׁהִיא שֶׁל שִׁבְעִים וְאֶחָד? שֶׁנֶּאֱמַר: „אֶסְפָה־לִּי שִׁבְעִים אִישׁ מִזִּקְנֵי יִשְׂרָאֵל", וּמֹשֶׁה עַל גַּבֵּיהֶן, הֲרֵי שִׁבְעִים וְאֶחָד. רַבִּי יְהוּדָה אוֹמֵר: שִׁבְעִים. וּמִנַּיִן לַקְּטַנָּה שֶׁהִיא שֶׁל עֶשְׂרִים וּשְׁלֹשָׁה? שֶׁנֶּאֱמַר: „וְשָׁפְטוּ הָעֵדָה ... וְהִצִּילוּ הָעֵדָה" — עֵדָה שׁוֹפֶטֶת וְעֵדָה מַצֶּלֶת; הֲרֵי כָּאן עֶשְׂרִים. וּמִנַּיִן לְעֵדָה שֶׁהִיא עֲשָׂרָה? שֶׁנֶּאֱמַר: „עַד מָתַי לָעֵדָה הָרָעָה הַזֹּאת" — יָצְאוּ יְהוֹשֻׁעַ וְכָלֵב.

ר' עובדיה מברטנורא

(ו) **ומשה על גביהם הרי שבעים ואחד.** דאמר קרא (במדבר יא, יז) ונשאו אתך, ואת בהדייהו: **רבי יהודה אומר שבעים.** דדריש אתך בדומין לך, ולא שיהיה הוא יושב עמהן בדין. ואין הלכה כרבי יהודה: **עדה שופטת.** עשרה מחייבין: **עדה מצלת.** עשרה מזכין. ושמעינן מינה דצריך שיהיו עשרים, שאם יחלקו יהיו עשרה מחייבין ועשרה מזכין:

יד אברהם

6.

סַנְהֶדְרִי גְדוֹלָה הָיְתָה שֶׁל שִׁבְעִים וְאֶחָד, וּקְטַנָּה שֶׁל עֶשְׂרִים וּשְׁלֹשָׁה. — *The Great Sanhedrin was composed of seventy-one [judges], and a lesser one of twenty- three.*

The Great Sanhedrin was the highest court of the land; the lesser sanhedrins were the courts of twenty-three for trying capital cases located in each city. The Great Sanhedrin of seventy-one sat in the לִשְׁכַּת הַגָּזִית [*Lishkas HaGazis*], *the Chamber of Hewn Stone*, a chamber in the Temple. Two additional courts also sat in the Temple area, one at the entrance to the courtyard and one at the entrance to the Temple Mount. These consisted of twenty-three judges each [see below, 11:2] (*Meiri*).

וּמִנַּיִן לַגְּדוֹלָה שֶׁהִיא שֶׁל שִׁבְעִים וְאֶחָד? שֶׁנֶּאֱמַר: „אֶסְפָה־לִּי שִׁבְעִים אִישׁ מִזִּקְנֵי יִשְׂרָאֵל", וּמֹשֶׁה עַל גַּבֵּיהֶן, הֲרֵי שִׁבְעִים וְאֶחָד. — *From where [do we know] that the great one was seventy-one? Because it says* (*Num.* 11:16): *"Gather to me seventy men from the leaders of Israel," and Moses [presided] over them; hence, seventy-one.*

The Torah says about these elders (ibid. v.17): *and they shall bear with you the burden of the nation,* thereby indicating that the court consisted of seventy in addition to Moses (*Rav* from *Gem.* 17a).

We do not apply here the principle that Moses alone was the equivalent to seventy-one, as we did above (mishnah 5, s.v. ולא את כהן גדול), and therefore require 141 for future generations, because that is only applicable when Moses filled the function of the High Court alone (*Tos. Yom Tov*).

1
6

6. The Great Sanhedrin was composed of seventy-one [judges], and a lesser one of twenty-three. From where [do we know] that the great one was seventy-one? Because it says: *Gather to me seventy men from the leaders of Israel,* and Moses [presided] over them; hence, seventy-one. R' Yehudah says: Seventy. And from where [do we know] that a lesser one is comprised of twenty-three? Because it says: *And the congregation shall judge ... and the congregation shall save* — a congregation which judges and a congregation which saves; we thus arrive at twenty. And from where [do we know] that a congregation consists of ten? Because it says: *Until when, this evil congregation?* — which excludes Joshua and Caleb.

YAD AVRAHAM

רַבִּי יְהוּדָה אוֹמֵר: שִׁבְעִים. — *R' Yehudah says: Seventy.*

He contends that the seventy formed a complete court on their own, without the addition of Moses. The word *with you* is meant to imply that they must be similar to you in that they are of pure pedigree and free of physical blemishes (*Rav* on *Gem.* ibid.).

Although R' Yehudah generally concurs with the principle that a court cannot consist of an even number of judges, this case is different because the Torah sets the number explicitly (*Gem.* 3b; see *Tos. Yom Tov*).

וּמִנַּיִן לַקְּטַנָּה שֶׁהִיא שֶׁל עֶשְׂרִים וּשְׁלֹשָׁה? שֶׁנֶּאֱמַר: ,,וְשָׁפְטוּ הָעֵדָה . . . וְהִצִּילוּ הָעֵדָה" עֵדָה שׁוֹפֶטֶת וְעֵדָה מַצֶּלֶת; הֲרֵי כָּאן עֶשְׂרִים. — *And from where [do we know] that a lesser one is comprised of twenty-three? Because it says (Num. 35:24): "And the congregation shall judge ... and the congregation shall save" — a congregation which judges and a congregation which saves; we thus arrive at twenty.*

From the repetition of the word עֵדָה, *congregation,* in this verse, the Sages infer that there must be sufficient judges on the court which tries a man for a capital offense so that the equivalent of a "congregation" can judge — i.e., vote to condemn him — while another group the same size votes to save him by declaring him innocent (*Rav*). Since the minimum number qualifying as a "congregation" is ten, as the mishnah will proceed to explain, we can derive from this verse that the court must consist of at least twenty judges.

וּמִנַּיִן לָעֵדָה שֶׁהִיא עֲשָׂרָה? שֶׁנֶּאֱמַר: ,,עַד מָתַי לָעֵדָה הַזֹּאת" – יָצְאוּ יְהוֹשֻׁעַ וְכָלֵב. — *And from where [do we know] that a congregation consists of ten? Because it says (Num. 14:27): "Until when, this evil congregation?" — which excludes Yehoshua and Calev.*

סנהדרין א/ו וּמִנַּיִן לְהָבִיא עוֹד שְׁלֹשָׁה? מִמַּשְׁמַע שֶׁנֶּאֱמַר: „לֹא תִהְיֶה אַחֲרֵי רַבִּים לְרָעֹת", שׁוֹמֵעַ אֲנִי שֶׁאֶהְיֶה עִמָּהֶם לְטוֹבָה. אִם כֵּן, לָמָּה נֶאֱמַר: „אַחֲרֵי רַבִּים לְהַטֹּת"? לֹא כְהַטָּיָתְךָ לְטוֹבָה הַטָּיָתְךָ לְרָעָה. הַטָּיָתְךָ לְטוֹבָה עַל פִּי אֶחָד; הַטָּיָתְךָ לְרָעָה עַל פִּי שְׁנַיִם. וְאֵין בֵּית דִּין שָׁקוּל, מוֹסִיפִין עֲלֵיהֶן עוֹד אֶחָד, הֲרֵי כָאן עֶשְׂרִים וּשְׁלֹשָׁה.

ר' עובדיה מברטנורא

הטייתך לרעה על פי שנים. והכי קאמר קרא (שמות כג, ב) לא תהיה אחרי רבים לרעות, לחייב על פי אחד שיהיה יתר על המזכין, אבל אחרי רבים להטות בשנים, אפילו לרעות, כשהיו שנים מחייבין יותר על המזכין. הלכך על כרחך עשרים ושלשה בעינן, דבציר מעשרה מזכין ליכא למימר, דהא כתיב (במדבר לה, כה) והצילו העדה, ותו לא משכחת חובה בבציר מעשרים עשר: ואין בית דין שקול. אין עושין בית דין זוגות, שאם יחלקו לחלאים הוי להו פלגא ופלגא ולא משכחת לה הטייתך לטובה על פי אחד, הלכך מוסיפין עליהם עוד אחד והוו להו עשרים ושלשה: מאה ועשרים ושלשה. מפרש בגמרא (יז, ב), עשרים ושלשה סנהדרי

יד אברהם

This verse refers to God's condemnation of the spies whom Moses sent to spy the Land of Israel (*Rashi*). When they reported back to Moshe and the people, ten of the twelve spies defamed the Land, describing it as unconquerable. This caused the people to lose heart and reject the Land, which in turn brought God's wrath upon them and the decree that the generation of the exodus would not enter the Land but would die in the desert. The verse refers to these spies as an *evil congregation*. This designation must obviously exclude Yehoshua and Calev who portrayed the Land in glowing terms and sought to rally the people behind God's promise to conquer the Land for them. Thus, we see that the designation "congregation" may be applied to as few as ten people.

וּמִנַּיִן לְהָבִיא עוֹד שְׁלֹשָׁה? — *And from where do we [know to] include another three?*

[The mishnah now resumes its derivation of the law that a lesser sanhedrin must consist of twenty-three judges. Up to now, we have been able to prove only that it must consist of at least twenty.]

מִמַּשְׁמַע שֶׁנֶּאֱמַר: „לֹא תִהְיֶה אַחֲרֵי־רַבִּים לְרָעֹת," שׁוֹמֵעַ אֲנִי שֶׁאֶהְיֶה עִמָּהֶם לְטוֹבָה. אִם כֵּן, לָמָּה נֶאֱמַר: „אַחֲרֵי רַבִּים לְהַטֹּת"? — *From the implication of that which it says (Ex. 23:2): "Do not follow a majority to convict," I may infer that I should follow them to exonerate. If so, why does it say (ibid.): "according to the majority [the matter] shall be decided"?*

[The mishnah interprets the verse to be using the terms <div dir="rtl">רָעָה</div> (lit., *evil*)

1
6

And from where do we [know to] include another three? From the implication of that which it says: *Do not follow a majority to convict,* I may infer that I should follow them to exonerate. If so, why does it say: *according to the majority [the matter] shall be decided?* [This teaches that] the decision to convict is unlike the decision to exonerate. The decision to exonerate turns on the vote of one; [while] the decision to convict [must] turn on the vote of two. But since no court may consist of an even number, we must add another, for a total of twenty-three.

YAD AVRAHAM

and טוֹבָה (lit., *good*) to refer to verdict of guilt and innocence. Our translation of the verse follows *Rashi*'s explanation of it according to the understanding of the mishnah; see his comm. to *Chumash*.]

By stating that a simple majority is insufficient for deciding guilt, the verse clearly implies that a majority of one suffices to exonerate the accused person. Accordingly, the end of the verse, which states that the court's decision should follow the view of its majority, cannot refer to a verdict of innocence, since this would be redundant (*Rashi* 2a).

לֹא כְהַטָּיָתְךָ לְטוֹבָה הַטָּיָתְךָ לְרָעָה. הַטָּיָתְךָ לְטוֹבָה עַל פִּי אֶחָד; הַטָּיָתְךָ לְרָעָה עַל פִּי שְׁנַיִם. — *[This teaches that] the decision to convict is unlike the decision to exonerate. The decision to exonerate turns on the vote of one; [while] the decision to convict [must] turn on the vote of two.*

The end of the verse is understood to teach that while guilt can be decided by a majority vote, it must be a greater majority than that which decides a verdict of innocence. Thus, an accused may be exonerated by a simple majority of one, but to be convicted he must be found guilty by a majority of at least two. Accordingly, at least twenty-two judges are necessary, in order to allow for a congregation of ten on each side plus a majority of two to convict (*Rav*).

וְאֵין בֵּית דִּין שָׁקוּל, מוֹסִיפִין עֲלֵיהֶן עוֹד אֶחָד, הֲרֵי כָאן עֶשְׂרִים וּשְׁלֹשָׁה. — *But since no court may consist of an even number, we must add another, for a total of twenty-three.*

We cannot have an even number of judges on a court, because that would negate the possibility of a majority of one deciding to exonerate the accused (*Rav*).

The *Gemara* (17a) notes that this arrangement would seem to negate the possibility of a majority of two deciding against him, since an odd number does not allow for a majority of two. However, it would still be possible in a case in which one of the judges was unsure and did not vote, and the remainder were deadlocked. In such

סנהדרין
א/ו

וְכַמָּה יְהֵא בָעִיר וּתְהֵא רְאוּיָה לְסַנְהֶדְרִין? מֵאָה וְעֶשְׂרִים. רַבִּי נְחֶמְיָה אוֹמֵר: מָאתַיִם וּשְׁלֹשִׁים, כְּנֶגֶד שָׂרֵי עֲשָׂרוֹת.

ר׳ עובדיה מברטנורא

קטנה. ושלש שורות של עשרים ושלש יושבים לפניהם, שאם הוצרכו להוסיף על הדיינים מוסיפים מהם, ועשרה בטלנים, עשרה בני אדם בטלנים מכל מלאכה שיושבים תמיד בבית המדרש, ושני סופרים לכתוב דברי המזכין ודברי המחייבין, ושני חזנים שמשי בית דין להלקות החייב ולהזמין בעלי הדין, ושני בעלי דינין, ושני עדים, ושני זוממין, ושני זוממי זוממין, ושני גבאים, ושלישי לחלק הצדקה, שצדקה נגבית בשנים ומתחלקת בשלשה, ורופא אומן להקיז דם, ולבלר, ומלמד תינוקות, הרי מאה ועשרים: **מאתים ושלשים כנגד שרי עשרות.** דהיינו עשרים ושלשה עשריות, שיהא כל דיין שר של עשרה, דבציר משרי עשרה לא אשכחן שררה. ואין הלכה כרבי נחמיה:

יד אברהם

a situation, two more judges are added to the court (see below 5:5), thereby allowing for the possibility of a majority of two.

וְכַמָּה יְהֵא בָעִיר וּתְהֵא רְאוּיָה לְסַנְהֶדְרִין? מֵאָה וְעֶשְׂרִים. — *How many must be in a town to warrant a sanhedrin? One hundred and twenty.*

[This is the minimum number of people necessary to allow for the function of a town and a lesser sanhedrin, as follows:] The court itself consists of twenty-three members, plus three rows of twenty-three each which sit in reserve (see below, 4:4). In addition, every town required ten unemployed people who were constantly available to form the required *minyan* for prayer. Also, two scribes were necessary, one to record the opinion of those who held the defendant guilty and one for those who deemed him innocent; in addition to two marshals, who meted out punishment and summoned the de-

1
6

How many must be in a town to warrant a sanhedrin? One hundred and twenty. R' Nechemiah says: Two hundred and thirty, corresponding to the officers of the tens.

fendants; plus the two claimants themselves, and two witnesses. In addition, four more possible witnesses are required — two to discredit the testimony of the original witnesses — these two provide a deterrent against false testimony for witnesses will be afraid to lie if they could be discredited through *hazamah.* — and two more to be able to discredit the second set so that a litigant wll find it difficult to hire a second set of witnesses to discredit the first set. The second set will be reluctant to testify falsely lest they be discredited by a *third* set. Two charity collectors, and a third who helps dispense it, a doctor, a scribe to write Torah scrolls, and a teacher for the children are also vital for the function of a town. This adds up to a total of one hundred and twenty (*Rav* from *Gem.* 17b). [Any town that lacks sufficient population to fill these functions is not considered large enough to warrant a sanhedrin.]

רַבִּי נְחֶמְיָה אוֹמֵר: מָאתַיִם וּשְׁלֹשִׁים, כְּנֶגֶד שָׂרֵי עֲשָׂרוֹת. — *R' Nechemiah says: Two hundred and thirty, corresponding to the officers of the tens.*

Since the lowest level of judges mentioned in the Torah is that of officers of the tens — i.e., presiding over groups of ten (see *Ex.* 18:21) — a lesser sanhedrin must consist of members with at least that status. Thus, in order to allow for twenty-three judges, ten times as many residents — two hundred and thirty — are necessary (*Rav*).

The halachah follows the former view (*Rav; Rambam, Hil. Sanhedrin* 1:3).

פרק שני

Chapter Two

[א] **כֹּהֵן** גָּדוֹל דָּן וְדָנִין אוֹתוֹ. מֵעִיד, וּמְעִידִין אוֹתוֹ. חוֹלֵץ, וְחוֹלְצִין לְאִשְׁתּוֹ, וּמְיַבְּמִין אֶת אִשְׁתּוֹ. אֲבָל הוּא אֵינוֹ מְיַבֵּם, מִפְּנֵי שֶׁהוּא אָסוּר בְּאַלְמָנָה.

יד אברהם

1

Having discussed in the previous chapter (mishnah 5) some of the laws concerning the *Kohen Gadol*, the *Tanna* goes on to elaborate further on those laws (*Tos.*).

כֹּהֵן גָּדוֹל דָּן — *The Kohen Gadol may judge*

He may sit on the Sanhedrin, and we are not concerned that due to his status his colleagues may defer to his opinion against their better judgment (*Meiri*).

וְדָנִין אוֹתוֹ. — *and be judged.*

[He may be tried in court for any wrongdoing.]

There are two opinions in the *Gemara* (18a) as to the necessity for this seemingly obvious statement. Some maintain that it is said only to contrast it with the laws concerning a king, stated in the next mishnah. Another view is that it is necessary to inform us that he is subject to all of the regular penalties of judgment, specifically the punishment of exile in one of the cities of refuge for inadvertently killing someone. This is not self-evident. The Torah (*Numbers* 35:28) defines the length of the term of exile as until the death of the *Kohen Gadol*. In the case in which the *Kohen Gadol* is himself the murderer, however, there is no *Kohen Gadol* in office at that time whose death could set him free (*Rashi*). [The death of the *Kohen Gadol* appointed afterward would not free him.] Thus, sentencing him to exile is in effect a life sentence. The mishnah, therefore, teaches us that he is nevertheless subject to this penalty.

In monetary matters he is judged by a court of three like anyone else (*Gem.* 16a; *Rambam, Hil. Sanhedrin* 5:1). Similarly, if he commits a transgression which calls for flogging, he is judged by a court of three. This is in contrast to capital charges, for which the *Kohen Gadol* must be tried by the High Court of seventy-one, as stated in the previous chapter [mishnah 5] (*Gem.* 18b).

מֵעִיד, — *He may testify,*

Under normal circumstances, it is considered beneath the dignity of the *Kohen Gadol* to be required to testify in court, and he is therefore exempt from testifying. However, if the son of the king is on trial, the *Kohen Gadol* may be called. In such a case, the king himself comes to the court to hear the testimony, thereby making it fitting for the *Kohen* to testify, and then leaves to allow the judges to deliberate the case and decide it, since a king may not participate in judicial deliberations [mishnah 2] (*Gem.* 18b; *Rashi* ibid.).

Others contend that once the *Gemara* explains that the case of the mishnah is one in which the king

1. The *Kohen Gadol* may judge and be judged. He may testify, and he may be testified against. He may perform *chalitzah*, and *chalitzah* may be performed with his wife, and *yibum* may be performed with his wife. However, he may not perform *yibum*, because he is forbidden to [marry] a widow.

YAD AVRAHAM

himself is present for the testimony, it is no longer necessary to assume that it refers to a situation in which his son is on trial. Rather, any time the king is interested in the testimony of the *Kohen Gadol* being given, he may come to the court to sit in on its acceptance (*Yad Ramah;* see also *Rambam, Hil. Klei HaMikdash* 5:9).

Another time the *Kohen Gadol* may be called to testify is when the king himself is on trial. Although the next mishnah states that a king may not be tried, this refers only to the kings of Israel. Kings from the Davidic dynasty, however, may be judged, as will be explained in mishnah 2. In such a situation, the *Kohen Gadol* may be required to testify (*Meiri*). The *Gemara* does not explain the mishnah to be discussing such a case because the fact that the next mishnah states simply that a king may not be tried indicates that the kings under discussion in the mishnah are those of Israel, not those of the Davidic line. It would therefore be farfetched to assume that the *Tanna* is here discussing only the latter (*Tos.* to 18b, s.v. והא תנן מלך).

Moreover, *Tosafos* (s.v. מעיד) state that he would be required to testify on matters involving Torah prohibitions and observances, for example, concerning the sighting of the new moon (see above, 1:2).

וּמְעִידִין אוֹתוֹ. — *and he may be testified against.*

I.e., concerning any claim anyone may have against him (*Meiri*).

חוֹלֵץ, — *He may perform chalitzah,*

If his brother should die childless, the *Kohen Gadol* may not marry in *yibum* his widowed sister-in-law as would an ordinary person (see 1:3, s.v. החליצה) for the reason to be explained below. Nevertheless, she is considered bound to him and forbidden to marry out of the family. To release her of this bond, the *Kohen Gadol* is permitted to perform *chalitzah* with her (as does any man who refuses to marry his childless brother's widow in *yibum*).

וְחוֹלְצִין לְאִשְׁתּוֹ, וּמְיַבְּמִין אֶת אִשְׁתּוֹ. — *and chalitzah may be performed with his wife, and yibum may be performed with his wife.*

If the *Kohen Gadol* should die childless, his brother may either marry his widow in *yibum* or release her through *chalitzah.* We are not concerned with his honor to the degree that we are concerned with that of a king, regarding whom we do not allow *chalitzah* or *yibum* for him or his wife (*Meiri;* see comm. to mishnah 2).

אֲבָל הוּא אֵינוֹ מְיַבֵּם, מִפְּנֵי שֶׁהוּא אָסוּר בְּאַלְמָנָה. — *However, he may not perform yibum, because he is forbidden to [marry] a widow.*

In contrast to an ordinary *Kohen,* the Torah (*Lev.* 21:4) prohibits a *Kohen Gadol* to marry a widow.

מֵת לוֹ מֵת, אֵינוֹ יוֹצֵא אַחַר הַמִּטָּה; אֶלָּא הֵן נִכְסִין, וְהוּא נִגְלֶה; הֵן נִגְלִין, וְהוּא נִכְסֶה; וְיוֹצֵא עִמָּהֶן עַד פֶּתַח הָעִיר; דִּבְרֵי רַבִּי מֵאִיר. רַבִּי יְהוּדָה אוֹמֵר: אֵינוֹ יוֹצֵא מִן הַמִּקְדָּשׁ, שֶׁנֶּאֱמַר: „וּמִן הַמִּקְדָּשׁ לֹא יֵצֵא".

ר' עובדיה מברטנורא

פרק שני – כהן גדול. (א) כהן גדול. אינו יוצא אחר המטה. דלמא אתי למנגע מתוך טרדתו, ורחמנא אמר (ויקרא כא, יא) ועל כל נפשות מת לא יבא: **הן נכסין והוא נגלה.** כיון שנתכסו נושאי המטה מן המבוי כלומר שיצאו ממנו הוא נגלה ונכנס בתוכו, אבל כל זמן שהן נגלין ונראין במבוי הוא נכסה ממנו שאינו נכנס לתוכו: **ויוצא עמהן עד פתח העיר.** שבעיר מצויין מבואות ויכול להתכסות מהן, אבל חוץ לעיר ליכא הכירא: **שנאמר ומן המקדש לא יצא.** רבי יהודה דריש ומן המקדש לא יצא כל עיקר, ורבי מאיר דריש ומקדושתו לא יצא, כלומר יזהר שלא יבא לידי מגע, ובתוך העיר שיש מבואות איכא היכרא ומזדהר. והלכה כרבי יהודה:

יד אברהם

Additionally, there is a positive command that the woman he marries be a virgin (ibid.:3). Thus, he is forbidden to marry his widowed sister-in-law.

Actually, the *Gemara* (19a) notes that in certain instances a *Kohen Gadol* should be permitted to marry in *yibum* his widowed sister-in-law. This is because of the principle of עֲשֵׂה דוֹחֶה לֹא תַעֲשֶׂה, *a positive commandment supersedes a negative one.* This occurs in the case of a widow with whom the deceased husband had made only *erusin* (betrothal) — the first stage of marriage, after which she is considered his wife but they may not yet consummate their marriage — see comm. to 1:1, s.v. והמוציא שם רע. Since during the *erusin* stage she is still a virgin, the positive command that he marry a virgin does not stand in the way of his performing *yibum,* and the remaining negative command barring him from marrying a widow [which she is, despite being a virgin] may be superseded by the positive commandment of *yibum.*

The *Gemara* states that in such a case strict Torah law would indeed permit her to the *Kohen Gadol* for *yibum.* However, since the *mitzvah* of *yibum* is fulfilled with the first conjugal act, after which their relationship would have to be terminated because there is no longer any applicable positive commandment to supersede the negative one of a *Kohen Gadol* marrying a widow, the Rabbis prohibited her to him nonetheless, for fear that he might wish to continue to live with her and refuse to divorce her (*Gem.* 19a).

In the case of a widow who had been fully married — having had *erusin* and *nisuin* (see comm. to 1:1) — this prohibition is by Torah law. Since once *nisuin* has been performed the couple is permitted to engage in conjugal relations, it must be presumed that the widow is no longer a

2
1

[If] someone [close] to him dies, he may not follow the bier; rather, [once] they pass from view, he may appear; [where] they appear, he must remain concealed from view; and goes with them until the entrance to the town; [these are] the words of R' Meir. R' Yehudah says: He does not leave the Temple, as it is stated: *And from the Temple, he shall not depart.*

YAD AVRAHAM

virgin. Thus, her marriage to the *Kohen Gadol* is barred by both negative and positive commandments, and this cannot be superseded by a positive commandment.

מֵת לוֹ מֵת, — *[If] someone [close] to him dies* (lit., *a deceased died to him),*

[I.e., one of his relatives died. A *Kohen* is forbidden to render himself *tamei* (ritually contaminated) by contact with a human corpse (*Lev.* 21:1). Nevertheless, an ordinary *Kohen* is allowed to become *tamei* through contact with his seven closest relatives — his father, mother, brother, unmarried sister, son, daughter, or wife (ibid. 2,3). A *Kohen Gadol,* however, is forbidden to become *tamei* even to these (ibid. 11).]

אֵינוֹ יוֹצֵא אַחַר הַמִּטָּה; — *he may not follow the bier;*

He may not follow directly behind the bier in the funeral procession because we fear that in his distress he may come to touch the body, which would be forbidden (*Rav*). Rather, he may only follow the procession at a distance, as follows:

אֶלָּא הֵן נִכְסִין, וְהוּא נִגְלֶה; הֵן נִגְלִין, וְהוּא נִכְסֶה; — *rather, [once] they pass from view, he may appear* (lit., *they are concealed and he is revealed*); *[where] they appear, he must remain concealed from view;*

Once those carrying the bier pass from a street and disappear from sight, he may enter there, but as long as they are there, he may not (*Rav; Rashi*).

וְיוֹצֵא עִמָּהֶן עַד פֶּתַח הָעִיר; דִּבְרֵי רַבִּי מֵאִיר. — *and he goes out with them until the entrance to the town; [these are] the words of R' Meir.*

Within the town, there are streets and alleys which allow the bier to keep out of his sight and thereby serve as a reminder that he must avoid contact. Once they leave the town this is no longer possible, and the *Kohen Gadol* must therefore cease to follow the bier altogether (*Rav*).

רַבִּי יְהוּדָה אוֹמֵר: אֵינוֹ יוֹצֵא מִן הַמִּקְדָּשׁ, שֶׁנֶּאֱמַר: ,,וּמִן הַמִּקְדָּשׁ לֹא יֵצֵא". — *R' Yehudah says: He does not leave the Temple, as it is stated* (*Lev.* 21:12): *'And from the Temple he shall not depart.''*

This verse refers to a *Kohen Gadol* who is an אוֹנֵן, *onein,* one whose deceased close relative has not yet been buried (*Rashi*). R' Yehudah maintains that this means he may not leave the Temple at all, but must remain and continue his duties (*Rav*). R' Meir, however, contends that the

וּכְשֶׁהוּא מְנַחֵם אֲחֵרִים, דֶּרֶךְ כָּל הָעָם עוֹבְרִין בָּזֶה אַחַר זֶה, וְהַמְמֻנֶּה מְמַצְּעוֹ בֵּינוֹ לְבֵין הָעָם. וּכְשֶׁהוּא מִתְנַחֵם מֵאֲחֵרִים, כָּל הָעָם אוֹמְרִים לוֹ ,,אָנוּ כַּפָּרָתְךָ", וְהוּא אוֹמֵר לָהֶן ,,תִּתְבָּרְכוּ מִן הַשָּׁמַיִם". וּכְשֶׁמַּבְרִין אוֹתוֹ, כָּל הָעָם מְסֻבִּין עַל הָאָרֶץ וְהוּא מֵסֵב עַל הַסַּפְסָל.

ר' עובדיה מברטנורא

וכשהוא מנחם את אחרים. דבמת שאינו שלו כולי עלמא מודו דיכול הוא לילך, דלא טריד ולא אתי למגע, וכשחוזרין מן הקברות ועומדין בשורה לנחם האבלים, וכל העם עוברים זה אחר זה ומנחמין האבל שעומד במעמדו וכל אחד אומר לו תתנחם מן השמים: **הממונה ממצעו.** שהוא הולך לימין כהן גדול וכל העם משמאלו כמלא כהן גדול באמצע: **הממונה.** הוא הסגן שהוא ממונה לעבוד העבודה תחת כהן גדול אם יארע פסול בכהן גדול ביום הכפורים: **אנו בפרתך.** בנו תתכפר מתה, ואנחנו תחתיך לכל הראוי לבא עליך: **וכשמבּרין אותו.** שאבל אסור לאכול סעודה ראשונה משלו, וקרוביו ואוהביו מאכילין אותו: מסובין על **הארץ.** הן מצירין ומתאבלין בלעטרו: **והוא מיסב.** בכבוד על הספסל:

יד אברהם

word מִקְדַּשׁ is translated here to mean *consecration — from his consecration he shall not depart.* I.e., he may not do anything which would endanger his sanctity by allowing for the possibility of coming into contact with the corpse. Therefore, as long as he maintains the distance prescribed above, it is sufficient (*Rav* from *Gem. 19a*).

The *Gemara* concludes that even R' Yehudah agrees with this interpretation of the verse, but maintains that due to his distress at the death of his close relative, we fear that he may act irrationally and the normal precautions would not be sufficient (ibid.). [It is thus unclear why *Rav* explains R' Yehudah to have interpreted the verse literally (*Rashash*).]

Rambam (Hil. Klei HaMikdash 5:5) rules that the *Kohen Gadol* may not leave his home or the Temple when his relative dies. Thus, he follows the

conclusion of the *Gemara* that R' Yehudah agrees with the interpretation of R' Meir but requires a greater degree of precaution [since he prohibits him from leaving even his home] (*Kesef Mishneh* ibid.).

וּכְשֶׁהוּא מְנַחֵם אֲחֵרִים, — *When he comforts others,*

When accompanying the funeral of one who is not his relative, the precautions cited above are unnecessary, since he is not so deeply affected as to be in danger of allowing himself to become contaminated. He may therefore join the funeral procession in the normal manner (*Rav*).

דֶּרֶךְ כָּל הָעָם עוֹבְרִין בָּזֶה אַחַר זֶה, — *it is customary for all the people to pass along one after another,*

After the actual burial those assembled stand in a line to comfort the mourners who stand in place while all the others pass by and say,

2 When he comforts others, it is customary for all
1 the people to pass along one after another, and the appointed one places him between himself and the people. When he is comforted by others, all the people say to him, "We are your atonement," and he says to them, "May you be blessed from Heaven." When they feed him the mourner's meal, all the people sit on the ground and he sits on a stool.

YAD AVRAHAM

"May you be comforted from Heaven" (*Rav* from *Gem.* 19a).

[The *Gemara* (ibid.) relates that they later enacted that it be done in the opposite manner, with the comforters standing in line while the mourners pass by. Although it is unclear from the *Gemara* whether this remained the accepted approach and, indeed, *Rambam* does not describe the procedure in this manner, it is nevertheless the prevalent custom today.]

וְהַמְמֻנֶּה מְמַצְּעוֹ בֵּינוֹ לְבֵין הָעָם. — *and the appointed one places him between himself and the people.*

Although he comes to offer comfort, he does not mix with the general populace (*Meiri*). Rather, the assistant *Kohen Gadol*, who is appointed to take over in case the *Kohen Gadol* should become *tamei* just before *Yom Kippur* and be unable to perform the service of that day, places the *Kohen Gadol* between himself and the people, with the people to the left of the *Kohen Gadol* and himself to his right (*Rav* from *Gem.* 19a). This is in order to show him honor and deference (*Yad Ramah*).

וּכְשֶׁהוּא מִתְנַחֵם מֵאֲחֵרִים, כָּל הָעָם אוֹמְרִים לוֹ „אָנוּ כַּפָּרָתְךָ״, וְהוּא אוֹמֵר לָהֶן „תִּתְבָּרְכוּ מִן הַשָּׁמַיִם״. — *When he is comforted by others, all the people say to him, "We are your atonement," and he says to them, "May you be blessed from Heaven."*

When the *Kohen Gadol* is in mourning and the people come to comfort him, they express their wish that they be his atonement — i.e., they accept upon themselves whatever hardship is due him (*Rav; Rashi*). [He, in turn, blesses them for their sentiment.]

וּכְשֶׁמַּבְרִין אוֹתוֹ, — *When they feed him the mourner's meal,*

A mourner is forbidden to eat his first meal [after the burial] from his own food, and his friends and relatives therefore feed him from their provisions (*Rav* from *Moed Katan* 27b).

כָּל הָעָם מְסֻבִּין עַל הָאָרֶץ — *all the people sit on the ground*

To indicate that they share in his sorrow (*Rav*).

וְהוּא מֵסֵב עַל הַסַּפְסָל. — *and he sits on a stool.*

As befitting the honor of his position (ibid.).

[ב] **הַמֶּלֶךְ** לֹא דָן וְלֹא דָנִין אוֹתוֹ. לֹא מֵעִיד וְלֹא מְעִידִין אוֹתוֹ. לֹא חוֹלֵץ וְלֹא חוֹלְצִין לְאִשְׁתּוֹ. לֹא מְיַבֵּם

ר' עובדיה מברטנורא

(ב) **המלך לא דן ולא דנין אותו.** ודוקא מלכי ישראל שאינם נשמעים לדברי חכמים, אבל מלך ממלכי בית דוד, דן ודנין אותו, שנאמר (ירמיה כא, יב) בית דוד כה אמר ה' דינו לבקר משפט:

יד אברהם

2.

After discussing the ways in which a *Kohen Gadol* is treated differently than others, the mishnah goes on to focus on the laws concerning a king, who enjoys an even higher status and is therefore treated even more uniquely (*Tos.* 18a).

הַמֶּלֶךְ לֹא דָן — *The king may not judge*

This is derived from the verse (*Zephaniah* 2:1), *Be adorned and adorn* —which is interpreted by the *Gemara* to mean "Adorn yourself and then you may adorn others" — i.e., only one who may be judged by the courts is eligible to judge others. Since a king may not be judged, as stated below, he may not sit on a court in judgment on others (*Meiri* to Gem. 19b).

וְלֹא דָנִין אוֹתוֹ. — *nor be judged.*

This is a Rabbinic decree, due to the fear that he will not accede to the decision of the courts if it is against his interest [thereby weakening the authority of the courts]. The enactment was precipitated by an event in which Yannai, a king of Israel during the Second Temple era, was called to testify in court on behalf of one of his slaves, and the judges backed down when he challenged their authority. Shimon ben Shetach, the head of the court, was incensed by their action, and they were killed by the angel Gabriel (*Gem.* 19a,b).

This restriction applies only to kings of Israel who do not descend from King David. Those of the Davidic dynasty, however, were not included, because of the verse (*Jeremiah* 21:12) which states: *House of David, so says Hashem: Execute justice in the morning* (*Gem.* 19a). Since the prophet explicitly exhorted them to preside over judgment, the Rabbis did not include them in their ordinance to the contrary (*Kesef Mishneh* to *Hil. Melachim* 3:7; see *Tos. R' Akiva)* [and since they could not be banned from judging, they were not excluded from being judged either].

Alternatively, the kings from the House of David could be relied upon to heed the laws of the Torah and submit to the authority of the courts; therefore, there was no need to exempt them from that authority (*Rambam Comm.;* see *Lechem Mishneh* to *Hil. Melachim* loc. cit. for an explanation of how this can be resolved with the *Gemara*).

Although kings from the Davidic dynasty may sit in judgment, they may not sit on the Sanhedrin (*Rambam, Hil. Sanhedrin* 2:5 from *Gem.* 18b). This is due to the fact that it is prohibited for any member of the Sanhedrin to dispute the ruling of the outstanding member there. [For this reason

2
2

2. **T**he king may not judge nor be judged. He may not testify nor be testified against. He does not perform *chalitzah*, nor is *chalitzah* performed with his wife. He does not perform *yibum*, nor is *yibum*

the least prestigious member of the court states his decision first, followed by his immediate superior and so on (see mishnah 4:2).] Therefore, if the king were to sit on the Sanhedrin, his opinion would perforce be imposed upon the other judges (*Gem.* 18b; *Rashi*) because it would not accord with his honor for others to rule before him (*Meiri* ibid.; cf. *Ran*).

Others contend that they are never eligible to judge capital cases. The *Gemara's* ruling that Davidic kings may sit on a court refers only to monetary cases, in which the rule that one may not contradict the ruling of the highest authority on the court does not apply (*Tos.* to 19a, s.v. אבל מלכי בית דוד).

לֹא מֵעִיד — *He may not testify*

Similarly, kings of Israel may not testify in court, because they might not defer to the authority of the court. This, too, pertains only to kings who are not from the House of David (*Rambam, Hil. Melachim* 3:7). Others contend that it applies to all kings, because it is not considered consistent with royal dignity to have the king testify for someone else in court (*Yad Ramah; Meiri*).

There is a third view, that a king is ineligible to testify in court because of the law that a witness in court must stand before the judges (*Deut.* 19:17). To force a king to do so would be inconsistent with the commandment (*Deut.* 17:15): *You shall surely place upon yourself a king* — which the Rabbis interpret (mishnah 5) to mean that his awe should be upon you (*Rashi* to *Shevuos* 31a, s.v. כל שכן). [Thus apart from considerations of honor, this violates the basic relationship between the king and his subjects demanded by the Torah.]

וְלֹא מְעִידִין אוֹתוֹ. — *nor be testified against.*

Since he cannot be judged [there is no point in accepting testimony against him] (*Meiri*). [Obviously, this law does not apply to Davidic kings.]

לֹא חוֹלֵץ — *He does not perform chalitzah,*

If the king's brother died childless, the king may not perform *chalitzah* with his widow (see previous mishnah), because it does not befit his royal status to stand before the court and allow the *yevamah* to spit before him (*Rashi* to 19b). [Thus, if he is the only surviving brother, she remains permanently bound as a *yevamah*.]

וְלֹא חוֹלְצִין לְאִשְׁתּוֹ. — *nor is chalitzah performed with his wife.*

If the king should die childless, his wife does not undergo *chalitzah*. Since she is in any case forbidden to marry anyone else after having been the wife of a king (see below), there is no point in her undergoing *chalitzah*, whose entire purpose is to render her permissible for marriage (*Rashi; Meiri;* see *Rashash*).

לֹא מְיַבֵּם — *He does not perform yibum,*

It is also prohibited for him to perform *yibum* and marry his childless brother's widow. The Torah (*Deut.* 25:6,7) describes the purpose of *yibum* as being to establish a name

סנהדרין ב/ג

וְלֹא מְיַבְּמִין לְאִשְׁתּוֹ. רַבִּי יְהוּדָה אוֹמֵר: אִם רָצָה לַחֲלוֹץ אוֹ לְיַבֵּם, זָכוּר לְטוֹב. אָמְרוּ לוֹ: אֵין שׁוֹמְעִין לוֹ. וְאֵין נוֹשְׂאִין אַלְמְנָתוֹ. רַבִּי יְהוּדָה אוֹמֵר: נוֹשֵׂא הַמֶּלֶךְ אַלְמְנָתוֹ שֶׁל מֶלֶךְ, שֶׁכֵּן מָצִינוּ בְדָוִד שֶׁנָּשָׂא אַלְמְנָתוֹ שֶׁל שָׁאוּל, שֶׁנֶּאֱמַר: ,,וָאֶתְּנָה לְךָ אֶת בֵּית אֲדֹנֶיךָ וְאֶת נְשֵׁי אֲדֹנֶיךָ בְּחֵיקֶךָ״.

[ג] **מֵת** לוֹ מֵת, אֵינוֹ יוֹצֵא מִפֶּתַח פַּלְטְרִין שֶׁלּוֹ. רַבִּי יְהוּדָה אוֹמֵר: אִם רוֹצֶה לָצֵאת

ר׳ עובדיה מברטנורא

אין שומעין לו. דמלך שמחל על כבודו אין כבודו מחול, וגנאי הוא לו שיחלוץ וירקה בפניו, וכל שאינה בת חליצה אינה בת יבום. וכן הלכה: **מלך נושא אלמנתו של מלך.** והלכה כרבי יהודה בהא: (ג) **אינו יוצא מפתח פלטרין שלו.** שגנאי הוא למלך להראות עגומת נפש לפני העם:

יד אברהם

for his brother, and it is beneath the dignity of royalty for the king to be rendered subsidiary to his brother in this manner (*Rashi; Meiri*). Alternatively, since he may not perform *chalitzah,* as stated above, he is automatically ineligible for *yibum,* according to the mishnah's rule (*Yevamos* 4:10) that the two are interdependent (*Rav; Rambam, Hil. Melachim* 2:3; see *Tos. Yom Tov; Tos. R' Akiva; Kovetz He'aros* to Yevamos 2a 25).

וְלֹא מְיַבְּמִין לְאִשְׁתּוֹ. — *nor is yibum performed with his wife.*

Since it is forbidden to marry the widow of the king [see below] (*Meiri*).

רַבִּי יְהוּדָה אוֹמֵר: אִם רָצָה לַחֲלוֹץ אוֹ לְיַבֵּם, זָכוּר לְטוֹב. — *R' Yehudah says: If he wishes to perform chalitzah or yibum, he is remembered favorably.*

He maintains that the inability of a king to waive his dignity (see below) does not apply if it is for the sake of performing a *mitzvah.* Therefore, though he cannot be coerced to perform *yibum* or *chalitzah,* if he volunteers to do so, it is acceptable and indeed considered exemplary behavior on his part (*Gem.* 19b).

אָמְרוּ לוֹ: אֵין שׁוֹמְעִין לוֹ. — *They said to him: They do not listen to him.*

[The Rabbis (representing the view of the first *Tanna)* dispute R' Yehudah's ruling and assert that the king's waiver is ineffective.] In stating the commandment to fear the king (loc. cit.), the Torah uses the double wording ... שׂוֹם תָּשִׂים, *You shall surely place* ... but which translates literally as, *Place, you shall place.* From this the Rabbis derive that even if he waives his honor it is still binding (*Gem.* 19b), because the

2
3

performed with his wife. R' Yehudah says: If he wishes to perform *chalitzah* or *yibum*, the is remembered favorably. They said to him: They do not listen to him. No one may marry his widow. R' Yehudah says: A king may marry the widow of [another] king, as we find that David married the widow of Saul, as it is stated: *And I gave you the house of your master and the wives of your master in your bosom.*

3. [If] someone [close] to him dies, he does not leave the entrance of his palace. R' Yehudah says: If he wishes to go out

YAD AVRAHAM

double wording indicates a constant obligation to place his awe upon the people (*Rashi* to *Kesubos* 17a). [I.e., even after it has been waived by the king, there is still an obligation upon us to place it upon ourselves again.] The Rabbis maintain that this applies even in the face of a *mitzvah.*

The halachah follows the view of the first *Tanna* (*Rav; Rambam, Hil. Melachim* 2:3).

וְאֵין נוֹשְׂאִין אַלְמְנָתוֹ — *No one may marry his widow.*

The widow of a king may not remarry, even another king. The same applies to his divorcee (*Meiri*).

רַבִּי יְהוּדָה אוֹמֵר: נוֹשֵׂא הַמֶּלֶךְ אַלְמְנָתוֹ שֶׁל מֶלֶךְ, שֶׁכֵּן מָצִינוּ בְדָוִד שֶׁנָּשָׂא אַלְמְנָתוֹ שֶׁל שָׁאוּל, שֶׁנֶּאֱמַר: „וָאֶתְּנָה לְךָ אֶת בֵּית אֲדוֹנֶיךָ וְאֶת נְשֵׁי אֲדוֹנֶיךָ בְּחֵיקֶךָ״. — *R' Yehudah says: A king may marry the widow of [another] king, as we find that David married the widow of Saul, as it is stated (II Samuel 12:8): "And I gave you the house of your master and the wives of your master into your bosom."*

The Rabbis, however, dispute this and interpret the verse to refer to the women from the house of the king who were permissible to David — i.e., Merav and Michal, the daughters of Saul (*Gem.* 19b).

Some commentators state that the halachah follows the view of R' Yehudah in this matter (*Rav; Rambam Comm.*). However, the accepted ruling is that of the Rabbis (*Rambam, Hil. Melachim* 2:3; *Meiri; Likkutei Halachos*).

3.

מֵת לוֹ מֵת, אֵינוֹ יוֹצֵא מִפֶּתַח פַּלְטְרִין שֶׁלּוֹ. — *[If] someone [close] to him dies, he does not leave the entrance of his palace.*

If a relative of the king dies, he may not join the funeral procession because it detracts from the dignity of a king to express his pain publicly (*Rav*).

אַחַר הַמִּטָּה יוֹצֵא, שֶׁכֵּן מָצִינוּ בְדָוִד שֶׁיָּצָא אַחַר מִטָּתוֹ שֶׁל אַבְנֵר, שֶׁנֶּאֱמַר: „וְהַמֶּלֶךְ דָּוִד הֹלֵךְ אַחֲרֵי הַמִּטָּה״. אָמְרוּ לוֹ: לֹא הָיָה הַדָּבָר אֶלָּא לְפַיֵּס אֶת הָעָם. וּכְשֶׁמַּבְרִין אוֹתוֹ, כָּל הָעָם מְסֻבִּין עַל הָאָרֶץ וְהוּא מֵסֵב עַל הַדַּרְגָּשׁ.

[ד] **וּמוֹצִיא** לְמִלְחֶמֶת הָרְשׁוּת עַל פִּי בֵית דִּין שֶׁל שִׁבְעִים וְאֶחָד. וּפוֹרֵץ לַעֲשׂוֹת לוֹ דֶרֶךְ וְאֵין מְמַחִין בְּיָדוֹ. דֶּרֶךְ הַמֶּלֶךְ

ר׳ עובדיה מברטנורא

לפייס את העם. כדי שיכירו שלא בעצת דוד הרג יואב את אבנר. ואין הלכה כרבי יהודה: **דרגש.** מטה: **(ד) למלחמת הרשות.** מלחמה שאר אומות חוץ ממלחמת עמלק ומלחמת שבעה עממין: **ופורץ.** גדר של אחרים לעשות לו דרך ללכת לכרמו ולשדהו: **ואין ממחין בידו.** אין מעכבין עליו:

יד אברהם

רַבִּי יְהוּדָה אוֹמֵר: אִם רוֹצֶה לָצֵאת אַחַר הַמִּטָּה יוֹצֵא, שֶׁכֵּן מָצִינוּ בְדָוִד שֶׁיָּצָא אַחַר מִטָּתוֹ שֶׁל אַבְנֵר, שֶׁנֶּאֱמַר: „וְהַמֶּלֶךְ דָּוִד הֹלֵךְ אַחֲרֵי הַמִּטָּה״. — *R' Yehudah says: If he wishes to go out after the bier he may go out, for so we find concerning David that he went out after the bier of Abner, as it is stated* (*II Samuel* 3:31): *"And King David followed the bier."*

In addition to being the general of Saul and his son Ish Bosheth, Avner was a Torah scholar of note. Thus he was akin to being a relative of David, according to the Talmud's dictum: "When a wise man dies, all are [considered] his relatives" [and must mourn him] (*Meiri*). Although Avner initially supported Ish Bosheth in his attempt to hold on to the throne of his father Saul, he later abandoned him and attempted to bring the people over to David. When Yoav, commander of David's army, heard of the pact between David and Avner, he called him to a meeting and killed the unsuspecting Avner in revenge for Avner's killing of Yoav's brother Asahel in an earlier confrontation. David was greatly distressed over the unjust killing of Avner and led the mourners at his funeral (see *II Samuel* Ch. 3).

אָמְרוּ לוֹ: לֹא הָיָה הַדָּבָר אֶלָּא לְפַיֵּס אֶת הָעָם. — *They said to him: This was only to placate the people.*

The Rabbis [the anonymous, first opinion] replied that we cannot derive from that event that a king may follow the bier of a relative, because that was a unique event. It was necessary for David to make clear to the nation that Avner was not executed by Yoav at his behest (*Rav*), and to preserve thereby the peace of the kingdom and prevent a rebellion by those who were loyal to Avner (*Tos. Yom Tov*).

The halachah follows the view of

after the bier he may go out, for so we find concerning David that he went out after the bier of Abner, as it is stated: *And King David followed the bier*. They said to him: This was only to placate the people. When they feed him the mourner's meal, all the people sit on the floor and he sits on the *dargash*.

4. He may wage a discretionary war with the consent of the court of seventy-one. He may break through to make a path for himself and no one may impede him. The king's path

YAD AVRAHAM

the first *Tanna* (*Rav; Rambam, Hil. Melachim* 2:4).

וּכְשֶׁמַּבְרִין אוֹתוֹ, — *When they feed him the mourner's meal,*

A king is not exempt from the laws of mourning (*Meiri*) and must, like anyone else, receive his first post-funeral meal from others; see mishnah 2.

כָּל הָעָם מְסֻבִּין עַל הָאָרֶץ וְהוּא מֵסֵב עַל הַדַּרְגָּשׁ. — *all the people sit on the floor and he sits on the dargash.*

This is a type of couch in which the strapwork connects the actual couch [which was made from leather (*Rashi*] to the frame on the inside — through slits on the frame — rather than from the outside, like an ordinary couch (*Gem.* 20a). [A king is thus honored more than a *Kohen Gadol*, who may sit on a stool when being comforted but not on a couch.]

4.

וּמוֹצִיא לְמִלְחֶמֶת הָרְשׁוּת עַל פִּי בֵית דִּין שֶׁל שִׁבְעִים וְאֶחָד. — *He may wage a discretionary war with the consent of the court of seventy-one.*

Before entering in any war other than those commanded by the Torah — viz., the wars of conquest against the seven nations of Canaan or a war with Amalek (see *Sotah* 8:7) — he must first confer with and receive the approval of the Great Sanhedrin (*Rav;* see commentary to 1:5).

From that which the mishnah lists this among the rulings concerning a king, it would seem to indicate that waging war is considered a royal prerogative, and the Sanhedrin is not authorized to initiate a war without his consent. However, it is possible that the mishnah cites this not to include it among the powers of the king but only among his limitations — i.e., he may not wage a war on his own [despite the fact that this type of undertaking is usually the prerogative of a king] (*Tos. Yom Tov*).

וּפוֹרֵץ לַעֲשׂוֹת לוֹ דֶרֶךְ וְאֵין מְמַחִין בְּיָדוֹ. — *He may break through to make a path for himself and no one may impede him.*

The king has the right to break through the fences of the property of others and make a road to reach his

אֵין לוֹ שִׁעוּר. וְכָל הָעָם בּוֹזְזִין וְנוֹתְנִין לְפָנָיו, וְהוּא נוֹטֵל חֵלֶק בָּרֹאשׁ.

„לֹא יַרְבֶּה־לּוֹ נָשִׁים" — אֶלָּא שְׁמוֹנֶה עֶשְׂרֵה. רַבִּי יְהוּדָה אוֹמֵר: מַרְבֶּה הוּא לוֹ, וּבִלְבַד שֶׁלֹּא יְהוּ מְסִירוֹת אֶת לִבּוֹ. רַבִּי שִׁמְעוֹן אוֹמֵר: אֲפִלּוּ אַחַת, וּמְסִירָה אֶת לִבּוֹ, הֲרֵי זֶה לֹא יִשָּׂאֶנָּה.

ר' עובדיה מברטנורא

חלק בראש. חלק היפה בורר ראשון, ונוטל מחצה מכל הבזה: **אלא שמונה עשרה.** שהרי דוד היו לו שש נשים ואמר ליה נביא ואם מעט ואוסיפה לך כהנה וכהנה (שמואל ב יב, ח), כהנה קמא שית וכהנה בתרא שית, הרי שמנה עשרה: **מרבה הוא לו.** יותר משמנה עשרה. שלש מחלוקות יש בדבר, תנא קמא סבר נושא שמנה עשרה ואפילו פרוצות, ויותר משמנה עשרה לא ישא ואפילו כשרות, שכך הוא גזירת הכתוב, רבי יהודה סבר נושא שמנה עשרה ואפילו פרוצות, ויותר משמנה עשרה פרוצות לא ישא, וכשרות והגונות ישא כמו אביגיל, ופליג אתנא קמא בחדא, רבי שמעון סבר אפילו אחת פרוצה לא ישא, וכשרות והגונות לא ישא יותר משמנה עשרה, ופליג אתנא קמא בחדא ואדרבי יהודה בתרתי. והלכה כתנא קמא:

יד אברהם

own fields and vineyards (*Rav; Rashi;* see below). Others understand this to mean only that he has a right to ride through whenever he needs, but not that he may expropriate the land on a permanent basis (*Yad Ramah*). *Rambam* restricts this even further, limiting the king's right to trespass the property of others only to a situation in which he needs to do so for military purposes (*Hil. Melachim* 5:3; see *Lechem Mishneh* ibid.).

דֶּרֶךְ הַמֶּלֶךְ אֵין לוֹ שִׁעוּר. — *The king's path has no limits.*

He may make as wide a path through another's property as is necessary and, in addition, he need not route it around his fields if the more direct route goes through them (*Meiri*).

וְכָל הָעָם בּוֹזְזִין וְנוֹתְנִין לְפָנָיו, וְהוּא נוֹטֵל חֵלֶק בָּרֹאשׁ. — *All the people plunder and place [it] before him, and he takes the first portion.*

The spoils of war belong half to the king and half to the rest of the army — with the latter portion divided among those who did the actual fighting as well as those who guarded the camp. The king has the right to choose his portion first. In addition, anything taken from the enemy's royal treasuries belongs entirely to the king (*Rambam, Hil. Melachim* 4:9 from *Gem.* 20b).

That the king receives half is derived from the verse (*I Chron.* 29:22): *And they crowned Solomon the son of David a second time and anointed him as prince to Hashem, and Tzadok as Kohen.* The king is thus compared to the *Kohen Gadol;* just as the latter receives half of the *Panim* bread in the Temple, with the remainder being divided among the other *Kohanim,* so the king receives half the spoils of war (*Gem.* 21a). The rule that those guarding the camp

2
4

has no limits. All the people plunder and place [it] before him, and he takes the first portion.

Let him not take for himself many wives — only eighteen. R' Yehudah says: He may take for himself [even] many, as long as they do not turn his heart. R' Shimon says: Even one, if she turns his heart, he may not marry her.

YAD AVRAHAM

share equally with those doing the actual fighting is stated explicitly in *I Samuel* 30:23-25.

The remainder of this mishnah deals with the restrictions and special responsibilities of a king, as derived from the passage in *Deuteronomy* (Ch. 1 ; vs. 16-19), which reads as follows: *Only let him accumulate for himself many horses, so that he shall not return the nation to Egypt in order to accumulate many horses* [as Egypt was famed for its horses (*Rashi*)] ... *And let him not take for himself many wives, in order that his heart not turn away, and silver and gold let him not accumulate for himself greatly. And it shall be, when he will sit on his royal throne, that he shall write this second Torah ... and it shall be with him, and he shall read in it all the days of his life.*

,,לֹא יַרְבֶּה־לּוֹ נָשִׁים״ – אֶלָּא שְׁמוֹנֶה עֶשְׂרֵה. — *"Let him not take for himself many wives" — only eighteen.*

The maximum number of wives the king is permitted is eighteen. This is derived from the prophet's statement to King David (see *II Samuel* 12:8), who already had six wives: *And if it is too few, I will add to you as much and as much* — i.e., two more times the present total of your wives, equaling eighteen (*Rav* from *Gem.* 21a).

There is a dispute among the authorities concerning this restriction. *Rambam* (*Melachim* 3:2) holds that it includes both wives and concubines, whereas others maintain that it includes only full-fledged wives, but concubines are not limited (*Ravad*, ad loc.; *Meiri* to mishnah).

רַבִּי יְהוּדָה אוֹמֵר: מַרְבֶּה הוּא לוֹ, וּבִלְבַד שֶׁלֹּא יְהוּ מְסִירוֹת אֶת לִבּוֹ. — *R' Yehudah says: He may take for himself [even] many, as long as they do not turn his heart.*

R' Yehudah disagrees with the first *Tanna* and contends that since the Torah defines the reason for the restriction as the concern that he not lose the purity of his heart, only wives who are of poor character and may turn his head away from God are limited to eighteen, but those of good character are not (*Rav* from *Gem.* 21b).

רַבִּי שִׁמְעוֹן אוֹמֵר: אֲפִלּוּ אַחַת, וּמְסִירָה אֶת לִבּוֹ, הֲרֵי זֶה לֹא יִשָּׂאֶנָּה. — *R' Shimon says: Even one, if she turns his heart, he may not marry her.*

R' Shimon maintains throughout the Talmud the principle of דָּרְשִׁינַן טַעֲמָא דִקְרָא, *we expound the reason of Scripture*, i.e., that our understanding of the rationale of a Torah law can [within certain guidelines] be used to legally define its limits. Thus, if the

אִם כֵּן, לָמָּה נֶאֱמַר: „וְלֹא יַרְבֶּה־לּוֹ נָשִׁים״? — אֲפִלּוּ כַּאֲבִגַיִל. „לֹא־יַרְבֶּה־לּוֹ סוּסִים״ — אֶלָּא כְּדֵי מֶרְכַּבְתּוֹ. „וְכֶסֶף וְזָהָב לֹא יַרְבֶּה־לּוֹ מְאֹד״ — אֶלָּא כְּדֵי לִתֵּן אַסְפַּנְיָא. וְכוֹתֵב לוֹ סֵפֶר תּוֹרָה לִשְׁמוֹ —

ר׳ עובדיה מברטנורא

אלא כדי מרכבתו. דוקא סוסים בטלים להרחיב דעתו ולהתגדל ברוב סוסים [אסור], אבל כדי רכבו ופרשיו להלחם באויביו מותר: **אספניא.** שכר חילות הכנסים ויוצאים עמו כל השנה: **וכותב לו ספר תורה לשמו.** חוץ מספר תורה שחייב כל אדם מישראל להיות לו ספר תורה והוא מונח בבית גנזיו, וספר תורה שכותב לשמו כשהוא מלך נכנס ויוצא עמו תמיד:

יד אברהם

Torah were to write only that he may not take many wives, we would understand that this is because they may turn his heart away from God. Accordingly, there is no reason for the Torah to have explicated this rationale unless it is to indicate that he may not marry *any* woman whose character holds the potential to turn his heart, even if he does not have eighteen wives (*Gem.* 21a).

אִם כֵּן, לָמָּה נֶאֱמַר: „וְלֹא יַרְבֶּה־לּוֹ נָשִׁים״? — אֲפִלּוּ כַּאֲבִגַיִל. — *If so, why does it say* (*Deut.* 17:17): *"Let him not take for himself many wives"? Even [if they are] like Abigail.*

I.e., even wives as virtuous as Abigail (see *I Samuel* 25:3) are only permitted up to a total of eighteen (*Rav*).

The implications of this verse also include that the king should not become so involved with his wives that he is with them constantly and his heart is thus attached to them and not to God (*Meiri; Rambam*, ibid. 3:6).

Rav states that the halachah follows the view of the *Tanna Kamma*, that the limit of eighteen wives includes all types of women, with no distinction drawn between those who are virtuous and those who are not. *Rambam* (*Melachim* 3:3) also states the halachah that he may not take more than eighteen wives without distinguishing between the different types of women. However, he later adds (6) that even if he has only one wife he may not be with her constantly. This would seem to indicate that he rules in accordance with the view of R' Shimon; indeed *Radbaz* cites the view of R' Shimon as the source for the statement. Others, however, note that *Rambam* does not state that if he transgresses he is punished by lashes, as he does concerning the other restrictions. He thus indicates that although this exhortation can be derived from the Torah, it is not included in the actual prohibition (*Likkutei Halachos*).

All of the above discussion is based on the assumption that the statement of the first *Tanna* is in dispute with those of R' Yehudah and R' Shimon. There is another view, however, that both of these *Tannaim* come to explain the first statement, not dispute it (see *Yad Ramah*).

2
4

If so, why does it say: *Let him not take for himself many wives?* Even [if they are] like Abigail. *Let him not accumulate for himself many horses* — only enough for his chariots. *And silver and gold let him not accumulate for himself greatly* — only enough to pay his troops. He writes a Torah scroll for himself —

YAD AVRAHAM

,,לֹא־יַרְבֶּה לוֹ־סוּסִים" – אֶלָּא כְּדֵי מֶרְכַּבְתּוֹ. — *"Let him not accumulate for himself many horses"* (ibid. v. 16) — *only enough for his chariots.*

He is not permitted to maintain an abundance of horses for the pleasure of owning many horses or for the honor such ownership accords him. However, he may own as many horses as are necessary to provide for the chariots of his armies (*Rav* from *Gem.* 21b). This is derived from the word לוֹ, *for himself;* only horses for himself are limited, not those needed for the army (*Gem.* ibid.).

,,וְכֶסֶף וְזָהָב לֹא יַרְבֶּה־לוֹ מְאֹד" – אֶלָּא כְּדֵי לִתֵּן אַסְפַּנְיָא. — *"And silver and gold let him not accumulate for himself greatly"* (ibid. v.17) — *only enough to pay his troops.*

I.e., to pay the armies who serve him throughout the year (*Rav*) as well as the royal staff (*Rambam, Melachim* 3:4). This, too, is derived from the Torah's use of the word לוֹ, *for himself* (*Gem.* ibid.). However, this pertains only to the private treasury of the king; no limit is set on the money he may collect in the Temple treasury or in the public treasuries for the needs of the people (*Meiri; Rambam, Melachim* 3:4). This is evident from the actions of King David and other kings who collected large reserves for the sake of the nation (*Radbaz; Kesef Mishneh*).

Some say that this restriction applies only to wealth which the king actively pursues by taxing the people. However, if he acquires it through gifts and spoils of war it is permissible (*Yad Ramah*).

וְכוֹתֵב לוֹ סֵפֶר תּוֹרָה לִשְׁמוֹ – — *He writes a Torah scroll for himself —*

There is a *mitzvah* for the king to write a *Sefer Torah* for himself [either personally or through a designated agent], as stated in *Deut.* 17:18.

Actually, there is a *mitzvah* for every Jew to acquire a *Sefer Torah* for himself, as derived from the verse (*Deut.* 31:19): *Write for yourselves this shirah* (*Gem.* 21b). Although the word *shirah* literally means song, and could theoretically refer only to *Parashas Haazinu,* which is described there as a song, it is prohibited to write a Torah scroll in such small segments (*Gittin* 60a). Therefore, the verse must be referring to the Torah as a whole, thus exhorting every Jew to write for himself a *Sefer Torah* (*Meiri*). A king, however, is required to write a second Torah as well, so that in addition to keeping one at home in a cabinet, he will have another one to carry with him wherever he goes (*Rav* from *Gem.* ibid.).

יוֹצֵא לַמִּלְחָמָה, מוֹצִיאָהּ עִמּוֹ; נִכְנָס, מַכְנִיסָהּ עִמּוֹ; יוֹשֵׁב בַּדִּין, הִיא עִמּוֹ; מֵסֵב, הִיא כְנֶגְדּוֹ; שֶׁנֶּאֱמַר: ,,וְהָיְתָה עִמּוֹ וְקָרָא בוֹ כָּל־יְמֵי חַיָּיו״.

[ה] **אֵין** רוֹכְבִין עַל סוּסוֹ, וְאֵין יוֹשְׁבִין עַל כִּסְאוֹ, וְאֵין מִשְׁתַּמְּשִׁין בְּשַׁרְבִיטוֹ; וְאֵין רוֹאִין אוֹתוֹ כְּשֶׁהוּא מִסְתַּפֵּר, וְלֹא כְשֶׁהוּא עָרֹם, וְלֹא בְּבֵית הַמֶּרְחָץ; שֶׁנֶּאֱמַר: ,,שׂוֹם תָּשִׂים עָלֶיךָ מֶלֶךְ״ — שֶׁתְּהֵא אֵימָתוֹ עָלֶיךָ.

ר׳ עובדיה מברטנורא

מיסב. על השלחן: (ה) **כשהוא מסתפר.** כשמגלח שער ראשו:

יד אברהם

יוֹצֵא לַמִּלְחָמָה, מוֹצִיאָהּ עִמּוֹ; נִכְנָס, מַכְנִיסָהּ עִמּוֹ; — *[when] he goes out to war, he takes it with him; [when] he returns, he brings it back with him;*

It must therefore be small enough to hang on his arm at all times (*Meiri* from *Gem.* ibid.).

Others explain this last ruling of the *Gemara* figuratively, and maintain that is acceptable for the king to designate someone to carry the Torah and accompany him wherever he goes (*Ran; Rambam, Melachim* 2:1; see commentators ad loc.).

יוֹשֵׁב בַּדִּין, הִיא עִמּוֹ; — *[when] he sits in judgment, it is with him;*

Although it has been stated previously (mishnah 2) that a king may not sit in judgment, the mishnah here refers to monetary cases — which he is permitted to judge — or to matters of state which he himself judges. Alternatively, it refers to kings from the House of David, who are permitted to sit in judgment (*Ran;* see *Tos. Yom Tov*).

מֵסֵב, הִיא כְנֶגְדּוֹ; — *[when] he reclines, it is before him;*

I.e., when he sits down to eat (*Rav*). [It was the custom in ancient times to eat in a reclining position (see *Pesachim* 10:1).]

שֶׁנֶּאֱמַר: ,,וְהָיְתָה עִמּוֹ וְקָרָא בוֹ כָּל־יְמֵי חַיָּיו.״ — *as it is stated* (ibid. v. 19): *"And it shall be with him, and he shall read in it all the days of his life."*

From this verse we also derive that he may not enter a bathroom or bathhouse with the Torah scroll, as it is only to be with him in a place where it is permissible for him to read it (*Gem.* 21b).

5.

The mishnah now discusses the restrictions placed upon the people in relation to the king in order to maintain the level of honor and awe they must have for him.

אֵין רוֹכְבִין עַל סוּסוֹ, — *No one may ride on his horse,*

[Using his personal articles detracts from the sense of awe a person must

2 [when] he goes out to war, he takes it with him;
5 [when] he returns, he brings it back with him; [when] he sits in judgment, it is with him; [when] he reclines, it is before him; as it is stated: *And it shall be with him, and he shall read in it all the days of his life.*

5. **N**o one may ride on his horse, sit on his throne, or use his scepter; and no one may observe him when he takes a haircut, or when he is undressed, or when he is in the bathhouse; as it is stated: *You shall surely place upon yourselves a king* — [do so in a manner] that his awe shall be upon you.

YAD AVRAHAM

have for him. Accordingly, it is prohibited to ride on the horse designated for his personal use.] An exception to this is where it is necessary to do so in order to save the king himself from danger (*Meiri* from *Gem.* 95a).

וְאֵין יוֹשְׁבִין עַל כִּסְאוֹ, וְאֵין מִשְׁתַּמְּשִׁין בְּשַׁרְבִיטוֹ; — *sit on his throne, or use his scepter;*

This applies to any utensils which were used expressly by the king. Even after his death, it is forbidden to use them. Accordingly, all his personal articles are burned after his death (*Gem.* 52b; *Rambam, Melachim* 2:1). Also included in this prohibition are his slaves and servants. These, however, are permitted to another king (*Rambam, Melachim* 2:1), as are his concubines (*Meiri;* cf. *Rambam* ibid. and *Kesef Mishneh*).

וְאֵין רוֹאִין אוֹתוֹ כְּשֶׁהוּא מִסְתַּפֵּר, — *and no one may observe him when he takes a haircut,*

Until the haircut is completed his appearance is very unattractive, and it is therefore demeaning to him to be seen (*Tif. Yis.*).

וְלֹא כְּשֶׁהוּא עָרֹם, וְלֹא בְּבֵית הַמֶּרְחָץ; — *or when he is undressed, or when he is in the bathhouse;*

I.e., even in the bathhouse, where it is appropriate to appear undressed, it is still inappropriate for the king to be seen in this state, since it detracts from the sense of dignity people must feel for him. Alternatively, he should not be seen in the bathhouse even when he is clothed (*Meleches Shlomo*).

שֶׁנֶּאֱמַר: ,,שׂוֹם תָּשִׂים עָלֶיךָ מֶלֶךְ" – שֶׁתְּהֵא אֵימָתוֹ עָלֶיךָ. — *as it is stated* (ibid. v. 15): *"You shall surely place upon yourselves a king" — [do so in a manner] that his awe shall be upon you.*

All of these things detract from the sense of awe people must have for a king (*Meiri*).

פרק שלישי

Chapter Three

סנהדרין [א] **דִּינֵי** מָמוֹנוֹת בִּשְׁלֹשָׁה. זֶה בּוֹרֵר לוֹ אֶחָד
ג/א וְזֶה בּוֹרֵר לוֹ אֶחָד, וּשְׁנֵיהֶן בּוֹרְרִין
לָהֶן עוֹד אֶחָד, דִּבְרֵי רַבִּי מֵאִיר. וַחֲכָמִים אוֹמְרִים: שְׁנֵי הַדַּיָּנִין בּוֹרְרִין לָהֶן עוֹד אֶחָד. זֶה פּוֹסֵל דַּיָּנוֹ שֶׁל זֶה וְזֶה פּוֹסֵל דַּיָּנוֹ שֶׁל זֶה; דִּבְרֵי רַבִּי מֵאִיר. וַחֲכָמִים אוֹמְרִים: אֵימָתַי? בִּזְמַן שֶׁמֵּבִיא עֲלֵיהֶן רְאָיָה שֶׁהֵן קְרוֹבִין אוֹ פְסוּלִין. אֲבָל אִם הָיוּ כְשֵׁרִים אוֹ מֻמְחִין, אֵינוֹ יָכוֹל לְפָסְלָן.

ר' עובדיה מברטנורא

פרק שלישי – זה בורר. (א) זה בורר לו אחד. אחד מהבעלי דינין בורר לו דיין אחד לדונו ולהפוך בזכותו, וכן השני בורר לו דיין אחד, ושני הבעלי דינים ביחד בוררים להם עוד דיין שלישי, ומתוך כך יצא דין אמת לאמתו, דלייתי בעלי דינים דינא ואמרי קושטא קא דייני לן, דסבר החייב הרי אני בעצמי בררתי האחד ואם היה יכול להפך בזכותי היה מהפך, והדיין השלישי בעצמו נוח לו להפך בזכות שניהם מפני ששניהם ביררו אותו: **וחכמים אומרים שני הדיינים בוררים להם אחד.** בלא דעת הבעלי דינים, כדי שלא יהיה לבו של זה השלישי נוטה אצל אחד מהן. והלכה כחכמים: **זה פוסל דיינו של זה.** יכול הוא לומר לא אדון לפני בית דין שבררת: **בזמן שהביא עליהן ראיה.** שזה מביא ראיה על דיין שבירר זה, לפוסלו: **אבל אם הם בשרים ומומחים.** הכי קאמר, אבל אם היו כשרים שאינן לא קרובים ולא פסולים, אף על פי שהם יושבי קרנות, נעשו כמומחין ואינו יכול לפוסלן. ופסק ההלכה בזה, כשקבלו בעלי הדין מי שידין להם, בין יחיד בין רבים, ופסק עליהם את הדין, דינו דין, ואין סותרין דינו, ואף על פי שאינו מומחה לרבים, ואם נודע שטעה, אם בדבר משנה טעה או בדבר המפורש בגמרא, מחזירים הדבר כשהיה ודנין בו כהלכה, ואם אי אפשר להחזיר, כגון שהלך זה שנטל הממון שלא כדין למדינת הים, פטור הדיין מלשלם מאחר שקיבלוהו עליהם, שאף על פי שגרם להזיק, לא נתכוין להזיק, ואם טעה בשקול הדעת, והוא בדבר שנחלקו בו תנאים או אמוראים או גאונים, וסוגיא דעלמא כחד מנייהו, ודן זה הדיין כדברי אותו הגאון שאין סוגיית העולם כמותו, אם לא נשא ונתן ביד יחזור הדין, ואם אי אפשר להחזיר ישלם מביתו, ואם נשא ונתן ביד, מה שעשה עשוי וישלם מביתו. ודיין שלא קבלו אותו בעלי הדין,

יד אברהם

1.

Having digressed to elaborate on the laws of the *Kohen Gadol* and the king, the mishnah now reverts to its original topic of judicial law (*Ran*).

Any court of three judges can impose its authority on a defendant and coerce him to come to trial. However, if either of the litigants wishes, he has the right to insist that the trial judges be chosen by the process described in this mishnah rather than accepting the authority of any specific court (*Tos.* 5a, s.v. דן). Nevertheless, if there is an established official court in that town, they can require that the litigants come to them for trial (*Rama, Choshen Mishpat* 3:1).

3
1

1. **M**onetary cases [are judged] by three. Each one chooses one [judge], and they both choose another; [these are] the words of R' Meir. However, the Sages say: The two judges choose another. Each can disqualify the judges of the other; [these are] the words of R' Meir. However, the Sages say: When? When he proves that they are relatives or ineligible. But if they are eligible or experts, he cannot disqualify them.

YAD AVRAHAM

דִּינֵי מָמוֹנוֹת בִּשְׁלֹשָׁה. — *Monetary cases [are judged] by three.*

[I.e., a court consisting of at least three judges must preside over a monetary case.]

זֶה בּוֹרֵר לוֹ אֶחָד וְזֶה בּוֹרֵר לוֹ אֶחָד, — *Each one chooses one [judge]* (lit., *this one chooses for himself one and this one chooses for himself one),*

[Each of the litigants has the right to choose one of the three judges unilaterally.] In this way, each will feel assured that his interest is being considered and will therefore accept the verdict of the judges. In addition, each of the judges will be fully attuned to the perspective of the one who chose him and will thus not overlook any point in his favor (*Rosh; Rama* ibid. 13:1). Furthermore, if the deliberations seem to be hastily leaning to one side, the judge appointed by the other will delay the decision in order to be certain that no factors were overlooked (*Nimmukei Yosef*). All these factors will combine to ensure a thorough analysis of the case and a correct verdict (ibid.).

וּשְׁנֵיהֶן בּוֹרְרִין לָהֶן עוֹד אֶחָד; דִּבְרֵי רַבִּי מֵאִיר. — *and they both choose another; [these are] the words of R' Meir.*

[The two litigants decide together on the choice of the third judge,] who will thus pursue the interest of both litigants equally (*Rav*).

וַחֲכָמִים אוֹמְרִים: שְׁנֵי הַדַּיָּנִין בּוֹרְרִין לָהֶן עוֹד אֶחָד. — *However, the Sages say: The two judges choose another.*

The two appointed judges, rather than the litigants, appoint the third judge, so that there will be no question of partiality (*Rav*). The *Gemara* (23a) explains that all agree that the two judges must agree to the appointment of the third. The dispute concerns only the litigants; R' Meir maintains that they too have a say in this selection and the Sages insist that they do not.

זֶה פּוֹסֵל דַּיָּנוֹ שֶׁל זֶה וְזֶה פּוֹסֵל דַּיָּנוֹ שֶׁל זֶה; דִּבְרֵי רַבִּי מֵאִיר. — *Each can disqualify the judges of the other; [these are] the words of R' Meir.*

This refers to judges who are not fully expert in Torah law but it was nonetheless customary to try cases before them in that vicinity. R' Meir maintains that since they are not qualified to act as judges, either litigant can disqualify them from trying the case (*Gem.* ibid.).

וַחֲכָמִים אוֹמְרִים: אֵימָתַי? בִּזְמַן שֶׁמֵּבִיא עֲלֵיהֶן רְאָיָה שֶׁהֵן קְרוֹבִין אוֹ פְסוּלִין. אֲבָל אִם הָיוּ כְשֵׁרִים אוֹ מֻמְחִין, אֵינוֹ יָכוֹל לְפָסְלָן. — *However, the Sages say: When? When he proves that they are relatives or ineligible. But if they are eligible or*

זֶה פּוֹסֵל עֵדָיו שֶׁל זֶה וְזֶה פּוֹסֵל עֵדָיו שֶׁל זֶה; דִּבְרֵי רַבִּי מֵאִיר. וַחֲכָמִים אוֹמְרִים: אֵימָתַי? בִּזְמַן שֶׁהוּא מֵבִיא עֲלֵיהֶם רְאָיָה שֶׁהֵן קְרוֹבִים אוֹ פְּסוּלִים. אֲבָל אִם הָיוּ כְשֵׁרִים, אֵינוֹ יָכוֹל לְפָסְלָן.

ר׳ עובדיה מברטנורא

אלא שעמד מאליו או מנה אותו המלך או קלת זקני הקהל העמידוהו, אם אינו מומחה לרבים, אף על פי שנטל רשות מראש הגולה, אין דיניו דין, בין טעה בין לא טעה, ואינו בכלל הדיינין אלא בכלל בעלי זרוע, וכל אחד מבעלי דינין אם רצה סותר דינו וחוזר ודן בפני בית דין, ואם טעה ולא נשא ונתן ביד יחזיר הדין, ואם אי אפשר להחזיר ישלם מביתו כדין כל גורם להזיק, ואם נשא ונתן ביד ישלם מביתו וחוזר ונוטל מבעל דין זה שנתן לו שלא כהלכה. ומומחה לרבים שקבלו אותו בעלי דינים, או שנטל רשות מראש גולה אף על פי שלא קבלו אותו בעלי דינים, הואיל והוא מומחה, אם טעה בין בדבר משנה בין בשקול הדעת ואי אפשר להחזיר הדין, פטור מלשלם. ומומחה שנטל רשות מראש גולה יש לו לכוף לבעלי הדין שידונו לפניו, בין רצו בין לא רצו, בין בארץ בין בחוץ לארץ, ומי שנטל רשות מן הנשיא שבארץ ישראל, אינו יכול לכוף לבעלי הדין אלא בארץ ישראל בלבד. ומומחה הוא, מי שלמד בתורה שבכתב ושבעל פה ויודע לסבור להקיש ולהבין דבר מתוך דבר [הוא הנקרא מומחה], וכשהוא ניכר וידוע ויצא טבעו אצל אנשי דורו, נקרא מומחה לרבים, והוא יכול לדון יחידי ואפילו לא נקט רשות מראש גולה: **זה פוסל עדיו של זה.** פלוגתיהו דרבי מאיר ורבנן מוקי לה בגמרא (כג,ב), כשאמר בעל דין יש לי שתי כתי עדים בדבר, והביא כת ראשונה, ועמד בעל דין שכנגדו עם אחר ואמר פסולין הן, רבי מאיר אומר יכול הוא עם אחר לפוסלן, ולאו נוגע בעדותו הוא, שהרי אמר יש לי כת אחרת, ואם בקש ולא מצא, יפסיד, ורבנן סברי אף על גב דאמר תחלה יש לי שתי כתי עדים, יכול לחזור ולומר אין לי אלא אלו, ונמצא זה שבא לפסלן נוגע בעדותו הוא, ולא מפסלי אפומיה. והלכה כחכמים:

יד אברהם

experts, he cannot disqualify them.

The *Gemara* explains this to mean that although they are not fully expert, the fact that they are generally accepted as judges in this place as if they were expert is sufficient basis for their validity and they cannot be disqualified (*Gem., Meiri*). However, there are certain people who are legally unfit to serve as judges, regardless of their legal expertise, such as relatives of either the litigants or of another judge, or people known to be dishonest, as well as certain classes of people, such as slaves and their descendants. Only if it can be shown that the prospective judge falls into one of these categories do the Sages allow a litigant to disqualify the other litigant's choice.

The halachah follows the view of the Sages (*Choshen Mishpat* 13:4).

זֶה פּוֹסֵל עֵדָיו שֶׁל זֶה וְזֶה פּוֹסֵל עֵדָיו שֶׁל זֶה; דִּבְרֵי רַבִּי מֵאִיר. — *Each one can disqualify the witnesses of the other; [these are] the words of R' Meir.*

Obviously the mishnah cannot be understood literally, to mean that a litigant can arbitrarily disqualify the witnesses brought by his adversary, since this would make a mockery of the entire judicial process. The *Gemara* (23a,b) explains it to be referring to a situation in which one of the litigants

3
1

Each one can disqualify the witnesses of the other; [these are] the words of R' Meir. However, the Sages say: When? When he proves that they are relatives or ineligible. But if they are eligible, the cannot disqualify them.

YAD AVRAHAM

claims that one [or both] of the witnesses testifying against him was ineligible due to a family flaw — e.g., that he was descended from a family of slaves [slaves, as a class, are disqualified by Torah law from serving as witnesses regardless of whether they are in actual servitude]. He was supported in this allegation by another person as well. R' Meir contends that since this assertion does not pertain specifically to the witness testifying against him, but rather to his family as a whole — in regard to whom he has no self-interest — his testimony to that effect is valid. Thus, he and the person supporting his allegation combine to form a set of witnesses whose testimony is effective (if checked and accepted) in disqualifying that entire family, and along with them, the witness testifying against him (*Gem.* 23b, *Rashi*).

וַחֲכָמִים אוֹמְרִים: אֵימָתַי? בִּזְמַן שֶׁהוּא מֵבִיא עֲלֵיהֶם רְאָיָה שֶׁהֵן קְרוֹבִים אוֹ פְסוּלִים. אֲבָל — אִם הָיוּ כְשֵׁרִים, אֵינוֹ יָכוֹל לְפַסְלָן. *However, the Sages say: When? When he proves that they are relatives or ineligible. But if they are eligible, he cannot disqualify them.*

The Sages contend that since his testimony concerning these witnesses necessarily affects his case, he is not eligible to testify against them (*Meiri*).

In another interpretation, the *Gemara* explains the mishnah to be discussing a case in which one of the litigants claimed to have two pairs of witnesses to testify on his behalf. In R' Meir's view, there is a requirement for him to substantiate his word by producing both pairs in court, though the testimony of only one pair is sufficient to prove his claim. Accordingly, when the first pair testifies, the one against whom they testify can join together with another person to establish that one of the first pair of witnesses is an ineligible witness. This testimony is not considered by R' Meir self-serving because his opponent in this litigation must in any case produce the second pair of witnesses he claims to have [and there is no reason to suspect them of being invalid]; thus there is no reason not to accept it. The Sages, however, are of the opinion that even though one claims to have additional witnesses available to support his claim, he can subsequently retract that claim. Since he may never produce the second pair of witnesses, the litigant's invalidation of his opponent's first pair is a self-serving testimony, which is unacceptable (*Rav* from *Gem.* 23b; cf. *Rashi* ad loc., s.v. נמצאת כת שניה; *Rambam Comm.*).

2.

One who is related to either of the litigants, as well as one who is guilty of certain misdeeds, is not eligible to testify or to serve as a judge, as will be delineated in mishnayos 3 and 4. Nevertheless, if the two parties to the trial agree to accept the testimony or verdict of such persons they may do so, because any stipulation made between two parties concerning monetary

[ב] אָמַר לוֹ „נֶאֱמָן עָלַי אַבָּא״, „נֶאֱמָן עָלַי אָבִיךָ״, „נֶאֱמָנִין עָלַי שְׁלֹשָׁה רוֹעֵי בָקָר״, רַבִּי מֵאִיר אוֹמֵר: יָכוֹל לַחֲזוֹר בּוֹ. וַחֲכָמִים אוֹמְרִים: אֵינוֹ יָכוֹל לַחֲזוֹר בּוֹ.

ר׳ עובדיה מברטנורא

(ב) נאמן עלי אבא. להיות דיין, אף על פי שהוא פסול מן התורה לדונני לא לזכות ולא לחובה, כדנפקא לן (בגמרא כז,ב) מלא יומתו אבות על בנים (דברים כד,טז): **נאמנים עלי שלשה רועי בקר.** לדון, דאילו לעדות, רועי בקר כשרים הן: **רבי מאיר אומר יכול לחזור בו.** אפילו לאחר גמר דין, לאחר שקבל הדיין העדות ואמר איש פלוני אתה זכאי: **אינו יכול לחזור בו.** לאחר גמר דין בלבד הוא דפליגי רבנן עליה דרבי מאיר, דאילו קודם גמר דין מודים חכמים לרבי מאיר דיכול לחזור בו, ואם קנו מידו כמי שמקבל עליו עדות איש פלוני או דינו של איש פלוני, אפילו קודם גמר דין אינו יכול לחזור בו, שאין לאחר קנין כלום. וכן הלכה:

יד אברהם

matters is binding (*Aruch HaShulchan, Choshen Mishpat* 22:1). Since a person is free to give away his money, his willingness to abide by a ruling based on normally inadmissible testimony or one rendered by ineligible judges is acceptable. The following mishnah discusses the corollary issue — the right of one of the litigants to retract his consent to such an arrangement once it has been given.

אָמַר לוֹ „נֶאֱמָן עָלַי אַבָּא״, „נֶאֱמָן עָלַי אָבִיךָ״ — *[If] he declared to him, "My father is acceptable to me," [or] "Your father is acceptable to me,"*

He agreed to accept his father or his opponent's father as a judge (*Rav; Rashi*) or as a witness (*R' Chananel; Rambam, Hil. Eidus* 7:2).

„נֶאֱמָנִין עָלַי שְׁלֹשָׁה רוֹעֵי בָקָר״, — *[or] "Three cattle herders are acceptable to me"* —

Such people were generally not versed in Torah law and could therefore not preside over a trial. The mishnah cites cattle herders specifically because they usually lived far from settlements and were thus not exposed to dealings between people. Accordingly, they lacked even the knowledge of practical everyday law learned by most people in the course of their regular affairs (*Gem.* 25b). Nevertheless, if the litigants agreed to use them as judges they may not retract.

This particular case refers only to their acceptability as judges. As witnesses however, they are qualified by Torah law [since no specialized knowledge is required to testify] (*Rav* from *Gem.* 25b). However, the Rabbis later decreed that they may not testify either because they observed a tendency among them to graze their cattle in other people's lands [placing them in the category of thieves] (*Gem.*).

רַבִּי מֵאִיר אוֹמֵר: יָכוֹל לַחֲזוֹר בּוֹ. — *R' Meir says: He can retract.*

Even after a decision has been

3
2

2. [If] he declared to him, "My father is acceptable to me," [or] "Your father is acceptable to me," [or] "Three cattle herders are acceptable to me" — R' Meir says: He can retract. But the Sages say: He cannot retract.

reached by this court of ineligible judges, he may retract his consent to their authority (*Rav* from *Gem.* 24b). The *Gemara* (ibid.) explains, however, that this applies only to the defendant in the case. Although he agreed to pay the claim if these judges should decide against him, a verbal monetary agreement is not enforceable in Torah law. Thus, since he has not yet given anything to the claimant, or performed a *kinyan* (act of acquisition)[1] binding himself to abide by the judges' decision, he is legally free to change his mind. However, if the claimant lost the case, he can no longer retract his decision to abide by the ruling. Since his acceptance of this arrangement constitutes an agreement to forgive his claim should these judges decide against him, once their decision has been rendered his waiver takes immediate effect [since no act of acquisition is required to effect one's waiver of another's obligation to him], and it is thus too late to retract.

וַחֲכָמִים אוֹמְרִים: אֵינוֹ יָכוֹל לַחֲזוֹר בּוֹ. — *But the Sages say: He cannot retract.*

Once the decision has been reached by the court he can no longer retract his consent to abide by their decision (*Rav* from *Gem.* 24b).

The halachah follows the view of the Sages (*Rav; Rambam, Eidus* 7:2; *Choshen Mishpat* 22:1).

In the case of one who agreed to accept the testimony of ineligible witnesses, he loses his option to rescind his consent as soon as their testimony has been accepted by the court (*Rama, Choshen Mishpat* 22:1; see *Tos. Yom Tov*).[2]

Some authorities maintain that the principle of this mishnah, that one is bound by his consent to accept invalid judges or witnesses, applies only if he expressed his consent to accept them before a court (*Hagahos HaAshri; Shach; Choshen Mishpat*

1. A *kinyan* is a formal "act of acquisition" by means of which transactions are legally effected, in certain cases even without the physical transfer of the object or money in question. See General Introduction to ArtScroll *Bava Basra*.

2. Some maintain that the mishnah's ruling applies even if he agreed to accept the testimony of one of those ineligible people in place of three judges or two witnesses (*Rashi; Rambam, Hil. Eidus* 7:2) [thereby waiving two requirements — that a verdict be based on the testimony of eligible judges and witnesses, and that there be three judges and two witnesses]. Others contend that only if he accepts him to fill the role of one valid judge or witness is his consent binding, but if in place of two or three, in which case the judges' or witness' eligibility is doubly flawed, this halachah does not apply (*Tos.; Nimmukei Yosef; Rama,* loc. cit.). Rather, we assume that his commitment to pay if the decision goes against him was not made wholeheartedly (*Yad Ramah*) [but on the assumption that he was so clearly right that they would have to rule in his favor].

סנהדרין ג/ב

הָיָה חַיָּב לַחֲבֵרוֹ שְׁבוּעָה, וְאָמַר לוֹ ,,דֹּר לִי בְּחַיֵּי רֹאשְׁךָ״, רַבִּי מֵאִיר אוֹמֵר: יָכוֹל לַחֲזוֹר בּוֹ. וַחֲכָמִים אוֹמְרִים: אֵינוֹ יָכוֹל לַחֲזוֹר בּוֹ.

ר׳ עובדיה מברטנורא

דור לי בחיי ראשך. נדור לי בחיי ראשך ואתן לך מה שאתה תובע, ואין צריך לומר, ומחול לך מה שיש לי אצלך. ונדר לו או קנו מידו, אף על פי שעדיין לא נדר, אינו יכול לחזור בו, כדברי חכמים. וכן הלכה:

יד אברהם

22:1). Others disagree and contend that as long as it was stated before witnesses it is binding (*Meiri; Nimmukei Yosef* to *Bava Basra* 128a; *Urim VeTumim, Choshen Mishpat* ad loc.; *Nesivos HaMishpat* ibid.; *Aruch HaShulchan* ibid.).

הָיָה חַיָּב לַחֲבֵרוֹ שְׁבוּעָה, וְאוֹמֵר לוֹ ,,דֹּר לִי בְּחַיֵּי רֹאשְׁךָ״, — *[If] he was under an obligation of oath to another, and he said, "Vow to me by the life of your head,"*

There are cases in Torah law where a plaintiff may collect on his claim without proof, merely by swearing an oath (see *Shevuos* 7:1). The mishnah discusses a case in which the defendant in such a case agreed to accept the personal oath of the plaintiff in place of an oath in court [which is of greater moment and evokes a more severe punishment from Heaven if made falsely] and thus consented to pay the money in dispute if he made that oath (*Rav* from *Gem.* 24b). After the plaintiff made the vow, the defendant reneged and refused to pay unless the plaintiff swore an oath in court as the law requires.

רַבִּי מֵאִיר אוֹמֵר: יָכוֹל לַחֲזוֹר בּוֹ. — *R' Meir says: He can retract.*

[He can retract his consent and demand that the plaintiff swear in court, even though the latter already made the vow.]

וַחֲכָמִים אוֹמְרִים: אֵינוֹ יָכוֹל לַחֲזוֹר בּוֹ. — *The Sages, however, say: He cannot retract.*

Once the oath agreed upon was made, he can no longer retract his consent and demand that his disputant swear a regular oath in court (*Rav; Rambam, Eidus* 7:3; *Choshen Mishpat* 22:3).

Others contend that even if the oath was not actually made, as long as it was decided in court that he would do so, it is too late for the other litigant to rescind his consent (*Meiri; Shach, Choshen Mishpat* 22:16 citing *Ramban, Rashba,* and others; *Aruch HaShulchan* ibid.:9).

This case seems to be an unnecessary repetition of the dispute cited previously. However, the *Gemara* (24b) explains that both cases are necessary. In the first case he agreed to place the outcome of the trial in the hands of a third party, which allows for the possibility that he did not really mean it since he could easily lose. Thus it is necessary to state that even in this case the Sages obligate him to accept the decision. In the second case, however, he placed his fate in the hands of the opposing litigant himself. One might

3
2 [If] he was under an obligation of oath to another, and he said, "Vow to me by the life of your head," R' Meir says: He can retract. The Sages, however, say: He cannot retract.

YAD AVRAHAM

therefore reason that even R' Meir agrees that his consent was fully meant and consequently binding. The mishnah must therefore explain that R' Meir disputes the Sages even in this case.

The halachah follows the view of the Sages (*Rav; Rambam, Shulchan Aruch* loc. cit.).

Most cases involving oaths are the reverse — the defendant is required to swear an oath to free himself of the plaintiff's claim (which, though credible, lacks sufficient proof to collect). In such a case, if the plaintiff agreed to accept the defendant's personal oath in lieu of the formal oath in court required by the law, all would agree that once the oath was given, the waiver of the claim implicit in this agreement has taken effect and the plaintiff can no longer retract, as explained above (s.v. רבי מאיר אומר).

3.

Having cited in the first mishnah the Sages' opinion that one can disqualify judges or witnesses only if he can prove that they are relatives or ineligible to serve, the mishnah now goes on to discuss the specifics of these two categories.

The Torah states (*Ex.* 23:1): *You shall not place your hand with a* רָשָׁע *[evildoer] to be a witness for theft.* From this we derive that anyone who commits a transgression which is punishable by death or lashes is disqualified from testifying, since both of these are described in the Torah with the term רָשָׁע (*Num.* 35:31; *Deut.* 25:2). In addition, anyone who illicitly obtains the money of others, even if not through a transgression punishable by death or lashes, is also disqualified [since he has shown that he is willing to be dishonest for the sake of gain] (*Rav; Rambam, Hil. Eidus* 10:3,4).

If someone gained money in a manner which is prohibited by Rabbinic law, he is Rabbinically disqualified from testifying. However, there is a distinction between one disqualified by Torah law and one disqualified by Rabbinic law. The disqualification by Torah law takes effect upon the commission of the crime, whereas the disqualification resulting from Rabbinic law must be announced by the courts before it takes effect.

This mishnah limits its discussion to those who are disqualified by Rabbinic law (*Tos.* 24b), while the Biblical disqualifications noted above are assumed by the mishnah though spelled out by the *Gemara.* The disqualifications because of kinship are dealt with in the next mishnah. There are in addition other Biblical disqualifications — women (mentioned in *Shevuos* 4:1) and slaves (who are in general accorded the status of women).

[ג] **וְאֵלּוּ** הֵן הַפְּסוּלִין: הַמְשַׂחֵק בְּקֻבְיָא,
וְהַמַּלְוֶה בְּרִבִּית, וּמַפְרִיחֵי יוֹנִים,
וְסוֹחֲרֵי שְׁבִיעִית. אָמַר רַבִּי שִׁמְעוֹן:

ר' עובדיה מברטנורא

(ג) **וְאֵלּוּ הֵן הַפְּסוּלִים.** לְדוּן וּלְהָעִיד: **הַמְשַׂחֵק בְּקֻבְיָא.** פָּסוּל לְעֵדוּת, לְפִי שֶׁאֵינוֹ מִתְעַסֵּק בְּיִשּׁוּבוֹ שֶׁל עוֹלָם, וְאָסוּר לְאָדָם שֶׁיִּתְעַסֵּק בְּעוֹלָמוֹ אֶלָּא אוֹ בַּתּוֹרָה וּגְמִילוּת חֲסָדִים, אוֹ בִּסְחוֹרָה וְאוּמָנוּת וּמְלָאכָה שֶׁיֵּשׁ בָּהֶן יִשּׁוּבוֹ שֶׁל עוֹלָם: **וּמַלְוֵי בְּרִבִּית.** אֶחָד הַלֹּוֶה וְאֶחָד הַמַּלְוֶה שְׁנֵיהֶם פְּסוּלִין, דְּקַיְמָא לָן (בבא מציעא עה,ב) הַמַּלְוֶה וְהַלֹּוֶה שְׁנֵיהֶם עוֹבְרִים בְּלֹא תַעֲשֶׂה: **וּמַפְרִיחֵי יוֹנִים.** אִיכָּא דִמְפָרְשֵׁי, מִין מִמִּינֵי הַשְּׂחוֹק, אִם תַּקְדִּים יוֹנָתְךָ לְיוֹנָתִי אֶתֵּן לְךָ כָּךְ וְכָךְ. וְאִיכָּא דִמְפָרְשֵׁי, שֶׁמְּגַדֵּל יוֹנָה מְלוּמֶּדֶת לְהָבִיא יוֹנִים לְבֵית בְּעָלֶיהָ בְּעַל כָּרְחָן, וְיֵשׁ בָּהֶן גָּזֵל מִפְּנֵי דַּרְכֵי שָׁלוֹם וְלֹא גָזֵל גָּמוּר: **וְסוֹחֲרֵי שְׁבִיעִית.** עוֹשִׂין סְחוֹרָה בְּפֵירוֹת שְׁבִיעִית, וְהַתּוֹרָה אָמְרָה (ויקרא כה,ו) וְהָיְתָה שַׁבַּת הָאָרֶץ לָכֶם לְאָכְלָה, וְלֹא לִסְחוֹרָה:

יד אברהם

וְאֵלּוּ הֵן הַפְּסוּלִין: — *These are the ones who are disqualified:*

The following people are disqualified from testifying in court, and they may certainly not serve as judges (*Rav; Rashi*).

הַמְשַׂחֵק בְּקֻבְיָא, — *one who plays dice,*

[I.e., a gambler.] Such a man is disqualified from testifying because he is not occupied in a socially useful pursuit — i.e., he idles away his time with useless pursuits rather than involving himself in either Torah and acts of kindness, or a business or trade which would be beneficial to society (*Rav* from *Gem.* 24b and *Rambam Comm.*). [He is therefore considered to be of low moral character and thus not to be trusted to testify truthfully.] In addition, because of his idleness he is not sensitive to the difficulties which people endure and is therefore not careful with the money of others; nor is he embarrassed to lie, since his pursuit of gambling requires constant bluffing (*Meiri*).

Rambam (*Eidus* 10:4) explains this disqualification to be due to illicit acquisition of money in accordance with his view (*Hil. Gezeilah* 6:10) that one who gambles does so with the expectation of winning and does not willingly give his money to those he bets against if he loses. Therefore, someone who obtains money in this matter is considered by Rabbinic law tantamount to a thief (see *Kesef Mishneh*).[1]

וְהַמַּלְוֶה בְּרִבִּית, — *one who lends on interest,*

The Torah prohibits a Jew from taking interest on a loan to his fellow Jew (*Ex.* 22:24). One who lends money on interest is therefore disqualified by his transgression. This prohibition applies to the borrower as well — he is forbidden to pay interest to a fellow Jew. Therefore, he too is disqualified from serving as a witness or judge (*Rav* from *Gem.* 25b).

---

1. The question of whether a gambler is disqualified because he is not occupied in a socially useful pursuit or because he is considered akin to a thief is actually the subject of a dispute in the *Gemara* (24b). Although the *Gemara* here cites the majority view to be that gambling is not considered theft, several general statements elsewhere in the Talmud indicated to *Rambam* that the accepted view is otherwise (*Kesef Mishneh*).

3
3

3. These are the ones who are disqualified: one who plays dice, one who lends on interest, pigeon-flyers, and *sheviis*-merchants. Said R' Shimon:

YAD AVRAHAM

Rambam (*Eidus* 10:4) explains the mishnah to refer only to those who give or take interest which is prohibited by Rabbinic law.[1] Someone who lends or borrows with interest as defined by Biblical law, however, is disqualified Biblically from serving as a witness or judge. Others dispute this and contend that even Biblically prohibited interest only disqualifies the participants by Rabbinic law. Since it is paid by consent, the participants do not think of themselves as engaging in a dishonest activity for the sake of money (*Tos.* 24b).

A third view opines that although the lender, who profits from the interest, is disqualified by Biblical law, the borrower is only disqualified by Rabbinic law. If the interest involved is only defined as such Rabbinically, the lender becomes disqualified by Rabbinic law but the borrower remains a qualified witness (*Nimmukei Yosef*).

וּמַפְרִיחֵי יוֹנִים, — *pigeon-flyers,*

The *Gemara* (25a) offers two interpretations of this. Some explain it to refer to those who race pigeons for gambling purposes. Although this is similar to the case of dice players, in each case there is a different reason to believe that the owner may be relying on his ability to be victorious, and the winnings are thus not taken with the true consent of the loser.[2] Another interpretation is that it refers to those who fly special pigeons trained to lure other pigeons away from their cotes and bring them back to the "pigeon-flyers." This is prohibited by Rabbinic law because it can lead to arguments with those who put out the cotes and consider the pigeons to be theirs (*Rav*). [It is not actual theft, however, because the pigeons do not really belong to the ones who set out the cotes for them. The pigeons in these cotes are wild pigeons which the owners never legally acquired. Even their presence in the cotes is not sufficient to acquire them for the owners of the cotes, because they came on their own and are free to fly away any time.]

וְסוֹחֲרֵי שְׁבִיעִית. — *and sheviis-merchants.*

I.e., those who do business with produce of *sheviis* — the *Shemittah* [Sabbatical] year. The *Shemittah* year occurs every seventh year. During this year it is forbidden to cultivate the land of Eretz Yisrael and there are various restrictions on the use of produce that grows uncultivated as well. One of these prohibitions is to

1. For example, interest is Biblically prohibited only when the amount to be paid has been stipulated in advance of the loan; if the amount of the payment is fixed later, it is only Rabbinically prohibited interest.

2. *Meiri* points out that this explanation is only according to the opinion that the issue involved is the permissibility of taking the winnings. However, according to the opinion that the issue is the gamblers' idleness from any worthwhile pursuit, this explanation would not be viable and only the second interpretation remains.

סנהדרין
ג/ג

בַּתְּחִלָּה הָיוּ קוֹרִין אוֹתָן אוֹסְפֵי שְׁבִיעִית. מִשֶּׁרַבּוּ הָאַנָּסִין חָזְרוּ לִקְרוֹתָן סוֹחֲרֵי שְׁבִיעִית. אָמַר רַבִּי יְהוּדָה: אֵימָתַי? בִּזְמַן שֶׁאֵין לָהֶם אֻמָּנוּת אֶלָּא הִיא, אֲבָל יֵשׁ לָהֶן אֻמָּנוּת שֶׁלֹּא הִיא, כְּשֵׁרִין.

ר׳ עובדיה מברטנורא

רבי שמעון אומר וכו׳. בגמרא (כו,א) מפרש מלתיה דרבי שמעון הכי, בתחלה היו קוראים אותם אוספי שביעית, כלומר, אוספי פירות שביעית לעצמן היו פסולים לעדות כמו סוחרי פירות שביעית: **משרבו האנסין.** השואלין מנת המלך כך וכך כורין תבואה בכל שנה, והיו צריכין לאסוף תבואה של שביעית לפרוע ממנה מנת המלך, חזרו לומר סוחרי פירות שביעית בלבד הם פסולים, אבל אוספי תבואת שביעית לתת למלך כשרים לעדות, כיון שאין אוספים לאצור לעצמן. ולענין פסק הלכה, כל מי שעבר עברה שחייב עליה מיתת בית דין או כרת או מלקות, פסול לעדות, דמחוייב מיתה נקרא רשע, דכתיב (במדבר לה,לא) אשר הוא רשע למות, ובחייבי מלקות כתיב (דברים כה,ב) והיה אם בן הכות הרשע, והתורה אמרה (שמות כג,א) אל תשת ידך עם רשע להיות עד חמס, ודרשינן אל תשת רשע עד, ואם לקה חזר להכשרו, דכתיב (דברים כה,ג) ונקלה אחיך לעיניך, כיון שלקה הרי הוא כאחיך, ואם לקח ממון שלא כדין, אף על פי שאינו חייב ביה לא מיתה ולא מלקות, פסול לעדות, כגון גנב וגזלן ומלוה ברבית, ואם לקח ממון שיש בו איסור דרבנן, פסול לעדות מדרבנן, כגון מפריחי יונים, וחמסן דיהיב דמי ולוקח החפץ שאין הבעלים רוצים למכרו, והגבאים והמוכסים שלוקחים לעצמן, ומקבלי צדקה מן העכו״ם בפרהסיא, אלו וכיוצא בהן פסולין לעדות מדרבנן, ואין עדותן בטלה עד שיכריזו עליהם ויפרסמו אותן, אבל פסולי עדות של תורה אין צריכין הכרזה, וכל הפסולין לעדות בין של תורה בין של דבריהם, אם נודע מעניינם שעשו תשובה גמורה והממון שלקחו שלא כדין החזירוהו, ועשו סייג וגדר לעצמן באותו דבר שחטאו בו שלא יוסיפו לעשותו עוד, הרי אלו חזרו להכשרן, ומשחקי בקוביא אף על פי שאין בזה גזל אפילו מדבריהם, הם פסולים לעדות, לפי שאין מתעסקין בישובו של עולם ואין בהם יראת שמים, ודוקא שאין להם מלאכה ואומנות אלא היא, כדברי רבי יהודה. וכן הלכה. ואימתי חזרתן, משישברו פספסיהן ויקבלו עליהם דאפילו בחנם לא עבדי:

יד אברהם

trade in *sheviis*-produce. This is prohibited by Torah law, as derived from the verse (*Lev.* 25:6): *And the uncultivated produce [of the Sabbatical year] of the land shall be for you to eat* — but not for commerce (*Rav*). [See General Introduction to ArtScroll *Sheviis*.] Although this is prohibited by Biblical law, and should thus disqualify the merchant Biblically, the mishnah refers to those fruits which are included in the laws of *Shemittah* only by Rabbinic law (*Tos.*). Alternatively, since the Torah does not explicitly forbid this, people rationalize that as long as they use the money to purchase food it is included in the connotation of the phrase *for you to eat* and is permitted (*Meiri*). [Thus, their transgression of the law is not evidence of their inherent untrustworthiness.]

There is another approach to this case, that it refers to one who was idle until the *Shemittah* year and at that time began to sell produce. Since the evidence leads to the conclusion that he is selling *sheviis* produce, the Rabbis decreed that he may no longer testify (*Rambam* loc. cit. from *Yerushalmi* 3:5). [However, since the evidence is merely circumstantial, it does not invalidate him by Biblical law.] This interpretation is borne

3
3 Originally they called them *sheviis*-stockpilers. When the oppressors increased they changed to calling them *sheviis*-merchants. Said R' Yehudah: When? When they have no other trade, but if they have another trade, they are qualified.

YAD AVRAHAM

out by the mishnah's use of the phrase *sheviis-merchants* rather than the seemingly more appropriate phrase *merchants of sheviis produce* (*Meiri*).

אָמַר רַבִּי שִׁמְעוֹן: בַּתְּחִלָּה הָיוּ קוֹרִין אוֹתָן אוֹסְפֵי שְׁבִיעִית. מִשֶּׁרַבּוּ הָאַנָּסִין חָזְרוּ לִקְרוֹתָן סוֹחֲרֵי שְׁבִיעִית. — *Said R' Shimon: Originally they called them sheviis-stockpilers. When the oppressors increased they changed to calling them sheviis-merchants.*

Originally the Rabbis referred to the category of people disqualified because of *sheviis* infractions as *sheviis*-stockpilers because they disqualified even those who merely stockpiled the produce of *Shemittah*. [Stockpiling *Shemittah* produce was prohibited either because the Torah permits taking the produce only for *eating*, not long-term storage (*Tos. Yom Tov* to *Sheviis* 5:6, s.v. אבל מוכר), or because it gives the appearance of being done in order to sell it at some future date (*Chazon Ish*, *Sheviis* 12:9).] However, when the Roman tax collectors increased their demands upon the populace and required taxes to be paid even during *Shemittah*, it became necessary to produce crops in *Shemittah* to meet those demands. The Rabbis then permitted people to stockpile *Shemittah* produce in order to pay off the oppressive taxes. From then on they disqualified only those who dealt with *Shemittah* produce for gain (*Rav* from *Gem.* 26a).

The *Gemara* (26a) reports that in the days of R' Yannai, the Rabbis were forced to give permission even to sow the fields in *Shemittah* and raise a crop to pay the taxes.

Although plowing and sowing in *Shemittah* are prohibited by Torah law, the Rabbis permitted it because it was life threatening to refuse to meet the demands of the tax collectors. Alternatively, R' Yannai's decision was at a time when the laws of *Shemittah* were only Rabbinically in effect (*Tos.* ibid.). [See General Introduction to ArtScroll *Sheviis*, p. 13, concerning the current status of *Shemittah*.]

אָמַר רַבִּי יְהוּדָה: אֵימָתַי? — *Said R' Yehudah: When?*

I.e., when are dice-players disqualified from testifying (*Rav*)? According to those who explain the case of pigeon-flyers to refer to gamblers, that too is included in R' Yehudah's statement (*Tos. Yom Tov*). R' Yehudah is explaining the intent of the earlier statements of the mishnah, not disputing them (*Gem.* 24b).

בִּזְמַן שֶׁאֵין לָהֶם אֻמָּנוּת אֶלָּא הִיא, אֲבָל יֵשׁ לָהֶן אֻמָּנוּת שֶׁלֹּא הִיא, כְּשֵׁרִין. — *When they have no other trade, but if they have another trade, they are disqualified.*

[Only gamblers who have no other trade, and are thus not involved in any worthwhile pursuit, are disqualified. If they gamble in addition to other pursuits they are still eligible to serve as witnesses.]

Those who are disqualified because

סנהדרין [ד] **וְאֵלּוּ** הֵן הַקְּרוֹבִין: אָבִיו, וְאָחִיו וַאֲחִי אָבִיו,
ג/ד וַאֲחִי אִמּוֹ, וּבַעַל אֲחוֹתוֹ, וּבַעַל
אֲחוֹת אָבִיו, וּבַעַל אֲחוֹת אִמּוֹ, וּבַעַל אִמּוֹ, וְחָמִיו,

ר׳ עובדיה מברטנורא

(ד) **ובעל אחותו וכו׳.** משום דבעל כאשתו: **וגיסו.** בעל אחות אשתו:

יד אברהם

of their gambling regain their status only if they destroy their dice and accept upon themselves never again to play dice even without money (*Rav* from *Gem.* 25b). Similarly, all of the above categories must show clear evidence of having desisted completely from these occupations in order to become eligible again, as described in the *Gemara* (ibid.).

4.

The Torah states (*Deut.* 24:16): *Fathers shall not be killed due to sons and sons shall not be killed due to fathers.* The *Gemara* (27b) proves that the intent of this verse is that they shall not be put to death by virtue of the testimony of their sons or fathers. The *Gemara* further derives exegetically from this verse that all of the relatives cited in the mishnah are ineligible to testify either for or against the person to whom they are so related.

As explained by the *Gemara,* the disqualification of relatives applies to those who are within two levels of kinship to each other. The first level represents those whose kinship is primary; i.e., it does not owe its relationship to that of a still-closer relative. Such a primary relationship would be that of a father and son or two brothers. The relationship of these pairs is therefore said to be a first-level to first-level relationship [רִאשׁוֹן בְּרִאשׁוֹן]. Each succeeding generation that the relationship moves away from these primary relationships becomes a more distant level of relationship. Thus the children of two brothers — i.e., first cousins — are considered second-level to second-level relatives [שֵׁנִי בְּשֵׁנִי], because their relationship is through their parents. The children of first cousins are considered the third level of the relationship, since they are yet one more generation removed from the primary relationship.

The relationship of an uncle and nephew is considered a first-to-second-level relationship, because the nephew is one step removed from the primary relationship which his father had with the uncle. Since this relationship still falls within the second level, an uncle and nephew are disqualified by reason of kinship from judging or testifying about each other. The nephew's son is a third-level relative to his great-uncle [i.e., a first-to-third-level relationship]. The eligibility status of such a relationship is the subject of a dispute in the *Gemara* (28a), and the later authorities disagree as to which is the prevailing view (see *Choshen Mishpat* 33:2). It goes without saying that the children of first cousins are eligible to judge and testify for each other [third-to-third level] or even toward the cousins [second-to-third level] (*Meiri*).

3
4

4. These are the [ineligible] relatives: His father and brother, his father's brother and mother's brothers, his sister's husband, father's sister's husband and mother's sister's husband, his mother's husband, his father-in-law,

YAD AVRAHAM

In addition, the spouse of any of these people is treated the same as the relative himself.

וְאֵלּוּ הֵן הַקְּרוֹבִין: — *These are the [ineligible] relatives:*

I.e., those relatives who are disqualified from testifying about each other, whether to their benefit or detriment [and certainly from judging each other] (*Gem.* 28a). Similarly, two relatives cannot sit on the same court or testify together with each other in one set of witnesses (ibid.). In each of the cases cited below, the disqualification is reciprocal — e.g., one cannot testify for his father nor is his father eligible to testify for him (*Rashi*).

אָבִיו, — *His father*

Some versions of the mishnah do not include this case, because it is stated explicitly in the verse, and the mishnah comes to inform us only of those which are not explicitly stated (*Rambam Comm.*).

וְאָחִיו, וַאֲחִי אָבִיו, וַאֲחִי אִמּוֹ, — *and brother, his father's brother and mother's brother,*

[One's brother is his first-to-first-level relative, while his uncles are first-to-second level.] According to *Rambam,* all relatives from the mother's side are disqualified by Rabbinic law only (*Rambam, Hil. Eidus* 13:1 as interpreted by *Radbaz* ad loc. and *Rama, Choshen Mishpat* 33:2; see below, s.v. אמר רבי יוסי). Others contend that *Rambam* means only to differentiate between that which is stated explicitly in the Torah and that which is derived by the Rabbis through the exegetical process, but that all are in essence Biblically disqualified (*Kesef Mishneh, Eidus* ad loc.; *Shach, Choshen Mishpat* ad loc.).

וּבַעַל אֲחוֹתוֹ, וּבַעַל אֲחוֹת אָבִיו, וּבַעַל אֲחוֹת אִמּוֹ, וּבַעַל אִמּוֹ, — *his sister's husband, father's sister's husband and mother's sister's husband, his mother's husband,*

[I.e., one's brother-in-law, uncles through marriage to his aunts, and stepfather.] All of these relatives through marriage may not testify concerning him — nor he about them — because a man and his wife are considered one unit of kinship (*Rav* from *Gem.* 28b). This is derived from the laws of incest (*Lev.* Ch. 18) in which the Torah forbids the union of a man with his uncle's wife *because she is your aunt* (v. 14). Although she is actually only the wife of his uncle the Torah calls her his aunt, thus indicating that a husband and wife are treated as a single unit of kinship (*Gem.* ibid.).

וְחָמִיו, — *his father-in-law,*

[Since a husband and wife are treated as one unit, his wife's relatives are considered to be related to him.]

סנהדרין
ג/ד

וְגִיסוֹ; הֵן וּבְנֵיהֶן וְחַתְנֵיהֶן; וְחוֹרְגוֹ לְבַדּוֹ. אָמַר רַבִּי יוֹסֵי: זוֹ מִשְׁנַת רַבִּי עֲקִיבָא, אֲבָל מִשְׁנָה רִאשׁוֹנָה: דּוֹדוֹ וּבֶן דּוֹדוֹ וְכָל הָרָאוּי לְיָרְשׁוֹ.

ר׳ עובדיה מברטנורא

הם ובניהן וחתניהן. ודוקא בנים ובנות שיש לו לגיסו מאחות אשתו, אבל [אם] יש לו בנים מאשה אחרת, או חתנים נשואים לבנות שיש לו מאשה אחרת, אין חשובין קרובין: **וחורגו.** בן אשתו מאיש אחר, הוא בלבד חשוב קרוב, אבל בן חורגו וחתן חורגו לא, ואשת חורגו לא יעיד לה, דאשה כבעלה, והאחים זה עם זה, בין מן האב בין מן האם, הרי הן ראשון בראשון, ובניהם זה עם זה, שני בשני, ובני בניהם זה עם זה, שלישי בשלישי, ולעולם שלישי בראשון כשר, ואין צריך לומר שלישי בשני, אבל שני בשני ואין צריך לומר שני בראשון, שניהם פסולים, וכדרך שאתה מונה בזכרים כך אתה מונה בנקבות, וכל אשה שאתה פסול לה, כך אתה פסול לבעלה, וכל איש שאתה פסול לו, כך אתה פסול לאשתו: **אבל משנה ראשונה דודו ובן דודו.** ואין הלכה כמשנה ראשונה: **וכל הראוי ליורשו.** תשלום משנתו של רבי עקיבא היא ולא ממשנה ראשונה, וכל הראוי ליורשו, דהיינו קרובי האב, אבל קרובי האם כגון אחי אמו שהזכרנו, כשר לו, שהרי אין אחי אמו ראוי ליורשו, אבל הוא ראוי לירש אחי אמו, לפיכך הוא פסול להעיד לו:

יד אברהם

וְגִיסוֹ; — *and his brother-in-law;*

I.e., the husband of his wife's sister (*Rav*). Since the wives of these two men are sisters and thus related on a first-level to first-level basis, their husbands are also considered related.

His wife's brother is obviously also ineligible; he is included in the general statement which follows — *they, their sons,* etc. — since he is the son of his father-in-law (*Tif. Yis.*).

However, beyond this degree of closeness, the principle of wives and husbands being considered as one unit of kinship no longer applies, and thus the husbands of two cousins are not disqualified from testifying concerning one another (*Meiri;* see below).

הֵן וּבְנֵיהֶן וְחַתְנֵיהֶן; — *they, their sons, and their sons-in-law;*

The sons and sons-in-law of those relatives listed above are also disqualified from serving as witnesses for him, and he for them.

However, this principle does not necessarily apply in reverse; i.e., one's own sons and sons-in-law are not necessarily disqualified in regard to the relatives listed. For example, one's son is not disqualified from testifying concerning his uncle according to the mishnah [since he is a third-level relative to his great-uncle], but his uncle's son cannot testify for him [since he is his first cousin — a second-level relative] (*Tos.*).

These sons and sons-in-law refer only to those who are actually related to him. Thus, for example, in the case of one's brother-in-law, the son is only disqualified if he is also the son of his wife's sister but not if he is his brother-in-law's son from another marriage (*Rav*).

The *Gemara* (28b) cites the view of R' Yose, who disputes the mishnah and contends that the rule including both the sons and sons-in-law of his relatives in the category of disqualified relatives does not apply to the case of his wife's sister's husband. Although he agrees that the son of his

3 and his brother-in-law; they, their sons, and their
4 sons-in-law; and his stepson alone. Said R' Yose: This is the mishnah of R' Akiva, but the original mishnah [stated]: His uncle and his uncle's son and all who are eligible to inherit him.

wife's sister is ineligible, he maintains that the son-in-law of that relative is an eligible witness (*Rashi; Tos.; Rosh*). According to R' Yose, in a first-to-second-level relationship, kinship through marriage disqualifies only when one marriage is involved; if the principle of a couple's unity must be invoked doubly to establish the relationship — as in this case where he is related to his sister-in-law's son-in-law only through his own marriage to his wife and the marriage of his sister-in-law's daughter to her husband — the link is not sufficiently strong to disqualify. Only in a first-to-first-level relationship does this occur — such as the husbands of two sisters (*Meiri*). Accordingly, his sister-in-law's son-in-law is eligible to testify about him, while her son is not (*Rashi; Tos.; Rosh*). The halachah follows this view.

Others interpret the dispute differently. Whereas the mishnah disqualifies all sons and sons-in-law of one's wife's sister's husband, R' Yose contends that it applies only to those of his wife's sister but not to her husband's children from a different marriage (*Rif; Rambam, Eidus* 13:7; *Meiri*). Although he states this principle in regard to a brother-in-law, it actually pertains to all relatives through marriage (*Meiri*). [*Rav*, however, contends that our mishnah also agrees to this distinction, as stated above.]

.וְחוֹרְגוֹ לְבַדּוֹ — *and his stepson alone.*

His stepson is ineligible, but not the son or son-in-law of his stepson (*Rav*). [The stepfather's relationship to his stepson is a first-to-second-level relationship since they are related only through the wife/mother. Thus, the stepson's son is a third-level relative.[1]

Actually, the disqualification of a stepson has already been stated by the mishnah, since his relationship to his stepson is that of the *mother's husband* cited above. Nevertheless, the mishnah repeats the case to show it from the other relative's perspective (*Rashi*). Alternatively, the mishnah cites a stepson to emphasize that only he is disqualified but not his son or sin-in-law (*Tos.*).

Although the mishnah uses examples of males, the same laws apply to parallel female relationships. [Thus a man may neither judge nor testify on behalf of women related to him in any of the above-mentioned ways.] Also, just as the husband of his female relative is considered related to him, so is the wife of his male relative (*Rav*).

אָמַר רַבִּי יוֹסֵי: זוֹ מִשְׁנַת רַבִּי עֲקִיבָא, אֲבָל מִשְׁנָה רִאשׁוֹנָה: דּוֹדוֹ וּבֶן דּוֹדוֹ וְכָל הָרָאוּי לְיָרְשׁוֹ. — *Said R' Yose: This is the mishnah of R' Akiva, but the original mishnah [stated]: His uncle and his uncle's son and all who are eligible to inherit him.*

R' Yose contends that familial relations in regard to eligibility to

1. In the preface to this mishnah it was noted that there is a view in the *Gemara* that first-to-third-level relatives are also disqualified. This applies, however, only to blood relatives, not relatives through marriage (*Tos.* 28a, s.v. רב). Thus, the stepson's son is not disqualified.

וְכָל הַקָּרוֹב לוֹ בְּאוֹתָהּ שָׁעָה. הָיָה קָרוֹב וְנִתְרַחֵק, הֲרֵי זֶה כָּשֵׁר. רַבִּי יְהוּדָה אוֹמֵר: אֲפִלּוּ מֵתָה בִתּוֹ וְיֶשׁ לוֹ בָנִים מִמֶּנָּה, הֲרֵי זֶה קָרוֹב.

[ה] **הָאוֹהֵב** וְהַשּׂוֹנֵא: אוֹהֵב — זֶה

ר׳ עובדיה מברטנורא

היה קרוב. כגון חתנו וראוי ליורשו מחמת אשתו: **ונתרחק.** שמתה אשתו קודם שראה עדות זו: **רבי יהודה אומר וכו׳.** ואין הלכה כרבי יהודה: (ה) **שושבינו.** רעהו בימי חופתו, פסול לו כל ימי החופה: **לא נחשדו ישראל על כך.** להעיד שקר משום איבה ואהבה. וכן הלכה.

יד אברהם

serve as a witness are defined by the laws of inheritance. This eliminates most maternal relatives, since inheritance passes only to relatives through the father's side [see *Bava Basra* 8:1]. Thus, a man can testify concerning his sister's son, since a man cannot inherit his sister's children [because his sister — the boy's mother — cannot inherit her son]. However, the nephew cannot testify about the uncle, because it is possible for him to inherit his mother's brother (*Rashi*). [A sister can inherit her brother if he dies without children, provided that there were no other brothers; see *Bava Basra* 8:1,2.][1]

Others contend that as long as the possibility of inheritance exists between two relatives in any direction, neither is qualified to testify concerning the other. Thus, a man is disqualified from testifying for his sister's son just as the latter is disqualified from testifying for him. R' Yose's dispute with R' Akiva pertains only to his mother's husband, brother-in-law [i.e. wife's sister's husband], mother's sister's husband, and stepson (*Baal HaMaor; Meiri*). A third view considers R' Yose's statement to eliminate all relatives through his wife. Although his wife could inherit them and he her, this does not make him an heir of that relative of his wife (*Ramban*). [Thus, for example, he could testify about his father-in-law since he can never inherit him directly, only through his wife.]

There is another approach to this mishnah, that the words *and all who are eligible to inherit him* are not part of the original mishnah but rather a resumption of the words of the anonymous mishnah [which R' Yose attributes to R' Akiva]

1. When inheritance passes to any non-immediate relative, it is seen as passing through the line of immediate relatives — even though they are no longer alive — and from them to their immediate relatives until a living heir is reached. Thus, if a man dies without children (or grandchildren), the person next in line to inherit him is his father. The inheritance is seen as passing to the father even if the father is no longer alive and from him to his heirs. If his only other child was a daughter, she inherits the estate [as daughters inherit their fathers when there are no sons] and, if she is also no longer alive, it passes to her heir — viz., her son. In this manner it is possible for a man to inherit his mother's brother (see *Bava Basra* 8:2).

The reverse, however, is not possible, since in order for a man to inherit his sister's son, the inheritance would first have to pass from son to mother, which it does not do (ibid. 8:1).

3
5

[This applies to] all who were related at that time. [If] he was related and then became unrelated, he is eligible. R' Yehudah says: Even if his daughter died and he has children from her, he is a relative.

5. **A** friend and an enemy: "a friend" is one's

YAD AVRAHAM

(*Rav; Rambam Comm.*).[1] In this view, the distinction between relatives from the father's side and those of the mother's side is relevant to the halachah, since the halachah follows the view of R' Akiva (see above, s.v. אחיו). However, the later authorities do not accept this interpretation and maternal relatives are also thus disqualified (*Choshen Mishpat* 33:2).

וְכָל הַקָּרוֹב לוֹ בְּאוֹתָהּ שָׁעָה. — *[This applies to] all who were related at that time.*

Having concluded R' Yose's interjection, the mishnah now resumes its original discussion (*Tif. Yis.*). The mishnah now states the rule that one is disqualified by virtue of familial relationship only if he was related at the time of his being a witness — i.e., either at the time he witnessed the event or at the time he testifies about it in court (*Rashi*). [These are the two times at which he actually serves in the capacity of a witness.]

הָיָה קָרוֹב וְנִתְרַחֵק, הֲרֵי זֶה כָּשֵׁר. — *[If] he was related and then became unrelated* (lit., *was distanced*), *he is eligible.*

E.g., if someone's former son-in-law witnessed an event concerning him after his daughter (the former's wife) had died and they were thus no longer related, he may testify in court about what he saw (*Rav;* see *Tos. Yom Tov*).

רַבִּי יְהוּדָה אוֹמֵר: אֲפִלּוּ מֵתָה בִתּוֹ וְיֵשׁ לוֹ בָנִים מִמֶּנָּה, הֲרֵי זֶה קָרוֹב. — *R' Yehudah says: Even if his daughter died and he has children from her, he is a relative.*

[R' Yehudah contends that one's former son-in-law remains related to him even after the daughter/wife has died as long as children remain from that marriage. Although he is no longer his son-in-law, as the father of his grandchildren, he is still considered his relative.]

The halachah follows the view of the first *Tanna* (*Rambam, Eidus* 14:1; *Choshen Mishpat* 33:12).

5.

הָאוֹהֵב וְהַשּׂוֹנֵא: — *A friend and an enemy:*

This mishnah is a continuation of the previous one and is the conclusion of R' Yehudah's statement there. He maintains that a friend and an enemy, as defined below, are both disqualified from testifying (*Tos. Yom Tov*).

1. This explanation is very difficult to comprehend, because it contradicts several of the cases cited earlier in the mishnah (*Rashash*). [In addition, if these are the words of R' Akiva, R' Yose's quote from the original seems meaningless. If it is meant to convey that only relatives who inherit are disqualified, its citation is pointless, since R' Akiva also agrees to this.]

שׁוֹשְׁבִינוֹ, שׂוֹנֵא — כָּל שֶׁלֹּא דִבֵּר עִמּוֹ שְׁלֹשָׁה יָמִים בְּאֵיבָה. אָמְרוּ לוֹ: לֹא נֶחְשְׁדוּ יִשְׂרָאֵל עַל כָּךְ.

[ו] **כֵּיצַד** בּוֹדְקִים אֶת הָעֵדִים? הָיוּ מַכְנִיסִין אוֹתָן וּמְאַיְּמִין עֲלֵיהֶן. וּמוֹצִיאִין אֶת כָּל הָאָדָם לַחוּץ וּמְשַׁיְּרִין אֶת הַגָּדוֹל שֶׁבָּהֶן,

ר׳ עובדיה מברטנורא

ודוקא בעדות פליגי רבנן עליה, אבל בדין מודו רבנן דפסול לו לדון, דאי רחים ליה אינו רואה לו חובה, ואי סני ליה לא מצי לאפוכי בזכותיה: (ו) **ומאיימין עליהם.** מודיעים אותם שהשוכרים עדי שקר, הן עצמן מבזין אותן וקוראים להן רשעים, דכתיב (במלכים-א כא,י) בנבות, והושיבו שנים אנשים בני בליעל נגדו, שיועצי המלך שהיו יועצים לשכרן קוראים להן בני בליעל:

יד אברהם

אוֹהֵב - זֶה שׁוֹשְׁבִינוֹ, — *"a friend" is one's groomsman;*

I.e., a close friend who brings gifts of food and drink to one's wedding feast, as was the custom in those days (see *Bava Basra* 9:4). There is a dispute in the *Gemara* (29a) whether he is disqualified from testifying on the day of the wedding only or throughout the seven days of rejoicing which follow the wedding. [Beyond that time, the emotions involved are apparently not assumed to be so intense as to bring into question the reliability of testimony.] (See *Rav, Rashi.*)

Others explain the *Gemara* to be discussing the length of time one must participate in his friend's celebration to be considered a groomsman. [Once he attains that status he is disqualified from then on.] (*Yad Ramah*).

שׂוֹנֵא - כָּל שֶׁלֹּא דִבֵּר עִמּוֹ שְׁלֹשָׁה יָמִים בְּאֵיבָה. — *"an enemy" is one who did not speak to him for three days out of enmity.*

In delineating the laws of the unintentional murderer, the Torah qualifies its penalty of exile with the statement that *he was not his enemy, nor did he seek his misfortune* (*Numbers* 35:23). Although the simple meaning of the verse would seem to refer to the prior relationship between the murderer and his victim, R' Yehudah exegetically explains it to refer to the relationship of the witnesses and judges to the murderer (*Rashi*): *And he* [the witnesses] *was not his enemy* — then he may testify about him; *and he* [the judge] *did not seek his misfortune* — then he may judge him. Since an enemy is disqualified by the Torah due to his subjectivity, it stands to reason that the same applies to a friend (*Gem.* 29a).

אָמְרוּ לוֹ: לֹא נֶחְשְׁדוּ יִשְׂרָאֵל עַל כָּךְ. — *They said to him: The Jewish people are not suspected of this.*

They are not suspected of testifying falsely because of friendship or enmity (*Rav*). The Sages, however,

groomsman; "an enemy" is one who did not speak to him for three days out of enmity. They said to him: The Jewish people are not suspected of this.

6. **H**ow do they examine the witnesses? They bring them in and admonish them. They then send everyone out and retain the most prominent of them,

YAD AVRAHAM

agree that this verse applies to a judge, who is indeed disqualified from judging his friend or enemy (*Gem.* 29a).

The halachah follows this view, that one may testify concerning his friend or enemy but he may not judge him (see *Choshen Mishpat* 7:7). Some hold that this applies to any friend or enemy, not only ones defined by R' Yehudah above (*Rambam, Sanhedrin* 23:6; *Hagahos HaAshri* to 36b). Others maintain that there is nevertheless a distinction between the two categories: If one's ordinary friend or enemy judged him, the judgment is valid after the fact, but if a groomsman or an enemy as defined by R' Yehudah did so, it is null (*Tur, Choshen Mishpat* 7). Still others maintain that a regular friend or enemy is permitted by law to judge but is discouraged from so doing (see *Rama* ibid. 7:7; *Tos.* 8a, s.v. פסילנא).

6.

כֵּיצַד בּוֹדְקִים אֶת הָעֵדִים? — *How do they examine the witnesses?*

I.e., in monetary cases. Although the formal scrutiny required of witnesses in capital cases (see below, 4:1) is not necessary in monetary cases, they nevertheless examined them to clarify their testimony (*Meiri*).

הָיוּ מַכְנִיסִין אוֹתָן וּמְאַיְּמִין עֲלֵיהֶן. — *They bring them in and admonish them.*

They call the witnesses into the court and warn them forcefully before everyone present of the severity of false testimony (*Rambam, Eidus* 17:2). They tell them that if they testify falsely, they will suffer derision in this world even from those who hired them (*Rav* from *Gem.* 29a), in addition to the great shame they will suffer in the World to Come (*Rambam* ibid.; *Choshen Mishpat* 28:8).

וּמוֹצִיאִין אֶת כָּל הָאָדָם לַחוּץ וּמְשַׁיְּרִין אֶת הַגָּדוֹל שֶׁבָּהֶן, — *They then send everyone out and retain the most prominent of them,*

I.e., they send out everyone but the witnesses, whom they examine privately one at a time (see below). Such an examination offers them a better opportunity to examine them thoroughly (*Tos. Yom Tov* from *Levush, Choshen Mishpat* 28). However, they do not sent out the litigants themselves, since they are required to be present when the witnesses testify (*Tos. Yom Tov; Sema, Choshen Mishpat* 28:37; *Beur HaGra* ibid. 46).

וְאוֹמְרִים לוֹ ,,אֱמֹר הֵיאָךְ אַתָּה יוֹדֵעַ שֶׁזֶּה חַיָּב לָזֶה". אִם אָמַר ,,הוּא אָמַר לִי, שֶׁאֲנִי חַיָּב לוֹ", ,,אִישׁ פְּלוֹנִי אָמַר לִי שֶׁהוּא חַיָּב לוֹ", לֹא אָמַר כְּלוּם, עַד שֶׁיֹּאמַר ,,בְּפָנֵינוּ הוֹדָה לוֹ שֶׁהוּא חַיָּב לוֹ מָאתַיִם זוּז". וְאַחַר כָּךְ, מַכְנִיסִין אֶת הַשֵּׁנִי וּבוֹדְקִים אוֹתוֹ. אִם נִמְצְאוּ דִבְרֵיהֶם מְכֻוָּנִים, נוֹשְׂאִין וְנוֹתְנִין בַּדָּבָר.

ר' עובדיה מברטנורא

הוא אמר לי. הלוה אמר לי: **לא אמר כלום.** דעביד [איניש] דאמר פלוני נושה בי, כדי שלא יחזיקוהו עשיר: **הודה לו.** שהיו שניהם בפנינו ולהודות לו נתכוין, להיות לו עדים בדבר:

יד אברהם

Other versions of the mishnah state *and they send them out* — referring to the other witnesses, but not the other people assembled (*Rif; Rosh*). In this view, public examination is better suited to ascertaining the truth. The witnesses are separated from each other, however, to prevent their coordinating their answers to difficult questions (*Tos. Yom Tov*).

וְאוֹמְרִים לוֹ ,,אֱמֹר הֵיאָךְ אַתָּה יוֹדֵעַ שֶׁזֶּה חַיָּב לָזֶה". — *and they say to him, "State how you know that this one owes that one."*

The wording of the judges' question to the witness indicates that the mishnah takes for granted that the judges already heard the testimony of this witness and are examining him for the sake of clarification. Although formal examination of the type described in Chapter 4 is not required in monetary cases, the mishnah is discussing a situation in which the witnesses stated that the defendant owed the plaintiff money without specifying how they knew this. Since it is possible that their source of information is not acceptable to the court, as described below, the judges must inquire as to the basis of their testimony. However, if they were to say in their initial statement that they saw the money being borrowed, no further examination would be necessary (*Ran*).

Alternatively, the witnesses discussed in the mishnah did not say anything before they were asked this question. However, the fact that they were brought to court by the plaintiff sufficed to indicate to the judges that they intend to testify against the defendant, and the question quoted here is thus appropriate (cited ibid.).

אִם אָמַר ,,הוּא אָמַר לִי, שֶׁאֲנִי חַיָּב לוֹ", — *If he said, "He told me, 'I owe him,'*

The witness testifies that his source was the defendant himself, who told him that he owed the money (*Rav*).

,,אִישׁ פְּלוֹנִי אָמַר לִי שֶׁהוּא חַיָּב לוֹ", — *[or] 'so-and-so told me that he owes him,' "*

[I.e., he admits that his knowledge of the matter is secondhand, based on what he was told by someone else.] The term פְּלוֹנִי, *so-and-so,* denotes a person of stature (*Tos. Yom Tov*). [I.e., although their source is impeccable the testimony is not acceptable.]

3
6

and they say to him, "State how you know that this one owes that one." If he said, "He told me, 'I owe him,' [or] 'so-and-so told me that he owes him,' " he has said nothing, until he says, "He admitted to him before us that he owes him two hundred *zuz*." Afterward, they bring in the second one and examine him. If their words are found to coincide they take up the matter.

YAD AVRAHAM

לֹא אָמַר כְּלוּם, — *he has said nothing,*

This witness' testimony is not valid. Hearsay testimony which quotes another witness is in general not acceptable (*Meiri*), and even testimony which quotes the defendant's own words is not valid, because a man is occasionally prone to discuss non-existent debts in order to convey the impression that he is not wealthy (*Rav*). Even if the admission was made in response to the plaintiff's claim, it is not conclusive because he may have meant it facetiously (*Meleches Shlomo* from *Gem.* 29a).

עַד שֶׁיֹּאמַר ,,בְּפָנֵינוּ הוֹדָה לוֹ שֶׁהוּא חַיָּב לוֹ מָאתַיִם זוּז.״ — *until he says, "He admitted to him before us that he owes him two hundred zuz."*

I.e., he told the witnesses that they should attest to the fact that he is admitting his debt (*Gem.* 29a). This is evident from the fact that the mishnah describes the witness as saying that the admission took place *before us* rather than simply stating that he heard the admission (*Nimmukei Yosef*).

Obviously, if they claim to have actually witnessed the loan, that is also valid testimony (*Tif. Yis.*).

The sum of two hundred *zuz* is chosen merely as an example, representing the minimum sum considered sufficient for a person's needs for a year. Possession of such an amount renders a person ineligible for charity (*Tos. Yom Tov*).

Some derive from the wording of the mishnah — which uses the plural *before us* despite the fact that it is discussing the questioning of only one witness — that if he told only one of the two people present to witness his admission it is not binding (*Baal HaMaor*). Others contend that such an admission would also be acceptable, as evidenced by the fact that the mishnah does not include that among the examples of invalid testimony (*Ramban;* see *Ran; Choshen Mishpat* 81:10 and *Shach* ibid.).

וְאַחַר כָּךְ, מַכְנִיסִין אֶת הַשֵּׁנִי וּבוֹדְקִים אוֹתוֹ. — *Afterward, they bring in the second one and examine him.*

He must explain his testimony in the same manner as the first, and it is not sufficient for him to simply state that he concurs with the testimony of the other witness (*Meiri* from *Gem.* 60a).

אִם נִמְצְאוּ דִבְרֵיהֶם מְכֻוָּנִים, נוֹשְׂאִין וְנוֹתְנִין בַּדָּבָר. — *If their words are found to coincide they take up the matter.*

[If the testimony of the two witnesses agrees it is accepted, and the court considers the matter further.] Unlike capital cases, the testimony of these witnesses must concur only concerning the vital questions — e.g., the date and time (see 5:1) — but not in all other details (*Meiri*).

סנהדרין
ג/ז

שְׁנַיִם אוֹמְרִים: זַכַּאי, וְאֶחָד אוֹמֵר: חַיָּב — זַכַּאי. שְׁנַיִם אוֹמְרִים: חַיָּב, וְאֶחָד אוֹמֵר: זַכַּאי — חַיָּב. אֶחָד אוֹמֵר: זַכַּאי, וְאֶחָד אוֹמֵר: חַיָּב, וַאֲפִלּוּ שְׁנַיִם מְזַכִּין אוֹ שְׁנַיִם מְחַיְּבִין וְאֶחָד אוֹמֵר ,,אֵינִי יוֹדֵעַ" — יוֹסִיפוּ הַדַּיָּנִין.

[ז] **גָּמְרוּ** אֶת הַדָּבָר, הָיוּ מַכְנִיסִין אוֹתָן. הַגָּדוֹל שֶׁבַּדַּיָּנִים אוֹמֵר: ,,אִישׁ פְּלוֹנִי, אַתָּה זַכַּאי"; ,,אִישׁ פְּלוֹנִי, אַתָּה חַיָּב". וּמִנַּיִן לִכְשֶׁיֵּצֵא אֶחָד מִן הַדַּיָּנִים לֹא יֹאמַר ,,אֲנִי מְזַכֶּה וַחֲבֵרַי מְחַיְּבִין; אֲבָל מָה אֶעֱשֶׂה שֶׁחֲבֵרַי רַבּוּ עָלַי?" עַל זֶה נֶאֱמַר:

ר' עובדיה מברטנורא

אפילו שנים מזכין או מחייבים ואחד אומר איני יודע יוסיפו דיינים. ואף על גב דאי הוה פליג עלייהו היה בטל במיעוטו, כי אמר איני יודע הוי כמו שלא ישב בדין, ונמצא הדין בשנים, ואין שלש בעינן: **(ז) היו מכניסין אותן.** לבעלי דינין, [שלאחר] ששמעו טענותיהן היו מוציאין לחוץ כדי שישאו ויתנו בדבר ולא ישמעו הבעלי דינים מי מחייב ומי מזכה:

יד אברהם

שְׁנַיִם אוֹמְרִים: זַכַּאי, וְאֶחָד אוֹמֵר: חַיָּב – זַכַּאי. — *[If] two vote: not liable, and one votes: liable — he is not liable.*

As stated in the Torah (*Ex.* 23:2): *You shall follow the majority* (*Rashi*).

שְׁנַיִם אוֹמְרִים: חַיָּב, וְאֶחָד אוֹמֵר: זַכַּאי – חַיָּב. — *[If] two vote: liable, and one votes: not liable — he is liable.*

[As will be discussed below in mishnah 4:1.]

אֶחָד אוֹמֵר: זַכַּאי, וְאֶחָד אוֹמֵר: חַיָּב, וַאֲפִלּוּ שְׁנַיִם מְזַכִּין אוֹ שְׁנַיִם מְחַיְּבִין וְאֶחָד אוֹמֵר ,,אֵינִי יוֹדֵעַ" – יוֹסִיפוּ הַדַּיָּנִין. — *[If] one votes: not liable, and one votes: liable, or even [if] two exonerate or two obligate and one says, "I do not know" — they add more judges.*

[If an opinion is not given by all three judges, they continue to add judges, two at a time, until a majority opinion is reached.] Although in the case in which the two agree, the third would be outvoted even if he were to dispute their decision, he must nevertheless express an opinion in order for them to be considered a body of three judges; if he does not, they cannot render a ruling (*Rav*).

It is unclear why it is necessary to add two judges, since in monetary matters a majority of one is sufficient for any verdict (*Rabbeinu Yonah*).

If after adding judges they still have no majority, they continue to add two at a time until they reach a total of seventy-one judges. If they still have no majority, the money remains in the hands of the one in possession (*Rambam, Hil. Sanhedrin* 8:2; cf. *Meiri*).

[If] two vote: not liable, and one votes: liable — he is not liable. [If] two vote: liable, and one votes: not liable — he is liable. [If] one votes: not liable, and one votes: liable, or even [if] two exonerate or two obligate and one says, "I do not know" — they add more judges.

7. When they conclude the matter, they bring them in. The head judge says: "So-and-so, you are not liable"; [or] "so-and-so, you are liable."

From where [do we know] that when one of the judges leaves [the court] he should not say, "I exonerated and my colleagues obligated; but what could I do since my colleagues outnumbered me?" Concerning this it is stated:

YAD AVRAHAM

7.

גָּמְרוּ אֶת הַדָּבָר, הָיוּ מַכְנִיסִין אוֹתָן. — *When they conclude the matter, they bring them in.*

They must call the litigants back into the court, because the judges had previously sent them out after hearing the testimony. This is done in order for the judges to be able to discuss the matter privately, without the litigants knowing who expressed which opinion (*Rav* from *Gem.* 30a). This frees the judges of any pressures which may exist on any of them to support one litigant or another and the anonymity of their decision also insures that they remain popular with everyone [and their words are thus heeded] (*Rambam Comm.*).

הַגָּדוֹל שֶׁבַּדַּיָּנִים אוֹמֵר: „אִישׁ פְּלוֹנִי, אַתָּה זַכַּאי"; „אִישׁ פְּלוֹנִי, אַתָּה חַיָּב". — *The head judge says: "So-and-so, you are not liable"; [or] "so-and-so, you are liable."*

It is necessary for the head of the court to state the verdict so that the litigants should not be able to deduce from the identity of the spokesman what his personal view is in regard to the verdict (*Tur, Choshen Mishpat* 19). Alternatively, this is done to honor the head of the court, since it is inappropriate for a wise man to speak up in the place of his superiors (*Tos. Yom Tov;* cf. *Mahariach*).

If it is necessary for the court to record the verdict, they do not record which judges exonerated and which obligated but simply record the court's verdict: So-and-so was exonerated or obligated (*Choshen Mishpat* 19:2 from *Gem.* 30a).

וּמִנַּיִן לִכְשֶׁיֵּצֵא אֶחָד מִן הַדַּיָּנִים לֹא יֹאמַר „אֲנִי מְזַכֶּה וַחֲבֵרַי מְחַיְּבִין; אֲבָל מָה אֶעֱשֶׂה שֶׁחֲבֵרַי רַבּוּ עָלַי?" עַל זֶה נֶאֱמַר: „לֹא־תֵלֵךְ רָכִיל בְּעַמֶּיךָ". וְאוֹמֵר: „הוֹלֵךְ רָכִיל מְגַלֶּה־

„לֹא־תֵלֵךְ רָכִיל בְּעַמֶּיךָ". וְאוֹמֵר „הוֹלֵךְ רָכִיל מְגַלֶּה־סּוֹד".

[ח] **כָּל** זְמַן שֶׁמֵּבִיא רְאָיָה, סוֹתֵר אֶת הַדִּין. אָמְרוּ לוֹ: כָּל רְאָיוֹת שֶׁיֵּשׁ לְךָ הָבֵא מִכָּאן עַד שְׁלֹשִׁים יוֹם — מָצָא בְּתוֹךְ שְׁלֹשִׁים יוֹם סוֹתֵר; לְאַחַר שְׁלֹשִׁים יוֹם אֵינוֹ סוֹתֵר. אָמַר רַבָּן שִׁמְעוֹן בֶּן גַּמְלִיאֵל: מַה יַּעֲשֶׂה זֶה שֶׁלֹּא מָצָא בְּתוֹךְ שְׁלֹשִׁים, וּמָצָא לְאַחַר שְׁלֹשִׁים? אָמְרוּ לוֹ: הָבֵא עֵדִים, וְאָמַר: אֵין לִי עֵדִים; אָמְרוּ: הָבֵא רְאָיָה, וְאָמַר: אֵין לִי רְאָיָה;

ר' עובדיה מברטנורא

(ח) **הבא ראיה.** שטר זכות: **הרי זו אינו כלום.** שהרי אמר אין לי, וחיישינן שמא זייף, או שכר עדי שקר: **אמר רבן שמעון בן גמליאל וכו'.** ואין הלכה כרבן שמעון בן גמליאל:

יד אברהם

סוֹד". — *From where [do we know] that when one of the judges leaves [the court] he should not say, "I exonerated and my colleagues obligated; but what could I do since my colleagues outnumbered me?" Concerning this it is stated* (*Lev.* 19:16): *"You shall not go about among your people bearing tales." And it is stated* (*Prov.* 11:13): *"One who bears tales reveals secrets."*

From the first verse alone one might think that if someone reveals a secret in order to protect his reputation or relationship with another it is not considered talebearing. Therefore the verse from *Proverbs* is cited to indicate that anyone who reveals secrets is considered a talebearer (*Tos. Yom Tov*).

Other versions to the mishnah cite only the verse from *Proverbs*, not the one from *Leviticus* (*Rif; Rosh; Bava Kamma* 99; see *Tos. Yom Tov*).

8.

כָּל זְמַן שֶׁמֵּבִיא רְאָיָה, סוֹתֵר אֶת הַדִּין. — *Whenever he brings proof, he can overturn the verdict.*

There is no statute of limitations on the submission of evidence; even after the verdict has been issued, if a litigant finds new evidence to support his claim, he may submit it to the court and, on the strength of his evidence, compel the court to retract its verdict against him (*Rashi*).

אָמְרוּ לוֹ: כָּל רְאָיוֹת שֶׁיֵּשׁ לְךָ הָבֵא מִכָּאן עַד שְׁלֹשִׁים יוֹם – — *[If] they said to him: Produce any proofs you have within thirty days —*

3
8
You shall not go about among your people bearing tales. And it is stated: *One who bears tales reveals secrets.*

8. **W**henever he brings proof, he can overturn the verdict. [If] they said to him: Produce any proofs you have within thirty days — [if] he finds [evidence] within thirty days he can overturn [the verdict]; after thirty days he cannot overturn [it]. Said Rabban Shimon ben Gamliel: What should this [man] do if he could not find [evidence] within thirty days, but found after thirty [days]? [If] they said to him: Bring witnesses, and he said: I have no witnesses; [or] they said: Bring evidence, and he said: I have no evidence;

YAD AVRAHAM

I.e., the judges specifically demanded of him that he produce whatever witnesses or other evidence he may have within thirty days (*Tif. Yis.*).

However, it seems unlikely that any *Tanna* should consider it a matter of judicial prerogative whether to issue such a call or not. Rather, the mishnah must refer to a situation in which the judges found it necessary to pursue such a course (*Tif. Yis.*).

מָצָא בְתוֹךְ שְׁלֹשִׁים יוֹם סוֹתֵר; לְאַחַר שְׁלֹשִׁים יוֹם אֵינוֹ סוֹתֵר. — *[if] he finds [evidence] within thirty days he can overturn [the verdict); after thirty days he cannot overturn [it].*

In issuing such a demand, the court in effect nullifies his rights in the matter if he fails to produce the evidence by the thirty-day deadline (*Meiri*). [This is in accordance with the authority of the Jewish courts to confiscate people's possessions (הֶפְקֵר בֵּית דִּין הֶפְקֵר).]

אָמַר רַבָּן שִׁמְעוֹן בֶּן גַּמְלִיאֵל: מַה יַּעֲשֶׂה זֶה שֶׁלֹּא מָצָא בְתוֹךְ שְׁלֹשִׁים, וּמָצָא לְאַחַר שְׁלֹשִׁים? — *Said Rabban Shimon ben Gamliel: What should this [man] do if he could not find [evidence] within thirty days but found after thirty [days]?*

[Rabban Shimon ben Gamliel contends that the courts may not impose such a restriction on a litigant.] The halachah follows this view. Even if the money has already been paid over by court order, it may still be recovered on the basis of new evidence (*Gem.* 31a).

אָמְרוּ לוֹ: הָבֵא עֵדִים, וְאָמַר: אֵין לִי עֵדִים; אָמְרוּ: הָבֵא רְאָיָה, וְאָמַר: אֵין לִי רְאָיָה; — *[If] they said to him: Bring witnesses, and he said: I have no witnesses; [or] they said: Bring evidence, and he said: I have no evidence;*

He stated before the court that he had no witnesses or documents to support his position (*Rav*).

סנהדרין
ג/ח

וּלְאַחַר זְמַן הֵבִיא רְאָיָה וּמָצָא עֵדִים, הֲרֵי זֶה אֵינוֹ כְלוּם. אָמַר רַבָּן שִׁמְעוֹן בֶּן גַּמְלִיאֵל: מַה יַּעֲשֶׂה זֶה שֶׁלֹּא הָיָה יוֹדֵעַ שֶׁיֵּשׁ לוֹ עֵדִים וּמָצָא עֵדִים; לֹא הָיָה יוֹדֵעַ שֶׁיֵּשׁ לוֹ רְאָיָה וּמָצָא רְאָיָה? אָמְרוּ לוֹ הָבֵא עֵדִים, אָמַר: אֵין לִי עֵדִים; הָבֵא רְאָיָה וְאָמַר: אֵין לִי רְאָיָה; רָאָה שֶׁמִּתְחַיֵּב בַּדִּין וְאָמַר „קִרְבוּ פְלוֹנִי וּפְלוֹנִי וְהָעִידוּנִי״, אוֹ שֶׁהוֹצִיא רְאָיָה מִתּוֹךְ אֲפֻנְדָּתוֹ, הֲרֵי זֶה אֵינוֹ כְלוּם.

ר׳ עובדיה מברטנורא

קרבו פלוני ופלוני והעידוני. בהא אפילו רבן שמעון בן גמליאל מודה, דכיון שהיה יודע בהן ואמר אין לי, ודאי שקרן הוא, אבל הטוען יש לי עדים או ראיה במדינת הים, אין שומעין לו לענות הדין עד שישלח למדינת הים, אלא פוסקין את הדין כפי מה שרואין ממנו עכשיו, וכשיביא עדים או ראיה, סותר את הדין וחוזרים ודנים כפי העדים או הראיה שהביא: **אפונדתו.** חגורתו. ואית דמפרשי מלבוש הסמוך לבשרו:

יד אברהם

וּלְאַחַר זְמַן הֵבִיא רְאָיָה וּמָצָא עֵדִים, הֲרֵי זֶה אֵינוֹ כְלוּם. — *and subsequently he brought evidence or witnesses, it is nothing.*

Since he already admitted to having no further evidence, his subsequent discovery of witnesses or proof is suspicious and appears manufactured (*Rav; Rambam Comm.*).

There is a dispute whether this ruling applies only after the court has issued its verdict or even beforehand (see *Chidushei R' Akiva Eiger* to *Choshen Mishpat* 20:1; and *Rashash* to mishnah).

However, if he offers a plausible explanation for this — e.g., he claims to have discovered witnesses who had been away and thus unavailable to him at the time of his earlier court appearance — he is believed, and the evidence is accepted (*Gem.* 31b; *Hil. Sanhedrin* 7:8).

אָמַר רַבָּן שִׁמְעוֹן בֶּן גַּמְלִיאֵל: מַה יַּעֲשֶׂה זֶה שֶׁלֹּא הָיָה יוֹדֵעַ שֶׁיֵּשׁ לוֹ עֵדִים וּמָצָא עֵדִים; לֹא הָיָה יוֹדֵעַ שֶׁיֵּשׁ לוֹ רְאָיָה וּמָצָא רְאָיָה? — *said Rabban Shimon ben Gamliel: What should [this man] do if he did not know [at the time] that he had witnesses and he [later] discovered witnesses; [or] if he did not know [at the time] that he had evidence and he [later] discovered evidence?*

[I.e., his evidenc e is acceptable even if he offers no particular reason why this evidence was not previously available.]

and subsequently he brought evidence or witnesses, it is nothing. Said Rabban Shimon ben Gamliel: What should this [man] do if he did not know [at the time] that he had witnesses and he [later] discovered witnesses; [or] if he did not know [at the time] that he had evidence and he [later] discovered evidence? [If] they said to him: Bring witnesses, and he said: I have no witnesses; Bring proof, and he said: I have no proof; and [when] he saw that he was about to be judged liable he said, "Let so-and-so and so-and-so approach and testify for me," or he took out evidence from his belt, it is nothing.

YAD AVRAHAM

In this case, the halachah follows the former view (*Rav* from *Gem.* 31a), and without a plausible explanation of his earlier statement disclaiming any further evidence, he cannot submit new evidence or testimony (*Rambam* ibid.; *Choshen Mishpat* 20:1,2 from *Gem.* 31b).

אָמְרוּ לוֹ: הָבֵא עֵדִים, אָמַר: אֵין לִי עֵדִים; הָבֵא רְאָיָה, וְאָמַר: אֵין לִי רְאָיָה; רָאָה שֶׁמִּתְחַיֵּב בַּדִּין וְאָמַר „קִרְבוּ פְּלוֹנִי וּפְלוֹנִי וְהַעִידוּנִי״, אוֹ שֶׁהוֹצִיא רְאָיָה מִתּוֹךְ אֲפֻנְדָּתוֹ, הֲרֵי זֶה אֵינוֹ כְלוּם. — *[If] they said to him: Bring witnesses, and he said: I have no witnesses; Bring proof, and he said: I have no proof; and [when] he saw that he was about to be judged liable he said, "Let so-and-so and so-and-so approach and testify for me," or he took out evidence from his belt,*[1] *it is nothing.*

In this instance even Rabban Shimon ben Gamliel concurs, because the fact that he clearly must have been aware of the existence of these people or documents at the time he disclaimed knowledge of them [since nothing happened during these court proceedings that might have revealed to him the existence of new evidence] — and he nevertheless refrained from producing them until it became absolutely necessary — attests to the falseness of the evidence (*Rav*).

If one of the litigants claims to have witnesses who are not presently available, the verdict is reached based on the evidence at hand, and if and when the witnesses arrive, the verdict is overturned (*Rav; Rambam Comm.*).

1. This translation follows *Rav* and *Rashi*. Others translate אפנדה as an undershirt (*Rav* from *Rambam Comm.*).

פרק רביעי

Chapter Four

[א] **אֶחָד** דִּינֵי מָמוֹנוֹת וְאֶחָד דִּינֵי נְפָשׁוֹת בִּדְרִישָׁה וּבַחֲקִירָה, שֶׁנֶּאֱמַר: ,,מִשְׁפַּט אֶחָד יִהְיֶה לָכֶם״. מַה בֵּין דִּינֵי מָמוֹנוֹת לְדִינֵי נְפָשׁוֹת? דִּינֵי מָמוֹנוֹת בִּשְׁלשָׁה; וְדִינֵי נְפָשׁוֹת בְּעֶשְׂרִים וּשְׁלשָׁה. דִּינֵי מָמוֹנוֹת פּוֹתְחִין בֵּין לִזְכוּת בֵּין לְחוֹבָה;

ר׳ עובדיה מברטנורא

פרק רביעי – אחד דיני ממונות. (א) אחד דיני ממונות. שנאמר משפט אחד יהיה לכם. ובדיני נפשות כתיב (דברים יג,טו) ודרשת וחקרת, וזהו דין תורה, אבל אמרו חכמים שאין מאריכין בדרישה וחקירה בדיני ממונות, שלא תנעול דלת בפני לוין, אלא אם כן ראו בית דין שהדין מרומה, ודרישה וחקירה הוא השאלה בענין בעצמו, כגון כמה הלוהו ומתי הלוהו ובאיזה ענין הלוהו ובאיזה מקום הלוהו, ויש מין אחר מן השאלה שנקראת בדיקה ואינה בענין בעצמו, כגון שישאלו לו מה היה לבוש, כליו שחורים או כליו לבנים, עומד היה או יושב בשעה שהלוהו:

יד אברהם

1.

The mishnah now delineates the differences between civil cases and capital cases.

אֶחָד דִּינֵי מָמוֹנוֹת וְאֶחָד דִּינֵי נְפָשׁוֹת בִּדְרִישָׁה וּבַחֲקִירָה — *Both civil cases and capital cases require inquiry and examination,*

חֲקִירָה, *examination,* refers to the seven general questions which witnesses must answer in order to validate their testimony, as discussed in mishnah 5:1 (*Tif. Yis.*). דְּרִישָׁה, *inquiry,* includes additional inquiries into the facts which are pertinent to the issue of the case (*Meiri* to mishnah 5:1). Thus, in the case of a loan, for example, the witnesses would be asked how much was lent; when the loan was made; what conditions, if any, were attached; where it took place, etc. There is yet another category of questions — known as בְּדִיקָה, *interrogation* — dealing with matters which are of no intrinsic importance to the case but which help to establish the veracity of the witnesses — e.g., questions about the color of the clothing worn, etc. These apply only to capital cases, as will be explained in 5:2 (*Rav*; see comm. to 5:1, s.v. העובד עבודה זרה).

שֶׁנֶּאֱמַר: ,,מִשְׁפַּט אֶחָד יִהְיֶה לָכֶם״. — *as it is stated* (*Lev.* 24:22): *"One judgment you shall have for yourselves."*

[I.e., the rule for court judgments should be uniform. Thus, an analogy is drawn between capital cases and civil cases,] and concerning capital cases the Torah states (*Deut.* 13:15): *You shall inquire and you shall examine thoroughly* (*Rav; Rashi*).

This is the Biblical rule. However, the Rabbis ordained that witnesses to civil cases should not be subjected to too extensive an examination, so as not to discourage them from testifying [for fear of being tripped up on minor details even when they are telling the truth]. Any substantial

4
1

1. **B**oth civil cases and capital cases require inquiry and examination, as it is stated: *One judgment you shall have for yourselves.* What is the difference between civil cases and capital cases? Civil cases are [tried] by three; capital cases by twenty-three. Civil cases open [with the consideration] of either acquittal or liability;

YAD AVRAHAM

diminution of witnesses' willingness to testify would in turn cause people to refuse to lend money for fear of being unable to recover it in court (*Rav* from *Gem.* 32b).

The *Gemara* (24b) offers another possibility as well, namely that even the mishnah refers to the law as it stood after the Rabbinic ordinance had been instituted. However, that ordinance referred only to loans and the like, in which one is seeking to recover what is rightfully his, while the mishnah refers to a trial concerning a potential fine or penalty rather than recovering a loss. Accordingly, the Rabbinic ordinance is not applicable (since there is no reason to be lenient here); and the Torah law requiring inquiry and examination remains in place.

Additionally, the *Gemara* states, the mishnah's ruling requiring careful examination of the witnesses remains in effect even for monetary cases where the judges suspect possible deceit (*Rav*). [I.e., they may invoke the Biblical rule in an attempt to expose the fraud they suspect is taking place.]

The *Gemara* (*Shevuos* 30b) states that if the judges see that deceit is being perpetrated they should reject the case entirely. *Tosafos* (32b) explain that rule to refer to a case in which the duplicity is certain, whereas our mishnah is discussing a situation in which it is merely suspected. Careful examination of the witnesses is therefore called for to determine whether such is indeed the case.

Others, however, distinguish between instances in which the plaintiff is seen to be deceitful — in which case his claim is rejected by the court entirely — and cases in which the defendant is dishonest. To throw out the case in such an event would be counterproductive, since it would be tantamount to allowing the dishonest defendant to win the case because of his deceit. Therefore, the case is taken up and the witnesses are subjected to severe scrutiny (*Rosh*).

מַה בֵּין דִּינֵי מָמוֹנוֹת לְדִינֵי נְפָשׁוֹת? — *What is the difference between civil cases and capital cases?*

Although the verse cited above compares them, those laws which are based on the principle of "seeking to exonerate a suspect" — a principle stated by the Torah in regard to capital cases — do not apply to civil cases (*Tos.*), since one litigant's gain is his opponent's loss (*Meiri*).

דִּינֵי מָמוֹנוֹת בִּשְׁלֹשָׁה; וְדִינֵי נְפָשׁוֹת בְּעֶשְׂרִים וּשְׁלֹשָׁה. — *Civil cases are [tried] by three; capital cases by twenty-three.*

The difference in the number of judges required is derived from the Torah, as explained above (1:1; 1:6).

דִּינֵי מָמוֹנוֹת פּוֹתְחִין בֵּין לִזְכוּת בֵּין לְחוֹבָה; — *Civil cases open [with the consideration] of either acquittal or liability;*

The judges may begin their discussion of the case from the

סנהדרין
ד/א

וְדִינֵי נְפָשׁוֹת פּוֹתְחִין לִזְכוּת, וְאֵין פּוֹתְחִין לְחוֹבָה. דִּינֵי מָמוֹנוֹת מַטִּין עַל פִּי אֶחָד, בֵּין לִזְכוּת בֵּין לְחוֹבָה; וְדִינֵי נְפָשׁוֹת מַטִּין עַל פִּי אֶחָד לִזְכוּת וְעַל פִּי שְׁנַיִם לְחוֹבָה. דִּינֵי מָמוֹנוֹת מַחֲזִירִין בֵּין לִזְכוּת בֵּין לְחוֹבָה; דִּינֵי נְפָשׁוֹת מַחֲזִירִין לִזְכוּת וְאֵין מַחֲזִירִין לְחוֹבָה. דִּינֵי מָמוֹנוֹת, הַכֹּל מְלַמְּדִין זְכוּת וְחוֹבָה; וְדִינֵי נְפָשׁוֹת, הַכֹּל מְלַמְּדִין זְכוּת וְאֵין הַכֹּל מְלַמְּדִין חוֹבָה.

ר׳ עובדיה מברטנורא

פותחים. משאו ומתנו של דין, בין לזכות בין לחובה: **מחזירין.** סותרין את הדין אחר שגמרוהו וידעו שטעו: **ואין הכל מלמדים חובה.** שאם אמר אחד מן התלמידים יש לי ללמד עליו חובה, אין שומעין לו:

יד אברהם

standpoint of either rejecting or accepting the claim (*Rav*).

וְדִינֵי נְפָשׁוֹת פּוֹתְחִין לִזְכוּת, וְאֵין פּוֹתְחִין לְחוֹבָה. — *capital cases must open [with the consideration] of acquittal, not guilt.*

The judges begin their discussion of the case by telling the suspect that if he is innocent he has nothing to fear. This is derived from the Torah's description of the procedure for trying a *sotah* — a woman suspected of adultery (*Num.* 5:11ff) — in which the possibility of innocence is stated prior to that of guilt (*Gem.* 32b).

דִּינֵי מָמוֹנוֹת מַטִּין עַל פִּי אֶחָד, בֵּין לִזְכוּת בֵּין לְחוֹבָה; וְדִינֵי נְפָשׁוֹת מַטִּין עַל פִּי אֶחָד לִזְכוּת וְעַל פִּי שְׁנַיִם לְחוֹבָה. — *Civil cases are decided by a majority of one, whether for acquittal or liability; capital cases are decided by a majority of one for acquittal but by a majority of two for guilt.*

In capital cases, a majority of one suffices for a decision only if it is to the benefit of the suspect but not if it is to his detriment, as stated by the mishnah previously (1:6). However, in civil cases, no matter who is adversely affected by the decision, a majority of one is sufficient.

דִּינֵי מָמוֹנוֹת מַחֲזִירִין בֵּין לִזְכוּת בֵּין לְחוֹבָה; — *Civil decisions may be reversed in favor of acquittal or liability;*

If the judges decide that their decision was in error, they may reverse it (*Rav*). [The application of this law revolves around several different opinions among the commentators and varies in accordance with the factors of many separate cases. It is therefore highly complex and beyond the scope of this commentary. For further discussion, see the commentary to *Gemara* 33a; *Rambam, Hil. Sanhedrin* 6:8; *Choshen Mishpat* 25.]

דִּינֵי נְפָשׁוֹת מַחֲזִירִין לִזְכוּת וְאֵין מַחֲזִירִין לְחוֹבָה. — *capital decisions may be reversed [only] in favor of acquittal but not in favor of guilt.*

4 capital cases must open [with the consideration] of
1 acquittal, not guilt. Civil cases are decided by a majority of one, whether for acquittal or liability; capital cases are decided by a majority of one for acquittal but by a majority of two for guilt. Civil decisions may be reversed in favor of acquittal or liability; capital decisions may be reversed [only] in favor of acquittal but not in favor of guilt. [In] civil cases, anyone may argue either for acquittal or liability; [in] capital cases, anyone may argue for acquittal but not everyone may argue for guilt.

YAD AVRAHAM

The Torah says (*Ex.* 23:7): וְנָקִי וְצַדִּיק אַל תַּהֲרֹג, *an innocent person and a righteous person you shall not kill.* The dual nature of this admonition is understood by the *Gemara* (33b) to refer to two categories of innocence: The word נָקִי, *innocent*, refers to one who is in reality innocent of any wrongdoing, even if he was erroneously found guilty by the court — thereby teaching that a guilty verdict may be reversed. The term צַדִּיק, *righteous*, is taken to refer to one who was declared by the court to be righteous even though he is in truth guilty. The verse states that neither of these may be executed — thereby teaching that an erroneous verdict of innocence may not be reversed (*Gem.* 33b; *Rashi* ad loc.). However, the *Gemara* concludes that if the judges erred in overlooking a law stated explicitly in a verse in the Torah, even a decision of innocence is invalidated.

דִּינֵי מָמוֹנוֹת, הַכֹּל מְלַמְּדִין זְכוּת וְחוֹבָה; — *[In] civil cases, anyone may argue either for acquittal or liability;*

During the deliberations, not only the judges trying the case, but even students who are in attendance may present arguments for either side of the dispute (*Gem.* 33b).

דִּינֵי נְפָשׁוֹת, הַכֹּל מְלַמְּדִין זְכוּת וְאֵין הַכֹּל מְלַמְּדִין חוֹבָה. — *[in] capital cases, anyone may argue for acquittal but not everyone may argue for guilt.*

I.e., the attending disciples may present arguments on behalf of the accused but not against him (*Rav*). Nevertheless, if they went ahead and presented a sound argument, it is accepted (*Yad Ramah*).

The *Gemara* (ibid.) cites the opinion of R' Yose the son of R' Yehudah that the same rule applies to the witnesses in the case — they are barred from presenting an argument for guilt but they may present an argument for acquittal. This distinction is derived by him exegetically (see comm. to 5:4). The Sages, however, dispute his view and contend that they cannot be trusted in the matter even to present arguments in favor of acquittal, since, having testified against him, if he is sentenced and they are then discredited by *hazamah*, they stand to be punished (*Rashi;* see *Deut.* 19:16ff). Accordingly, the verse must be understood

סנהדרין
ד/א

דִּינֵי מָמוֹנוֹת, הַמְלַמֵּד חוֹבָה מְלַמֵּד זְכוּת, וְהַמְלַמֵּד זְכוּת מְלַמֵּד חוֹבָה; דִּינֵי נְפָשׁוֹת, הַמְלַמֵּד חוֹבָה מְלַמֵּד זְכוּת, אֲבָל הַמְלַמֵּד זְכוּת אֵינוֹ יָכוֹל לַחֲזוֹר וּלְלַמֵּד חוֹבָה. דִּינֵי מָמוֹנוֹת דָּנִין בַּיּוֹם וְגוֹמְרִין בַּלַּיְלָה; דִּינֵי נְפָשׁוֹת דָּנִין בַּיּוֹם וְגוֹמְרִין בַּיּוֹם. דִּינֵי מָמוֹנוֹת גּוֹמְרִין בּוֹ בַּיּוֹם, בֵּין לִזְכוּת בֵּין לְחוֹבָה; דִּינֵי נְפָשׁוֹת גּוֹמְרִין בּוֹ בַּיּוֹם לִזְכוּת, וּבְיוֹם שֶׁלְּאַחֲרָיו לְחוֹבָה. לְפִיכָךְ

ר׳ עובדיה מברטנורא

דנים ביום וגומרין בלילה. דכתיב (שמות יח,כב) ושפטו את העם בכל עת, וכתיב (דברים כא,טז) והיה ביום הנחילו את בניו, הא כיצד, יום לתחילת דין, ולילה לגמר דין: **דנין ביום וגומרין ביום.** דכתיב (במדבר כה,ד) והוקע אותם לה׳ נגד השמש: **גומרים בו ביום בין לזכות בין לחובה** [וכו׳]. דאמר קרא (ישעיה א,כא) מלאתי משפט צדק ילין בה:

יד אברהם

to exclude witnesses from offering arguments in favor of either side of the case (*Yad Ramah; Rambam, Eidus* 5:8). The halachah follows the latter view (*Rambam*, ibid.; see mishnah 5:4).

Some maintain that the same ruling applies to civil cases since the same factors come into play (*Ramban*, cited by *Ran; Meiri*). Others contend that only the fear of the death penalty would impel the witnesses to present false arguments, but not fear of monetary punishment. Therefore, in such a case, the witnesses too may present their views (*Rambam, Hil. Eidus* 5:8 as explained by *Meiri; Ran*).

דִּינֵי מָמוֹנוֹת, הַמְלַמֵּד חוֹבָה מְלַמֵּד זְכוּת, וְהַמְלַמֵּד זְכוּת מְלַמֵּד חוֹבָה; דִּינֵי נְפָשׁוֹת, הַמְלַמֵּד חוֹבָה מְלַמֵּד זְכוּת, אֲבָל הַמְלַמֵּד זְכוּת אֵינוֹ יָכוֹל לַחֲזוֹר וּלְלַמֵּד חוֹבָה. — *[In] civil cases, one who argued for acquittal may argue for liability, and one who argued for liability may argue for acquittal; [in] capital cases, one who argued for guilt may argue for acquittal, but one who argued for acquittal may not argue for guilt.*

During the deliberations, a judge who began the discussion of a civil case by arguing the side of one litigant may then switch and put forth arguments in support of the other. In capital cases, however, he may switch only from a position of guilty to one of innocent but not the reverse. This is based on the verse (*Num.* 34:25) concerning capital cases which states וְהִצִּילוּ, *and they [the judges] shall save* — indicating that it is the obligation of the judges to seek to exonerate the suspect (*Rashi*).

However, this applies only during the deliberations. At the time of decision, every judge must vote in accordance with his conviction at that time (*Gem.* 34b).

דִּינֵי מָמוֹנוֹת דָּנִין בַּיּוֹם וְגוֹמְרִין בַּלַּיְלָה; — *Civil cases are tried by day and may be concluded by night;*

[I.e., they are begun by day and, if necessary, may be concluded at night.] This is derived from the

4 [In] civil cases, one who argued for acquittal may
1 argue for liability, and one who argued for liability may argue for acquittal; [in] capital cases, one who argued for guilt may argue for acquittal, but one who argued for acquittal may not argue for guilt. Civil cases are tried by day and may be concluded by night; capital cases must be tried by day and concluded by day. Civil cases may be concluded on that day, whether for acquittal or liability; capital cases may be concluded on that day for acquittal but only on the following day for guilt. Therefore,

apparent contradiction between the verse (*Ex.* 18:22) which states: *And they shall judge the nation at all times, and* the verse which states (*Deut.* 21:16) — in reference to judgment concerning inheritance (*Rashi*) — *on the day in which he gives over inheritance to his sons,* implying that it may be done only by day. The resolution is, as stated in the mishnah, that the case must begin by day but it may continue into the night (*Rav* from *Gem.* 34b).

דִּינֵי נְפָשׁוֹת דָּנִין בַּיּוֹם וְגוֹמְרִין בַּיּוֹם. — *capital cases must be tried by day and concluded by day.*

When the people of Israel began sinning with the women of Moab and were thereby led astray to worship their idol, God commanded Moses to take the heads of the nation [i.e., convene them in courts (*Gem.*)] and have them try the offenders and *hang them* [the culprits] *before Hashem toward the sun* [*Num.* 25:4] (*Rav* from *Gem.* ibid.). [The corpses of all those executed by stoning are hung for people to see (*Rashi* to *Num.*; see below 6:4). Since the verse states that they be hung *toward the sun,* we learn that the sentence has to be carried out while the sun is still in view. And since a death sentence must be implemented as soon as the conviction is announced (see below, 6:1), we learn that the conviction itself must be by day.]

דִּינֵי מָמוֹנוֹת גּוֹמְרִין בּוֹ בַּיּוֹם, בֵּין לִזְכוּת בֵּין לְחוֹבָה; — *Civil cases may be concluded on that day, whether for acquittal or liability;*

Civil cases may be decided on the same day on which they are begun (*Rashi*).

דִּינֵי נְפָשׁוֹת גּוֹמְרִין בּוֹ בַּיּוֹם לִזְכוּת, וּבְיוֹם שֶׁלְּאַחֲרָיו לְחוֹבָה. — *capital cases may be concluded on that day for acquittal, but only on the following day for guilt.*

A decision of innocence in a capital case should be rendered immediately, so as not to prolong the agony of the accused (*Tif. Yis.*). A decision of guilt, however, must be delayed until the following day, to allow the judges one more opportunity to discover a basis for acquittal (*Rashi*). This is derived from the verse (*Isaiah* 1:21): *It was filled with justice; righteousness*

אֵין דָּנִין לֹא בְעֶרֶב שַׁבָּת וְלֹא בְעֶרֶב יוֹם טוֹב.

[ב] דִּינֵי הַטֻּמְאוֹת וְהַטְּהָרוֹת, מַתְחִילִין מִן הַגָּדוֹל; דִּינֵי נְפָשׁוֹת מַתְחִילִין מִן הַצַּד. הַכֹּל כְּשֵׁרִין לָדוּן דִּינֵי מָמוֹנוֹת, וְאֵין הַכֹּל

ר׳ עובדיה מברטנורא

לפיכך אין דנים לא בערב שבת. שנמצא גמר דינו בשבת, ולהשהותו אחר שבת אי אפשר, מפני ענוי הדין, ולדונו בו ביום אי אפשר, שאין ארבע מיתות בית דין דוחין את השבת, שנאמר (שמות לה,ג) לא תבערו אש בכל מושבותיכם ביום השבת, למד על מחוייבי שריפה שאין שורפין אותן בשבת, והוא הדין לשאר חייבי מיתות: **(ב) מן הצד.** מן הקטנים בחכמה שהיו יושבים בצד, דאמר קרא (שם כג,ב) לא תענה על ריב, וכתיב רב, כלומר לא תענה על מופלא שבבית דין ולנטות מדבריו, לפיכך אין שומעין דבריו אלא בסוף: **הכל כשרים לדון.** ואפילו גר, והוא שתהא אמו מישראל, וממזר נמי כשר לדון דיני ממונות:

יד אברהם

resided in it. The word לָן, *resided,* literally means staying overnight, thus conveying that justice was served by that which the courts allowed capital cases to be left overnight before rendering a decision (*Rav* from *Gem.* 35a). [Thus, a capital case can only be concluded on the day it begins if the verdict is innocent, but if the verdict is for guilt, it must continue into the following day.]

לְפִיכָךְ אֵין דָּנִין לֹא בְעֶרֶב שַׁבָּת וְלֹא בְעֶרֶב יוֹם טוֹב. — *Therefore, trials are not held on Friday or on the day before a Festival.*

A capital case cannot be initiated on the day before the Sabbath or a Festival because if the decision is to convict it must be delayed until the next day, and executions may not be performed on the Sabbath or Festival. They cannot convict and then delay the execution until the following day, because it is prohibited to keep someone who has been sentenced to death waiting in agony for his punishment (*Rav* from *Gem.* 35a). The verdict itself cannot be postponed an extra day, because such a delay would cause the judges to lose the absolute clarity of their previously arrived-at positions (*Gem.* ibid.).

However, the Rabbis prohibited the initiation of even civil cases on these days (*Yerushalmi* cited by *Rif; Nimmukei Yosef*).

2.

דִּינֵי הַטֻּמְאוֹת וְהַטְּהָרוֹת, — *[In judging] cases of tumah and taharah,*

I.e., if a question concerning *tumah* (ritual contamination) and *taharah* (ritual purity) came before the court for a ruling (*Rashi*). The rule stated below also applies to other areas of ritual law, such as questions of *kashrus* (*Tos. Yom Tov*).

The version of the mishnah brought in the Gemara reads: [In] civil cases and cases of ritual ...

מַתְחִילִין מִן הַגָּדוֹל; — *they begin from the most eminent;*

The most eminent of the judges is the first to express his opinion on the

trials are not held on Friday or on the day before a Festival.

2. [In judging] cases of *tumah* and *taharah,* they begin from the most eminent; [in] capital cases they begin from the side.

All are eligible to judge civil cases, but not all

YAD AVRAHAM

matter (*Rashi*), because it is the custom of wise men to refrain from expressing their view before their betters (*Tos. Yom Tov*).

.דִּינֵי נְפָשׁוֹת מַתְחִילִין מִן הַצַּד — *[in] capital cases they begin from the side.*

I.e., from the least eminent judges, who sit on the side of the judges' row (see mishnah 3). This is based on the verse (*Ex.* 23:2): וְלֹא תַעֲנֶה עַל רִב, *Do not respond to an argument* — which [due to the lack of the letter *yud* in the word רִב] the Sages interpret exegetically to read: לֹא תַעֲנֶה עַל רַב, *Do not respond to a master* — i.e., do not dispute his words. Since it is prohibited for the lesser judges to dispute the words of the preeminent one, the former must express their view first in order to allow for a vote (*Rav, Rambam Comm.* from *Gem.* 36a). However, once a lesser judge has legitimately stated his view, he is not required to rescind it because of the opposing view offered afterward by the greater judge (*Yad Ramah*).

The primary concern here is that the greatest member of the court may voice an opinion in favor of guilt which his lesser colleagues will not dispute. Since we are commanded to try and save the defendant (see previous mishnah), we must take measures to prevent such a situation from coming to pass. Accordingly, this is a consideration only in capital cases, not in civil or ritual ones (*Tos.* 36a as interpreted by *Maharsha;* cf. *Maharam*).

It is also possible that the rule derived from this verse refers only to capital cases, not civil or other types of cases. Accordingly, these types of cases can begin, as is proper, from the preeminent member of the court (*Tos.*).

There is another view, that it is not actually forbidden for a lesser judge to dispute a preeminent one. Indeed, even a student is not supposed to remain silent before his superior if he sees injustice being done (*Gem.* 6b). However, the verse teaches that we should take precautionary measures in capital cases against the possibility of a judge feeling inadequate to express his view in the suspect's defense in the face of an opposing view by a preeminent judge (*Nimmukei Yosef; Rambam, Hil. Sanhedrin* 10:6; see *Rashi* 32a).

,הַכֹּל כְּשֵׁרִין לָדוּן דִּינֵי מָמוֹנוֹת — *All are eligible to judge civil cases,*

I.e., no Jewish male is disqualified by reason of pedigree from serving as a judge in civil cases, even one who has the genealogical status of a convert [i.e., he comes from a line which began with a convert and never intermarried with families of regular Jews (see *Kiddushin* 4:6,7)]. As long as his mother was already Jewish when he was born he is eligible [thus making him a born Jew, not an actual convert] (*Rav, Rambam Comm.* from *Gem.* 36b). The same applies to a

כְּשֵׁרִין לָדוּן דִּינֵי נְפָשׁוֹת — אֶלָּא כֹהֲנִים, לְוִיִּם, וְיִשְׂרְאֵלִים הַמַּשִּׂיאִין לַכְּהֻנָּה:

[ג] **סַנְהֶדְרִין** הָיְתָה כַּחֲצִי גֹרֶן עֲגֻלָּה, כְּדֵי שֶׁיְּהוּ רוֹאִין זֶה אֶת זֶה. וּשְׁנֵי סוֹפְרֵי הַדַּיָּנִין עוֹמְדִין לִפְנֵיהֶם, אֶחָד מִיָּמִין וְאֶחָד מִשְּׂמֹאל, וְכוֹתְבִין דִּבְרֵי הַמְזַכִּין וְדִבְרֵי הַמְחַיְּבִין. רַבִּי יְהוּדָה אוֹמֵר: שְׁלֹשָׁה: אֶחָד כּוֹתֵב דִּבְרֵי הַמְזַכִּין; וְאֶחָד כּוֹתֵב דִּבְרֵי הַמְחַיְּבִין; וְהַשְּׁלִישִׁי כּוֹתֵב דִּבְרֵי הַמְזַכִּין וְדִבְרֵי הַמְחַיְּבִין.

ר׳ עובדיה מברטנורא

ואין הכל כשרים לדון דיני נפשות. דכתיב (שמות יח,כב) והקל מעליך ונשאו אתך, בדומין לך, מה משה רבינו מיוחס אף בית דין מיוחסים: (ג) **בחצי גורן עגולה כדי שיהו רואים זה את זה.** דאמר קרא (שיר השירים ז,ג) שררך אגן הסהר, שררך אגן זו סנהדרי שיושבת בטבורו של עולם ומגינה על כל העולם כולו, והיא דומה לסהר, שיושבים בעגול כחצי ירח, תרגום ירח, סיהרא, ובעגולה שלימה אין יושבים מפני שצריכים בעלי דינים והעדים ליכנס ולדבר בפני כולם: **רבי יהודה אומר שלשה היו.** כדי שיהיו שני עדים על המזכין ושני עדים על המחייבין. ואין הלכה כרבי יהודה:

יד אברהם

I.e., those whose genealogical status allows them to marry their daughters to *Kohanim* (*Rashi;* see *Kiddushin* 4:1). This is derived from the verse (*Ex.* 18:22) which quotes Yisro's words to Moshe, *and it shall be easier upon you and they will bear with you.* From the unnecessary word *with you,* the *Gemara* (36b) derives that they must be similar to Moshe in the purity of their genealogical status (*Rav*).

mamzer [an illegitimate child] (*Rav* from *Gem.* ibid.).

Even a convert who was not born to a Jewish mother is qualified to judge such cases if the litigants involved are also of the same status (*Tos.; Meiri*).

וְאֵין הַכֹּל כְּשֵׁרִין לָדוּן דִּינֵי נְפָשׁוֹת - אֶלָּא כֹהֲנִים, לְוִיִּם, וְיִשְׂרְאֵלִים הַמַּשִּׂיאִין לַכְּהֻנָּה. — *but not all are eligible to judge capital cases — only Kohanim, Leviim, and Yisraelim who are eligible to have [their daughters] marry Kohanim.*

3.

הָיְתָה כַּחֲצִי גֹרֶן עֲגֻלָּה, כְּדֵי שֶׁיְּהוּ רוֹאִין זֶה אֶת זֶה. — *was [seated] in the shape of a semicircular threshing floor so that they should see one another.*

[The judges sat in a semicircle in

סַנְהֶדְרִין — *The Sanhedrin*

This ruling applies to both the Great Sanhedrin of seventy-one and the lesser sanhedrins of twenty-three (*Rashi;* see 1:1).

4 are eligible to judge capital cases — only *Kohanim,*
3 *Leviim,* and *Yisraelim* who are eligible to have [their daughters] marry *Kohanim.*

3. The Sanhedrin was [seated] in the shape of a semicircular threshing floor so that they should see one another. Two judicial scribes stand before them, one to the right and one to the left, and they record the words of those who defend and those who convict. R' Yehudah says: Three: One records the words of those who defend; one records the words of those who convict; and the third records the words [both] of those who defend and those who convict.

YAD AVRAHAM

order to be able to see one another when they discussed the case.] The *Gemara* (37a) bases this on a verse (*Shir HaShirim* 7:3) which is interpreted to compare the Sanhedrin to a circle. A full circle would not be viable, however, because the litigants and witnesses must face the judges and in a circle they would have their backs to some of them. They must therefore sit in a semicircle (*Rav; Rashi*).

וּשְׁנֵי סוֹפְרֵי הַדַּיָּנִין עוֹמְדִין לִפְנֵיהֶם, אֶחָד מִיָּמִין וְאֶחָד מִשְּׂמֹאל, וְכוֹתְבִין דִּבְרֵי הַמְזַכִּין וְדִבְרֵי הַמְחַיְּבִין. — *Two judicial scribes stand before them, one to the right and one to the left, and they record the words of those who defend and those who convict.*

I.e., one of them records the statements of those who argue for acquittal, while the other records those of the judges who take the opposing view during the deliberations (*Rambam, Hil. Sanhedrin* 1:9; *Meiri;* see *Rav,* cited below).

Others contend that both record both views, so that if either made an error it could be corrected from the notes of the other (*Rashi; Rama*).

Although the judges are permitted to change their opinions when they come to a vote (see mishnah 1), it is necessary to record their deliberations nonetheless. The views of those who condemn must be recorded because if they retract their reasoning and wish to convict the accused for a reason other than the one they advanced during the deliberations, the decision must be delayed and considered for another day (see below, 5:15). Even the arguments of those who acquit the accused must be recorded since, if the judges argue for the same decision but base their views on two different sources [which are mutually exclusive (see *Rashi* to 34a, s.v. אין מונין להן אלא)], their opinions cannot be combined to equal two votes in the final decision (*Gem.* 34a; cf. *Rambam, Hil. Sanhedrin* 10:5, 12:3).

רַבִּי יְהוּדָה אוֹמֵר; שְׁלֹשָׁה: אֶחָד כּוֹתֵב דִּבְרֵי הַמְזַכִּין; וְאֶחָד כּוֹתֵב דִּבְרֵי הַמְחַיְּבִין; וְהַשְּׁלִישִׁי כּוֹתֵב דִּבְרֵי הַמְזַכִּין וְדִבְרֵי הַמְחַיְּבִין. — *R' Yehudah says: Three: One records the words of those who defend; one records the words of those who convict; and the third records the words [both] of those who defend and those who convict.*

R' Yehudah requires three scribes,

[ד] וְשָׁלֹשׁ שׁוּרוֹת שֶׁל תַּלְמִידֵי חֲכָמִים יוֹשְׁבִין לִפְנֵיהֶם, כָּל אֶחָד וְאֶחָד מַכִּיר אֶת מְקוֹמוֹ. הָיוּ צְרִיכִין לִסְמוֹךְ, סוֹמְכִין מִן הָרִאשׁוֹנָה; אֶחָד מִן הַשְּׁנִיָּה בָּא לוֹ לָרִאשׁוֹנָה, וְאֶחָד מִן הַשְּׁלִישִׁית בָּא לוֹ לַשְּׁנִיָּה, וּבוֹרְרִין לָהֶן עוֹד אֶחָד מִן הַקָּהָל וּמוֹשִׁיבִין אוֹתוֹ בַּשְּׁלִישִׁית. וְלֹא הָיָה יוֹשֵׁב בִּמְקוֹמוֹ שֶׁל רִאשׁוֹן אֶלָּא יוֹשֵׁב בַּמָּקוֹם הָרָאוּי לוֹ.

ר׳ עובדיה מברטנורא

(ד) **ושלש שורות.** וכל שורה של עשרים ושלשה תלמידי חכמים, שמא יחלקו הדיינים ויהיו רובן מחייבין ומיעוטן מזכין, והטיה לרעה אינה על פי אחד כדכתיב (שמות כג,ב) לא תהיה אחרי רבים לרעות, וצריך להוסיף שנים שנים עד שבעים ואחד, שלעולם אין מוסיפין על הדיינים יותר משבעים ואחד, הלכך צריך להושיב לפניהם ארבעים ושמונה להשלמת שבעים ואחד, ולאו אורח ארעא לעשות שורות תלמידים מרובה משל דיינים, הלכך עבדינן שלש שורות: **וכל אחד מכיר את מקומו.** לפי שכסדר חכמתם היו מושיבים אותם, לפיכך היה כל אחד צריך להכיר את מקומו: **הוצרכו לסמוך.** כגון שמת אחד מן הדיינים: **ולא היה יושב במקומו של ראשון.** ולא היה אותו שנברר מן הקהל יושב במקומו של ראשון, אלא במקום הראוי לו בסוף שורה השלישית, לפי שהקטן מן התלמידים שבשורות, גדול מן הגדול שבקהל:

יד אברהם

one each to record each of the opposing views, and a third to record both of them together, so that there will be two witnesses to each view presented (*Rav; Rambam Comm.*).

According to the approach of *Rashi* (see above), each of the first two scribes records only one opinion so that each view should be recorded accurately by someone who focused on that alone. A third scribe records both so that any error can be checked (*Rashi*).

4.

וְשָׁלֹשׁ שׁוּרוֹת שֶׁל תַּלְמִידֵי חֲכָמִים יוֹשְׁבִין לִפְנֵיהֶם, — *Three rows of scholars sat before them,*

I.e., three rows of scholars who were not yet ordained (*Yad Ramah*), each row consisting of twenty-three people [paralleling the court itself) (*Rav; Rashi*), sat before a sanhedrin of twenty-three. According to some, these three rows also sat in a semicircle (*Rashi; Meiri*); others maintain that they sat in a straight line (*Yad Ramah*).

The purpose of these extra rows was to prepare for the possibility that the presiding judges would be deadlocked and would require the inclusion of additional judges (see 3:6 and comm. ibid.). Since the largest possible number of judges on a court is

4
4

4. **T**hree rows of scholars sat before them, each one recognizing his place. [If] they need to ordain, they ordain from the first [row]; one from the second row [then] moves up to the first, one from the third [row] moves up to the second, and they choose one from the congregation and sit him in the third [row]. He does not sit in the place of the first but in the place appropriate to him.

YAD AVRAHAM

seventy-one, forty-eight potential judges were needed. However, it would not be respectful to make the rows of students larger than that of the judges themselves nor to seat them in small rows. Therefore, a third row was added to the forty-six students making up the first two (*Rav; Rashi*).

כָּל אֶחָד וְאֶחָד מַכִּיר אֶת מְקוֹמוֹ. — *each one recognizing his place.*

The scholars sat in order of their eminence — with the most eminent sitting to the extreme right, the second to his left, etc. (*Meiri*). It was thus necessary for each one to recognize his correct place (*Rav*).

הָיוּ צְרִיכִין לִסְמוֹךְ, סוֹמְכִין מִן הָרִאשׁוֹנָה; — *[If] they need to ordain, they ordain from the first [row];*

I.e., if they needed to add a judge, for example, if one of the judges died (*Rav; Rashi*),[1] they promoted the most prominent member of the first row of scholars.

אֶחָד מִן הַשְּׁנִיָּה בָּא לוֹ לָרִאשׁוֹנָה, וְאֶחָד מִן הַשְּׁלִישִׁית בָּא לוֹ לַשְּׁנִיָּה, — *one from the second row [then] moves up to the first, one from the third [row] moves up to the second,*

[With the first seat of the first row now vacant, each scholar moved over one seat to his right, with those on the extreme right of each row moving up to the higher row.]

וּבוֹרְרִין לָהֶן עוֹד מִן הַקָּהָל וּמוֹשִׁיבִין אוֹתוֹ בַּשְּׁלִישִׁית. — *and they choose one from the congregation and sit him in the third [row].*

[The seat left vacant at the extreme left of the last row was filled by someone from the congregation.]

וְלֹא הָיָה יוֹשֵׁב בִּמְקוֹמוֹ שֶׁל רִאשׁוֹן אֶלָּא יוֹשֵׁב בַּמָּקוֹם הָרָאוּי לוֹ. — *He does not sit in the place of the first but in the place appropriate to him.*

The individual who was added from the congregation to the last row of scholars did not simply take the place left vacant by the scholar who moved up to the row of judges because he was less eminent than the last of the seated scholars (*Rav*).

Those who moved up from the head of one row to the end of the higher row did not suffer any loss of stature, since it is better to be as "the tail of a lion than the head of a fox" (*Gem.* 37a from *Avos* 4:15).

1. The ruling cited here would also apply in case of a deadlock (see 5:8). However, the mishnah discusses a situation in which only one of the disciples is promoted to sit on the court, and in a case of an indecisive vote, two are added (*Margoliyos HaYam*).

[ה] **כֵּיצַד** מְאַיְּמִין אֶת הָעֵדִים עַל עֵדֵי נְפָשׁוֹת? הָיוּ מַכְנִיסִין אוֹתָן וּמְאַיְּמִין עֲלֵיהֶן: שֶׁמָּא תֹאמְרוּ מֵאֹמֶד וּמִשְּׁמוּעָה, עֵד מִפִּי עֵד, וּמִפִּי אָדָם נֶאֱמָן שְׁמַעְנוּ; אוֹ שֶׁמָּא אִי אַתֶּם יוֹדְעִין שֶׁסּוֹפֵנוּ לִבְדּוֹק אֶתְכֶם בִּדְרִישָׁה וּבַחֲקִירָה. הֱווּ יוֹדְעִין שֶׁלֹּא כְדִינֵי מָמוֹנוֹת דִּינֵי נְפָשׁוֹת — דִּינֵי מָמוֹנוֹת, אָדָם נוֹתֵן מָמוֹן וּמִתְכַּפֵּר לוֹ;

ר' עובדיה מברטנורא

(ה) **מאיימין על העדים.** שלא יעידו שקר: **מאומד.** שהדעת נוטה שהוא כן: **דיני ממונות.** אם העיד לחייב לזה ממון שלא כדין, מחזירו לו ומתכפר:

יד אברהם

5.

כֵּיצַד מְאַיְּמִין אֶת הָעֵדִים עַל עֵדֵי נְפָשׁוֹת? — *How do they admonish* (lit., *put fear into*) *the witnesses in capital* [*cases*]?

[When witnesses come to court to testify that someone committed a transgression which is punishable by the death penalty, they are admonished about the severity of the crime of testifying falsely and thereby wrongly causing someone's execution. Indeed, a similar procedure is required even in civil cases, as explained above in mishnah 3:6. The mishnah now describes what the judges say to the witnesses to inspire them with a fear of testifying falsely.]

הָיוּ מַכְנִיסִין אוֹתָן וּמְאַיְּמִין עֲלֵיהֶן: — *They admit them and admonish them [saying to them]:*

Actually, this brief statement condenses several steps into one. The full procedure, as described by *Rambam* (*Hil. Sanhedrin* 12:1,3), is as follows: When the witnesses were admitted to the court and testified that they saw the accused transgress a certain capital offense, the court first asks them if they are sure they recognize the accused and if they warned him before he committed his transgression. [These two preliminary questions, which establish the essential relevance of their testimony to supporting a capital charge, are noted by the mishnah below in 5:1.] If the witnesses reply in the affirmative, they are then asked the following:

שֶׁמָּא תֹאמְרוּ מֵאֹמֶד — *Perhaps what you say is conjecture*

They ask the witnesses if the testimony they are reporting is perhaps something they concluded happened from the evidence at hand, but did not actually see (*Rav*). For example, the witnesses may have seen someone with a knife in his hand chasing someone else into a cave and come out with the knife dripping

4
5

5. **H**ow do they admonish the witnesses in capital [cases]? They admit them and admonish them [saying to them]: Perhaps what you say is conjecture or hearsay, or testimony from the mouth of another witness, [or something] you heard from a reliable person; or perhaps you do not realize that we will check you through inquiry and examination. Know that capital cases are not like civil cases — [in] civil cases, a person pays [back the] money and receives atonement;

YAD AVRAHAM

with blood. Upon investigating the cave, they discover the body of the person who had been chased. Despite the preponderance of circumstantial evidence that the pursuer is the murderer, they cannot testify that he actually committed the murder (*Gem.* 37b).

Although this rule applies to civil cases as well, the judges nevertheless stress this fact to the witnesses in capital cases [due to the severity of the punishment] (*Gem.* ibid.).

וּמִשְּׁמוּעָה, — *or hearsay,*

I.e., it was widely accepted that the accused committed the alleged act, and the witnesses assumed that so widespread a rumor must be true (*Yad Ramah*).

עֵד מִפִּי עֵד, — *or testimony from the mouth of another witness,*

I.e., perhaps the two witnesses are testifying something they merely heard from two others (ibid.).

וּמִפִּי אָדָם נֶאֱמָן שֶׁמַּעְנוּ; — *[or something] you heard from a reliable person;*

This translation follows the interpretation of *Yad Ramah*. Others explain that this is part of the previous case — i.e., the witnesses heard it from other witnesses whom they consider reliable (*Meiri*).

אוֹ שֶׁמָּא אִי אַתֶּם יוֹדְעִין שֶׁסּוֹפֵנוּ לִבְדּוֹק אֶתְכֶם בִּדְרִישָׁה וּבַחֲקִירָה. — *or perhaps you do not realize that we will check you through inquiry and examination.*

I.e., perhaps you came with the intention of testifying falsely, and you are unaware of the rigorous investigation you will undergo before your testimony is accepted (*Yad Ramah*).

הֱווּ יוֹדְעִין שֶׁלֹּא כְדִינֵי מָמוֹנוֹת דִּינֵי נְפָשׁוֹת – דִּינֵי מָמוֹנוֹת, אָדָם נוֹתֵן מָמוֹן וּמִתְכַּפֵּר לוֹ; — *Know that capital cases are not like civil cases — [in] civil cases, a person pays [back the] money and receives atonement;*

If someone testified falsely concerning a monetary matter, the false witness can achieve atonement merely by returning the money to the person whom he wrongly caused to lose the case (*Rav*).

דִּינֵי נְפָשׁוֹת, דָּמוֹ וְדַם זַרְעִיּוֹתָיו תְּלוּיִן בּוֹ עַד סוֹף הָעוֹלָם. שֶׁכֵּן מָצִינוּ בְקַיִן שֶׁהָרַג אֶת אָחִיו, שֶׁנֶּאֱמַר: ,,דְּמֵי אָחִיךָ צֹעֲקִים". אֵינוֹ אוֹמֵר ,,דַּם אָחִיךָ אֶלָּא דְּמֵי אָחִיךָ" — דָּמוֹ וְדַם זַרְעִיּוֹתָיו. דָּבָר אַחֵר: ,,דְּמֵי אָחִיךָ" — שֶׁהָיָה דָמוֹ מֻשְׁלָךְ עַל הָעֵצִים וְעַל הָאֲבָנִים. לְפִיכָךְ נִבְרָא אָדָם יְחִידִי, לְלַמֶּדְךָ שֶׁכָּל הַמְאַבֵּד נֶפֶשׁ אַחַת מִיִּשְׂרָאֵל מַעֲלֶה עָלָיו הַכָּתוּב כְּאִלּוּ אִבֵּד עוֹלָם מָלֵא; וְכָל הַמְקַיֵּם נֶפֶשׁ אַחַת מִיִּשְׂרָאֵל מַעֲלֶה עָלָיו הַכָּתוּב כְּאִלּוּ קִיֵּם עוֹלָם מָלֵא. וּמִפְּנֵי שְׁלוֹם הַבְּרִיּוֹת, שֶׁלֹּא יֹאמַר אָדָם לַחֲבֵרוֹ, ,,אַבָּא גָדוֹל מֵאָבִיךָ".

ר' עובדיה מברטנורא

לפיכך נברא יחידי. להראותך שמאדם אחד נתישב מלואו של עולם: **רשויות הרבה.**

יד אברהם

דִּינֵי נְפָשׁוֹת, דָּמוֹ וְדַם זַרְעִיּוֹתָיו תְּלוּיִן בּוֹ עַד סוֹף הָעוֹלָם. — *[but in] capital cases, his blood and the blood of his descendants are his responsibility until eternity.*

[The false witness is held responsible for the blood of the victim and of all the descendants who would have been born had he not been unjustly executed] and there is no way to rectify the situation (*Tif. Yis.*).

שֶׁכֵּן מָצִינוּ בְקַיִן שֶׁהָרַג אֶת אָחִיו, שֶׁנֶּאֱמַר: ,,דְּמֵי אָחִיךָ צֹעֲקִים". אֵינוֹ אוֹמֵר ,,דַּם אָחִיךָ" אֶלָּא דָּמוֹ וְדַם זַרְעִיּוֹתָיו. — *For so we find with Cain who killed his brother, as it is stated* (*Gen.* 4:10): *"The bloods of your brother cry out." It does not say "the blood of your brother" but "the bloods of your brother" — his blood and that of his descendants.*

[The use of the plural form דְּמֵי of the word blood alludes to those who would have descended from Abel had he not been murdered.]

דָּבָר אַחֵר: ,,דְּמֵי אָחִיךָ" – שֶׁהָיָה דָמוֹ מֻשְׁלָךְ עַל הָעֵצִים וְעַל הָאֲבָנִים. — *Alternatively, "the bloods of your brother" — because his blood was splattered over the trees and stones.*

[Another possible explanation of the plural form of the word *blood* is that it was spattered over trees and stones as if it came from more than one source.] This is not part of the speech the judges make to the witnesses but merely an interjection of the *Tanna* of the mishnah to point out that there are alternative approaches to the verse (*Yad Ramah; Rambam, Hil. Sanhedrin* 12:3).

לְפִיכָךְ נִבְרָא אָדָם יְחִידִי, — *Therefore was man created singly,*

This, too, was said by the judges (*Rashi*).

לְלַמֶּדְךָ שֶׁכָּל הַמְאַבֵּד נֶפֶשׁ אַחַת מִיִּשְׂרָאֵל מַעֲלֶה עָלָיו הַכָּתוּב כְּאִלּוּ אִבֵּד עוֹלָם מָלֵא; וְכָל הַמְקַיֵּם נֶפֶשׁ אַחַת מִיִּשְׂרָאֵל מַעֲלֶה עָלָיו

4 [but in] capital cases, his blood and the blood of
5 his descendants are his responsibility until eternity. For so we find with Cain who killed his brother, as it is stated : *The bloods of your brother cry out.* It does not say *the blood of your brother* but *the bloods of your brother* — his blood and that of his descendants. Alternatively, the bloods of your brother — because his blood was spattered over the trees and stones. Therefore was man created singly, to teach you that whoever destroys a single life from Israel is considered by Scripture as if he had destroyed an entire world; and that whoever preserves a single life from Israel is considered by Scripture as if he had preserved an entire world. Also for the sake of peace among people, so that no man should [be able to] say to another, "My father was greater than yours."

YAD AVRAHAM

הַכָּתוּב כְּאִלּוּ קִיֵּם עוֹלָם מָלֵא. — *to teach you that whoever destroys a single life from Israel is considered by Scripture as if he had destroyed an entire world; and that whoever preserves a single life from Israel is considered by Scripture as if he had preserved an entire world.*

I.e., to teach that a single individual is capable of fathering an entire world (*Rav*) [thus showing the immense potential and worth of each individual].

Other versions do not specify the destruction or preservation of a soul from Israel (see *Rambam* loc. cit.).[1]

וּמִפְּנֵי שְׁלוֹם הַבְּרִיּוֹת, שֶׁלֹּא יֹאמַר אָדָם לַחֲבֵרוֹ, ,,אַבָּא גָדוֹל מֵאָבִיךָ״. — *Also for the sake of peace among people, so that no man should [be able to] say to another, "My father was greater than yours."*

[Since all men are descended from the same ancestor — Adam — no one can reasonably claim that his ancestry is inherently superior to another's.] Here, again, the *Tanna* interjects an alternative interpretation in the middle of describing the words of the judges, but this is not part of their statement (*Yad Ramah; Rambam* loc. cit.).

1. The latter approach would seem to be supported by the fact that Adam was not a Jew. However, it is possible that once the Jewish people were chosen to fulfill the primary role of mankind by accepting and fulfilling the Torah, the validity of this lesson applies only to them.

סנהדרין
ד/ה

וְשֶׁלֹּא יְהוּ מִינִין אוֹמְרִים הַרְבֵּה רְשׁוּיוֹת בַּשָּׁמַיִם. וּלְהַגִּיד גְּדֻלָּתוֹ שֶׁל הַקָּדוֹשׁ בָּרוּךְ הוּא, שֶׁאָדָם טוֹבֵעַ כַּמָּה מַטְבְּעוֹת בְּחוֹתָם אֶחָד וְכֻלָּן דּוֹמִין זֶה לָזֶה, וּמֶלֶךְ מַלְכֵי הַמְּלָכִים הַקָּדוֹשׁ בָּרוּךְ הוּא טָבַע כָּל אָדָם בְּחוֹתָמוֹ שֶׁל אָדָם הָרִאשׁוֹן וְאֵין אֶחָד מֵהֶן דּוֹמֶה לַחֲבֵרוֹ. לְפִיכָךְ, כָּל אֶחָד וְאֶחָד חַיָּב לוֹמַר „בִּשְׁבִילִי נִבְרָא הָעוֹלָם״.

וְשֶׁמָּא תֹאמְרוּ „מַה לָּנוּ וְלַצָּרָה הַזֹּאת?״ וַהֲלֹא כְבָר נֶאֱמַר: „וְהוּא עֵד אוֹ רָאָה אוֹ יָדָע, אִם־לוֹא יַגִּיד״ וְגוֹמֵר. וְשֶׁמָּא תֹאמְרוּ, „מַה לָּנוּ לָחוּב בְּדָמוֹ שֶׁל זֶה?״ וַהֲלֹא כְבָר נֶאֱמַר: „וּבַאֲבֹד רְשָׁעִים רִנָּה״.

ר׳ עובדיה מברטנורא

אלהות הרבה יש, וכל אחד ברא את שלו: **מה לנו ולצרה הזאת.** להכניס ראשינו בדאגה זו, ואפילו על האמת: **והלא כבר נאמר והוא עד.** וחייבין אתם להגיד מה שראיתם: **ושמא תאמרו מה לנו לחוב.** להיות מחוייבים בדמו של זה, נוח לנו לעמוד באם לא יגיד: **הרי הוא אומר ובאבוד רשעים רנה.** ואם רשע הוא, אין כאן עון כלל:

יד אברהם

וְשֶׁלֹּא יְהוּ מִינִין אוֹמְרִים הַרְבֵּה רְשׁוּיוֹת בַּשָּׁמַיִם. — *And so that heretics should have no [reason to] say there are many powers in Heaven.*

Had several men been created in the beginning, people would cite these separate creations as evidence that there are many gods, each of which created his own first man (*Rav*).

וּלְהַגִּיד גְּדֻלָּתוֹ שֶׁל הַקָּדוֹשׁ בָּרוּךְ הוּא, — *And to teach the greatness of the Holy One, Blessed is He,*

I.e., to teach the following lesson to future generations [who were not present at creation] (*Rashi*).

שֶׁאָדָם טוֹבֵעַ כַּמָּה מַטְבְּעוֹת בְּחוֹתָם אֶחָד וְכֻלָּן דּוֹמִין זֶה לָזֶה, וּמֶלֶךְ מַלְכֵי הַמְּלָכִים הַקָּדוֹשׁ בָּרוּךְ הוּא טָבַע כָּל אָדָם בְּחוֹתָמוֹ שֶׁל אָדָם הָרִאשׁוֹן וְאֵין אֶחָד מֵהֶן דּוֹמֶה לַחֲבֵרוֹ. — *for a man mints many coins from one mold and they are all alike, but the King of kings, the Holy One, Blessed is He, minted all men from the mold of Adam and not one is like another.*

All men, being descended from Adam, share the same basic form which defines them as men: yet they all differ in a multitude of specific characteristics (*Rambam Comm.*).

לְפִיכָךְ, כָּל אֶחָד וְאֶחָד חַיָּב לוֹמַר „בִּשְׁבִילִי נִבְרָא הָעוֹלָם״. — *Therefore, everyone is obligated to say, "For my sake was the world created."*

Since every man is the potential progenitor of an entire race (*Yad Ramah*), he must consider himself the equivalent of a world and therefore be careful not to bring about its downfall by committing so severe a transgres-

4
5
And so that heretics should have no [reason to] say there are many powers in Heaven. And to teach the greatness of the Holy One, Blessed be He, for a man mints many coins from one mold and they are all alike, but the King of kings, the Holy One, Blessed be He, minted all men from the mold of Adam and not one is like another. Therefore, everyone is obligated to say, "For my sake was the world created."

Perhaps you will say, "What need have we for this trouble?" But it has already been stated: *And he is a witness who saw or knew, if he will not attest, etc.* And perhaps you will say, "What need have we to incur responsibility for this man's blood?" But it has already been stated: *When the wicked perish there is joy.*

YAD AVRAHAM

sion [as testifying falsely that another committed a capital offense] (*Rashi*).

Alternatively, this phrase is connected to the previous idea of the value of human life. A person must view himself as if the entire world was created for him and then extend that concept to include others as well, thereby preventing him from causing the death of an innocent man with his testimony (*Meiri*).

וְשֶׁמָּא תֹאמְרוּ ,,מַה לָּנוּ וְלַצָּרָה הַזֹּאת?" — *Perhaps you will say, "What need have we for this trouble?"*

After hearing the terrible responsibility witnesses carry for false or inaccurate testimony, it would be only natural for them to refuse to testify even to what they did see (*Tos. Yom Tov*) in order to avoid any chance of incurring the heavy punishment (*Rav*). Anticipating this, the judges remind them of their responsibility to testify.

וַהֲלֹא כְּבָר נֶאֱמַר: ,,וְהוּא עֵד אוֹ רָאָה אוֹ יָדָע, אִם־לוֹא יַגִּיד" וְגוֹמֵר. — *But it has already been stated* (lit., *but does it not already state) (Lev.* 5:1): *"And he is a witness who saw or knew, if he will not attest, etc."*

I.e., the Torah obligates you to testify to that which you witnessed (*Rav*).

וְשֶׁמָּא תֹאמְרוּ, ,,מַה לָּנוּ לָחוּב בְּדָמוֹ שֶׁל זֶה?" — *And perhaps you will say, "What need have we to incur responsibility for this man's blood?"*

I.e., the witnesses may feel that it is better to accept the consequences of transgressing the commandment to testify rather than to have blood on their hands (*Rav*).

וַהֲלֹא כְּבָר נֶאֱמַר: ,,וּבַאֲבֹד רְשָׁעִים רִנָּה". — *But it has already been stated (Proverbs* 11:10): *"When the wicked perish there is joy."*

Thus, if the accused is indeed guilty, there is no fault whatsoever attached to you for bringing about his just punishment (*Rav*).

פרק חמישי

Chapter Five

This chapter continues the discussion begun in the previous one concerning capital cases. After impressing upon the witnesses the severity of the crime of false testimony, the judges proceed to examine them (*Rashi*), in accordance with the Biblical dictum (*Deut.* 13:15), *And you shall investigate and inquire thoroughly* (*Rambam, Hil. Eidus* 1:4).

Once the testimony of witnesses has been examined and accepted by the court, it can be shown to be false only by a process known as הֲזָמָה, *hazamah*.[1] This is where a second set of witnesses comes to court and testifies that they observed the first witnesses at one location at the very moment they claim to have witnessed the alleged act at another location (*Makkos* 1:4). In such a case, the Torah decrees that these latter witnesses are to be believed and the first ones are thus thoroughly discredited. This not only refutes their testimony but, as a penalty for their false testimony, renders them liable to whatever punishment or loss their false testimony would have inflicted (*Deut.* 19:19). [If the testimony is merely contradicted by other witnesses, the first witnesses are not proven to be false, since we have no reason to believe the later witnesses any more than the earlier ones. Thus, although the court must, out of doubt, reject both testimonies, neither set of witnesses is discredited and both may be accepted by a court in regard to some other case (*Bava Basra* 31b).]

It follows that a primary objective of the examination of the witnesses must be to establish the precise time and place of the act about which they testify, so that their testimony may be subject to refutation by *hazamah*. Moreover, any testimony which is by its very nature not susceptible to refutation by *hazamah* [עֵדוּת שֶׁאִי אַתָּה יָכוֹל לַהֲזִימָהּ] is not acceptable in the first place. Therefore, if the time and place of the alleged event cannot be precisely fixed, the testimony must be rejected (*Gem.* 41b).

1. The witnesses themselves can be impeached by showing that they are relatives or otherwise ineligible to testify, as explained in Chapter 3. The testimony itself, however, can only be proven false by *hazamah*.

[א] הָיוּ בּוֹדְקִין אוֹתָן בְּשֶׁבַע חֲקִירוֹת: בְּאֵיזֶה שָׁבוּעַ? בְּאֵיזוֹ שָׁנָה? בְּאֵיזֶה חֹדֶשׁ? בְּכַמָּה בַחֹדֶשׁ? בְּאֵיזֶה יוֹם? בְּאֵיזוֹ שָׁעָה? בְּאֵיזֶה מָקוֹם? רַבִּי יוֹסֵי אוֹמֵר: בְּאֵיזֶה יוֹם? בְּאֵיזוֹ שָׁעָה? בְּאֵיזֶה מָקוֹם? מַכִּירִין אַתֶּם אוֹתוֹ?

ר׳ עובדיה מברטנורא

פרק חמישי – היו בודקין אותן. (א) היו בודקין אותן. אחר שקיימו עליהן היו בודקין אותן בשבע חקירות, כנגד שבעה לשונות שנאמרו במקרא בחייבי מיתות בית דין, ודרשת וחקרת ושאלת היטב (דברים יג,טו) הרי כאן שלשה, ושאלת אינו מן המנין שממנו למדנו בדיקות, ובמקום אחר הוא אומר (שם יז,ד) והוגד לך ושמעת ודרשת היטב, יש כאן שנים אחרים, הרי לך חמשה, ובמקום אחר אומר (שם יט,יח) ודרשו השופטים היטב, שנים אחרים, הרי כאן שבעה: **באיזה שבוע.** של יובל: **באיזו שנה.** של שבוע: **באיזה יום.** של שבת: **באיזו שעה.** של יום, שכל שבע חקירות הללו מביאות אותן לידי הזמה, ושמא אין עדים להזימן לכל היום ויש עדים להזימן לאותה שעה: **רבי יוסי אומר.** אין צריך אלא שלשה חקירות, באיזה יום באיזו שעה באיזה מקום. ואין הלכה כרבי יוסי, אלא אפילו אמרו העדים אתמול הרגו, בודקין אותם בשבע חקירות, כדי שתטרף דעתן עליהן ויודו אם יש פסול בעדותן: **מכירין אתם אותו.** ההרוג,

יד אברהם

1.

הָיוּ בּוֹדְקִין אוֹתָן — *They interrogate them*

They questioned each of the witnesses separately, beginning with the most eminent of them (see above, 3:6), in the manner described below (*Meiri*).

The word בּוֹדְקִין, *interrogate,* is used here in the general sense of questioning witnesses, not in the specific sense noted above (4:1) of testing their veracity by checking them on less relevant questions. They are discussed in the next mishnah (*Margaliyos HaYam*).

בְּשֶׁבַע חֲקִירוֹת: — *with seven questions:*

The *Gemara* derives exegetically from seven different references to the judges' investigation of the witnesses in three different places in the Torah (*Deut.* 13:15, 17:4, 19:18) that seven basic questions must be asked (*Rav* from *Gem.* 40b). The primary purpose of these questions is to pinpoint the time and place of the alleged event so as to allow for the possibility of the witnesses being refuted through the process of *hazamah* (*Rashi* from *Gem.* 41b).

בְּאֵיזֶה שָׁבוּעַ? — *In which septenary?*

I.e., in which of the seven-year *Shemittah* cycles within the fifty-year cycle of *Yovel* (*Rav*). [Every seventh year, a *Shemittah* (Sabbatical) year was observed. After seven *Shemittah* years had passed (i.e., forty-nine years), the following year (the fiftieth) was observed as a *Yovel* (Jubilee) year. Thus the eighteenth year after *Yovel,* for example, was dated as the fourth year of the third *Shemittah* cycle.]

This particular question was asked only when the laws of *Yovel* were in force. These applied only when the majority of Israel resided in the Land, and this situation never again pertained after the destruction of the First Temple, according to most opinions. Since in other eras *Yovel* is not observed, it would be unrealistic to expect witnesses to

5
1

1. **T**hey interrogate them with seven questions: In which septenary? In which year? In which month? On which day of the month? On which day? In which hour? In which place? R' Yose says: On which day? In which hour? In which place? Did you recognize him?

YAD AVRAHAM

know which *Shemittah* period it would be if the *Yovel* cycle would be in effect. In any given era, the witnesses must be able to pinpoint the date in accordance with the prevalent system of recording dates in that time (*Minchas Chinuch, Mitzvah* 463).

בְּאֵיזוֹ שָׁנָה? — *In which year?*

In which year of the seven-year cycle (*Rav*).

בְּאֵיזֶה חֹדֶשׁ? בְּכַמָּה בַחֹדֶשׁ? בְּאֵיזֶה יוֹם? — *In which month? On which day of the month? On which day?*

I.e., the calendar date, as well as the day of the week (*Rav*). Although they already identified the date of the event, other witnesses who come to refute them may remember only the day of the week but not that of the month; therefore, they must state both (*Rashi*).

בְּאֵיזוֹ שָׁעָה? — *In which hour?*

This is necessary because there may be witnesses to discredit them on the basis of their having been seen in some other location for only part of the day, and thus the specification of the hour is needed to fully establish the possibility of refutation (*Rav*).

בְּאֵיזֶה מָקוֹם? — *In which place?*

This is vital, since it allows other witnesses to discredit their claim to having been in that place at that time (*Rashi*).

רַבִּי יוֹסֵי אוֹמֵר: בְּאֵיזֶה יוֹם? בְּאֵיזוֹ שָׁעָה? בְּאֵיזֶה מָקוֹם? — *R' Yose says: On which day? In which hour? In which place?*

He maintains that only these three questions are necessary (*Rav*), since all of the pertinent information can be ascertained from these alone (*Tos. Yom Tov*). The *Gemara* (40b) explains R' Yose's position to be that since it is common for witnesses to come to testify shortly after the event takes place, it is unnecessary to pinpoint the date from such a broad perspective. However, if the date could not be clarified without the other questions, R' Yose agrees that they are necessary (*Tos. Yom Tov*).

The first *Tanna*, however, contends that even if the questions are not necessary they must be asked, in order to expose the witnesses to a sufficient degree of harassment and confusion to induce them to retract their testimony if it is false (*Gem.* ibid.).

The halachah follows the view of the first *Tanna* (*Rav; Rambam, Eidus* 1:4).

Others contend that the mishnah is discussing a situation in which the witnesses testified to the event without giving any time reference. In such a case, the first *Tanna* holds that they must be asked all seven questions, while R' Yose considers just the last three sufficient, since in most cases the event took place recently. However, if the witnesses specified a time frame in their original testimony, it is not necessary to question them about that time frame — e.g., if they specified the year, the questioning begins with the month (*Yad Ramah; Baal HaMaor*, cited by *Ran*).

מַכִּירִין אַתֶּם אוֹתוֹ? — *Did you recognize him?*

They further ask the witnesses if

הִתְרֵיתֶם בּוֹ? הָעוֹבֵד עֲבוֹדָה זָרָה, אֶת מִי עָבַד
וּבַמֶּה עָבַד?

[ב] **כָּל** הַמַּרְבֶּה בִבְדִיקוֹת הֲרֵי זֶה מְשֻׁבָּח.
מַעֲשֶׂה וּבָדַק בֶּן זַכַּאי בְּעֻקְצֵי תְאֵנִים.

━━━━━━━━━ ר' עובדיה מברטנורא ━━━━━━━━━

שמא עכו"ס הוא, וזו אינה מן התקירות שמביאות לידי הזמה, אלא כשאר בדיקות שאינן אלא
לעשות העדות מוכחשת, שמא לא יאמר האחד כדברי חבירו, והוא והן יהיו פטורים: [**אֶת מִי**]
עָבַד. לפטור או למרקולים: **וּבַמֶּה עָבַד.** בזבוח או בהשתחויה: (ב) **בֶּן זַכַּאי.** רבן יוחנן בן
זכאי, ותלמיד דן לפני רבו היה באותה שעה, לכך קורהו בן זכאי: **בְּעֻקְצֵי תְאֵנִים.** שהיו
מעידים אותו שהרגו תחת התאנה, ובדק בן זכאי אותה זו, עוקציה דקיס או גסים, עוקץ, זנב
הפרי מקום חיבורו לאילן:

━━━━━━━━━━ **יד אברהם** ━━━━━━━━━━

they recognized the victim well
enough to determine with certainty
whether he was Jewish or Gentile
(*Rav* from *Gem.* 40b). [This is not part
of R' Yose's opinion but a continuation of the general text of the
mishnah.]

Others explain this to refer to the
accused. Did you recognize him well
enough [to be able to identify him
with certainty]? (*Rambam, Hil. Sanhedrin* 12:1.)

As noted earlier (comm. to 4:5),
Rambam explains that this question,
as well as the following one, were
asked before the judges admonished
the witnesses.

הִתְרֵיתֶם בּוֹ? — *Did you warn him?*
Did you warn him prior to his
commission of the crime that the act
he was about to perform was
forbidden and punishable by death
(*Rambam, Hil. Sanhedrin* 12:2)? And
did he acknowledge your warning
and declare his intention to carry out
the forbidden act nonetheless (*Gem.*
40b; *Rambam*, ibid.)? This is required
because it is derived from the Torah
that such a warning and response are

necessary before capital punishment
may be imposed (*Gem.* ibid.).

הָעוֹבֵד עֲבוֹדָה זָרָה, אֶת מִי עָבַד וּבַמֶּה עָבַד?
— *[In the case of] an idolater [they
ask], what did he worship and how did
he worship [it]?*

[If the witnesses testify that someone practiced idolatry, the judges ask
them the identity of the idol he served
and the manner in which he served it.]
Similarly, if the alleged act was the
desecration of the Sabbath, they must
specify the labor performed and the
manner in which it was done. If he
killed, they must describe the weapon
with which he did so. The same
applies to all cases (*Rambam, Eidus*
1:4).

These questions which are pertinent to the innocence or guilt of the
accused are analogous to the seven
inquiries listed above and must be
clarified for the testimony to be valid
(*Rambam, Eidus* 1:5; *Meiri*). These fall
into the category of דְּרִישׁוֹת, *inquiries*
[see 4:1] (*Meiri*).

According to others, however,
these questions are actually included
in the category of בְּדִיקוֹת,

Did you warn him? [In the case of] an idolater [they ask], what did he worship and how did he worship [it]?

2. **W**hoever expands the interrogations is praiseworthy. It [once] happened that Ben Zakkai interrogated concerning the stems of figs.

YAD AVRAHAM

interrogations. These are secondary questions designed to test the reliability of the witnesses and they need not answer all of them for their testimony to be valid [see next mishnah] (*Rav*). Although their inability to answer the questions listed in this mishnah must obviously invalidate their testimony — since if he was not warned or if the victim was not Jewish he is not punishable by death, and if they cannot describe which idol he served they cannot be assumed to have seen him do so — nevertheless, if the judges neglect to ask these questions the testimony is valid. Since the crux of their testimony is that the accused is liable for execution, it is implicit in their testimony that he was properly warned and that the act warrants the death penalty. In the case of the seven inquiries, however, if the questions were not asked, the testimony is not valid (*R' Dovid,* cited by *Ran*).[1]

A third view maintains that questions which are pertinent to the innocence or guilt of the accused are analogous to the seven inquiries, but not those which deal with the manner in which the act was allegedly committed (*Baal HaMaor,* cited by *Ran*).

2.

The mishnah now discusses additional questions which the judges ask the witnesses to test their veracity, although they are not actually pertinent to the case itself (*Meiri;* see above).

כָּל הַמַּרְבֶּה בִבְדִיקוֹת הֲרֵי זֶה מְשֻׁבָּח. — *Whoever expands the interrogations is praiseworthy.*

[A judge who interviews the witnesses in greater detail is to be lauded, since it further tests their reliability.]

מַעֲשֶׂה וּבָדַק בֶּן זַכַּאי בְּעֻקְצֵי תְאֵנִים. — *It [once] happened that Ben Zakkai interrogated concerning the stems of figs.*

Rabban Yochanan ben Zakkai — who was still a student at the time and was thus referred to simply as Ben

1. [Once their testimony has been accepted on the reasonable assumption that they meant that the obvious factors necessary for a death penalty were present, they can no longer be questioned about it, since even if they were later to state that some of these factors were absent they would not be believed. This is based on the rule that once a witness has testified, he cannot alter his testimony (כֵּיוָן שֶׁהִגִּיד שׁוּב אֵינוֹ חוֹזֵר וּמַגִּיד; see *Kesubos* 18b). This includes not only his actual words but their implications as well.]

וּמַה בֵּין חֲקִירוֹת לִבְדִיקוֹת? חֲקִירוֹת, אֶחָד אוֹמֵר „אֵינִי יוֹדֵעַ", עֵדוּתָן בְּטֵלָה. בְּדִיקוֹת, אֶחָד אוֹמֵר „אֵינִי יוֹדֵעַ", וַאֲפִלּוּ שְׁנַיִם אוֹמְרִים „אֵין אָנוּ יוֹדְעִין", עֵדוּתָן קַיֶּמֶת. אֶחָד חֲקִירוֹת וְאֶחָד בְּדִיקוֹת, בִּזְמַן שֶׁמַּכְחִישִׁין זֶה אֶת זֶה, עֵדוּתָן בְּטֵלָה.

ר' עובדיה מברטנורא

אמר אחד איני יודע עדותן בטלה. דשוב אי אתה יכול להזימן באותה חקירה, וכל זמן שאי אפשר לקיים תורת הזמה באחד מן העדים, כל העדות בטלה, ואפילו הן מאה, דאין העדים נעשים זוממים עד שיזומו כולן: **בדיקות.** אפילו אמרו כולן אין אנו יודעים, מצות הזמה ראויה להתקיים, דאין הזמה תלויה אלא בחקירה, לומר עמנו הייתם באותה שעה במקום אחר: **עדותן בטלה.** כל עדותן בטלה [שבגמרא], הוא והן פטורים:

יד אברהם

Zakkai — questioned witnesses who testified to an act of murder which took place under a fig tree, as to whether the figs had thick or thin stems (*Rav* from *Gem.* 41a). This is cited as an example of the extent to which judges may go in questioning witnesses.

וּמַה בֵּין חֲקִירוֹת לִבְדִיקוֹת? — *What [difference] is there between examinations and interrogations?*

[I.e., in what way do their laws differ?]

חֲקִירוֹת, אֶחָד אוֹמֵר „אֵינִי יוֹדֵעַ", עֵדוּתָן בְּטֵלָה. — *[In the case of] examinations, [if] one says, "I do not know," their testimony is null.*

Any witness who is unable to answer any of the seven points of examination is disqualified, because he can no longer be refuted through *hazamah.* For example, if he cannot pinpoint the precise date of the alleged crime, it is impossible to prove his testimony false by showing that he was somewhere else at that time. Thus his testimony is automatically unacceptable [as noted above in the preface to mishnah 1] (*Rav* from *Gem.* 41b).

בְּדִיקוֹת, אֶחָד אוֹמֵר „אֵינִי יוֹדֵעַ", וַאֲפִלּוּ שְׁנַיִם אוֹמְרִים „אֵין אָנוּ יוֹדְעִין", עֵדוּתָן קַיֶּמֶת. — *[In the case of] interrogations, [if] one says, "I do not know," or even [if] two say, "We do not know," their testimony is upheld.*

In the case of the secondary questions designed to check the general veracity of the witnesses, even if none of the witnesses can answer these questions their testimony is admissible since their inability to answer does not affect the possibility of refuting their testimony through *hazamah* (*Rav*). Only if a question elicits a contradictory response does it invalidate their testimony, as the mishnah states below.

The *Gemara* (41b) states that the phrase or *even two who do not know* is unnecessary, since in a case of two witnesses there is no reason to

5
2
What [difference] is there between examinations and interrogations? [In the case of] examinations, [if] one says, "I do not know," their testimony is null. [In the case of] interrogations, [if] one says, "I do not know," or even [if] two say, "We do not know," their testimony is upheld. Whether [in the case of] examinations or [in the case of] interrogations, if they contradict each other, their testimony is null.

YAD AVRAHAM

distinguish between one who does not know and two who do not. The *Gemara* concludes, therefore, that this refers back to the previous case of examinations and should be emended[1] (*Yad Ramah; Chidushei HaRan*) to read as follows: *Even [in the case of] examinations, if two say, "We know," and one says, "I do not know," their testimony is upheld* — unlike the previous case in which there were only two witnesses and the disqualification of one automatically invalidates the testimony of both. Although the mishnah says in *Makkos* (1:7) that all of the witnesses in the group are interdependent, and thus the impossibility of refuting even one of them by *hazamah* renders them all impervious to the punishment for false testimony — and therefore invalidates them as a group from testifying in this case (as explained above) — this mishnah disputes that principle (*Gem.* ibid. as explained by *Rashi*).

Tosafos contend that there is no dispute over this rule between this mishnah and the one in *Makkos* since, in this situation, the witness who does not know the answers to the seven points of examination is severed from the rest of the group and is no longer considered a witness at all. Thus, the inability to subject him to *hazamah* is irrelevant. The *Gemara's* statement that our mishnah disputes the ruling of the mishnah in *Makkos* refers instead to the rule stated there in mishnah 1:8, that if one of a group of witnesses is discovered to be a relative or otherwise invalid to testify, the entire group is disqualified (*Tos.*).

אֶחָד חֲקִירוֹת וְאֶחָד בְּדִיקוֹת, בִּזְמַן שֶׁמַּכְחִישִׁין זֶה אֶת זֶה, עֵדוּתָן בְּטֵלָה. — *Whether [in the case of] examinations or [in the case of] interrogations, if they contradict each other, their testimony is null.*

[Any time the witnesses contradict each other on any point whatsoever) the accused goes free. However, the witnesses are not punished for their contradictory testimony [since punishment for witnesses is mandated only for cases of *hazamah*] (*Rav*). Even if there are three witnesses, and one contradicts the other two, the entire group is disqualified (*Rambam, Eidus* 2:3).

1. *Rashi*, however, explains this not as an emendation of the mishnah but merely as an interpretation of the frame of reference of the phrase *even two say*.

[ג] **אֶחָד** אוֹמֵר בִּשְׁנַיִם בַּחֹדֶשׁ וְאֶחָד אוֹמֵר בִּשְׁלֹשָׁה בַּחֹדֶשׁ, עֵדוּתָן קַיֶּמֶת, שֶׁזֶּה יוֹדֵעַ בְּעִבּוּרוֹ שֶׁל חֹדֶשׁ וְזֶה אֵינוֹ יוֹדֵעַ בְּעִבּוּרוֹ שֶׁל חֹדֶשׁ. אֶחָד אוֹמֵר בִּשְׁלֹשָׁה וְאֶחָד אוֹמֵר בַּחֲמִשָּׁה, עֵדוּתָן בְּטֵלָה. אֶחָד אוֹמֵר בִּשְׁתֵּי שָׁעוֹת וְאֶחָד אוֹמֵר בְּשָׁלֹשׁ שָׁעוֹת, עֵדוּתָן קַיֶּמֶת.

ר׳ עובדיה מברטנורא

(ג) **שזה ידע בעבורו של חודש.** זה שאמר בשנים ידע שהחדש שעבר מלא היה, ויום ראשון של חודש שהוא יום שלשים, מחדש שעבר היה, ודוקא עד חצי החדש, אבל מחצי החדש ואילך עדותן בטילה, שחזקה אין עובר חצי החדש עד שכל העולם יודעים מתי קדשו בית דין את החדש:

יד אברהם

3.

Although the preceding mishnah has established that contradictory testimony disqualifies a group of witnesses even if they disagree in regard to a trivial point, there are instances when minor disagreements concerning even the seven basic inquiries do not invalidate their testimony.

אֶחָד אוֹמֵר בִּשְׁנַיִם בַּחֹדֶשׁ וְאֶחָד אוֹמֵר בִּשְׁלֹשָׁה בַּחֹדֶשׁ, — *[If] one says [it happened] on the second of the month and one says [it happened] on the third of the month,*

[I.e., they disagree about the date of the alleged act, but the discrepancy is only one day.] They do not, however, dispute which day of the week it was — e.g., one says it happened on Wednesday the second of the month, while the other says it was Wednesday the third (*Rambam, Eidus* 2:4; *Tos.* 41b). [As stated in mishnah 1, the witnesses are asked not only for the date of the event, but for the day of the week as well.]

עֵדוּתָן קַיֶּמֶת, שֶׁזֶּה יוֹדֵעַ בְּעִבּוּרוֹ שֶׁל חֹדֶשׁ וְזֶה אֵינוֹ יוֹדֵעַ בְּעִבּוּרוֹ שֶׁל חֹדֶשׁ. — *their testimony is upheld, because this one is aware of the intercalation of the month and this one is not aware of the intercalation of the month.*

We do not view their testimony as contradictory but rather assume that the witness who said that the act took place on the third is unaware that the previous month had been extended to thirty days (see 1:2), and the day he assumes to have been the third of the new month was actually only the second (*Rav*).

Although we do not generally accept testimony to impose the death penalty if there is any doubt about its legitimacy, since it is common for people to be unaware of the extension of a month, it is legitimate to assume this explanation of the discrepancy (*Gem.* 69a). It is not even necessary to interview them to verify this assumption, because the fact that they both cited the same day of the week is ample basis to accept it (*Tos.* 41b, s.v. שזה; see *Aruch LaNer*).

3. [If] one says [it happened] on the second of the month and one says [it happened] on the third of the month, their testimony is upheld, because this one is aware of the intercalation of the month and this one is not aware of the intercalation of the month. [If] one says [it happened] on the third and one says [it happened] on the fifth, their testimony is null. [If] one says [it happened] in the second hour [of the day] and one says [it happened] in the third hour [of the day], their testimony is upheld.

YAD AVRAHAM

However, this holds true only during the first half of the month. Beyond that time we take for granted that everyone is aware of the extension of the previous month, and the discrepancy between the two testimonies is thus sufficient basis to disqualify them entirely (*Rav* from *Gem.* 41b). This is so even though they agree about which day of the week it took place — e.g., one says it happened on Wednesday the sixteenth, while the other maintains it was on Wednesday the seventeenth (*Rambam, Eidus* 2:4). [Although it is clear in this case that the second witness is making a mistake, since Wednesday was in fact the sixteenth, once the middle of the month has passed we can no longer assume that his mistake was in regard to the date rather than the day of the week. Since in the latter case their testimonies contradict, we cannot accept their testimony.]

אֶחָד אוֹמֵר בִּשְׁלֹשָׁה וְאֶחָד אוֹמֵר בַּחֲמִשָּׁה, עֵדוּתָן בְּטֵלָה. — *[If] one says [it happened] on the third and one says [it happened] on the fifth, their testimony is null.*

[If one witness says that the event occurred on the third of the month and the other contends that it was the fifth, the testimony is rejected.] We do not assume that the latter was unaware of the last two times that the month had been extended, since that is not a mistake which is likely to occur (*Gem.* 41b). [As noted above, even a one-day discrepancy is attributed to lack of knowledge of the extension of the month only until midmonth.]

The mishnah uses an example of the third and the fifth, rather than following the structure of the previous case by saying the second and the fourth, in order for this case to coincide with the following one involving a discrepancy in hours (*Meleches Shlomo;* cf. *Tos. Yom Tov; Tif. Yis.*).

אֶחָד אוֹמֵר בִּשְׁתֵּי שָׁעוֹת וְאֶחָד אוֹמֵר בְּשָׁלֹשׁ שָׁעוֹת, עֵדוּתָן קַיֶּמֶת. — *[If] one says [it happened] in the second hour [of the day]* (lit., *at two hours*) *and one says [it happened] in the third hour [of the day]* (lit., *at three hours*), *their testimony is upheld.*

[The system of chronology employed in those days was to divide the day — regardless of its length — into twelve equal parts and to label events as occurring in a certain "hour" of the day. Thus each "hour" represented one-twelve of the day's length, not

סנהדרין
ה/ד

אֶחָד אוֹמֵר בְּשָׁלֹשׁ וְאֶחָד אוֹמֵר בְּחָמֵשׁ, עֵדוּתָן בְּטֵלָה. רַבִּי יְהוּדָה אוֹמֵר: קַיֶּמֶת. אֶחָד אוֹמֵר בְּחָמֵשׁ וְאֶחָד אוֹמֵר בְּשֶׁבַע, עֵדוּתָן בְּטֵלָה, שֶׁבְּחָמֵשׁ חַמָּה בַּמִּזְרָח וּבְשֶׁבַע חַמָּה בַּמַּעֲרָב.

[ד] **וְאַחַר** כָּךְ, מַכְנִיסִין אֶת הַשֵּׁנִי וּבוֹדְקִין אוֹתוֹ. אִם נִמְצְאוּ דִבְרֵיהֶם מְכֻוָּנִין, פּוֹתְחִין בִּזְכוּת. אָמַר אֶחָד מִן הָעֵדִים „יֶשׁ לִי לְלַמֵּד עָלָיו זְכוּת״, אוֹ אֶחָד

ר׳ עובדיה מברטנורא

רבי יהודה אומר קיימת. דעביד אינש דטעי כולי האי: **חמה במזרח.** ממקום זריחת החמה עד אמצע הרקיע קרוי מזרח, ומאמצע הרקיע עד מקום השקיעה קרוי מערב: (ד) **נמצאו דבריהם מכוונים.** ומעתה צריכין לישא וליתן בדבר: **פותחין בזכות.** אם לא עברת אל תירא: **אמר אחד מן העדים יש לי ללמד עליו זכות.** אפילו זכות, וכל שכן חובה. משתקים אותו, דכתיב (במדבר לה,ל) ועד אחד לא יענה, בין לזכות בין לחובה:

יד אברהם

sixty minutes.] The *Gemara* (*Pesachim* 12a) explains that a person is prone to make an error of up to two hours in assessing the time of day. Therefore, if one of the witnesses claims that the event took place in the second hour of the day — which may mean at the very beginning of the second hour — and one says in the third hour — which could refer to the end of the third hour — the maximum discrepancy comes to only two hours. We can therefore assume that their testimony is valid and one of them erred in assessing the time.

It is impossible to investigate by asking the witnesses, since, if one of them erred in assessing the time, he has no way of clarifying that now (*Mahariach*).

אֶחָד אוֹמֵר בְּשָׁלֹשׁ וְאֶחָד אוֹמֵר בְּחָמֵשׁ, עֵדוּתָן בְּטֵלָה. — *[If] one says [it happened] in the third [hour] and one says in the fifth, their testimony is null.*

[This is because the one who said the third hour may mean the beginning of the third hour and the one who said the fifth hour may be referring to the end of the fifth, making for the discrepancy of more than two hours, which is irreconcilable.]

Actually, the possibility exists that one witness is referring to the end of the third hour and the other to the beginning of the fifth, which would make testimony acceptable. Nevertheless, we do not interview them to discover if this is indeed the case, because the court scrutinizes witnesses only if it may help exonerate the accused, not to establish his guilt (*Tos.* 41b). Similarly, although an error of up to two hours is acceptable, we cannot assume that when they disagree by three or four hours, that each is making a mistake of up to two hours in a different direction (ibid.).

רַבִּי יְהוּדָה אוֹמֵר: קַיֶּמֶת. — *R' Yehudah says: It is upheld.*

He contends that a person is prone to err up to three hours in the day, and a discrepancy between the beginning

5 [If] one says [it happened] in the third [hour] and
4 one says in the fifth, their testimony is null. R' Yehudah says: It is upheld. [But if] one says [it happened] in the fifth [hour] and one says in the seventh, their testimony is null, because in the fifth [hour] the sun is to the east while in the seventh [hour] it is to the west.

4. After this, they admit the second [witness] and examine him. [If] their words concur, they open with [the consideration of] acquittal. [If] one of the witnesses says, "I can present grounds for his acquittal," or one

YAD AVRAHAM

of the third and the end of the fifth is thus not cause for disqualification of the witnesses (*Rav* from *Pesachim* 12a).

The halachah follows the view of the first *Tanna* (*Rambam, Eidus* 2:5).

אֶחָד אוֹמֵר בְּחָמֵשׁ וְאֶחָד אוֹמֵר בְּשֶׁבַע, עֵדוּתָן בְּטֵלָה, שֶׁבְּחָמֵשׁ חַמָּה בַּמִּזְרָח וּבְשֶׁבַע חַמָּה בַּמַּעֲרָב — *[But if] one says [it happened] in the fifth [hour] and one says in the seventh, their testimony is null, because in the fifth [hour] the sun is to the east while in the seventh [hour] it is to the west.*

[In this case, even R' Yehudah agrees that the two statements cannot be reconciled. Since time was measured by the relative position of the sun in the sky it is not likely that anyone would confuse these two times.] Similarly, if one said that it occurred before sunrise and the other during or after sunrise, their testimony is disqualified (*Gem.* 42a).

4.

וְאַחַר כָּךְ, מַכְנִיסִין אֶת הַשֵּׁנִי וּבוֹדְקִין אוֹתוֹ. — *After this, they admit the second [witness] and examine him.*

The use of the singular — *they examined him* — in mishnah 1 indicated that the witnesses were examined separately, something the mishnah stated explicitly in regard to civil cases (mishnah 3:6). The mishnah therefore states now that after completing the examination of the first witness, they bring in the second witness for his examination (*Tos. Yom Tov* to mishnah 1).

אִם נִמְצְאוּ דִבְרֵיהֶם מְכֻוָּנִין, פּוֹתְחִין בִּזְכוּת. — *[If] their words concur, they open with [the consideration of] acquittal.*

[If the testimonies of the two witnesses concur, the judges discuss the case. They begin his discussion by focusing on the possibility of the innocence of the accused (see 4:1).]

אָמַר אֶחָד מִן הָעֵדִים „יֵשׁ לִי לְלַמֵּד עָלָיו זְכוּת״, — *[If] one of the witnesses says, "I can present grounds for his acquittal,"*

The witnesses may not intercede to

סנהדרין
ה/ד

מִן הַתַּלְמִידִים „יֵשׁ לִי לְלַמֵּד עָלָיו חוֹבָה״, מְשַׁתְּקִין אוֹתוֹ. אָמַר אֶחָד מִן הַתַּלְמִידִים „יֵשׁ לִי לְלַמֵּד עָלָיו זְכוּת״, מַעֲלִין אוֹתוֹ וּמוֹשִׁיבִין אוֹתוֹ בֵּינֵיהֶן, וְלֹא הָיָה יוֹרֵד מִשָּׁם כָּל הַיּוֹם כֻּלּוֹ. אִם יֵשׁ מַמָּשׁ בִּדְבָרָיו, שׁוֹמְעִין לוֹ. וַאֲפִלּוּ הוּא אוֹמֵר „יֵשׁ לִי לְלַמֵּד עַל עַצְמִי זְכוּת״, שׁוֹמְעִין לוֹ, וּבִלְבַד שֶׁיֵּשׁ מַמָּשׁ בִּדְבָרָיו.

ר׳ עובדיה מברטנורא

אמר אחד מן התלמידים. היושבים לפני הדיינים, יש לי ללמד עליו חובה, משתקין אותו, דכתיב (שם) [ועד] אחד לא יענה בנפש למות, למות הוא דאינו עונה, הא לזכות עונה: **אינו יורד משם כל היום.** ואפילו שאין ממש בדבריו, אבל יש ממש בדבריו, אינו יורד משם לעולם:

יד אברהם

או אֶחָד מִן הַתַּלְמִידִים „יֵשׁ לִי לְלַמֵּד עָלָיו חוֹבָה״, מְשַׁתְּקִין אוֹתוֹ. — *or one of the disciples [says], "I can present grounds for his conviction," they silence him.*

The disciples who sit before the judges (see 4:4) may not argue against the accused. This too is exegetically derived from the above verse (ibid.).

אָמַר אֶחָד מִן הַתַּלְמִידִים „יֵשׁ לִי לְלַמֵּד עָלָיו זְכוּת״, מַעֲלִין אוֹתוֹ וּמוֹשִׁיבִין אוֹתוֹ בֵּינֵיהֶן, — *[If] one of the disciples says, "I can present grounds for his acquittal," they elevate and seat him among them,*

[Unlike the witnesses, the disciples may argue on *behalf* of the accused.] This is derived from the same verse (see *Gem.* 34a). [He therefore moves up from the students' row to take a seat among the judges to express his view.]

argue on behalf of the accused — and certainly not to argue against him. This is exegetically derived from the verse (*Num.* 35:30): *A single witness shall not answer* ... i.e., a witness may not argue for either acquittal or conviction when the case is under discussion (*Rav, Rambam Comm.* from *Gem.* 34a).

Although the verse concludes *for death,* it cannot be understood to exclude the witnesses from offering arguments only in favor of conviction, since they are also prejudiced in trying to acquit the defendant, as explained above in the comm. to 4:1 [s.v. דיני נפשות הכל מלמדין] (*Tos. Yom Tov*). Thus, that part of the verse must be understood to refer only to students, and to exclude them from offering arguments in favor of conviction, but not arguments in favor of acquittal. Witnesses, however, are excluded from offering arguments in favor of either position (*Yad Ramah* to *Gem.* 34a).

5 of the disciples [says,] "I can present grounds
4 for his conviction," they silence him. [If] one of the disciples says, "I can present grounds for his acquittal," they elevate and seat him among them, and he does not descend from there the entire day. If there is substance to his words, they listen to him. Even if he says, "I can present grounds for my own acquittal," they listen to him, as long as there is substance to his words.

YAD AVRAHAM

וְלֹא הָיָה יוֹרֵד מִשָּׁם כָּל הַיּוֹם כֻּלּוֹ. — *and he does not descend from there the entire day.*

[He remains seated among the judges for the duration of the day,] even if they find no substance to his argument (*Rav* from *Gem.* 42a), so as not to cause him embarrassment (*Gem.; Rashi* ibid.).

אִם יֵשׁ מַמָּשׁ בִּדְבָרָיו, שׁוֹמְעִין לוֹ. — *If there is substance to his words, they listen to him.*

If his point is well taken, he may vote in the decision for this case (*Tif. Yis.*), and he remains seated with the judges from that time on (*Rav* from *Gem.* ad loc.). However, he does not participate in other decisions [until he is called upon to replace a judge who leaves the court] (*Tos. Yom Tov*).

Others interpret the *Gemara* to mean that he remains seated with the judges only for the duration of that case but not afterward (*Meiri*).

וַאֲפִלּוּ הוּא אוֹמֵר „יֵשׁ לִי לְלַמֵּד עַל עַצְמִי זְכוּת", שׁוֹמְעִין לוֹ, וּבִלְבַד שֶׁיֵּשׁ מַמָּשׁ בִּדְבָרָיו. — *Even if he says, "I can present grounds for my own acquittal," they listen to him, as long as there is substance to his words.*

[Even the accused himself is heeded if he offers a coherent argument.] Although the witnesses are not permitted to intercede on his behalf, we cannot prevent a person from arguing in his own behalf. Furthermore, if witnesses present arguments in his favor, some of the judges may not remain aware of the fact that these witnesses have a vested interest in the outcome — since if he is convicted they are subject to *hazamah* — and they may be unduly influenced by their words. The subjectivity of the accused himself, however, is clear to all, and no such mistake will be made (*Yad Ramah*).

Rambam states that if the argument of the accused is accepted, he is permitted to participate in the decision of the court (*Hil. Sanhedrin* 10:8). However, this position is difficult to comprehend (*Yad Ramah; Lechem Mishneh* ad loc.).

[ה] **אִם** מָצְאוּ לוֹ זְכוּת, פְּטָרוּהוּ; וְאִם לָאו, מַעֲבִירִין דִּינוֹ לְמָחָר. הָיוּ מִזְדַּוְּגִין זוּגוֹת זוּגוֹת — וּמְמַעֲטִין בְּמַאֲכָל וְלֹא הָיוּ שׁוֹתִין יַיִן כָּל הַיּוֹם — וְנוֹשְׂאִין וְנוֹתְנִין כָּל הַלַּיְלָה. וְלַמָּחֳרָת מַשְׁכִּימִין וּבָאִין לְבֵית דִּין. הַמְזַכֶּה אוֹמֵר „אֲנִי מְזַכֶּה וּמְזַכֶּה אֲנִי בִּמְקוֹמִי". וְהַמְחַיֵּב אוֹמֵר „אֲנִי מְחַיֵּב וּמְחַיֵּב אֲנִי בִּמְקוֹמִי". הַמְלַמֵּד חוֹבָה מְלַמֵּד זְכוּת, אֲבָל הַמְלַמֵּד זְכוּת אֵינוֹ יָכוֹל לַחֲזוֹר וּלְלַמֵּד חוֹבָה.

ר' עובדיה מברטנורא

(ה) [**מעבירין אותו למחר**]. מעבירין את הדין עד למחר, משום הלנת הדין:

יד אברהם

5.

The mishnah now discusses the process of deciding a capital case.

אִם מָצְאוּ לוֹ זְכוּת, פְּטָרוּהוּ; וְאִם לָאו, מַעֲבִירִין דִּינוֹ לְמָחָר. — *If they find a reason to acquit him, they acquit him; if not, they postpone his verdict until the next day.*

[As explained in mishnah 4:1, a verdict of innocence can be returned in one day; a verdict of guilty may not.]

The text of the mishnah found in the *Gemara* reads מַעֲבִירִין אוֹתוֹ לְמָחָר. This seems to have been *Rambam*'s version, who translates *they imprisoned him* [the accused] *until the next day.*

הָיוּ מִזְדַּוְּגִין זוּגוֹת זוּגוֹת - — *They then pair off —*

After recessing the court until the next day, the judges leave the court and gather in groups of two or three (*Meiri*) in their homes or in some public place to discuss the case further (*Rashi*).

וּמְמַעֲטִין בְּמַאֲכָל וְלֹא הָיוּ שׁוֹתִין יַיִן כָּל הַיּוֹם - — *limiting their [consumption of] food and abstaining from wine the entire day —*

The *Gemara* (42a) cites the verse (*Proverbs* 31:4): *It is not for kings to drink wine, nor for princes to ask where is strong drink* — which the *Gemara* interprets to mean: Those who are involved in [investigating] the secrets of the world [exegetically interpreting the word רוֹזְנִים (lit., *princes*) in that verse from the root רָז, *secrets*] may not drink intoxicants.

וְנוֹשְׂאִין וְנוֹתְנִין כָּל הַלַּיְלָה. — *and analyze the matter through the night.*

They continued to analyze the case, either with one another or each one on his own, the entire night (*Rambam, Hil. Sanhedrin* 12:3; cf. *Rashi; Yad Ramah*).

וְלַמָּחֳרָת מַשְׁכִּימִין וּבָאִין לְבֵית דִּין. — *On the following morning they arise early and come to court.*

They return to court early the following morning and continue to deliberate the case until near sundown (*Tif. Yis.* from *Gem.* 46b).

5
5

5. If they find a reason to acquit him, they acquit him; if not, they postpone his verdict until the next day. They then pair off — limiting their [consumption of] food and abstaining from wine the entire day — and analyze the matter through the night. On the following morning they arise early and come to court. The one who argued for acquittal declares, "I argued for acquittal and I maintain my position in favor of acquittal." The one who argued for conviction says, "I argued for conviction and I maintain my position in favor of conviction." One who argued for conviction may argue for acquittal, but one who argued for acquittal may not reverse [himself] and argue for conviction.

YAD AVRAHAM

הַמְזַכֶּה אוֹמֵר ,,אֲנִי מְזַכֶּה וּמְזַכֶּה אֲנִי בִּמְקוֹמִי״. — *The one who argued for acquittal declares, "I argued for acquittal and I maintain my position in favor of acquittal."*

The one who argued for acquittal on the first day reiterates his view, as he is obligated by law to do (*Rashi;* see 4:1).

Although if he had originally argued for conviction he would nevertheless be able to change his view to argue for acquittal — as stated below — it is nevertheless necessary for him to mention that his position is consistent with his view from the previous day. This is so that if the number of judges arguing for acquittal corresponds with that of the day before, but one or more does not declare his consistency with his previous position, the scribes will know that one of the judges has changed his position from innocence to guilt, which is not permissible during this state of the deliberations (*Yad Ramah*).

וְהַמְחַיֵּב אוֹמֵר ,,אֲנִי מְחַיֵּב וּמְחַיֵּב אֲנִי בִּמְקוֹמִי״. — *The one who argued for conviction says, "I argued for conviction and I maintain my position in favor of conviction."*

The judge favoring conviction is *not* required to maintain his position the next day. The mishnah means only that if he did not find cause to change his view overnight, he declares that he maintains his opinion that the accused is guilty (*Rashi*).

הַמְלַמֵּד חוֹבָה מְלַמֵּד זְכוּת, אֲבָל הַמְלַמֵּד זְכוּת אֵינוֹ יָכוֹל לַחֲזוֹר וּלְלַמֵּד חוֹבָה. — *One who argued for conviction may argue for acquittal, but one who argued for acquittal may not reverse [himself] and argue for conviction.*

During the remainder of the deliberations, one who had previously supported a verdict of innocence may not advocate a ruling in favor of guilt. However, when it comes time to vote on a verdict, each judge must vote in accordance with his view at the time of the vote (*Tos. Yom Tov* from *Gem.* 34b).

סנהדרין
ה/ה

טָעוּ בַדָּבָר, שְׁנֵי סוֹפְרֵי הַדַּיָּנִין מַזְכִּירִין אוֹתָן. אִם מָצְאוּ לוֹ זְכוּת, פְּטָרוּהוּ; וְאִם לָאו, עוֹמְדִים לַמִּנְיָן. שְׁנֵים עָשָׂר מְזַכִּין וְאַחַד עָשָׂר מְחַיְּבִין, זַכַּאי. שְׁנֵים עָשָׂר מְחַיְּבִין וְאַחַד עָשָׂר מְזַכִּין, וַאֲפִלּוּ אַחַד עָשָׂר מְזַכִּין וְאַחַד עָשָׂר מְחַיְּבִין, וְאֶחָד אוֹמֵר „אֵינִי יוֹדֵעַ", וַאֲפִלּוּ עֶשְׂרִים וּשְׁנַיִם מְזַכִּין אוֹ מְחַיְּבִין, וְאֶחָד אוֹמֵר „אֵינִי יוֹדֵעַ" — יוֹסִיפוּ הַדַּיָּנִין. עַד כַּמָּה מוֹסִיפִין? שְׁנַיִם שְׁנַיִם עַד שִׁבְעִים וְאֶחָד.

ר' עובדיה מברטנורא

שנים עשר מחייבין ואחד עשר מזכין. והטייתך לרעה על פי אחד ליתא, הלכך יוסיפו דיינים: **ואפילו שנים ועשרים מזכין או מחייבין ואחד אומר איני יודע יוסיפו דיינים.** דהאי דאמר איני יודע כמאן דליתא דמי, ואין דנין דיני נפשות לא לזכות ולא לחובה בפחות משלשה ועשרים. **שנים שנים.** אם נחלקו השנים שהוסיפו, זה לכאן וזה לכאן, דהאכתי ליכא הטיה לא לטובה על פי אחד ולא לרעה על פי שנים, צריך להוסיף עוד שנים, וכן עד שבעים ואחד:

יד אברהם

טָעוּ בַדָּבָר, שְׁנֵי סוֹפְרֵי הַדַּיָּנִין מַזְכִּירִין אוֹתָן. — *[If] they erred, the two judicial scribes remind them.*

If the judges themselves do not recall who argued for conviction and who for acquittal (*Meiri*) — or they do not remember the reasons previously given for these positions — they rely on the records of the scribes [see 4:3].

אִם מָצְאוּ לוֹ זְכוּת, פְּטָרוּהוּ; וְאִם לָאו, עוֹמְדִים לַמִּנְיָן. — *If they find an argument to acquit him, they acquit him; if not, they take a vote.*

[If some of those who had argued for conviction change their position, and there is now a majority in favor of acquittal, he is acquitted.] Similarly, if those who had argued for acquittal change their view and a majority now votes that he is guilty, he is convicted (*Meiri*).

שְׁנֵים עָשָׂר מְזַכִּין וְאַחַד עָשָׂר מְחַיְּבִין, זַכַּאי. — *[If] twelve vote for acquittal and eleven for conviction, he is acquitted.*

[Since a majority of the court voted to acquit him, he is acquitted. As explained above (4:1), even in capital cases a majority of one (i.e., twelve out of the requisite twenty-three) is sufficient for acquittal.]

שְׁנֵים עָשָׂר מְחַיְּבִין וְאַחַד עָשָׂר מְזַכִּין, — *[If] twelve vote for conviction and eleven for acquittal,*

As explained in 4:1, a bare majority of one is not sufficient to convict; rather, a majority of two is required (*Rav*).

וַאֲפִלּוּ אַחַד עָשָׂר מְזַכִּין וְאַחַד עָשָׂר מְחַיְּבִין, וְאֶחָד אוֹמֵר „אֵינִי יוֹדֵעַ", — *or even eleven vote for acquittal and eleven for conviction, and one says, "I do not know,"*

Although the one who is unsure could not effect a conviction even if he were to vote for it, since that would still be a majority of only one, his

5
5

[If] they erred, the two judicial scribes remind them. If they find an argument to acquit him, they acquit him; if not, they take a vote. [If] twelve vote for acquittal and eleven for conviction, he is acquitted. [If] twelve vote for conviction and eleven for acquittal, or even eleven vote for acquittal and eleven for conviction, and one says, "I do not know," or even twenty-two vote for acquittal or conviction, and one says, "I do not know" — they add judges. Up to how many do they add? Two by two until [they reach] seventy-one.

YAD AVRAHAM

abstention cannot be combined with the vote of those who would acquit to create a majority for that view (*Tos. Yom Tov*).

וַאֲפִלּוּ עֶשְׂרִים וּשְׁנַיִם מְזַכִּין אוֹ מְחַיְּבִין, וְאֶחָד אוֹמֵר ,,אֵינִי יוֹדֵעַ" - יוֹסִיפוּ הַדַּיָּנִין. — *or even twenty-two vote for acquittal or conviction, and one says, "I do not know" — they add judges.*

Even if there is a unanimous vote for either view, if one of the judges does not express an opinion he effectively excludes himself from active participation in the decision. Therefore, this is no longer considered a full court of twenty-three members and no decision concerning a capital case may be rendered (*Rav*). [Consequently, judges are added to the court in order to reach the required number and come to a decision.]

Although the two additional judges are unable to affect the decision, since even if they disagree with the others they will be outvoted, their inclusion in the court is nevertheless considered to be relevant, since the possibility exists that they will influence the others to change their view (*Tif. Yis.*).[1]

עַד כַּמָּה מוֹסִיפִין? — *Up to how many do they add?*

If judges were added because of a tie vote and the two additional judges split in their opinions, thereby maintaining the tie vote, so that more judges had to be added, what is the maximum number of judges which may be added (*Rav*)?

שְׁנַיִם שְׁנַיִם עַד שִׁבְעִים וְאֶחָד. — *Two by two until [they reach] seventy-one.*

They continue adding judges in pairs until a decisive vote is obtained or until they reach a total of seventy-one (*Meiri*).

1. This would seem to be applicable only in the case of twenty-two who agree to acquit. Had they agreed to convict, the additional judges, who are taken from the front row of disciples (see 4:4), could have offered any arguments they had in the defendant's favor even before they were included in the court, as stated above. Perhaps their elevation to the bench would make them more forceful and make them see the case more clearly (since they must now vote).

שְׁלֹשִׁים וְשִׁשָּׁה מְזַכִּין וּשְׁלֹשִׁים וַחֲמִשָּׁה מְחַיְּבִין, זַכַּאי. שְׁלֹשִׁים וְשִׁשָּׁה מְחַיְּבִין וּשְׁלֹשִׁים וַחֲמִשָּׁה מְזַכִּין, דָּנִין אֵלּוּ כְּנֶגֶד אֵלּוּ עַד שֶׁיִּרְאֶה אֶחָד מִן הַמְחַיְּבִין דִּבְרֵי הַמְזַכִּין.

ר' עובדיה מברטנורא

עד שיראה אחד מן המחייבים דברי המזכין. דאיכא הטיה לטובה על פי אחד, והוא הדין אם יראה אחד מן המזכים דברי המחייבים, דבשעת גמר דין קיימא לן, דאף המלמד זכות יכול ללמד חובה, והאי דלא תני או עד שיראה אחד מן המזכין דברי המחייבין, דתנא אזכות קמהדר:

יד אברהם

The reason two judges at a time are added is because we wish the outcome of the case to be decided by their votes, and it is therefore necessary to add enough judges to decide the issue either for acquittal or conviction (*Yad Ramah*).

שְׁלֹשִׁים וְשִׁשָּׁה מְזַכִּין וּשְׁלֹשִׁים וַחֲמִשָּׁה מְחַיְּבִין, זַכַּאי. — *[If] thirty-six vote for acquittal and thirty-five for conviction, he is acquitted.*

[If, upon reaching the maximum number of judges, thirty-six vote to acquit, the accused is acquitted, since a majority of one is sufficient for acquittal, as stated above.]

שְׁלֹשִׁים וְשִׁשָּׁה מְחַיְּבִין וּשְׁלֹשִׁים וַחֲמִשָּׁה מְזַכִּין, דָּנִין אֵלּוּ כְּנֶגֶד אֵלּוּ עַד שֶׁיִּרְאֶה אֶחָד מִן הַמְחַיְּבִין דִּבְרֵי הַמְזַכִּין. — *[If] thirty-six vote for conviction and thirty-five for acquittal, they debate one another until one of those voting for conviction agrees with the opinion of those voting for acquittal.*

Since a guilty verdict cannot be rendered on the basis of a bare

[If] thirty-six vote for acquittal and thirty-five for conviction, he is acquitted. [If] thirty-six vote for conviction and thirty-five for acquittal, they debate each other until one of those voting for conviction agrees with the opinion of those voting for acquittal.

YAD AVRAHAM

majority of one for conviction, and since the maximum number of judges allowable has been reached, there is no alternative but for the seventy-one judges to continue debating the issue until one of those voting for conviction changes his vote to one for acquittal. This creates a majority of one for acquittal, which is sufficient. Alternatively, if one of the judges who favors acquittal changes his position, a verdict of guilty can be rendered. The mishnah mentions the first alternative only because that is the favorable one (*Rav*).

If they cannot come to a decisive vote, the accused is acquitted. However, they first seek to reach a majority view so as to avoid the humiliation to the court of being unable to come to a clear decision (*Gem.* 42a; *Rashi* ad loc.).

According to some, the same ruling would apply if thirty-five argue for acquittal, thirty-five for conviction, and one is unsure. Since no verdict has been reached, the accused goes free (*Rambam, Hil. Sanhedrin* 9:2). Others contend that in such a situation the one who is unsure would be replaced by another judge (*Ran*).

פרק ששי
Chapter Six

[א] **נִגְמַר** הַדִּין, מוֹצִיאִין אוֹתוֹ לְסָקְלוֹ. בֵּית הַסְּקִילָה הָיָה חוּץ לְבֵית דִּין, שֶׁנֶּאֱמַר: „הוֹצֵא אֶת הַמְקַלֵּל". אֶחָד עוֹמֵד עַל פֶּתַח בֵּית דִּין וְהַסּוּדָרִין בְּיָדוֹ, וְאָדָם אֶחָד רוֹכֵב הַסּוּס רָחוֹק מִמֶּנּוּ, כְּדֵי שֶׁיְּהֵא רוֹאֵהוּ. אוֹמֵר אֶחָד „יֵשׁ לִי לְלַמֵּד עָלָיו זְכוּת", הַלָּה מֵנִיף בַּסּוּדָרִין וְהַסּוּס רָץ וּמַעֲמִידוֹ.

ר' עובדיה מברטנורא

פרק שישי – נגמר הדין. (א) נגמר הדין. חוץ לבית דין. רחוק מבית דין, שמא בעוד שמוליכין אותו לבית הסקילה, ימצאו לו זכות ויפטר: **והסודרין בידו.** להניף, והוא סימן להחזירו:

יד אברהם

1.

The mishnah now discusses the procedure to be followed if a guilty verdict has been reached in a capital case. The first case discussed is that of stoning, since that is the first of the four types of execution mentioned in the Torah (*Rashi;* cf. *Yad Ramah; Ran; Meiri*).

נִגְמַר הַדִּין, מוֹצִיאִין אוֹתוֹ לְסָקְלוֹ. — *Once the case has been decided, they take him out to stone him.*

I.e., if the case was decided and a guilty verdict was reached (*Tif. Yis.*), he is taken out and executed immediately (*Rambam, Hil. Sanhedrin* 12:4; see below, 11:4). Although the mishnah discusses stoning, the same basic procedure pertains to all four methods of execution (*Rambam Comm.; Meiri*).

[The Torah prescribes four different methods of execution for different capital offenses. These are: stoning, burning, beheading, and strangulation. In the upcoming chapters the mishnah will discuss the particular procedures and laws pertaining to each of them, as well as which offenses are punishable by which method. However, the overall execution procedure described here is applicable to all of them.]

בֵּית הַסְּקִילָה הָיָה חוּץ לְבֵית דִּין, — *The stoning place was outside the court [area],*

A specific place was designated in which to carry out any sentence of stoning. This place was set far from the courts, in order to allow time to halt the proceedings if someone should come forward and provide any basis to reconsider the decision (*Rav* from *Gem.* 42b). In addition, if it were close to the court it would appear as if the judges were anxious to carry out the death penalty and therefore allowed for no interval between their sentencing and execution (*Gem.* ibid.). The distance allowed was six *mil,*[1] equal to the distance between the court of Moses

1. A *mil* is two thousand *amos.* There are various opinions as to the length of an *amah,* ranging from eighteen to twenty-four inches.

6
1

1. Once the case has been decided, they take him out to stone him. The stoning place was outside the court [area], as it is stated: *Take out the blasphemer.* One [man] stands at the courthouse door with flags in his hand, and [another] man sits astride a horse at a distance from him within his sight. [If] someone says, "I have grounds for his acquittal," that one waves the flags and the horse runs and halts him.

YAD AVRAHAM

and the end of the encampment in the desert (*Rambam, Hil. Sanhedrin* 12:3; see *Tos. Yom Tov*).

שֶׁנֶּאֱמַר: ,,הוֹצֵא אֶת הַמְקַלֵּל״. — *as it is stated (Lev.* 24:14): *"Take out the blasphemer."*

Actually, he must be stoned outside the entire city, not only outside the court area, since the full verse (quoted here in part) states *take the blasphemer outside the camp.* However, the mishnah specifies the court to teach that even if the court convenes outside the city, the stoning must nevertheless take place at a distance from the court (*Gem.* 42b) for the reasons given.

Tos. (42b) note two exceptions to this rule. The Torah states that a betrothed *naarah* — a girl between the ages of twelve and twelve and a half who has been betrothed through *erusin* but has not yet completed her marriage with *nisuin* (see ArtScroll *Nedarim* 10:1) — who commits adultery is executed at the entrance of her father's house (*Deut.* 22:21). The mishnah in *Kesubos* 4:3 states that if her father does not own a house, she is executed anyway, at the gate of the city — unless the city is predominantly Gentile, in which case she is executed at the entrance of the courthouse (*Kesubos* 45b). Similarly, one who engaged in idolatry in a city inhabited primarily by Gentiles is executed at the entrance of the courthouse [instead of the city gates] [ibid.; cf. *Ran; Tos.* to *Kesubos* 45b (s.v. על פתח) seem to dispute this].

אֶחָד עוֹמֵד עַל פֶּתַח בֵּית דִּין וְהַסּוּדָרִין בְּיָדוֹ, — *One [man] stands at the courthouse door with flags in his hand,*

A man was appointed by the court to stand outside the courthouse with flags in his hand, in order to be able to wave them as a signal to return the prisoner to court should new grounds for acquittal arise (*Rav*).

וְאָדָם אֶחָד רוֹכֵב הַסּוּס רָחוֹק מִמֶּנּוּ, כְּדֵי שֶׁיְּהֵא רוֹאֵהוּ. — *and [another] man sits astride a horse at a distance from him within his sight.*

A man sits astride a horse as far as possible from the one with the flags [in the direction of the place of execution] so that if the latter waves them to signal that the case has been reopened, the former will have the best possible chance to reach the prisoner in time to prevent his execution. Obviously, he must remain within sight of the man with the flags so that he will see him if he signals (*Rashi*).

אוֹמֵר אֶחָד ,,יֵשׁ לִי לְלַמֵּד עָלָיו זְכוּת״, הַלָּה מֵנִיף בַּסּוּדָרִין וְהַסּוּס רָץ וּמַעֲמִידוֹ. — *[If] someone says, "I have grounds for his acquittal," that one waves the flags and the horse runs and halts him.*

If one of the judges feels that he has

סנהדרין
ו/א

וַאֲפִלּוּ הוּא אוֹמֵר „יֵשׁ לִי לְלַמֵּד עַל עַצְמִי זְכוּת״, מַחֲזִירִין אוֹתוֹ, אֲפִלּוּ אַרְבָּעָה וַחֲמִשָּׁה פְעָמִים, וּבִלְבַד שֶׁיֵּשׁ מַמָּשׁ בִּדְבָרָיו. מָצְאוּ לוֹ זְכוּת, פְּטָרוּהוּ; וְאִם לָאו, יוֹצֵא לִסָּקֵל. וְכָרוֹז יוֹצֵא לְפָנָיו: אִישׁ פְּלוֹנִי בֶּן פְּלוֹנִי יוֹצֵא לִסָּקֵל עַל שֶׁעָבַר עֲבֵרָה פְּלוֹנִית, וּפְלוֹנִי וּפְלוֹנִי עֵדָיו. כָּל מִי שֶׁיּוֹדֵעַ לוֹ זְכוּת יָבוֹא וִילַמֵּד עָלָיו.

ר׳ עובדיה מברטנורא

ובלבד שיהא ממש בדבריו. ואם אין ממש בדבריו, פעם ראשונה ושניה בלבד מחזירין אותו, דלמא מחמת בעתותא נסתתמו טענותיו, ואולי תתישב דעתו עליו ויזכור טענותיו, יותר על כך אין מחזירין אותו, ומוסרין לו שני תלמידי חכמים שיעיינו אם יש ממש בדבריו, שאז מחזירין אותו ארבעה וחמשה פעמים: **ופלוני ופלוני עדיו.** שעבר עבירה פלונית ביום פלוני בשעה פלונית, במקום פלוני, דלמא איכא דמזים להו:

יד אברהם

a new theory to present which could alter the verdict, the flagman signals the horseman, who races to the execution party to stop the proceedings (*Rashi*), and to return the suspect to court where his case is then reconsidered (*Meiri; Rambam, Hil. Sanhedrin* 13:1). It is necessary to return the condemned man to court because a person may be tried only in his presence (*Mahariach;* cf. *Tos. Yom Tov*).

וַאֲפִלּוּ הוּא אוֹמֵר „יֵשׁ לִי לְלַמֵּד עַל עַצְמִי זְכוּת״, מַחֲזִירִין אוֹתוֹ, אֲפִלּוּ אַרְבָּעָה וַחֲמִשָּׁה פְּעָמִים, — *Even if he says, "I have grounds for my own acquittal," they return him, even four or five times,*

[Even if the condemned man offers his own grounds for acquittal as he is being led out to the place of execution, he is returned for the consideration of his arguments. Even if this should occur four or five times, he is returned each time.] These numbers are used arbitrarily; there is actually no limit to the number of times he may be brought back for reconsideration of his case [as long as the situation meets the requirements specified below] (*Tos. Yom Tov*).

וּבִלְבַד שֶׁיֵּשׁ מַמָּשׁ בִּדְבָרָיו. — *as long as there is substance to his words.*

If he presents an argument which has some basis for validity, he is returned to the court for the consideration of his argument (*Rashi*). This requisite applies only after the first two times which he claims to have a new argument to present. The first two times, however, he is returned even if he offers no coherent point since it is possible that he has a valid argument to present but is overcome by fear and unable to express himself coherently. After two times, however, the judges send along the Torah scholars who decide whether there is any possible weight to his arguments whatsoever. If there is, they return him again; if not, they

6
1 Even if he says, "I have grounds for my own acquittal," they return him, even four or five times, as long as there is substance to his words. [If] they found an argument for his acquittal, they acquit him; if not, he goes out to be stoned. A proclamation goes out before him: So-and-so the son of so-and-so is going out to be stoned because he transgressed such-and-such a prohibition, and so-and-so and so-and-so are his witnesses. Whoever knows any grounds for his acquittal should come forward and present them.

YAD AVRAHAM

proceed with the execution (*Rav* from *Gem.* 43a).

מָצְאוּ לוֹ זְכוּת, פְּטָרוּהוּ; וְאִם לָאו, יוֹצֵא לִסָּקֵל. — *[If] they found an argument for his acquittal, they acquit him; if not, he goes out to be stoned.*

[If the consideration of the new argument does not yield any valid reason for overturning the verdict of guilt, they take him back out to be executed, without requiring a new verdict by the court with the entire process that it entails.]

וְכָרוֹז יוֹצֵא לְפָנָיו: — *A proclamation goes out before him:*

Whenever someone is taken out to be executed, whether following the original verdict or after subsequent reconsideration, someone is sent from the court to go before him and shout the following proclamation (*Meiri*).

אִישׁ פְּלוֹנִי בֶּן פְּלוֹנִי יוֹצֵא לִסָּקֵל עַל שֶׁעָבַר עֲבֵרָה פְּלוֹנִית, וּפְלוֹנִי וּפְלוֹנִי עֵדָיו. — *So-and-so the son of so-and-so is going out to be stoned because he transgressed such and such a prohibition, and so-and-so and so-and-so are his witnesses.*

Official criers went ahead of the procession (*Tif. Yis.*) to announce who was being executed and for what transgression, as well as who the witnesses are whose testimony convicted him. They also announced that they testified that he committed the transgression on such and such a day at such and such an hour in such and such a place. These last details were added to allow an opportunity for *hazamah* (*Rav* from *Gem.* 43a; see 5:1).

For the purpose of this announcement, it is sufficient to clarify the precise day without explicitly stating the *Shemittah* cycle, year, month, and day of the month, since the issue of confusing the witnesses is not pertinent here (*Tos. Yom Tov;* see 5:1).

כָּל מִי שֶׁיּוֹדֵעַ לוֹ זְכוּת יָבֹא וִילַמֵּד עָלָיו. — *Whoever knows any grounds for his acquittal should come forward and present them.*

[This is the conclusion and purpose of the proclamations. If someone does, in fact, present new facts or arguments, the case is reconsidered, as described above.]

סנהדרין
ו/ב

[ב] **הָיָה** רָחוֹק מִבֵּית הַסְּקִילָה כְּעֶשֶׂר אַמּוֹת, אוֹמְרִים לוֹ „הִתְוַדֵּה, שֶׁכֵּן דֶּרֶךְ הַמּוּמָתִין מִתְוַדִּין, שֶׁכָּל הַמִּתְוַדֶּה יֵשׁ לוֹ חֵלֶק לָעוֹלָם הַבָּא״. שֶׁכֵּן מָצִינוּ בְּעָכָן, שֶׁאָמַר לוֹ יְהוֹשֻׁעַ: „בְּנִי שִׂים נָא כָבוֹד לַה׳ אֱלֹהֵי יִשְׂרָאֵל וְתֶן־לוֹ תוֹדָה, וְגוֹ׳. וַיַּעַן עָכָן אֶת־יְהוֹשֻׁעַ וַיֹּאמַר אָמְנָה אָנֹכִי חָטָאתִי ... וְכָזֹאת, וגו׳. וּמִנַּיִן שֶׁכִּפֵּר לוֹ וִדּוּיוֹ? שֶׁנֶּאֱמַר: „וַיֹּאמֶר יְהוֹשֻׁעַ מֶה עֲכַרְתָּנוּ יַעְכָּרְךָ ה׳ בַּיּוֹם הַזֶּה״ — הַיּוֹם הַזֶּה אַתָּה עָכוּר, וְאִי אַתָּה עָכוּר לָעוֹלָם הַבָּא.

ר׳ עובדיה מברטנורא

(ב) **היה רחוק מבית הסקילה.** דקרוב לבית הסקילה שמא תטרוף דעתו ולא יכול להתודות: **ותן לו תודה.** ואף על גב דאין אדם נהרג על פי עצמו, הריגת עכן הוראת שעה היתה: **וכזאת וכזאת עשיתי.** בגמרא (מג,ב) מפרש שמעל בחרמים בימי משה: **שהוא**

יד אברהם

2.

הָיָה רָחוֹק מִבֵּית הַסְּקִילָה כְּעֶשֶׂר אַמּוֹת, — *[When] he was approximately ten cubits from the stoning place,*

The confession must be made before actually reaching the stoning place, because the prisoner may be so overcome by fear when he arrives there that he will be unable to make the necessary confession (*Rav*).

אוֹמְרִים לוֹ „הִתְוַדֵּה, — *they say to him, "Confess,*

They tell him to confess to this transgression, as well as to any others he may have committed (*Tif. Yis.; Rashash*).

שֶׁכֵּן דֶּרֶךְ הַמּוּמָתִין מִתְוַדִּין, — *as it is the practice of those who are executed to confess,*

This is included in their statement to induce him to confess (*Tif. Yis.*).

שֶׁכָּל הַמִּתְוַדֶּה יֵשׁ לוֹ חֵלֶק לָעוֹלָם הַבָּא״. — *because anyone who confesses has a share in the World to Come."*

I.e., if he repents and confesses, his execution atones for his sin and enables him to gain a share of the World to Come despite the severity of his crime. Without both sincere repentance and confession, his execution does not atone for his sin [and he thus is punished in the World to Come as well] (*Rambam, Hil. Teshuvah* 1:1).

שֶׁכֵּן מָצִינוּ בְּעָכָן, — *For so we find concerning Achan,*

When the Jewish nation began their conquest of Israel and destroyed the city of Jericho, they were forbidden by Divine decree to rebuild it or to take any of its spoils. Achan transgressed this prohibition by taking some valuables from the city and was sentenced to death for it (*Joshua* Ch. 7).

6
2
2. [When] he was approximately ten cubits from the stoning place, they say to him, "Confess, as it is the practice of those who are executed to confess, because anyone who confesses has a share in the World to Come." For so we find concerning Achan, that Joshua said to him: *My son, please give honor to the God of Israel and render confession to him, etc. And Achan answered Joshua and said: I have sinned ... thus [have I done], etc.* From where do we know that his confession brought him atonement? Because it says: *And Joshua said, "Why have you troubled us? Hashem shall trouble you on this day"* — on this day you are troubled, but you will not be troubled in the World to Come.

YAD AVRAHAM

שֶׁאָמַר לוֹ יְהוֹשֻׁעַ: „בְּנִי שִׂים־נָא כָבוֹד לַה׳ אֱלֹהֵי יִשְׂרָאֵל וְתֶן־לוֹ תוֹדָה, וגו׳. — *that Joshua said to him (Joshua 7:19): "My son, please give honor to the God of Israel and render confession to him, etc."*

Although a man may not be executed on the basis of his own confession, this was a הוֹרָאַת שָׁעָה, *temporary ruling,* for an exceptional case which was judged in accordance with the compelling need of the situation (*Rav; Rambam Comm.*). [The Sanhedrin is allowed to act in extralegal ways on a temporary basis when there is a compelling reason to do so; *Yevamos* 90b.]

וַיַּעַן עָכָן אֶת־יְהוֹשֻׁעַ וַיֹּאמַר אָמְנָה אָנֹכִי חָטָאתִי ... וְכָזֹאת, וגו׳.״ — *"And Achan answered Joshua and said: I have sinned ... thus [have I done], etc."*

In addition to the transgression at hand, he had also previously transgressed bans which had been issued by Moses (*Rav* from *Gem.* 43b) on taking spoils from the cities he had conquered [*Numbers* 23:1-3] (*Rashi*). Until now he had gone unpunished, because no one knew about it, and thus the nation as a whole had not been affected by his actions. After crossing the Jordan, however, they became responsible even for hidden acts transgressed in their midst, and it thus became the responsibility of the nation to eradicate the evil from their midst (*Gem.* ibid.).

There are those who dispute this principle and contend that hidden acts are never the nation's responsibility. According to that view, it must be assumed that the act committed under Joshua's rule was known to some members of Achan's family (*Gem.* ibid.).

וּמִנַּיִן שֶׁכִּפֵּר לוֹ וִדּוּיוֹ? שֶׁנֶּאֱמַר: „וַיֹּאמֶר יְהוֹשֻׁעַ מֶה עֲכַרְתָּנוּ יַעְכָּרְךָ ה׳ בַּיּוֹם הַזֶּה״ - הַיּוֹם הַזֶּה אַתָּה עָכוּר, וְאִי אַתָּה עָכוּר לְעוֹלָם הַבָּא. — *From where do we know that his confession brought him atonement? Because it says (ibid. v.25): "And Joshua said, 'Why have you troubled us? Hashem shall trouble you on this day'" — on this day you are troubled, but you will not be troubled in the World to Come.*

[Joshua's emphasizing that Achan's

וְאִם אֵינוֹ יוֹדֵעַ לְהִתְוַדּוֹת, אוֹמְרִים לוֹ „אֱמֹר: תְּהֵא מִיתָתִי כַּפָּרָה עַל כָּל עֲוֹנוֹתַי״. רַבִּי יְהוּדָה אוֹמֵר: אִם הָיָה יוֹדֵעַ שֶׁהוּא מְזֻמָּם, אוֹמֵר „תְּהֵא מִיתָתִי כַּפָּרָה עַל כָּל עֲוֹנוֹתַי חוּץ מֵעָוֹן זֶה״. אָמְרוּ לוֹ: אִם כֵּן, יְהוּ כָל אָדָם אוֹמְרִים כָּךְ כְּדֵי לְנַקּוֹת אֶת עַצְמָן.

[ג] **הָיָה** רָחוֹק מִבֵּית הַסְּקִילָה אַרְבַּע אַמּוֹת, מַפְשִׁיטִין אוֹתוֹ אֶת בְּגָדָיו. הָאִישׁ, מְכַסִּין אוֹתוֹ מִלְּפָנָיו, וְהָאִשָּׁה,

ר׳ עובדיה מברטנורא

מזומם. שעדיו הן זוממין: **לנקות את עצמן.** מן הבריות, ויוציאו לעז על הדיינים ועל העדים. ואין הלכה כרבי יהודה: (ג) **מפשיטין את בגדיו.** דכתיב (ויקרא כד,יד) ורגמו אותו, בלא כסותו: [**מכסין אותו מלפניו**]. פרק אחד, כלומר מעט ממנו מלפניו. ואין הלכה כרבי יהודה:

יד אברהם

troubles would be *on this day* implies that after this day was over (i.e., after his execution) he would no longer be troubled, but would attain his share in the World to Come. Thus we see that anyone who confesses before his execution receives a share in the World to Come despite the transgression for which he was executed.]

וְאִם אֵינוֹ יוֹדֵעַ לְהִתְוַדּוֹת, — *If he does not know how to confess,*

I.e., he does not recall his other misdeeds (*Tif. Yis.*).

אוֹמְרִים לוֹ „אֱמֹר: תְּהֵא מִיתָתִי כַּפָּרָה עַל כָּל עֲוֹנוֹתַי״. — *they said to him, "Say: Let my death be an atonement for all my sins."*

He may express his confession with a general statement. However, he must still specify the sin for which he is being executed (ibid.).

רַבִּי יְהוּדָה אוֹמֵר: אִם הָיָה יוֹדֵעַ שֶׁהוּא מְזֻמָּם, — *R' Yehudah says: If he knows that he is the victim of a plot,*

If the condemned man knows that he is innocent and that the witnesses who testified against him testified falsely (*Rav*). The word מְזֻמָּם is derived from the word *hazamah.* The verse concerning false witnesses (*Deut.* 19:19) states וַעֲשִׂיתֶם לוֹ כַּאֲשֶׁר זָמַם, *and you shall do to him as he plotted to do* (*Tos. Yom Tov*).

אוֹמֵר „תְּהֵא מִיתָתִי כַּפָּרָה עַל כָּל עֲוֹנוֹתַי חוּץ מֵעָוֹן זֶה״. — *he should say, "Let my death be an atonement for all my sins except for this one."*

I.e., he is permitted to say this [in order to try to clear his name, though he is executed anyway] (*Tif. Yis.*).

אָמְרוּ לוֹ: אִם כֵּן, יְהוּ כָל אָדָם אוֹמְרִים כָּךְ כְּדֵי לְנַקּוֹת אֶת עַצְמָן. — *They said to*

6
3

If he does not know how to confess, they said to him, "Say: Let my death by an atonement for all my sins." R' Yehudah says: If he knows that he is the victim of a plot, he should say, "Let my death be an atonement for all my sins except for this one." They said to him: If so, everyone will say so in order to clear himself.

3. When he was four cubits from the stoning place, they removed his clothing. They cover a man in front, and a woman

him: If so, everyone will say so in order to clear himself.

[If such a statement were permitted, all who are executed by the courts, even those who are actually guilty, will declare their innocence in order to clear their name,] and it will cause people to malign the witnesses and judges who executed them (*Rav*).

The halachah does not follow the view of R' Yehudah (*Rav; Rambam, Sanhedrin* 13:1).

Yerushalmi (*Chagigah* 2) recounts an episode in which the head of the Sanhedrin (see *Avos* 1:8), Shimon ben Shetach, eradicated a nest of witches in Israel by executing eighty of them at one time. Their relatives took vengeance by hiring witnesses to testify that Shimon ben Shetach's son was guilty of a capital crime. Upon being taken out to be stoned, he declared, "If I am guilty of this sin, my death should not be an atonement for me; if not, let my death be an atonement for all my sins and a collar hanging around the necks of the witnesses." The witnesses were moved by this to repent and confess their crime, but it was too late to exonerate him [as witnesses may not recant their testimony once it has been accepted by the courts] and he was executed (*Rashi* 44b).

3.

הָיָה רָחוֹק מִבֵּית הַסְּקִילָה אַרְבַּע אַמּוֹת, מַפְשִׁיטִין אוֹתוֹ אֶת בְּגָדָיו. — *When he was four cubits from the stoning place, they removed his clothing.*

This is derived from the verse (*Lev.* 24:14): *and they shall stone him,* which implies just him, without his clothing (*Rav* from *Gem.* 45a). This was done in order to hasten his death [since the clothing softens the impact of the fall to some extent, making for the possibility that he will not die immediately) (*Rambam Comm.*).

Four cubits is considered the immediate area of the stoning place. Therefore, his clothes must be removed when he arrives within those four cubits so that it should not appear that he is going to be stoned with them on, in transgression of the law requiring that he be unclothed (*Yad Ramah* to mishnah 2).

הָאִישׁ, מְכַסִּין אוֹתוֹ מִלְּפָנָיו, — *They cover a man in front,*

I.e., they cover his genitals with a piece of material (*Rashi*).

מִלְּפָנֶיהָ וּמֵאַחֲרֶיהָ; דִּבְרֵי רַבִּי יְהוּדָה. וַחֲכָמִים אוֹמְרִים: הָאִישׁ נִסְקָל עָרֹם וְאֵין הָאִשָּׁה נִסְקֶלֶת עֲרֻמָּה.

[ד] **בֵּית** הַסְּקִילָה הָיָה גָבוֹהַּ שְׁתֵּי קוֹמוֹת. אֶחָד מִן הָעֵדִים דּוֹחֲפוֹ עַל מָתְנָיו; נֶהְפַּךְ עַל לִבּוֹ, הוֹפְכוֹ עַל מָתְנָיו. אִם מֵת בָּהּ, יָצָא;

ר׳ עובדיה מברטנורא

(ד) **היה גבוה שתי קומות.** ומפילו משם לארץ: **הופכו על מתניו.** שכשהוא מושכב פרקדן מגונה יותר:

יד אברהם

וְהָאִשָּׁה, מִלְּפָנֶיהָ וּמֵאַחֲרֶיהָ; דִּבְרֵי רַבִּי יְהוּדָה — *and a woman [both] in front and back; [these are] the words of R' Yehudah.*

A woman who is about to be stoned also has her clothing removed, but since her genital area is visible even from behind (*Rashi*, *Sotah* 8a), another piece of material is attached to cover her in back as well (*Gem.* 45a).

וַחֲכָמִים אוֹמְרִים: הָאִישׁ נִסְקָל עָרֹם וְאֵין הָאִשָּׁה נִסְקֶלֶת עֲרֻמָּה — *But the Sages say: A man is stoned unclothed but a woman is not stoned unclothed.*

Since being stripped of her clothing is a great humiliation to a woman, she is not subjected to such treatment, even though leaving them on may prolong her death agony. This is based on the Biblical dictum, וְאָהַבְתָּ לְרֵעֲךָ כָּמוֹךָ, *Love your friend as yourself.* The Rabbis understood this verse to apply to the imposition of capital punishment, to teach that it be carried out with the minimal degree of pain and humiliation possible [to the extent allowed by the other requirements of the Torah] (*Gem.* 45a). A man, however, is not as humiliated as a woman by nudity, and it is therefore preferable to a man that he be subjected to this indignity in order to avoid prolonging the agony of death (*Meiri* ibid.).[1]

R' Yehudah, however, maintains that even a woman is understood to prefer this humiliation to the prolonging of her pain (*Gem.* ibid.).

4.

The mishnah now describes the procedure for execution by stoning.

בֵּית הַסְּקִילָה הָיָה גָבוֹהַּ שְׁתֵּי קוֹמוֹת — *The stoning place was elevated twice the height [of a man].*

[As the mishnah goes on to explain, the execution referred to as stoning actually requires that the condemned

1. [This reasoning is not necessary to explain why a man is unclothed, since that is required by the Torah, as explained above. However, were it not for this rationale, there would be no basis to differentiate between a man and a woman in this matter and the rules governing the process of execution would overrule the concern for her embarrassment, just as it does for a man.]

6 [both] in front and back; [these are] the words of R'
4 Yehudah. But the Sages say: A man is stoned unclothed but a woman is not stoned unclothed.

4. The stoning place was elevated twice the height [of a man]. One of the witnesses shoves him by his hips; [if] he falls onto his chest, he is turned onto his hips. If he dies from this, it is sufficient;

YAD AVRAHAM

first be pushed from an elevation twice the height of the average man] — i.e., from a height of six cubits (*Tif. Yis.;* see comm. to ArtScroll *Bava Basra* 6:8, s.v. וכוכין ארכן ארבע אמות). He stands on the edge of this elevation and is pushed off to fall on the ground below (*Meiri*). This height is sufficient to allow for a quick death without smashing his body and thereby adding to the indignity of his execution as would a fall from a greater height (*Gem.* 45a).

אֶחָד מִן הָעֵדִים דּוֹחֲפוֹ עַל מָתְנָיו; — *One of the witnesses shoves him by his hips;*

The condemned is made to stand at the edge of the elevation where one of the witnesses approaches him from behind and gives him a shove on his hips, propelling him over the edge (*Tif. Yis.*).

נֶהְפַּךְ עַל לִבּוֹ, הוֹפְכוֹ עַל מָתְנָיו. — *[if] he falls onto his chest* (lit., *heart*), *he is turned onto his hips.*

If he falls to the ground with his face downward, he must be turned over on his side so that the stones can be thrown onto his chest, as described below. He cannot be turned over onto his back, because it would be too great an indignity for him to lie facing up. Therefore, he is positioned on his side so that stones can be thrown onto his chest but he does not face upward (*Rav; Rashi* as interpreted by *Aruch LaNer*).[1]

Rambam (*Sanhedrin* 15:1) apparently renders the mishnah in the following manner: *He shoves him by his hips so that he turns over and falls on his chest,* without mentioning that he must be turned over after falling. Nevertheless, it is clear that he must then be turned over since if he does not die from the impact of the fall, stones must be thrown onto his chest, as the mishnah will state below (*Kesef Mishneh,* ad loc.).

אִם מֵת בָּהּ, יָצָא; — *If he dies from this, it is sufficient;*

[If the condemned dies from this alone, without being stoned at all, the *mitzvah* of execution has nonetheless been fulfilled.]

This is derived from the punishment which was designated at the

1. Others interpret *Rashi* to mean that he is originally pushed in a manner which causes him to fall face down, because it would be an indignity for him to fall facing up while still alive. Once he has fallen, he is turned face up, since if he has already expired it is no longer an indignity [indeed, this is the position in which a corpse is burned], and if he is still alive, this indignity is necessary to hasten his death (*Shevus Yaakov* 1:5, cited by *R' Akiva Eiger* to 45a).

סנהדרין
ו/ד

וְאִם לָאו, הַשֵּׁנִי נוֹטֵל אֶת הָאֶבֶן וְנוֹתְנָהּ עַל לִבּוֹ. אִם מֵת בָּהּ, יָצָא. וְאִם לָאו, רְגִימָתוֹ בְּכָל יִשְׂרָאֵל, שֶׁנֶּאֱמַר: „יַד הָעֵדִים תִּהְיֶה בּוֹ בָרִאשׁוֹנָה לַהֲמִיתוֹ וְיַד כָּל הָעָם בָּאַחֲרֹנָה״.

כָּל הַנִּסְקָלִין נִתְלִין; דִּבְרֵי רַבִּי אֱלִיעֶזֶר. וַחֲכָמִים אוֹמְרִים: אֵינוֹ נִתְלֶה אֶלָּא הַמְגַדֵּף וְהָעוֹבֵד עֲבוֹדָה זָרָה. הָאִישׁ תּוֹלִין אוֹתוֹ פָּנָיו כְּלַפֵּי הָעָם, וְהָאִשָּׁה פָּנֶיהָ כְּלַפֵּי הָעֵץ; דִּבְרֵי רַבִּי אֱלִיעֶזֶר. וַחֲכָמִים אוֹמְרִים: הָאִישׁ נִתְלֶה וְאֵין הָאִשָּׁה נִתְלֵית.

ר׳ עובדיה מברטנורא

המגדף. מברך את ה׳: **ועובד עבודה זרה.** כמי מגדף הוא, דכתיב (במדבר טו,ל) והנפש אשר תעשה ביד רמה וגו׳ את ה׳ הוא מגדף, ואותה פרשה בעבודה זרה מדברת:

יד אברהם

time of the giving of the Torah for any man or beast who would touch Mt. Sinai — *No hand shall touch it, for [who does so] shall be stoned or hurled down; be he man or beast he shall not live* (*Ex.* 19:13). This verse clearly equates execution by stoning with execution by falling. Moreover, the verse is worded in such a manner as to emphasize its future tense, thereby indicating that the same principle applies to the execution by stoning to be meted out in future generations (*Gem.* 45a; *Rashi*).

וְאִם לָאו, הַשֵּׁנִי נוֹטֵל אֶת הָאֶבֶן וְנוֹתְנָהּ עַל לִבּוֹ. — *if not, the second [witness] takes the stone and throws it upon his chest.*

This stone had to be of a weight requiring two people to lift it. The two witnesses lift the stone together, and one of them [i.e., the one who did not push him down] throws it down upon the condemned (*Gem.* 45b).

אִם מֵת בָּהּ, יָצָא. וְאִם לָאו, רְגִימָתוֹ בְּכָל יִשְׂרָאֵל, שֶׁנֶּאֱמַר: „יַד הָעֵדִים תִּהְיֶה בּוֹ בָרִאשׁוֹנָה לַהֲמִיתוֹ וְיַד כָּל הָעָם בָּאַחֲרֹנָה״. — *If he dies from this, it is sufficient; if not, his stoning is by all of Israel, as it is stated* (*Deut.* 17:7): *"The hand of the witnesses shall be upon him first to put him to death, and the hand of the entire nation afterward."*

[Although this is a Biblical decree and thus not subject to critical analysis, its rationale is nevertheless very understandable.] Since the witnesses actually saw the crime being committed, their knowledge of the guilt of this person is much more certain than that of anyone else. Therefore, the Torah placed upon

6 4 if not, the second [witness] takes the stone and throws it upon his chest. If he dies from this, it is sufficient; if not, his stoning is by all of Israel, as it is stated: *The hand of the witnesses shall be upon him first to put him to death, and the hand of the entire nation afterward.*

All those who are stoned are hanged; [these are] the words of R' Eliezer. The Sages say: No one is hanged except for the blasphemer and the idolater. A man is hanged facing the people, and a woman facing the gibbet; [these are] the words of R' Eliezer. But the Sages say: A man is hanged but a woman is not hanged.

YAD AVRAHAM

them the primary responsibility to carry out the appropriate punishment (*Rambam Comm.* to 7:3).

כָּל הַנִּסְקָלִין נִתְלִין; דִּבְרֵי רַבִּי אֱלִיעֶזֶר. — *All those who are stoned are hanged; [these are] the words of R' Eliezer.*

[When someone is executed in accordance with the *mitzvah* of stoning, his body is subsequently hanged in the manner described below.] This is derived from the verse (*Deut.* 21:22): *And if there be in a man a sin for which he is condemned to death and he is put to death, you shall hanged him upon a tree.* Although this verse does not specify stoning, the *Gemara* (45b) nevertheless derives exegetically that only someone executed by stoning is hanged.

וַחֲכָמִים אוֹמְרִים: אֵינוֹ נִתְלֶה אֶלָּא הַמְגַדֵּף וְהָעוֹבֵד עֲבוֹדָה זָרָה. — *The Sages say: No one is hanged except for the blasphemer and the idolater.*

The specification of these particular offenses to require hanging is derived exegetically by the *Gemara* (45b; see *Rav, Rambam Comm.; Tos. Yom Tov*).

הָאִישׁ תּוֹלִין אוֹתוֹ פָּנָיו כְּלַפֵּי הָעָם, וְהָאִשָּׁה פָּנֶיהָ כְּלַפֵּי הָעֵץ; דִּבְרֵי רַבִּי אֱלִיעֶזֶר. — *A man is hanged facing the people, and a woman facing the gibbet; [these are] the words of R' Eliezer.*

A woman, for whom the disgrace of being hanged facing the populace would be great, is hanged with her back to them facing the gibbet [the type of gallows described below]. For a man, however, it is not as great a disgrace and he is therefore hanged facing the people in order to leave a deeper impression upon them (*Yad Ramah*).

וַחֲכָמִים אוֹמְרִים: הָאִישׁ נִתְלֶה וְאֵין הָאִשָּׁה נִתְלֵית. — *But the Sages say: A man is hanged but a woman is not hanged.*

The Sages derive this from the fact that the verse cited above for hanging specifies a man. R' Eliezer sees this as meant for a different point altogether (see *Gem.* 46a).

סנהדרין
ו/ד

אָמַר לָהֶן רַבִּי אֱלִיעֶזֶר: וַהֲלֹא שִׁמְעוֹן בֶּן שָׁטָח תָּלָה נָשִׁים בְּאַשְׁקְלוֹן? אָמְרוּ לוֹ: שְׁמוֹנִים נָשִׁים תָּלָה, וְאֵין דָּנִין שְׁנַיִם בְּיוֹם אֶחָד.

כֵּיצַד תּוֹלִין אוֹתוֹ? מְשַׁקְּעִין אֶת הַקּוֹרָה בָּאָרֶץ, וְהָעֵץ יוֹצֵא מִמֶּנָּה. וּמַקִּיף שְׁתֵּי יָדָיו זוֹ עַל גַּבֵּי זוֹ, וְתוֹלֶה אוֹתוֹ. רַבִּי יוֹסֵי אוֹמֵר: הַקּוֹרָה מֻטָּה עַל הַכֹּתֶל, וְתוֹלֶה אוֹתוֹ כְּדֶרֶךְ שֶׁהַטַּבָּחִין עוֹשִׂין. וּמַתִּירִין אוֹתוֹ מִיָּד. וְאִם לָן, עוֹבֵר עָלָיו בְּלֹא תַעֲשֶׂה, שֶׁנֶּאֱמַר: „לֹא־תָלִין נִבְלָתוֹ עַל־הָעֵץ

ר' עובדיה מברטנורא

ואין דנין שנים ביום אחד. בבית דין אחד, משום דלא מצי לאפוכי בזכותייהו דכל חד וחד, אלא תלייתן של נשים הללו הוראת שעה היתה ואין למדים ממנה. ואין הלכה כרבי אליעזר: **משקיעין.** נועצים: **והעץ יוצא ממנה.** כמין יתד היה יוצא מן הקורה סמוך לראשה: **ומקיף.** סומך זו אצל זו. כמו לתרום שלא מן המוקף [עירובין לב]: **ותולין אותו.** בידיו: **הקורה מוטה על הכותל.** לא היתה נעוצה בארץ, אלא ראשה אחד [על הארץ וראשה אחד] מוטה ונסמך על הכותל, וטעמא דרבי יוסי, לפי שהעץ שנתלה עליו נקבר עמו, ואמרה תורה (דברים כא,כג) כי קבור תקברנו, מי שאינו מחוסר אלא קבורה, יצא זה שמחוסר חפירה תלישה וקבורה, ורבנן, חפירה לאו כלום היא, ולא מיעטה תורה אלא שלא יהיה העץ במחובר מעיקרו. והלכה כחכמים:

יד אברהם

אָמַר לָהֶן רַבִּי אֱלִיעֶזֶר: וַהֲלֹא שִׁמְעוֹן בֶּן שָׁטָח תָּלָה נָשִׁים בְּאַשְׁקְלוֹן? — *Said R' Eliezer to them: Did not Shimon ben Shatach hang women in Ashkelon?*

[In support of his position, R' Eliezer cites the precedent of Shimon ben Shatach — the head of the Sanhedrin in his time (see *Avos* 1:8) — who had eighty women executed by stoning for practicing witchcraft (see 7:7) and then hanged, as described above, mishnah 2, s.v. אמרו לו).]

אָמְרוּ לוֹ: שְׁמוֹנִים נָשִׁים תָּלָה, וְאֵין דָּנִין שְׁנַיִם בְּיוֹם אֶחָד. — *They said to him: He hanged eighty women, and one may not try [even] two in one day.*

By law, a court may not perform more than one execution in a single day, so that they devote ample time to investigate thoroughly the possibility of innocence. Thus, Shimon ben Shatach's act was obviously an exception, since he executed eighty women in one day (*Rav; Rashi*). The reason he did so was to prevent their relatives from gathering together to free them (*Rashi*), or to forestall their using witchcraft to escape (*Yad Ramah*).

The rule against executing more than one person in a single day applies only if they are convicted of different transgressions. In the case of Shimon ben Shatach we must say, therefore, that although the eighty women were all practicing witchcraft, they were involved in several different types of sorcery, each of which is prohibited by virtue of separate negative commandments (*Rashi*).

The halachah follows the view of the Sages, that a woman is not hanged following

6
4

Said R′ Eliezer to them: Did not Shimon ben Shatach hang women in Ashkelon? They said to him: He hanged eighty women, and one may not try [even] two in one day.

How do they hang him? They sink a post into the ground, with a beam protruding from it. He places his two hands one upon the other, and hangs him. R′ Yose says: The post is leaned against the wall, and he hangs him in the way that butchers do it.

They release him immediately. If he is left overnight, this constitutes a transgression of a negative commandment, as it is stated: *And you shall not leave his body hanging overnight*

YAD AVRAHAM

her execution by stoning (*Rav; Rambam, Sanhedrin* 15:6).

כֵּיצַד תּוֹלִין אוֹתוֹ? מְשַׁקְּעִין אֶת הַקּוֹרָה בָּאָרֶץ, וְהָעֵץ יוֹצֵא מִמֶּנָּה. — *How do they hang him? They sink a post into the ground, with a beam protruding from it.*

As sunset approaches, the court sentences the criminal to death and carries out his execution, after which they proceed to hang his corpse (*Gem.* 46b). [For this purpose, a post is fixed in the ground,] and a crossbeam is attached to the top of the post so that it extends outward from it (*Yad Ramah*) to form a gibbet.

וּמַקִּיף שְׁתֵּי זוֹ עַל גַּבֵּי זוֹ, וְתוֹלֶה אוֹתוֹ. — *He places his two hands one upon the other, and hangs him.*

The corpse's hands are tied together, with the palm of one hand on top of the back of the other hand. The other end of that rope is tied to the beam (ibid.).

רַבִּי יוֹסֵי אוֹמֵר: הַקּוֹרָה מֻטָּה עַל הַכֹּתֶל, וְתוֹלֶה אוֹתוֹ כְּדֶרֶךְ שֶׁהַטַּבָּחִין עוֹשִׂין. — *R′ Yose says: The post is leaned against the wall, and he hangs him in the way that butchers do it.*

The post is stood diagonally against a wall, and the corpse is hanged from it (*Rav*) — i.e., from beneath the diagonal, with the body dangling freely by the rope, not leaning on the slope of the post (*Tif Yis.*).

From the seeming redundance in the phrase (*Deut.* 21:23): קָבוֹר תִּקְבְּרֶנּוּ, literally, *bury, you shall bury him,* the *Gemara* derives that the post upon which the convict is hanged must be buried with him, and that the burial must take place immediately after the hanging. R′ Yose therefore maintains that the post cannot be sunk into the ground since taking it out would result in a considerable delay between hanging and burial. The Sages, however, do not consider this delay substantial (*Rav* from *Gem.* 46b).

וּמַתִּירִין אוֹתוֹ מִיָּד. — *They release him immediately.*

As soon as one person hangs the

סנהדרין
ו/ה

כִּי קָבוֹר־תִּקְבְּרֶנּוּ בַּיּוֹם הַהוּא כִּי־קִלְלַת אֱלֹהִים תָּלוּי, וגו׳״; כְּלוֹמַר, מִפְּנֵי מַה זֶה תָּלוּי? מִפְּנֵי שֶׁבֵּרַךְ אֶת הַשֵּׁם, וְנִמְצָא שֵׁם שָׁמַיִם מִתְחַלֵּל.

[ה] **אָמַר** רַבִּי מֵאִיר: בְּשָׁעָה שֶׁאָדָם מִצְטַעֵר, שְׁכִינָה מַה הַלָּשׁוֹן אוֹמֶרֶת? כִּבְיָכוֹל ,,קַלַּנִי מֵרֹאשִׁי; קַלַּנִי מִזְּרוֹעִי״. אִם

ר׳ עובדיה מברטנורא

(ה) **בזמן שאדם מצטער.** שפורענות באה עליו בעונו: **מה לשון אומרת.** באיזה לשון שכינה קובלת ומתודדת עליו: **קלני מראשי.** ראשי כבד עלי וזרועי כבד עלי, כאדם שהוא עיף: **קלני.** איני קל מראשי:

יד אברהם

corpse, another takes it down (*Gem.* 46b). Two people are employed in order to speed its removal (*Rashi*). Alternatively, this is done in order to avoid the possibility that the one tying him up will become so involved in his actions that he will forget to release him (*Yad Ramah*).

וְאִם לָן, עוֹבֵר עָלָיו בְּלֹא תַעֲשֶׂה, שֶׁנֶּאֱמַר: ,,לֹא־תָלִין נִבְלָתוֹ עַל־הָעֵץ כִּי־קָבוֹר תִּקְבְּרֶנּוּ בַּיּוֹם הַהוּא כִּי־קִלְלַת אֱלֹהִים תָּלוּי, וגו׳״; — *If he is left overnight, this constitutes a transgression of a negative commandment, as it is stated (Deut.* 21:23*): "And you shall not leave his body hanging overnight for you shall bury him on that day, for one who is hanged is [like] a curse to* H*ASHEM, etc.";*

In addition to transgressing the positive commandment to bury him, those who leave the corpse hanging overnight also transgress a negative commandment (*Meiri; Rambam, Hil. Sanhedrin* 15:8).

There is a difference between the two commandments, however, in that the latter is not transgressed unless the body is left until daybreak the following morning, whereas the former takes effect immediately with nightfall (*Aruch LaNer*).

כְּלוֹמַר, מִפְּנֵי מַה זֶה תָּלוּי? מִפְּנֵי שֶׁבֵּרַךְ אֶת הַשֵּׁם, וְנִמְצָא שֵׁם שָׁמַיִם מִתְחַלֵּל. — *that is to say, why was this person hanged? Because he blasphemed* H*ASHEM; thus the name of* H*ASHEM is profaned.*

When people see him hanging there it reminds them of his sin and thus brings further desecration of God's honor (*Rashi*). This phrase in the Torah is used specifically in regard to the hanging following execution for blaspheming [but the same point can be made in regard to all executions] (*Meiri*).

The *Gemara* (46b) cites a *Baraisa* which offers another explanation by way of a parable for the verse's depiction of a hanging corpse as like a curse to HASHEM: There were once twin brothers, one of whom became king while the other became a highwayman. The highwayman was eventually captured and the king sentenced him to hang for his crimes. When the populace saw the corpse

for you shall bury him on that day, for one who is hanged is [like] a curse to Hashem, etc.; that is to say, why was this person hanged? Because he blasphemed Hashem; thus the name of Hashem is profaned.

5. **S**aid R' Meir: At a time when a person suffers, what expression does the *Shechinah* use? So to speak, "I am burdened by my head; I am burdened by my arm." If

YAD AVRAHAM

swinging from the gallows they thought that the king himself had been hanged, bringing disgrace upon the king. So he ordered the body cut down (*Gem.* 46b). Similarly, when a hanging person — who was created in the image of God — (*Gen.* 1:26) — is left on public display, he brings disgrace to God's honor (*Rashi,* ad loc.).

5.

Having cited the verse which states that one who is hanged is like a curse to HASHEM, the mishnah goes on to record R' Meir's interpretation of that verse.

אָמַר רַבִּי מֵאִיר: בְּשָׁעָה שֶׁאָדָם מִצְטַעֵר, — *Said R' Meir: At a time when a person suffers,*

I.e., when he undergoes the deserved punishment for his sins (*Rav*), specifically execution for his transgression of a capital offense (*Meiri*).

שְׁכִינָה מַה הַלָּשׁוֹן אוֹמֶרֶת? — *what expression does the Shechinah use?*

How does the Divine Presence express its anguish for the suffering of that person (*Rav*)?

Other versions do not mention the *Shechinah,* and some commentators understand the mishnah to refer to the comments of other people in response to one who bewails his suffering (*Rambam Comm.*).

כִּבְיָכוֹל — *So to speak* (lit., *as if it were possible*),

I.e., as if it were possible to speak of HASHEM in these terms. Though in reality it is impossible to ascribe human emotions to God, such anthropomorphisms are used as mere figures of speech to describe the indescribable (*Tif. Yis.*).

„קַלַּנִי מֵרֹאשִׁי; קַלַּנִי מִזְּרוֹעִי." — *"I am burdened by my head; I am burdened by my arm."*

It is as if the *Shechinah* were exhausted from the weight of its "head" and "arm" (*Rav*) — i.e., that God is troubled by the punishment of the wicked and would greatly prefer that they repent. Therefore, people should take heed and rectify their deeds rather than undergo unnecessary suffering (*Meiri*).

סנהדרין
ו/ה

כֵּן הַמָּקוֹם מִצְטַעֵר עַל דָּמָם שֶׁל רְשָׁעִים שֶׁנִּשְׁפָּךְ, קַל וָחֹמֶר עַל דָּמָן שֶׁל צַדִּיקִים.

וְלֹא זוֹ בִלְבַד, אֶלָּא כָּל הַמֵּלִין אֶת מֵתוֹ עוֹבֵר בְּלֹא תַעֲשֶׂה. הֱלִינוֹ לִכְבוֹדוֹ, לְהָבִיא לוֹ אָרוֹן וְתַכְרִיכִים, אֵינוֹ עוֹבֵר עָלָיו. וְלֹא הָיוּ קוֹבְרִין אוֹתוֹ בְּקִבְרוֹת אֲבוֹתָיו. אֶלָּא, שְׁנֵי בָתֵּי קְבָרוֹת הָיוּ מְתֻקָּנִין לְבֵית דִּין; אֶחָד לַנֶּהֱרָגִין וְלַנֶּחֱנָקִין, וְאֶחָד לַנִּסְקָלִין וְלַנִּשְׂרָפִין.

ר׳ עובדיה מברטנורא

ולא זה בלבד. עובר בלא תעשה אם הלינו: **לא היו קוברין אותן בקברות אבותיהן.** לפי שאין קוברין רשע אצל צדיק: **שני קברות היו מתוקנין לבית דין.** לפי שאין קוברים מי שנתחייב מיתה חמורה אצל מי שנתחייב מיתה קלה, והלכתא גמירא לה, שנים ולא ארבעה:

יד אברהם

אִם כֵּן הַמָּקוֹם מִצְטַעֵר עַל דָּמָם שֶׁל רְשָׁעִים שֶׁנִּשְׁפָּךְ, קַל וָחֹמֶר עַל דָּמָן שֶׁל צַדִּיקִים. — *If the Omnipresent is pained so for the blood of the wicked which is spilled, how much more so for the blood of the righteous.*

[This is the conclusion of R' Meir's interpretation of the verse cited above.] If this is how God reacts to the death of those whose actions have brought such retribution upon themselves, how much more so is He upset at those who unjustly kill the righteous (*Rambam Comm.*).

וְלֹא זוֹ בִלְבַד, אֶלָּא כָּל הַמֵּלִין אֶת מֵתוֹ עוֹבֵר בְּלֹא תַעֲשֶׂה. — *Not only this, but anyone who leaves his deceased [relative] overnight transgresses a negative commandment.*

I.e., the prohibition on leaving an executed corpse hanging overnight applies by extension to leaving any dead body overnight, even one who died of natural causes (*Gem.* 46b).

הֱלִינוֹ לִכְבוֹדוֹ, לְהָבִיא לוֹ אָרוֹן וְתַכְרִיכִים, אֵינוֹ עוֹבֵר עָלָיו. — *If he left him overnight for the sake of his honor, in order to bring him a casket or shrouds, he does not transgress.*

Although one is not usually permitted to transgress a Biblical injunction for the sake of someone's honor, in this case the prohibition itself is due to the desecration of the deceased's honor, and it is therefore permissible to leave him if deference to his honor so dictates (*Aruch LaNer*).

The same ruling applies if delay is necessary in order for relatives to gather for his funeral (*Tif. Yis.*).

6 the Omnipresent is pained so for the blood of
5 the wicked which is spilled, how much more so for the blood of the righteous.

Not only this, but anyone who leaves his deceased [relative] overnight transgresses a negative commandment. If he left him overnight for the sake of his honor, in order to bring him a casket or shrouds, he does not transgress. They do not bury him in his ancestral plot. Rather, there were two cemeteries set aside for the court; one for those who were beheaded or strangled, and one for those who were stoned or burned.

YAD AVRAHAM

וְלֹא הָיוּ קוֹבְרִין אוֹתוֹ בְּקִבְרוֹת אֲבוֹתָיו. — *They do not bury him in his ancestral plot.*

One who has been executed by the court may not be buried in the regular cemetery because an evildoer is not permitted to be buried together with the righteous (*Rav*). This is derived by the *Gemara* (74a) (from the Biblical incident (*II Kings* 13:21) in which an evildoer whose body was cast away came to rest on the grave of the prophet Elisha. Scripture describes how, upon touching the grave, the man miraculously came back to life briefly, to walk away and fall down again at another plot (*Gem.*).

אֶלָּא, שְׁנֵי בָתֵּי קְבָרוֹת הָיוּ מְתֻקָּנִין לְבֵית דִּין; אֶחָד לַנֶּהֱרָגִין וְלַנֶּחֱנָקִין, וְאֶחָד לַנִּסְקָלִין וְלַנִּשְׂרָפִין. — *Rather, there were two cemeteries set aside for the court; one for those who were beheaded or strangled, and one for those who were stoned or burned.*

In addition to separating the burial places of those who were executed from others, those executed were themselves divided into two separate sections of graves. This is because beheading and strangulation are less severe forms of execution than stoning and burning and are given to perpetrators of lesser capital crimes. [Thus it would not be proper to bury those executed for more severe transgressions next to those executed for lesser transgressions.] However, the Sages had a tradition from Sinai that only two distinct categories be set in regard to this matter, rather than allocating a separate cemetery for each of the four methods of execution (*Rav* from *Gem.* 47a).

[ו] נִתְעַכֵּל הַבָּשָׂר, מְלַקְּטִין אֶת הָעֲצָמוֹת וְקוֹבְרִין אוֹתָן בִּמְקוֹמָן. וְהַקְּרוֹבִים בָּאִים וְשׁוֹאֲלִין בִּשְׁלוֹם הַדַּיָּנִים וּבִשְׁלוֹם הָעֵדִים, כְּלוֹמַר: שֶׁאֵין בְּלִבֵּנוּ עֲלֵיכֶם כְּלוּם, שֶׁדִּין אֱמֶת דַּנְתֶּם. וְלֹא הָיוּ מִתְאַבְּלִין, אֲבָל אוֹנְנִין, שֶׁאֵין אֲנִינוּת אֶלָּא בַלֵּב.

ר׳ עובדיה מברטנורא

(ו) **נתעכל הבשר.** כבר נתכפר לו במיתתו ובבזיונו: **מלקטין את העצמות.** וקוברים אותן בקברות אבותן: **ולא היו מתאבלים.** כדי שיהא בזיונן כפרה להם. ואית דאמרי, לפי שהאבלות חלה משיסתם הגולל, ובאותה שעה אין מתאבלים עליהם, שלא נגמרה כפרתן עד שיתעכל הבשר, והואיל ואדחי האבלות, אדחי:

יד אברהם

6.

נִתְעַכֵּל הַבָּשָׂר, מְלַקְּטִין אֶת הָעֲצָמוֹת וְקוֹבְרִין אוֹתָן בִּמְקוֹמָן. — *[When] the flesh has decomposed, they gather the bones and bury them in their place.*

The body's decay and disgrace brings the final atonement to the deceased and his body may now be taken for burial in the ancestral plot (*Rav* from *Gem.* 47b).

There is another view in the *Gemara* (ibid.), that of Rav Ashi, who holds that atonement occurs as soon as the corpse has experienced the anguish of internment. Nevertheless, the body is not moved until after its decay because to do so earlier is not feasible due to the stench.

וְהַקְּרוֹבִים בָּאִים וְשׁוֹאֲלִין בִּשְׁלוֹם הַדַּיָּנִים וּבִשְׁלוֹם הָעֵדִים, כְּלוֹמַר: שֶׁאֵין בְּלִבֵּנוּ עֲלֵיכֶם כְּלוּם, שֶׁדִּין אֱמֶת דַּנְתֶּם. — *The relatives come to inquire after the welfare of the judges and the witnesses, as if to say: We have nothing in our hearts against you, because you have judged correctly.*

This refers to those relatives who would be obligated to mourn if he had died under normal circumstances (*Meiri*). They express their agreement with the judgment by means of a symbolic gesture, rather than stating it explicitly, for the sake of the honor of the deceased (*Tif. Yis.*).

וְלֹא הָיוּ מִתְאַבְּלִין, — *They do not mourn,*

The laws of mourning do not apply to one who has been executed by law, because this is part of the disgrace which he must undergo in order to achieve atonement (*Rav; Rashi*). Alternatively, as long as atonement has not been achieved, it is inappropriate to express grief over the loss of such an evildoer (*Rambam Comm.*).

6
6

6. [When] the flesh has decomposed, they gather the bones and bury them in their place. The relatives come to inquire after the welfare of the judges and the witnesses, as if to say: We have nothing in our hearts against you, because you have judged correctly. They do not mourn, but they grieve, for grieving is only in the heart.

YAD AVRAHAM

Even when moving the bones and reburying them [which takes place after atonement has been achieved, as stated above], there is no mourning, because once it has been deferred it is not reinstated (*Rav; Rambam Comm.*).

Others contend that the mishnah refers only to the mourning generally following after burial. Those laws of mourning which apply upon the reburial of one's relative's bones[1] apply in this case as well, since the bones are disinterred after atonement (*Tos. Yom Tov*).

אֲבָל אוֹנְנִין, שֶׁאֵין אֲנִינוּת אֶלָּא בַלֵּב. — *but they grieve, for grieving is only in the heart.*

They are permitted to dwell on their grief inside their hearts because this does not honor the deceased, since it is not overtly expressed; accordingly, it does not impede his atonement (*Rashi*).

According to the alternate interpretation cited above, only mourning which is observed by others is inappropriate for an evildoer, but not that which one grieves for him within his heart (*Tos. Yom Tov*). In addition it would be impossible to demand of the relatives that they restrain themselves to such an extent (*Yad Ramah*).

There is another approach, that the grieving here refers to the laws of *aninus* — the special rules of mourning which apply to the day of death until the burial, i.e., that one who loses a relative may not partake of food from sacrifices or *maaser sheni* (second tithe). Since it is impossible for them to suppress their inner grief, these restrictions apply (*Yad Ramah*).

1. In Mishnaic times it was customary to bury in a deep moist grave to hasten the decay of the flesh. Afterward, the bones were gathered and reburied in a coffin (see *Moed Katan* 1:6; *Yerushalmi* ad loc.). When the bones were disinterred for reburial, a one-day mourning period applied (see *Yoreh Deah* 403).

פרק שביעי

Chapter Seven

[א] אַרְבַּע מִיתוֹת נִמְסְרוּ לְבֵית דִּין: סְקִילָה, שְׂרֵפָה, הֶרֶג, וָחֶנֶק. רַבִּי שִׁמְעוֹן אוֹמֵר: שְׂרֵפָה, סְקִילָה, חֶנֶק, וָהֶרֶג. זוֹ מִצְוַת הַנִּסְקָלִין.

[ב] מִצְוַת הַנִּשְׂרָפִין: הָיוּ מְשַׁקְּעִין אוֹתוֹ בְּזֶבֶל עַד אַרְכּוּבוֹתָיו, וְנוֹתְנִין סוּדָר קָשָׁה לְתוֹךְ הָרַכָּה וְכוֹרֵךְ עַל צַוָּארוֹ.

ר׳ עובדיה מברטנורא

פרק שביעי – ארבע מיתות. (א) ארבע מיתות. סקילה שרפה הרג וחנק. סקילה חמורה משרפה, ושתיהן מהרג, ושלשתן מחנק, ונפקא מינה למי שנתחייב שתי מיתות, דקיימא לן דנדון בחמורה: **רבי שמעון אומר וכו׳.** ואין הלכה כרבי שמעון: **זו מצות הנסקלין.** הא דפרישנא בפרקין דלעיל: **(ב) משקעין אותו.** שלא יתהפך אנה ואנה ותפול הפתילה על בשרו: **קשה לתוך הרכה.** כורכים סודר קשה לתוך הרכה, קשה מבפנים לחנוק, ורכה מבחוץ להגין:

יד אברהם

1.

אַרְבַּע מִיתוֹת נִמְסְרוּ לְבֵית דִּין; — *Four executions* (lit., *deaths*) *were given to the courts:*

[The Torah mandates four different methods of execution for various capital offenses.]

סְקִילָה, שְׂרֵפָה, הֶרֶג, וָחֶנֶק. — *stoning, burning, beheading, and strangulation.*

The mishnah lists the four methods of execution allowed by Jewish law in declining order of their severity (*Gem.* 49b). This first *Tanna* considers stoning to be more severe than burning and beheading worse than strangulation. The practical difference of this is in a situation in which one committed several capital offenses, each of which renders him liable to a different type of execution. Since one can obviously not be executed twice, he receives the more severe type of execution for which he is liable [see below, 9:4] (*Rav; Rashi*).

Another difference would be if several people who had been convicted of capital crimes, each of them meriting a different type of death, were held together, and it was forgotten which prisoner was being held for which execution. In such circumstances, they all receive the lesser sentence since we cannot inflict upon a condemned prisoner a more severe punishment than the one he deserves; we can, however, execute him by a less severe one if the one he deserves cannot be imposed [see below, 9:3] (*Meiri;* see *Tos. Yom Tov; Mahariach; Rashash; Meleches Shlomo*).

רַבִּי שִׁמְעוֹן אוֹמֵר: שְׂרֵפָה, סְקִילָה, חֶנֶק, וָהֶרֶג. — *R' Shimon says: Burning, stoning, strangulation, and beheading.*

[R' Shimon contends that burning is considered more severe than stoning and strangulation more severe than beheading (*Gem.* 49b).

1. **F**our executions were given to the courts: stoning, burning, beheading, and strangulation. R' Shimon says: Burning, stoning, strangulation, and beheading. This is the procedure for those who are stoned.

2. **[T**his is] the procedure for those who are burned: They place him in manure up to his knees, and place a coarse scarf inside a soft one and wind it around his neck.

YAD AVRAHAM

.זוֹ מִצְוַת הַנִּסְקָלִין — *This is the procedure for those who are stoned.*

This is in effect a summation of the previous chapter. The procedure described there is the proper procedure for execution by stoning. The next mishnayos will delineate the others (*Rashi*).

2.

Execution by burning in Torah law is a far different procedure — and far quicker death — than the burnings at the stake which were practiced by other nations. The mishnah now describes this method of execution.

:מִצְוַת הַנִּשְׂרָפִין — *[This is] the procedure* (lit., *mitzvah*) *for those who are burned:*

[The mishnah's reference to the *mitzvah* of burning applies to the *mitzvah* incumbent upon the courts to mete out this punishment when it is called for.]

,הָיוּ מְשַׁקְּעִין אוֹתוֹ בְּזֶבֶל עַד אַרְכּוּבוֹתָיו — *They place* (lit., *sink*) *him in manure up to his knees,*

The condemned is made to stand in a pile of manure up to his knees. This prevents him from jumping around and thereby causing the molten lead (see below) to pour out on his flesh rather than down his throat (*Rav; Rashi*). Alternatively, this is done to protect those who execute him from being defecated upon by the condemned man during his death throes. Placing him in this situation prevents him from turning around and forces his executioners to be careful in positioning themselves (*Yad Ramah*).[1]

.וְנוֹתְנִין סוּדָר קָשָׁה לְתוֹךְ הָרַכָּה וְכוֹרֵךְ עַל צַוָּארוֹ — *and place a coarse* (lit., *hard*) *scarf inside a soft one and wind it around his neck.*

They wrap a soft scarf around a coarse one and then tighten it around his throat to force open his mouth. A soft scarf alone would not achieve the desired result while a strong, coarse cloth would abrade his neck. Therefore, this combination is used (*Rav; Rashi*). In

1. *Yad Ramah* explains the mishnah to require the use of manure; the silence of other commentators indicates their agreement. *Meiri*, however, states that even dirt or sand can be used to anchor him in place.

זֶה מוֹשֵׁךְ אֶצְלוֹ וְזֶה מוֹשֵׁךְ אֶצְלוֹ, עַד שֶׁפּוֹתֵחַ אֶת פִּיו. וּמַדְלִיק אֶת הַפְּתִילָה וְזוֹרְקָהּ לְתוֹךְ פִּיו; וְיוֹרֶדֶת לְתוֹךְ מֵעָיו וְחוֹמֶרֶת אֶת בְּנֵי מֵעָיו. רַבִּי יְהוּדָה אוֹמֵר: אַף הוּא אִם מֵת בְּיָדָם לֹא הָיוּ מְקַיְּמִין בּוֹ מִצְוַת שְׂרֵפָה. אֶלָּא פּוֹתְחִין אֶת פִּיו בִּצְבָת שֶׁלֹּא בְטוֹבָתוֹ; וּמַדְלִיק אֶת הַפְּתִילָה וְזוֹרְקָהּ לְתוֹךְ פִּיו, וְיוֹרֶדֶת לְתוֹךְ מֵעָיו וְחוֹמֶרֶת אֶת בְּנֵי מֵעָיו. אָמַר רַבִּי אֶלְעָזָר בֶּן צָדוֹק: מַעֲשֶׂה בְּבַת כֹּהֵן אַחַת שֶׁזִּנְּתָה, וְהִקִּיפוּהָ חֲבִילֵי זְמוֹרוֹת וּשְׂרָפוּהָ.

ר׳ עובדיה מברטנורא

את הפתילה. פתילה של אבר מדליק, ומתיך לתוך פיו: **וחומרת.** כוולת, לשון חמרמרו מעי (איכה ב,יא), וילפינן מבני אהרן שנאמר בהם (ויקרא י,ו) וכל בית ישראל יבכו את השרפה, ולא נשרפו גופתם, דהא כתיב (שם פסוק ה) ויקרבו וישאום בכותנותם, הכא נמי מתקיימת מצות שרפה אף על פי שאין נשרפים אלא בני מעים בלבד, והכי עדיף טפי, דכתיב (שם יט,יח) ואהבת לרעך כמוך, ברור לו מיתה יפה: **אף הוא אם מת בידם.** כלומר אם היה מת בידם על ידי חניקתם קודם זריקת הפתילה, לא היו מקיימים מצות שרפה, לפיכך לא היו חונקים אותו, אלא פותחים את פיו בצבת, טנאלוויי״א בלע״ז. ואין הלכה כרבי יהודה:

יד אברהם

addition, if only the coarse scarf were used it might choke him to death, and the obligation is to execute him by burning, not choking (*Yad Ramah*).

זֶה מוֹשֵׁךְ אֶצְלוֹ וְזֶה מוֹשֵׁךְ אֶצְלוֹ, עַד שֶׁפּוֹתֵחַ אֶת פִּיו. — *This one pulls toward himself and this one pulls toward himself until he opens his mouth.*

Each of the two witnesses who testified to his crime takes one end of the doubled cloth and pulls it toward himself, thereby forcing the condemned to open his mouth (*Meiri; Rambam, Sanhedrin* 15:3).

וּמַדְלִיק אֶת הַפְּתִילָה וְזוֹרְקָהּ לְתוֹךְ פִּיו; — *One melts a bar [of lead]* (lit., *lights a wick*) *and pours* (lit., *throws*) *it into his mouth;*

I.e., a hard piece of lead (*Gem.* 52a) is melted down (*Rashi*) to produce a liquefied mass which is then poured down the condemned's throat to kill him. [Although the sequence in which this point is presented in the mishnah is after the condemned's mouth was forced open, this was presumably done in advance, with a flame held to it continuously to keep it molten (*Tif. Yis.*).]

Yad Ramah, noting that the word פְּתִילָה usually means *wick,* suggests that the lead used for his purpose was shaped into long rods resembling wicks, to make it easier to melt. Since such rods are referred to as wicks, the *Tanna* refers to the process of applying a flame to them to melt them as *lighting the wick.*

וְיוֹרֶדֶת לְתוֹךְ מֵעָיו וְחוֹמֶרֶת אֶת בְּנֵי מֵעָיו. — *and it descends into his bowels and burns his intestines.*

This one pulls toward himself and this one pulls toward himself until he opens his mouth. One melts a bar [of lead] and pours it into his mouth; and it descends into his bowels and burns his intestines. R' Yehudah says: If he dies in their hands they have not fulfilled the commandment of burning. Rather, they force open his mouth with tongs; one melts the bar and pours it into his mouth, and it descends into his bowels and burns his intestines. Said R' Elazar ben Tzadok: It once occurred with the daughter of a *Kohen* that she committed adultery, and they surrounded her with bundles of branches and burned her.

YAD AVRAHAM

This results in a quick death and is what the Torah means when it decrees execution by burning. This is derived from the deaths of Nadav and Avihu, the sons of Aaron, when *they brought a strange fire before HASHEM*. The Torah (*Lev.* 10:6) describes their death as *burning*, despite the fact that only their insides were burnt but their bodies remained intact, as may be seen from the fact that they were carried out in their clothing (*Rav* from *Gem.* 52a).

רַבִּי יְהוּדָה אוֹמֵר: אַף הוּא אִם מֵת בְּיָדָם לֹא הָיוּ מְקַיְּמִין בּוֹ מִצְוַת שְׂרֵפָה. — R' Yehudah *says: If he dies in their hands they have not fulfilled the commandment of burning.*

He maintains that the process described above is not tenable, because it allows for the possibility that the condemned will die from choking, thereby negating the fulfillment of the court's obligation to execute him by burning (*Rav*).

אֶלָּא פוֹתְחִין אֶת פִּיו בִּצְבַת שֶׁלֹּא בְטוֹבָתוֹ; וּמַדְלִיק אֶת הַפְּתִילָה וְזוֹרְקָהּ לְתוֹךְ פִּיו, וְיוֹרֶדֶת לְתוֹךְ מֵעָיו וְחוֹמֶרֶת אֶת בְּנֵי מֵעָיו. — *Rather, they force open his mouth with tongs; one melts the bar and pours it into his mouth, and it descends into his bowels and burns his intestines.*

[By using tongs to force open his mouth, they avoid the possibility of choking him.]

The halachah, however, follows the first view (*Rav*; *Rambam*, loc. cit.).

אָמַר רַבִּי אֶלְעָזָר בֶּן צָדוֹק: מַעֲשֶׂה בְּבַת כֹּהֵן אַחַת שֶׁזִּנְּתָה, — *Said R' Elazar ben Tzadok: It once occurred with the daughter of a Kohen that she committed adultery,*

Unlike an ordinary woman who commits adultery, whose execution is strangulation (11:1), the punishment dictated by the Torah for an adulteress who is the daughter of a *Kohen* is burning (*Lev.* 21:9; mishnah 9:1).

וְהִקִּיפוּהָ חֲבִילֵי זְמוֹרוֹת וּשְׂרָפוּהָ. — *and they surrounded her with bundles of branches and burned her.*

[R' Eliezer ben Tzadok cites this precedent to prove that the proper

אָמְרוּ לוֹ: מִפְּנֵי שֶׁלֹּא הָיָה בֵית דִּין שֶׁל אוֹתָהּ שָׁעָה בָּקִי.

[ג] **מִצְוַת** הַנֶּהֱרָגִים: הָיוּ מַתִּיזִין אֶת רֹאשׁוֹ בְּסַיִף, כְּדֶרֶךְ שֶׁהַמַּלְכוּת עוֹשָׂה. רַבִּי יְהוּדָה אוֹמֵר: נִוּוּל הוּא זֶה. אֶלָּא מַנִּיחִין אֶת רֹאשׁוֹ עַל הַסַּדָּן וְקוֹצֵץ בְּקוֹפִיץ. אָמְרוּ לוֹ: אֵין מִיתָה מְנֻוֶּלֶת מִזּוֹ.

מִצְוַת הַנֶּחֱנָקִין: הָיוּ מְשַׁקְּעִין אוֹתוֹ בְּזֶבֶל עַד אַרְכּוּבוֹתָיו, וְנוֹתְנִין סוּדָר קָשָׁה לְתוֹךְ הָרַכָּה

ר׳ עובדיה מברטנורא

שלא היה בית דין של אותה שעה בקי. צדוקין היו, שאין להם [גזירה שוה], אלא קרא כמשמעו: (ג) **רבי יהודה אומר ניוול הוא זה.** שהורגו מעומד ונופל: **סדן.** עץ עבה תקוע בארץ כמות של נפחים, ובברייתא (נב,ב) פירש, דטעמא דפליג רבי יהודה אדרבנן, מפני שאמרה תורה (שם יח,ג) ובחוקותיהם לא תלכו, ואמרי ליה רבנן, כיון דכתיב סייף באורייתא, דאמר קרא נקום ינקם (שמות כא,כ), לא מינייהו גמרינן. והלכה כחכמים:

יד אברהם

means of carrying out the obligation to execute through burning is to set the person on fire.]

אָמְרוּ לוֹ: מִפְּנֵי שֶׁלֹּא הָיָה בֵית דִּין שֶׁל אוֹתָהּ שָׁעָה בָּקִי. — *They said to him: Because the court at that time was not expert.*

This was done by a court of Sadducees, who rejected the Oral Tradition and explained the Written Torah in whatever manner it seemed to them to mean literally (*Rav* from *Gem.* 52b). Having no tradition on which to base themselves, they burned her in this manner. Our tradition extending back to Moshe at Sinai, however, is to burn in the manner described in the mishnah.

3.

מִצְוַת הַנֶּהֱרָגִים: הָיוּ מַתִּיזִין אֶת רֹאשׁוֹ בְּסַיִף, כְּדֶרֶךְ שֶׁהַמַּלְכוּת עוֹשָׂה. — *[This is] the procedure for those who are beheaded: They decapitate him with a sword, in the manner in which the government does.*

While the condemned is standing, they cut off his head from the front, severing his trachea and esophagus and killing him instantly (*Meiri*). This was the manner in which civil authorities [i.e., the Roman government] of that time would behead their convicts (*Tif. Yis.*).

רַבִּי יְהוּדָה אוֹמֵר: נִוּוּל הוּא זֶה. — *R' Yehudah says: This is a disgrace.*

It is too great a disgrace to the condemned for his head to be chopped so that it falls to the ground from a standing position (*Rav; Rashi*).

They said to him: Because the court at that time was not expert.

3. [This is] the procedure for those who are beheaded: They decapitate him with a sword, in the manner in which the government does. R' Yehudah says: This is a disgrace. Rather, they place his head on a block and cut it off with an axe. They said to him: There is no more disgraceful manner of death than this.

[This is] the procedure for those who are strangled: They place him in manure up to his knees, and place a coarse scarf inside a soft one

YAD AVRAHAM

Actually the method he proposes is also a disgrace (see below). However, since that of the first *Tanna* entails the example of the Roman government, it is preferable to carry out the execution in a different way, in line with the prohibition (*Lev.* 18:3) against following the customs of the gentiles (*Gem.* 52b; *Meiri*).

Alternatively, the disgrace meant by R' Yehudah is to the Torah, to execute in the manner of the government and thereby violate the prohibition on imitating the gentile customs (*Tos.; Yad Ramah*).

אֶלָּא מַנִּיחִין אֶת רֹאשׁוֹ עַל הַסַּדָּן וְקוֹצֵץ בְּקוֹפִיץ. — *Rather, they place his head on a block and cut it off with an axe.*

אָמְרוּ לוֹ: אֵין מִיתָה מְנֻוֶּלֶת מִזּוֹ. — *They said to him: There is no more disgraceful manner of death than this.*

The Sages contend that the method of execution proposed by R' Yehudah is an even more disgraceful manner of death, because the blade of an axe is not as sharp as that of a sword and it smashes part of the neck rather than cutting it cleanly (*Yad Ramah*). They are not deterred by that which the method they propose is used by the gentiles, since they derive it from the Torah (*Deut.* 13:16) and not from following the example of the Romans (*Gem.* loc. cit.).

According to the alternate interpretation of R' Yehudah cited above, that he considers it a disgrace to the Torah, the Rabbis misunderstood his statement and therefore replied that the method he proposes is even more disgraceful (*Yad Ramah*).

The halachah follows the view of the Sages (*Rav; Rambam, Sanhedrin* 15:4).

מִצְוַת הַנֶּחֱנָקִין: הָיוּ מְשַׁקְּעִין אוֹתוֹ בְּזֶבֶל עַד אַרְכּוּבוֹתָיו, — *[This is] the procedure for those who are strangled: They place* (lit., *sink*) *him in manure up to his knees,*

It is necessary to immobilize him in this manner to prevent him from flopping around and thereby prolonging his execution, thus caus-

וְכוֹרֵךְ עַל צַוָּארוֹ. זֶה מוֹשֵׁךְ אֶצְלוֹ וְזֶה מוֹשֵׁךְ אֶצְלוֹ, עַד שֶׁנַּפְשׁוֹ יוֹצְאָה.

[ד] **אֵלּוּ** הֵן הַנִּסְקָלִין: הַבָּא עַל הָאֵם, וְעַל אֵשֶׁת הָאָב, וְעַל הַכַּלָּה, וְעַל הַזָּכוּר, וְעַל הַבְּהֵמָה, וְהָאִשָּׁה הַמְּבִיאָה אֶת הַבְּהֵמָה; וְהַמְגַדֵּף, וְהָעוֹבֵד עֲבוֹדָה זָרָה, וְהַנּוֹתֵן מִזַּרְעוֹ לַמֹּלֶךְ,

ר׳ עובדיה מברטנורא

(ד) **אלו הן הנסקלין.** אית מינייהו דכתיב בהו סקילה בהדיא, והנך דלא כתיבא בהו סקילה, כתיב בהו דמיו בו דמיהם בם, וכל מקום שנאמר דמיו בו דמיהם בם, אינו אלא סקילה, דילפינן מאוב וידעוני, דכתיב (ויקרא כ,כז) באבן ירגמו אותם דמיהם בם: **והנותן מזרעו למולך.** קסבר האי תנא מולך לאו עבודה זרה הוא, אלא חק האומות בעלמא הוא, מדתנא עבודה זרה, ותנא מולך:

יד אברהם

ing unnecessary suffering (*Tif. Yis.*; cf. *Lechem Mishneh* to *Hil. Sanhedrin* 15:3).

Alternatively, this was done to prevent the condemned from defecating on his executioners during his death throes, as explained in the previous mishnah (*Yad Ramah* to mishnah 2).

וְנוֹתְנִין סוּדָר קָשָׁה לְתוֹךְ הָרַכָּה וְכוֹרֵךְ עַל צַוָּארוֹ. זֶה מוֹשֵׁךְ אֶצְלוֹ וְזֶה מוֹשֵׁךְ אֶצְלוֹ, עַד שֶׁנַּפְשׁוֹ יוֹצְאָה. — *and place a coarse scarf inside a soft one and wind it around his neck. This one pulls toward himself and this one pulls toward himself until his life departs.*

[The two witnesses wind this scarf combination around the condemned's neck and pull in opposite directions until he dies of strangulation. This is the same procedure as that used to force open the condemned's mouth for burning (mishnah 2), except that in this case they continue to pull until he is strangled to death. Here, too, the combination of a soft and coarse cloth is necessary, because the soft one would not effect the strangulation and the coarse one would abrade his neck (cf. *Lechem Mishneh* loc. cit.).]

4.

Having described the four methods of execution mandated by the Torah, the mishnah now goes on to list the specific offenses for which each of these punishments is incurred, beginning with stoning. After listing them, the mishnah will discuss each one in greater detail.

אֵלּוּ הֵן הַנִּסְקָלִין: — *These are the ones who are stoned:*

In some of the cases listed, the Torah explicitly specifies stoning as the method of execution. Concerning others, it uses the terms דָּמָיו בּוֹ or דְּמֵיהֶם בָּם, *their blood is upon them.* This same term is used in reference to a necromancer or wizard, for whom the Torah explicitly mandates the

and wind it around his neck. This one pulls toward himself and this one pulls toward himself until his life departs.

4. **T**hese are the ones who are stoned: one who cohabits with his mother, or his father's wife, or [his] daughter-in-law, or with a male, or an animal, or a woman who brings an animal [upon herself]; a blasphemer, an idolater, one who offers of his children to *Molech,*

YAD AVRAHAM

punishment of stoning. We thus infer that whenever these terms are used, stoning is the appropriate punishment. Still others from among those listed are derived exegetically to require this method of execution (*Rav*).

הַבָּא עַל הָאֵם, וְעַל אֵשֶׁת הָאָב, — *one who cohabits with his mother* (lit., *one who comes upon his mother*), *or his father's wife,*

One is forbidden to his father's wife even if she is not his mother, and even if his father is no longer married to her (see below). These two prohibitions are stated in *Lev.* 18:7,8. Both the man and the woman are subject to the punishment (*Gem.* 54b) [if she was a willing partner to it].

וְעַל הַכַּלָּה, — *or [his] daughter-in-law,*

See *Lev.* 18:15, 20:12. This is even if she is no longer married to his son; see below. Here too both parties are subject to this punishment (*Gem.*).

וְעַל הַזְּכוּר, וְעַל הַבְּהֵמָה, — *or with a male, or an animal,*

Unnatural acts between two men are expressly forbidden in *Lev.* 18:22 and 20:13. The prohibition of bestiality is stated in 18:23 and 20:15.

Although the mishnah specifies a בְּהֵמָה, *domesticated animal,* the same applies to one who commits bestiality with a wild animal or fowl (*Meiri;* see *Margoliyos HaYam* to 54a).

וְהָאִשָּׁה הַמְּבִיאָה אֶת הַבְּהֵמָה; — *or a woman who brings an animal [upon herself];*

The previous case referred to a man who commits an act of bestiality; this one refers to a woman who does so; see *Lev.* 18:23, 20:16.

וְהַמְגַדֵּף, וְהָעוֹבֵד עֲבוֹדָה זָרָה, וְהַנּוֹתֵן מִזַּרְעוֹ לַמֹּלֶךְ, — *a blasphemer, an idolater, one who offers of his children to Molech,*

The blasphemer is stated in *Lev.* 24:16, the idolater in several places (see below, mishnah 6).

Molech was a pagan practice in which a man passed his children over a flame in honor of an entity called *Molech* (see mishnah 7). The Torah forbids this practice in *Lev.* 18:21. The *Tanna* of this mishnah follows the view that *Molech* was not deemed a deity, and its service is thus not included in the category of idolatry (*Rav* from *Gem.* 64a).

וּבַעַל אוֹב וְיִדְּעוֹנִי; וְהַמְחַלֵּל אֶת הַשַּׁבָּת; וְהַמְקַלֵּל אָבִיו וְאִמּוֹ; וְהַבָּא עַל נַעֲרָה הַמְאֹרָסָה; וְהַמֵּסִית, וְהַמַּדִּיחַ, וְהַמְכַשֵּׁף, וּבֵן סוֹרֵר וּמוֹרֶה.

הַבָּא עַל הָאֵם חַיָּב עָלֶיהָ מִשּׁוּם אֵם וּמִשּׁוּם אֵשֶׁת אָב. רַבִּי יְהוּדָה אוֹמֵר:

ר׳ עובדיה מברטנורא

והמקלל אביו ואמו. חמור ממכה, דאיכא תרתי, קלון אביו ואמו ומוציא שם שמים לבטלה, דהא תנן (לעיל משנה ח׳) אינו חייב עד שיקללם בשם: **והמסית.** את היחידים: **והמדיח.** עיר הנדחת: **מכשף.** דכתיב (שמות כב,יז) מכשפה לא תחיה, וסמיך ליה (שם פסוק יח) כל שוכב עם בהמה מות יומת, מה שוכב עם בהמה בסקילה, אף מכשפה בסקילה: **הבא על האם חייב עליה.** שתי חטאות, דבכולהו עריות [כתיב בהו כרת וכתיב בהו] חלוק חטאות, ואפילו בגוף אחד. וכן הלכה:

יד אברהם

וּבַעַל אוֹב וְיִדְּעוֹנִי; — *a practitioner of Ov or a Yidoni;*

[These were different ways of communicating with the dead. The practitioners of these black arts were subject to the death penalty. This will be more fully described below in mishnah 7.]

וְהַמְחַלֵּל אֶת הַשַּׁבָּת; — *one who desecrates the Sabbath;*

[I.e., he performs one of the prohibited labors; see below, mishnah 8.]

וְהַמְקַלֵּל אָבִיו וְאִמּוֹ; — *one who curses his father or mother;*

[I.e., he curses them using the name of God (see mishnah 8).]

This is considered a more serious offense than one who assaults them physically [who is punished with the less severe execution of strangulation (11:1)] because it involves the desecration of God's Name as well as the humiliation of his parents (*Rav; Rashi*).

וְהַבָּא עַל נַעֲרָה הַמְאֹרָסָה; — *one who cohabits with a betrothed naarah;*

[The first six months of a girl's maturity are governed by different laws than those which apply to adult women. This period is known as *naarus.* A girl becomes a *naarah* at the age of twelve provided she has at least two pubic hairs, and she retains that classification until a half year later.

In Torah law, marriage takes place in two stages — *erusin,* betrothal, and *nisuin,* full marriage. *Erusin,* the first stage of the marriage process, prevents the woman from marrying anyone else and renders relations with any other man adulterous; however, until *nisuin* has been performed, she may not yet live with her husband. Today, both these procedures are done at the same time — *erusin* with the giving of the ring and *nisuin* with the *chupah* and seclusion in the bridal chamber. In earlier times, however, these two procedures were separated by a significant amount of time, often as much

a practitioner of *Ov* or a *Yidoni;* one who desecrates the Sabbath; one who curses his father or mother; one who cohabits with a betrothed *naarah;* one who instigates [an individual to idolatry], one who leads astray [an entire town], a sorcerer, and a *ben sorer umoreh.*

One who cohabits with [his] mother is liable for [having transgressed the prohibitions of] a mother and a father's wife. R' Yehudah says:

YAD AVRAHAM

as a year (see ArtScroll Introduction to *Kiddushin*). Thus, a betrothed *naarah* is a physically mature girl between the ages of twelve and twelve and a half who is betrothed to a man through *erusin* but has not yet completed her marriage with *nisuin.*]

וְהַמֵּסִית, וְהַמַּדִּיחַ, — *one who instigates [an individual to idolatry], one who leads astray [an entire town],*

[I.e., someone who influences others to practice idolatry — either an individual or an entire city. See mishnah 10 for a full explanation.]

וְהַמְכַשֵּׁף, — *a sorcerer,*

See below, mishnah 11.

וּבֵן סוֹרֵר וּמוֹרֶה. — *and a ben sorer umoreh.*

The Torah decrees that a delinquent son immediately past his bar mitzvah can, under certain conditions, be executed for his delinquencies (*Deut.* 21:18-21); see Chapter 8.

There are thus a total of eighteen offenses which call for the punishment of stoning; seven involve illicit intimate relations, eight are related to issues of faith, two to one's relationship with his parents and one with the Sabbath. The mishnah now elaborates upon them (*Meiri*).

הַבָּא עַל הָאֵם חַיָּב עָלֶיהָ מִשּׁוּם אֵם וּמִשּׁוּם אֵשֶׁת אָב. — *One who cohabits with [his] mother is liable for [having transgressed the prohibitions of] a mother and a father's wife.*

[If one has relations with his father's wife, who is also his mother] he has transgressed two distinct prohibitions. If he did so deliberately, this point is moot, since he can only be executed once. The mishnah teaches, however, that if someone inadvertently cohabits with his mother (e.g., thinking she was someone else), he must bring two sin-offerings, one for transgressing the prohibition of cohabiting with his mother and one for cohabiting with the wife of his father, which is a separate prohibition in the Torah (*Lev.* 18:8).

These two prohibitions, in common with all the forbidden relationships for which there is a death penalty, are also subject to the penalty of *kares* (Divinely imposed premature death) if the court-mandated death penalty cannot be invoked for some reason (e.g., lack of witnesses or proper warning). As such, their inadvertent transgression is subject to the requirement of a sin-offering for atonement (*Rav*).

אֵינוֹ חַיָּב אֶלָּא מִשּׁוּם הָאֵם בִּלְבָד. הַבָּא עַל אֵשֶׁת אָב חַיָּב עָלֶיהָ מִשּׁוּם אֵשֶׁת אָב וּמִשּׁוּם אֵשֶׁת אִישׁ, בֵּין בְּחַיֵּי אָבִיו בֵּין לְאַחַר מִיתַת אָבִיו, בֵּין מִן הָאֵרוּסִין בֵּין מִן הַנִּשּׂוּאִין. הַבָּא עַל כַּלָּתוֹ חַיָּב עָלֶיהָ מִשּׁוּם כַּלָּתוֹ וּמִשּׁוּם אֵשֶׁת אִישׁ, בֵּין בְּחַיֵּי בְנוֹ בֵּין לְאַחַר מִיתַת בְּנוֹ, בֵּין מִן הָאֵרוּסִין בֵּין מִן הַנִּשּׂוּאִין.

ר' עובדיה מברטנורא

בין מן האירוסין. דכיון שקדשה, אשתו היא, דכתיב (ויקרא כב,יג) ואיש כי יקח אשה, משמע לקיחה נקראת אשתו, והך קיחה קדושין הן, דגמר קיחה קיחה משדה עפרון:

יד אברהם

Although he performed only one illicit act, the *Gemara* (*Makkos* 14a) derives that one deed which includes two transgressions obligates a person to bring two offerings (*Rav; Rashi*).[1]

This ruling has application in a case of intentional transgression as well, in that in order to be liable for the death penalty, one must be warned in advance of the transgression. If he was warned by the witnesses in regard to either of the prohibitions involved, it is a valid warning and he is punished for the deed (*Yerushalmi*, cited by *Meiri*).

The mishnah does not cite the additional prohibition of adultery, because it is discussing a case in which the perpetrator's father was no longer alive; the two prohibitions of a mother and father's wife, however, apply even after his death (*Tos.*).

רַבִּי יְהוּדָה אוֹמֵר: אֵינוֹ חַיָּב אֶלָּא מִשּׁוּם הָאֵם בִּלְבָד. — *R' Yehudah says: He is liable only for a mother.*

[R' Yehudah contends that only the prohibition against relations with one's mother applies.] This is derived by him from the words (*Lev.* 17:7): She is your mother, which he construes as a limiting clause indicating that he is liable for that prohibition and no other (*Gem.* 53b).

הַבָּא עַל אֵשֶׁת אָב חַיָּב עָלֶיהָ מִשּׁוּם אֵשֶׁת אָב וּמִשּׁוּם אֵשֶׁת אִישׁ, — *One who cohabits with his father's wife is liable for a father's wife and for adultery,*

[His father's wife is prohibited to him even if she is not his mother, as noted above. In addition, if she is presently married to his father, he is liable for adultery as well.] R' Yehudah, however, disagrees in this case as well and contends that only the prohibition against cohabiting with one's father's wife applies, as derived from that which the Torah stresses (ibid.): *She is the nakedness of your father* (*Gem.* 54a).

בֵּין בְּחַיֵּי אָבִיו בֵּין לְאַחַר מִיתַת אָבִיו, — *both during his father's lifetime and after his death,*

This refers only to the prohibition against his father's wife, which continues to apply even after the father

1. If his father was never married to his mother, however, he is liable only for the prohibition of a mother (see *Yevamos* 11:1; *Rambam, Issurei Biah* 2:1).

He is liable only for a mother. One who cohabits with his father's wife is liable for a father's wife and for adultery, both during his father's lifetime and after his death, whether she was betrothed or married. One who cohabits with his daughter-in-law is liable for his daughter-in-law and for adultery, both during his son's lifetime and after his death, whether she was betrothed or married.

YAD AVRAHAM

has died [or divorced her; *Rambam, Isurei Biah* 2:1]. The adultery prohibition, however, applies only as long as the woman is still married (*Rashi*).

.בֵּין מִן הָאֲרוּסִין בֵּין מִן הַנְּשׂוּאִין — *whether she was betrothed or married.*

Whether the woman had been fully married to his father through the process of *nisuin* or had only undergone the initial procedure of *erusin,* these prohibitions apply, because once a woman has undergone *erusin* she is considered the man's wife by Torah law, and all prohibitions relating to that state take effect immediately (*Rav; Rashi*).

הַבָּא עַל כַּלָּתוֹ חַיָּב עָלֶיהָ מִשּׁוּם כַּלָּתוֹ וּמִשּׁוּם אֵשֶׁת אִישׁ, — *One who cohabits with his daughter-in-law is liable for his daughter-in-law and for adultery,*

The Torah states explicitly (*Lev.* 18:15): *You shall not reveal the nakedness of your daughter-in-law; she is the wife of your son; do not reveal her nakedness.* Transgression of this injunction is punishable by stoning, as derived from the words דְּמֵיהֶם בָּם, *their blood is upon them* (*Lev.* 20:12). [As in the previous case, if he had relations with her while she was still married to his son, he also transgresses the prohibition against adultery.]

Although the verse cited seems to express two distinct prohibitions, one due to that which she is his daughter-in-law [i.e., and thus his relative] and one for the fact of her being married to his son, the phrase she is the wife of your son indicates that this is all one prohibition (*Gem.* 54a; *Rashi* ibid.).

The distinction drawn between this case and that of one's mother [in which she is prohibited for that which she is his mother as well as for that which she is his father's wife] is easily understood, since the relationships of mother and father's wife can exist independently of each other [i.e., one's mother can have conceived him out of wedlock and his father's wife is obviously not necessarily his mother], whereas those of daughter-in-law and son's life are inseparable (*Meiri*).

בֵּין בְּחַיֵּי בְנוֹ בֵּין לְאַחַר מִיתַת בְּנוֹ, בֵּין מִן הָאֲרוּסִין בֵּין מִן הַנְּשׂוּאִין. — *both during his son's lifetime and after his death, whether she was betrothed or married.*

Here, too, the first statement refers only to the prohibition of daughter-in-law and not that of adultery (*Meiri*). I.e., the daughter-in-law prohibition remains in effect even after the marriage to his son has terminated and even if she had only been betrothed to his son and never completed the marriage.

סנהדרין
ז/ה

הַבָּא עַל הַזְּכוּר, וְעַל הַבְּהֵמָה, וְהָאִשָּׁה הַמְבִיאָה אֶת הַבְּהֵמָה: אִם אָדָם חָטָא, בְּהֵמָה מֶה חָטָאת? אֶלָּא לְפִי שֶׁבָּאת לָאָדָם תַּקָּלָה עַל יָדָהּ, לְפִיכָךְ אָמַר הַכָּתוּב תִּסָּקֵל. דָּבָר אַחֵר, שֶׁלֹּא תְהֵא הַבְּהֵמָה עוֹבֶרֶת בַּשּׁוּק וְיֹאמְרוּ ,,זוֹ הִיא שֶׁנִּסְקַל פְּלוֹנִי עַל יָדָהּ״.

[ה] **הַמְגַדֵּף** אֵינוֹ חַיָּב עַד שֶׁיְּפָרֵשׁ אֶת הַשֵּׁם. אָמַר רַבִּי יְהוֹשֻׁעַ בֶּן

ר׳ עובדיה מברטנורא

(ה) **עד שיפרש את השם.** ויברך השם בשם, שנאמר (שם כד,טז) ונוקב שם ה׳ בנקבו שם, שיקוב השם בשם: **בכל יום.** כל זמן שהיו נושאים ונותנים בבדיקת העדים:

יד אברהם

הַבָּא עַל הַזְּכוּר, וְעַל הַבְּהֵמָה, וְהָאִשָּׁה הַמְּבִיאָה אֶת הַבְּהֵמָה: — *One who cohabits with [another] man, or an animal, and a woman who brings an animal [upon herself]:*

The verse (*Lev.* 20:13) states in regard to homosexual activity דְּמֵיהֶם בָּם, *their blood is upon them,* thereby teaching that both participants are stoned. The punishment for bestiality is given there (vs. 15,16) in terms of מוֹת יוּמָת, *shall be put to death,* which is interpreted exegetically to refer to stoning.

[These three cases are listed here to introduce the mishnah's elaboration on them.] Although no new information is added concerning the first of these, it is repeated along with the others in order to follow the order of the cases as cited (*Meiri;* cf. *Yad Ramah; Meleches Shlomo*).

אִם אָדָם חָטָא, בְּהֵמָה מֶה חָטָאת? — *If the person sinned, what did the animal sin?*

The Torah decrees in reference to bestiality (*Lev.* 23:15) that the animal which participated in the act be executed along with the transgressor (*Meiri*). [Since an animal is obviously not bound to the commandments of the Torah, why should it be destroyed for this act?]

אֶלָּא לְפִי שֶׁבָּאת לְאָדָם תַּקָּלָה עַל יָדָהּ, לְפִיכָךְ אָמַר הַכָּתוּב תִּסָּקֵל. — *But because a person came to disaster through it, Scripture said that it should be stoned.*

Since this animal was the object of a man's sin (*Rashi*), it too is destroyed.

דָּבָר אַחֵר, שֶׁלֹּא תְהֵא הַבְּהֵמָה עוֹבֶרֶת בַּשּׁוּק וְיֹאמְרוּ ,,זוֹ הִיא שֶׁנִּסְקַל פְּלוֹנִי עַל יָדָהּ״. — *In addition, so that it should not occur that the animal passes in the street and people say, "This is the one through whom so-and-so was stoned."*

The Torah is concerned with the dignity of even the sinner, and therefore requires that the animal be executed to preclude the possibility of his posthumous disgrace by having people reminded by the continued presence of the animal of the shameful act he committed (*Tif. Yis.*).

One who cohabits with [another] man, or an animal, and a woman who brings an animal [upon herself]: If the person sinned, what did the animal sin? But because a person came to disaster through it, Scripture said that it should be stoned. In addition, so that it should not occur that the animal passes in the street and people say, "This is the one through whom so-and-so was stoned."

5. The blasphemer is not liable unless he utters the [Divine] Name. Said R' Yehoshua ben

YAD AVRAHAM

The *Gemara* notes that this second explanation actually includes both reasons for executing the animal, i.e., in addition to the humiliation clearly mentioned, the reference to the stoning also denotes the idea of the animal being the means whereby someone came to disaster. Thus, the first explanation is redundant, and is stated only to indicate that one of these two reasons is sufficient by itself to warrant the execution of the animal (*Rashi*). However, the *Gemara* is unable to reach a conclusion as to which of the two is intended. Therefore, in any case in which only one of the reasons applies — e.g., the act was performed by a minor, who is not responsible for his actions and cannot be considered to have sinned — the animal cannot be executed, since it is uncertain whether the reason which is applicable in this case is sufficient to warrant his execution (*Rambam, Hil. Melachim* 9:6; *Kesef Mishneh* ad loc.).

5.

הַמְגַדֵּף — *The blasphemer*

[I.e., one who curses the Name of God.] The prohibition against doing so is stated in *Exodus* (22:27), and the punishment of stoning is stated explicitly (*Lev.* 24:16).

.אֵינוֹ חַיָּב עַד שֶׁיְּפָרֵשׁ אֶת הַשֵּׁם — *is not liable unless he utters the [Divine] Name.*

He is punished by stoning only if he actually said the Name of God and cursed it, not if he heard others mention it and reacted with a curse (*Rashi*).

The name under discussion is the four-letter Name spelled *yud, kei, vav, kei* (*Meiri*). According to *Rambam* (*Hil. Avodah Zarah* 2:7), the same ruling applies if he uttered in its place the name *alef, daleth, nun, yud* [i.e., the way the four-letter Name is commonly pronounced]. *Yad Ramah*, however, disputes this.

This punishment applies only if he blasphemed the Name with the Name — viz., "May *Yose* smite *Yose*." [As the mishnah will explain below, the name *Yose* was substituted for the Name of *HASHEM* in the discussions of blasphemy to avoid the mention of anything blasphemous during the legal proceeding.] This is derived from the verse (*Lev.* 24:16), *And one who curses the Name of HASHEM shall be put to death ... upon his cursing the Name he shall be put to death.* The repetition of the verse is meant to indicate that

סנהדרין
ז/ה

קָרְחָה: בְּכָל יוֹם דָּנִין אֶת הָעֵדִים בְּכִנּוּי — ,,יַכֶּה יוֹסֵי אֶת יוֹסֵי״. נִגְמַר הַדִּין, לֹא הוֹרְגִים בְּכִנּוּי. אֶלָּא, מוֹצִיאִים אֶת כָּל הָאָדָם לַחוּץ וְשׁוֹאֲלִים אֶת הַגָּדוֹל שֶׁבָּהֶן וְאוֹמְרִים לוֹ ,,אֱמֹר מַה שֶּׁשָּׁמַעְתָּ בְּפֵרוּשׁ״, וְהוּא אוֹמֵר. וְהַדַּיָּנִים עוֹמְדִין עַל רַגְלֵיהֶן וְקוֹרְעִין וְלֹא מְאַחִין.

ר׳ עובדיה מברטנורא

היו דנין אותן בבינוי. כל אדם שמהפך דבר ומדבר כמו שמקלל ותולה באחר, קרוי כינוי בלשון חכמים, ובלשון מקרא, כי לא ידעתי אכנה (איוב לב,כב): **יכה יוסי את יוסי.** אני שמעתי מפני שהוא בן ארבע אותיות ועולה בגימטריא אלהי״ם, לכך מכנים שם בן ארבע אותיות ליוסי: **נגמר הדין.** ובאים בית דין לומר חייב הוא, לא היו יכולים להרגו על פי עדות זו ששמעו, שהרי לא שמעו מפיהם אלא קללת כנוי: **אלא מוציאים את כל האדם לחוץ.** דגלאי הוא להשמיע ברכת השם לרבים: **וקורעין ולא מאחין.** עולמית, תפירה אלכסנדרית, שאין הקריעה ניכרת, אבל שאר תפירות מותר:

יד אברהם

only if the Name is blasphemed with the Name is it punishable by death (*Rav* from *Gem.* 56a). Some maintain that this requires that the Sacred Name of *yud, kei,* etc. be cursed in that name; if any other name is used the punishment is flogging but not death (*Yad Ramah*). Others contend that if the Sacred Name is cursed using any of the seven Names of HASHEM which may not be erased (see *Rambam, Hil. Yesodei HaTorah* 6:2), the blasphemer is subject to death by stoning (*Rambam,* loc. cit.; see *Meiri*).

אָמַר רַבִּי יְהוֹשֻׁעַ בֶּן קָרְחָה: בְּכָל יוֹם דָּנִין אֶת הָעֵדִים בְּכִנּוּי — *Said R' Yehoshua ben Karchah: Each day they examine the witnesses by means of a pseudonym —*

Throughout the time in which the judges investigate the case and interview the witnesses, reference to the alleged transgression is made without actually mentioning the Name of HASHEM (*Meiri*).

,,יַכֶּה יוֹסֵי אֶת יוֹסֵי״. — (i.e.) "May Yose smite Yose."

The name Yose is substituted for the Name of *Hashem* to avoid repeating the terrible blasphemy in court (*Tif. Yis.*). This name was chosen to substitute for the name of God because it too consists of four letters and adds up numerically to the same value as the name *Elokim* (*Rav; Rashi*).

נִגְמַר הַדִּין, לֹא הוֹרְגִים בְּכִנּוּי. — *[When] the case is completed, they may not kill [based] upon a pseudonym.*

The court may not sentence the accused to death based on the testimony they have heard, since it has not yet been stated explicitly that he actually blasphemed the Name of God (*Rav*). It is possible that he, too, uttered only the name *Yose* in place of that of Hashem, and that the witnesses are trying to have him put to death illicitly without actually giving false testimony (*Meiri*).

אֶלָּא, מוֹצִיאִים אֶת כָּל הָאָדָם לַחוּץ — *Rather, they send everyone out*

7
5

Karchah: Each day they examine the witnesses by means of a pseudonym — "May Yose smite Yose." [When] the case is completed, they may not kill [based] upon a pseudonym. Rather, they send everyone out and ask the most eminent of them and say to him, "State explicitly what you heard," and he says [it]. The judges stand on their feet and rend [their garments] and do not repair [them].

YAD AVRAHAM

The courtroom is cleared of everyone but the witnesses and judges — even those who usually remain inside when testimony is received, such as the scribes (*Tif. Yis.*) — so that the desecration of Hashem's Name should not be expressed in front of more people than absolutely necessary (*Rav*).

וְשׁוֹאֲלִים אֶת הַגָּדוֹל שֶׁבָּהֶן — *and ask the most eminent of them*

They make the following request to the chief witness, in the presence of the others (*Meiri*).

וְאוֹמְרִים לוֹ ,,אֱמֹר מַה שֶּׁשָּׁמַעְתָּ בְּפֵרוּשׁ", וְהוּא אוֹמֵר. — *and say to him, "State explicitly what you heard," and he says [it].*

This one time the witness must repeat the actual words of the blasphemer (*Meiri; Rambam, Avodah Zarah* 2:8).

Yerushalmi states that he does not repeat his actual words but rather cites the Name of God which was cursed and then states that the suspect cursed this Name by this Name. However, the wording of our mishnah does not seem to convey this interpretation (*Meiri*), nor does our *Gemara* mention it (*Tos. Yom Tov*).

וְהַדַּיָּנִים עוֹמְדִין עַל רַגְלֵיהֶן — *The judges stand on their feet*

This is derived from the story in prophets (*Judges* 3), in which Eglon, the king of Moab, rose at the mention of the Name of Hashem, even though the Sacred Name was not mentioned. Certainly we, the Jewish people, must rise at the mention of the Sacred Name (*Gem.* 60a).

וְקוֹרְעִין — *and rend [their garments]*

[As a sign of anguish over this terrible desecration of Hashem's Name.] This, too, is derived from an episode in *Prophets*. When the king of Assyria who was besieging Jerusalem sent back the messengers of King Hezekiah with a message of blasphemy, all who heard rent their garments (*II Kings* 18:37), as did Hezekiah upon receiving that message (ibid. 19:1).

The law concerning the rending of garments differs from that of the punishment of stoning, in that it is not necessary for one to hear the Name blasphemed with the Name to be obligated to rend (*Ran*). Some maintain that this obligation applies only if one hears the Sacred Name or one of the seven Names which may not be erased blasphemed (*Meiri*). Others contend that any blasphemy of God calls for this response, even if no such Name is used (*Rambam, Hil. Avodah Zarah* 2:10).

וְלֹא מְאַחִין. — *and do not repair [them].*

I.e., this rip may never be repaired. However, it is permitted to sew the rip in a manner which does not totally obviate the effects of it having been torn (*Rav; Rambam Comm.*). [This

וְהַשֵּׁנִי אוֹמֵר: אַף אֲנִי כָּמוֹהוּ; וְהַשְּׁלִישִׁי אוֹמֵר: אַף אֲנִי כָּמוֹהוּ.

[ו] **הָעוֹבֵד** עֲבוֹדָה זָרָה — אֶחָד הָעוֹבֵד, וְאֶחָד הַזּוֹבֵחַ, וְאֶחָד הַמְקַטֵּר, וְאֶחָד הַמְנַסֵּךְ, וְאֶחָד הַמִּשְׁתַּחֲוֶה, וְאֶחָד הַמְקַבְּלוֹ עָלָיו לֶאֱלוֹהַּ, וְהָאוֹמֵר לוֹ „אֵלִי אַתָּה״.

ר׳ עובדיה מברטנורא

אף אני שמעתי כמוהו. ואינו צריך להזכיר ברכת שם בשם: **והשלישי אומר.** אתיא כמאן דאמר מה שנים עדות אחת אף שלשה עדות אחת: **(ו) אחד העובד עבודה זרה.** בדבר שדרך עבודתה בכך: **ואחד המזבח כו׳.** ואף על פי שאין דרך עבודתה באחת מארבע עבודות הללו, חייב, וכל שאר עבודות חוץ מאלו, אינו חייב עד שיעבוד כדרך עבודתה: **והמקבלו עליו באלוה.** אפילו באמירה בעלמא, דאתקש לזביחה, דכתיב (שמות לב,ח) ויזבחו לו ויאמרו אלה אלהיך: **והאומר לו אלי אתה.** בפניו, ואתא סיפא לגלויי רישא, דאי תנא רישא, הוי אמינא הני מילי בפניו אבל שלא בפניו לא, תנא סיפא בפניו, מכלל דרישא שלא בפניו, ואפילו הכי חייב:

יד אברהם

rent is thus treated in the same fashion as that torn over the death of a parent — see *Yoreh Deah* 340:15.]

וְהַשֵּׁנִי אוֹמֵר: אַף אֲנִי כָּמוֹהוּ; — *The second says: I too [heard] as he did;*

Since a person can be convicted only on the testimony of two witnesses, it is necessary for the second witness as well to state his testimony unambiguously. However, it is not necessary for him to repeat the actual blasphemy but merely to testify that he too heard that which the first repeated (*Rav*). Although it is generally required of each witness to repeat the testimony on his own, that is a Rabbinic enactment which is waived to avoid further desecration of God's Name (*Gem.* 60a).

וְהַשְּׁלִישִׁי אוֹמֵר: אַף אֲנִי כָּמוֹהוּ. — *and the third says: I too [heard] as he did.*

I.e., if there was a third witness to the blasphemy, he too repeats what the second one said. The necessity to interview a third witness who comes with the others is based upon the view of R' Akiva, who maintains (*Makkos* 1:7) that if a group of witnesses contains more than two members, their testimonies must be considered interrelated with the validity of any one of them [see above, 6:2] (*Rav* from *Gem.* 60a). Consequently, the court must examine even the third witness and determine his validity since his failure to qualify would invalidate the testimony of the others as well (*Rashi*).

6.

הָעוֹבֵד עֲבוֹדָה זָרָה — *The idolater [is liable]*

[The mishnah now lists the various practices which render a person liable for serving a false god.]

אֶחָד הָעוֹבֵד, — *whether he serves,*

The second says: I too [heard] as he did; and the third says: I too [heard] as he did.

6. The idolater [is liable] whether he serves, slaughters, burns [an offering], pours a libation, bows down, accepts it upon himself as a deity, or says to it, "You are my god."

YAD AVRAHAM

I.e., he serves a false god in the manner in which it is generally worshiped — whatever its ritual (*Rav* from *Gem.* 60b). This is prohibited by the verse (*Deut.* 12:30): *Lest you investigate their gods saying, "How do these nations worship their gods ..."* The punishment of stoning for idolatry is specified explicitly in the Torah (*Deut.* 17:5).

וְאֶחָד הַזּוֹבֵחַ, — *slaughters,*

[I.e., slaughters an animal as a sacrifice to an idol.]

וְאֶחָד הַמְקַטֵּר, — *burns [an offering],*

He burns a sacrifice to an idol, whether an animal sacrifice or incense (*Tif. Yis.*).

וְאֶחָד הַמְנַסֵּךְ, — *pours a libation,*

[It was the custom of many ancient religions to pour out wine libations as an offering to their deities.] Included in this category is one who throws blood on the altar to a false god (*Tif. Yis.* from *Gem.* 60b).

וְאֶחָד הַמִּשְׁתַּחֲוֶה, — *bows down,*

One is liable for bowing down to an idol even if he does not prostrate himself completely but merely bows his head to the ground (*Meiri*). All four of these services — slaughtering, burning an offering, pouring a libation, and bowing down — were common forms of worship and should thus be included in the first category of *serves.* In specifying these four, the mishnah means to teach that one is liable for them even if he performed them for a deity for whom such practices are not the accepted method of service. This is because these are services which are designated for worshiping the Almighty in the Temple (*Rav* from *Gem.* loc. cit.), as derived exegetically by the *Gemara* (ibid.) from verses in the Torah. However, if one uses some other practice to serve a deity in a manner not customary to it, he is not liable, as the mishnah will state below.

וְאֶחָד הַמְקַבְּלוֹ עָלָיו לֶאֱלוֹהַּ, — *accepts it upon himself as a deity,*

I.e., he states his acceptance of another god. This case refers to one who makes his acceptance not in the presence of its idol (*Rashi;* see below), even with mere words to that effect (*Rav; Rashi*).

וְהָאוֹמֵר לוֹ ,,אֵלִי אַתָּה". — *or says to it, "You are my god."*

I.e., he accepts it upon himself in its presence (*Rashi*). The mishnah specifies both of these cases to avoid the misconception that only acceptance in the presence of an idol is considered tantamount to worshiping it (*Rav; Rashi*). On the other hand, were the mishnah to mention only the case of acceptance in its absence, one might think that only explicit

אֲבָל הַמְגַפֵּף, וְהַמְנַשֵּׁק, וְהַמְכַבֵּד, וְהַמְרַבֵּץ, וְהַמַּרְחִיץ, הַסָּךְ, הַמַּלְבִּישׁ, וְהַמַּנְעִיל עוֹבֵר בְּלֹא תַעֲשֶׂה. הַנּוֹדֵר בִּשְׁמוֹ וְהַמְקַיֵּם בִּשְׁמוֹ עוֹבֵר בְּלֹא תַעֲשֶׂה. הַפּוֹעֵר עַצְמוֹ לְבַעַל פְּעוֹר — זוֹ הִיא עֲבוֹדָתוֹ. הַזּוֹרֵק אֶבֶן

ר׳ עובדיה מברטנורא

המגפף. מחבק: **עובר בלא תעשה.** לא תעבדם יתירה כתיב: **הנודר בשמו.** קונם עלי כל פירות שבעולם בשם עבודה זרה פלוני: **המקיים.** נשבע: **עובר בלא תעשה.** ושם אלהים אחרים לא תזכירו (שם כג,יג): **הפוער עצמו.** מתריז רעי לפניו: **זו היא עבודתו.** ואפילו נתכוין לבזותו, הואיל וזו היא עבודתו, חייב חטאת:

יד אברהם

acceptance of its authority is considered idolatry, but not mere acknowledgment of it as his god (*Yad Ramah*).

אֲבָל הַמְגַפֵּף, וְהַמְנַשֵּׁק, וְהַמְכַבֵּד, וְהַמְרַבֵּץ, וְהַמַּרְחִיץ, הַסָּךְ, הַמַּלְבִּישׁ, וְהַמַּנְעִיל עוֹבֵר בְּלֹא תַעֲשֶׂה. — *However, one who embraces, kisses, sweeps, sprinkles, washes, anoints, clothes, or shoes [it] transgresses a negative commandment.*

[I.e., one who embraces or kisses an idol, sweeps the floor around it, sprinkles the ground in front of it to wash away the dust, or washes it or anoints it with oil, or one who places clothes or shoes upon it, is not liable to the death penalty,] provided this is not its normal manner of worship (*Rashi*). He has, however, transgressed the negative commandment of: *You shall not serve them.* The Torah's repetition of this injunction (*Ex.* 20:2; ibid. 23:13) indicates that even when it is not punishable by death it is nevertheless prohibited (*Rav; Rashi*). This also includes any form of honor granted them (*Meiri*).

הַנּוֹדֵר בִּשְׁמוֹ — *One who vows in its name*

[A *neder* is a vow by which one prohibits something to himself by saying that it be to him like something holy (see General Introduction to ArtScroll *Nedarim*).] It is prohibited for one to makes a *neder* in the name of a false god — e.g., "I forbid upon myself such and such an item like something which is designated for that idol" (*Rav; Rashi*).

וְהַמְקַיֵּם בִּשְׁמוֹ — *or upholds in its name*

I.e., he supports his words by swearing to their veracity in the name of an idol (*Rav; Rashi*). Others explain this to refer to one who upholds the *neder* to which another adjured him in the name of an alien deity (*Yad Ramah*).

עוֹבֵר בְּלֹא תַעֲשֶׂה. — *transgresses a negative commandment.*

I.e., he is not liable to the death penalty, but he has violated the prohibition (Ex. 23:13): *And the name of other gods you shall not* mention (*Rav; Rashi*). This prohibition actually includes any explicit mention of a false god by name; the mishnah specifies vows only to teach that even in such a case there is no capital punishment (*Yad Ramah*).

7
6 However, one who embraces, kisses, sweeps, sprinkles, washes, anoints, clothes, or shoes [it] transgresses a negative commandment. One who vows in its name or upholds in its name transgresses a negative commandment. Defecating to Baal Peor — this is its service. Throwing a stone

YAD AVRAHAM

There is a dispute in the *Gemara* (63a) as to the repercussions for one who honors a false god in any of these ways. One view is that for all of these actions he is flogged, except for swearing and vowing, since these are perpetrated by word alone [and the punishment of lashes can generally not be imposed for verbal transgressions]. The other view contends just the opposite: that he receives lashes only for swearing and vowing, not for the others. This view contends that even a prohibition which is transgressed by mere speech receives lashes. However, all the other forms of honoring false gods are derived from a prohibition which includes many other issues as well (לאוו שבכללות), and a generalized Torah prohibition covering many matters does not carry with it a punishment of flogging for any particular infraction.

Rambam (*Hil. Avodah Zarah* 3:6; 5:10,11) decides in favor of the second opinion. Although in regard to all other issues he rules that transgression by mere speech does not incur a punishment of flogging, vows are an exception to this rule. This may be seen from the fact that false oaths made in the name of Hashem carry a punishment of flogging [see *Rambam, Hil. Shevuos* 1:3] (*Kesef Mishneh,* ad loc.). *Ravad* (ibid.) disputes this ruling and maintains that only worship through deed is punishable by lashes but not mere lip service.

הַפּוֹעֵר עַצְמוֹ לְבַעַל פְּעוֹר – — *Defecating to Baal Peor —*

I.e., in front of the idol of this name (*Rav; Rashi*). Others explain that he merely uncovers himself and extends his buttocks toward it as if he were about to defecate in its direction (*Yad Ramah*).

זוֹ הִיא עֲבוֹדָתוֹ. — *this is its service.*

Even though defecating before an idol would ordinarily be considered disgracing it and would certainly not constitute service, since this was the manner in which the idol of Baal Peor was generally worshiped, one who does so is liable. Consequently, even if he does so in order to disgrace it, he is liable (*Rav* from *Gem.* 64a). However, in such a case, he would be liable only to a sin-offering [for unintentional worship), not stoning, since his intention was to disgrace it rather than to worship it (*Rav; Rambam, Avodah Zarah* 3:5; see *Kesef Mishneh*).

Others contend that it is possible to explain the mishnah to mean that he is stoned for worshiping in this manner, even though he meant to disgrace it (*Rashi* to *Gem.* ibid.; *Meiri*). This happens in a case in which he meant to disgrace it and thereby serve it (*Tos.* to 64a, s.v. אעיג). This apparently contradictory intention is feasible if he accepted it as a deity and meant to disgrace it in defiance (Ran to *Gem.* ibid.). Alternatively, since the accepted method of worshiping that idol was by humiliating it, such an intent is not considered contradictory

לְמַרְקוּלִיס זוֹ הִיא עֲבוֹדָתוֹ.

[ז] **הַנּוֹתֵן** מִזַּרְעוֹ לַמֹּלֶךְ אֵינוֹ חַיָּב עַד שֶׁיִּמְסֹר לַמֹּלֶךְ וְיַעֲבִיר בָּאֵשׁ. מָסַר לַמֹּלֶךְ וְלֹא הֶעֱבִיר בָּאֵשׁ, הֶעֱבִיר בָּאֵשׁ וְלֹא מָסַר לַמֹּלֶךְ, אֵינוֹ חַיָּב — עַד שֶׁיִּמְסֹר לַמֹּלֶךְ וְיַעֲבִיר בָּאֵשׁ.

ר׳ עובדיה מברטנורא

והזורק אבן למרקוליס. שעובדים אותו בזריקת אבנים, והמסלק אבן מלפניו נמי חייב, שעובדים אותו נמי בסלוק אבנים: **מרקוליס.** חילוף השבח, מר לשון חלוף הוא, [כמו] במר דכנתא, במר דשחוטה, קלוס, שבח: **זו היא עבודתו.** ואפילו נתכוין לרוגמו, חייב חטאת: (ז) **עד שימסור למולך.** מוסרו ביד הכומרים: **ויעביר באש.** מעבירו מצד זה לצד זה: **עד שימסור ויעביר באש.** שנאמר (ויקרא יח,כא) [לא] תתן להעביר, וכתיב התם (דברים יח,י) לא ימצא בך מעביר בנו ובתו באש, מה העברה האמורה שם באש, אף העברה האמורה כאן באש:

יד אברהם

to its service (*Teshuvos Rivash,* 110).

הַזּוֹרֵק אֶבֶן לְמַרְקוּלִיס — *Throwing a stone at Markolis —*

Two stones were placed on the ground with a third placed atop both of them, and that was designated [to represent] the deity Markolis. The idol was served by throwing other stones at it (*Rashi*). Removing stones from before it was also a form of worship and is thus prohibited as well (*Rav* from *Gem.* 64a).

The word *Markolis* comes from the root *kilos,* meaning praise, which was the name given to it by its worshipers. The Sages added the prefix *mar* — bitter — to denigrate it (*Rav; Tos.*).

זוֹ הִיא עֲבוֹדָתוֹ. — *this is its service.*

Therefore, even one who does so with the intent of disgracing it is liable (*Rav;* see above).

7.

הַנּוֹתֵן מִזַּרְעוֹ לַמֹּלֶךְ — *One who gives of his children to Molech*

This was a pagan rite prohibited in the Torah (ibid. 18:21), with a punishment of stoning decreed for it (*Lev.* 20:2).

The *Gemara* explains (64b) that the child was made to jump over the flames rather than walking through them (*Rashi;* ibid.). Others interpret that the manner in which the child passed through was not important as long as it was only the child himself and not the parent with the child on his shoulders (*Rambam, Hilchos Avodas Kochavim* 6:3; *Kesef Mishneh* ad loc., citing *Maharik*).

Yad Ramah's view is that the service of *Molech* required that the father take the child in his arms and jump with him over the flames.

Although the service did not call for burning the child to death (*Rambam Comm.*), the act of passing

at Markolis — this is its service.

7. One who gives of his children to *Molech* is not liable unless he hands [him] over to *Molech* and passes [him] through the fire. [If] he hands [him] over to *Molech* but does not pass [him] over the fire, [or] he passes [him] over the fire but does not hand [him] over to *Molech*, he is not liable — unless he hands [him] over to *Molech* and passes [him] over the fire.

YAD AVRAHAM

him through the flames generally caused him to be singed, at least on his clothing and hair. At times the act was repeated over and over, often bringing about the child's death (*Ramban*, ibid. 18:21).

אֵינוֹ חַיָּב – עַד שֶׁיִּמְסֹר לַמֹּלֶךְ וְיַעֲבִיר בָּאֵשׁ. — *is not liable unless he hands [him] over to Molech and passes [him] through the fire.*

From the verse (ibid. 18:21): *And you shall not give from your children to pass to Molech,* we derive that the prohibition applies to one who first gives his child over to the priests of *Molech* before he is passed through the flames. Although this verse does not explicitly state that passing to *Molech* means passing it through a fire, this detail emerges from the verse (*Deut.* 18:10): *There shall not be found among you one who passes his son or daughter through fire* (*Rav* from *Gem.* 64b).

It is *Rashi's* understanding that the passage through the fire was performed by the priests, not the father. However, *Rambam's* view (*Hil. Avodah Zarah* 6:3) is that the priests returned the child to the father, who then passed the child over the flames himself. Thus, the mishnah means that the father is not liable unless he both handed over the child to the priests and then passed the child through himself.

מָסַר לַמֹּלֶךְ וְלֹא הֶעֱבִיר בָּאֵשׁ, הֶעֱבִיר בָּאֵשׁ וְלֹא מָסַר לַמֹּלֶךְ, אֵינוֹ חַיָּב – עַד שֶׁיִּמְסֹר לַמֹּלֶךְ וְיַעֲבִיר בָּאֵשׁ. — *[If] he hands [him] over to Molech but does not pass [him] over the fire, [or] he passes [him] over the fire but does not hand [him] over to Molech, he is not liable — unless he hands [him] over to Molech and passes [him] over the fire.*

[It is unclear why this repetition is necessary.]

As noted previously (comm. to mishnah 4), there is a dispute among *Tannaim* whether *Molech* was viewed as a deity and its worship as a form of idolatry, or not. According to the former view, the Torah's unnecessary specification of this prohibition — despite the fact that it is already prohibited as idolatry — teaches us that this form of worship is punishable by death even when done to a different idol for which it is not the standard mode of worship (*Gem.* 64a). The halachah follows the latter view, and such ritual is punishable by death

סנהדרין
ז/ח

בַּעַל אוֹב זֶה פִּיתוֹם הַמְדַבֵּר מִשֶּׁחְיו, וְיִדְּעוֹנִי זֶה הַמְדַבֵּר בְּפִיו. הֲרֵי אֵלּוּ בִסְקִילָה, וְהַנִּשְׁאָל בָּהֶם בְּאַזְהָרָה.

[ח] **הַמְחַלֵּל** אֶת הַשַּׁבָּת — בְּדָבָר שֶׁחַיָּבִין עַל זְדוֹנוֹ כָּרֵת וְעַל שִׁגְגָתוֹ חַטָּאת.

ר׳ עובדיה מברטנורא

אוב זה פיתום. לוקח גולגולת של מת לאחר שנתאכל הבשר, ומקטיר לה, ושואל ממנה עתידות, והיא משיבה: **והמדבר משחיו.** ויש שעושים שישיב המת דרך בית השחי: **וידעוני.** חיה ששמה ידוע, וצורתה כצורת אדם בפניה וידיה ורגליה, והיא מחוברת בטבורה לחבל היוצא מן השורש הנשרש בארץ, שמשם חיותה, וכשרוצים לצוד אותה מורים בחצים אל החבל עד שהוא נפסק והיא מתה מיד, והיא קרויה בלשון חכמים בר נש דטור: **והנשאל בהם.** שבא ושואל ליודע בהם להגיד לו דבר העתיד [כגון שאול]: **באזהרה.** דאל תפנו אל האובות:

יד אברהם

only when performed in service of *Molech* (*Rambam, Hil. Avodas Kochavim* 6:3; see *Kesef Mishneh* ad loc.).

בַּעַל אוֹב זֶה פִּיתוֹם הַמְדַבֵּר מִשֶּׁחְיו, — *A practitioner of Ov is a necromancer who speaks from his armpit,*

The prohibition against this type of communication with the dead, as well as that of the *Yidoni*, is specified in the Torah (*Lev.* 19:31) along with the fact that it is punishable by stoning (ibid. v. 27).

Ov refers to a specific type of necromancy — a *pitom* — one who raises the spirit of the dead person being consulted and causes it to take up residence under his armpit, from where its voice emanates (*Rashi*).

Tiferes Yisrael identifies the word *pitom* with the Greek *python*, meaning a soothsayer [such as those who delivered the oracles in ancient Greece].

There is a variant reading of the mishnah followed by *Rav* which adds a prefix *vav* to the word הַמְדַבֵּר and thus divides this statement of the mishnah into two cases: *A practitioner of Ov is a pitom* (necromancer) *and one who speaks from his armpit.* The *pitom* in this view is a type of necromancy in which one takes a skull and offers sacrifices to it, after which it answers questions put to it. The case of one who raises a spirit under his armpit is a second example of an Ov practice (*Rav;* cf. *Meiri; Rambam, Hil. Avodas Kochavim* 6:2).[1]

Whatever these may be, they are not identical with the prohibition defined in the Torah as *inquiring of the dead* (*Deut.* 18:11). That category refers to one who does no deed of necromancy but merely fasts and dwells in the cemetery until he feels himself possessed of the spirit of darkness which enables him to

1. See footnote to mishnah 11.

A practitioner of *Ov* is a necromancer who speaks from his armpit, and a *Yidoni* is one who speaks through his mouth. These receive stoning, and one who inquires of them [transgresses] a prohibition.

8. One who desecrates the Sabbath [is] with something which is punishable by *kares* if done intentionally and obligates a sin-offering if done inadvertently.

YAD AVRAHAM

communicate with the dead (*Gem.* 65b).

וְיִדְּעוֹנִי זֶה הַמְדַבֵּר בְּפִיו. — *and a Yidoni is one who speaks through his mouth.*

Yidoni is a variant form of necromancy in which the practitioner takes the bone of a certain animal (*Rashi*) or bird (*Rambam*) called a *yedua* and places it in his mouth, from where the voice of the spirit emanates (*Gem.* 65b; cf. *Rav*).

הֲרֵי אֵלּוּ בִסְקִילָה, — *These receive stoning,*

I.e., those who actually perform these magical rites are stoned (*Meiri*).

וְהַנִּשְׁאָל בָּהֶם בְּאַזְהָרָה. — *and one who inquires of them [transgresses] a prohibition.*

The person who comes to inquire of them to predict the future has transgressed the prohibition (*Lev.* 19:31): *Do not turn to the Ovos and Yidonim* (*Rav, Rashi;* cf. *Tos.*).

8.

הַמְחַלֵּל אֶת הַשַּׁבָּת – — *One who desecrates the Sabbath*

The prohibition to labor on the Sabbath is stated explicitly (*Ex.* 20:10). The punishment of stoning is derived from the incident in the desert in which one of the Jewish people gathered wood on the Sabbath and was punished by stoning in accordance with an explicit Divine command (*Num.* 15:36).

בְּדָבָר שֶׁחַיָּבִין עַל זְדוֹנוֹ כָּרֵת וְעַל שִׁגְגָתוֹ חַטָּאת. — *[is] with something which is punishable by kares if done intentionally and obligates a sin-offering if done inadvertently.*

[Not all violations of Sabbath law incur the penalty of stoning. This is incurred only for those acts for which the Torah decrees a penalty of *kares* (Divinely decreed premature death) if done intentionally and a sin-offering if done by mistake. Such acts, if done intentionally, before witnesses, and after proper warning, are punishable by stoning. (*Kares* is the Divinely imposed penalty for intentional transgression which cannot be punished by the courts — e.g., if there was no valid witnesses or the witnesses failed to warn him. Although the courts cannot act in such cases — because the degree of his guilt and culpability cannot be legally estab-

הַמְקַלֵּל אָבִיו וְאִמּוֹ אֵינוֹ חַיָּב עַד שֶׁיְּקַלְּלֵם בַּשֵּׁם. קִלְּלָם בְּכִנּוּי, רַבִּי מֵאִיר מְחַיֵּב, וַחֲכָמִים פּוֹטְרִין.

[ט] **הַבָּא** עַל נַעֲרָה הַמְאֹרָסָה אֵינוֹ חַיָּב עַד שֶׁתְּהֵא נַעֲרָה,

ר' עובדיה מברטנורא

(ח) עד שיקלל בשם. באחד מן השמות המיוחדים: **קללם בכנוי.** רחום, וחנון, וארך אפים: **(ט) עד שתהא נערה.** ולא קטנה פחותה מבת שתים עשרה שנה ויום אחד, ולא בוגרת שעברו עליה שתים עשרה שנה וששה חדשים ויום אחד:

יד אברהם

lished — God, Who knows the truth of these matters, punishes him accordingly.)]

This description includes all the categories of forbidden labor on the Sabbath, with the exception of lighting a fire which, in the opinion of R' Yose, is not punishable by *kares* and is therefore excluded from the laws of stoning. Also excluded is the violation of the law of *techumin* — the prohibition against walking more than a certain distance from a settlement on the Sabbath. In the view of R' Akiva, this prohibition is of Biblical origin, but even he agrees that is not punishable by *kares*. The mishnah's stipulation, therefore, must reflect one of these two opinions and exclude that particular case (*Gem.* 66a).

Both these views, however, are considered minority opinions, and the halachah does not follow either of them. There is a liability of *kares* and stoning for lighting a fire on the Sabbath (*Rambam, Hil. Shabbos* 7:1), and the prohibition of walking beyond the *techum* is considered to be only a Rabbinic prohibition, not a Biblical one [and thus excluded on these grounds from *kares* and stoning). See General Introduction to ArtScroll *Eruvin* p.10, for a more detailed discussion of this last point.

הַמְקַלֵּל אָבִיו וְאִמּוֹ — *One who curses his father or mother*

Concerning this prohibition it is stated (*Lev.* 20:9): *His blood is upon himself*, which indicates a punishment of stoning (see preface to mishnah 4).

אֵינוֹ חַיָּב עַד שֶׁיְּקַלְּלֵם בַּשֵּׁם. — *is not liable unless he curses them with the Name of Hashem.*

I.e., with one of the specific Names of God (*Rav; Rambam, Hil. Mamrim* 5:2) — i.e., the seven Names which may not be erased (*Radbaz* ad loc.). Others contend that this refers to the Sacred Name alone (*Yad Ramah; Meiri*).

קִלְּלָם בְּכִנּוּי, — *[If] he cursed them with a secondary Name,*

This includes all the terms used to describe God by his attributes — e.g., Merciful, the Almighty (*Rav*). According to the second view cited above it includes only those Names

One who curses his father or mother is not liable unless he curses them with the Name of *Hashem*. [If] he cursed them with a secondary Name, R' Meir holds [him] liable, but the Sages acquit [him].

9. **O**ne who cohabits with a betrothed *naarah* is not liable unless she is a *naarah*,

YAD AVRAHAM

which may not be erased (*Yad Ramah*).

רַבִּי מֵאִיר מְחַיֵּב, וַחֲכָמִים פּוֹטְרִין. — *R' Meir holds [him] liable, but the Sages acquit [him].*

I.e., they acquit him of being stoned, but he is nevertheless subject to lashes — the penalty imposed on one who curses any Jew with the Name of God (*Meiri*). The halachah follows the view of the Sages (*Rambam, Mamrim* 5:2; cf. *Yad Ramah; Ran; Kesef Mishneh* to *Rambam* ad loc.; see *Lechem Mishneh* ad loc.; *Tos. Yom Tov* for discussion of contradictory rulings of *Rambam*).

9.

The Torah (*Deut.* 22:21) treats adultery with a betrothed *naarah* more severely than adultery with other betrothed or married women. Whereas the usual punishment for adultery is strangulation, for adultery with a betrothed *naarah* the Torah mandates the punishment of stoning (the most severe form of execution — see mishnah 1). The following mishnah delineates the various conditions that must pertain at the time of the adultery for stoning to be imposed.

הַבָּא עַל נַעֲרָה הַמְאֹרָסָה — *One who cohabits with a betrothed naarah*

I.e., a girl between the ages of twelve and twelve and a half who has undergone *erusin* (see comm. to mishnah 5).

אֵינוֹ חַיָּב — *is not liable*

The man who commits adultery with her (as well as the girl herself) is not liable to execution by stoning unless the following conditions are met. They are, however, still liable to strangulation in common with all adulterers (see below).

עַד שֶׁתְּהֵא נַעֲרָה, — *unless she is a naarah,*

I.e., and not a minor of less than twelve years of age, nor a *bogeres* — a girl beyond the half-year stage of *naarus* (*Rav* from *Gem.* 66b). If one sinned with a betrothed *bogeres*, they are liable only to strangulation (*Rambam, Isurei Biah* 3:4).

There is a dispute in the *Gemara* whether this mishnah is of the opinion that one who has relations with a betrothed minor[1] is executed by strangulation or whether he is not

1. A girl up to the age of twelve and a half can be betrothed through her father (*Kiddushin* 2:1).

בְּתוּלָה, מְאֹרָסָה, וְהִיא בְּבֵית אָבִיהָ. בָּאוּ עָלֶיהָ שְׁנַיִם, הָרִאשׁוֹן בִּסְקִילָה וְהַשֵּׁנִי בְּחֶנֶק.

ר׳ עובדיה מברטנורא

בתולה. ולא בעולה, ואם נבעלה שלא כדרכה, עדיין בתולה היא, ואפילו באו עליה עשרה בני אדם, כלם שלא כדרכה, כלם בסקילה: **מאורסה.** ולא נשואה: **והיא בבית אביה.** שאם מסר האב לשלוחי הבעל, הבא עליה אחר כך אינו בסקילה אלא בחנק:

יד אברהם

punished whatsoever (since the girl, being a minor, cannot be punished). However, there is yet another view cited by the *Gemara* (ibid.) that disputes the ruling of our mishnah in regard to a minor. In this view, attributed to the Sages, although the minor herself cannot be held liable for her adultery, the man who cohabits with her is stoned, the same as if she had been a *naarah*. The halachah follows this view (*Rambam, Hil. Isurei Biah* 3:5).

בְּתוּלָה, — *a virgin,*

Relations with a betrothed *naarah* render one punishable by stoning only if she has had no previous relations (*Rav* from *Gem.* 66b).

מְאֹרָסָה, — *betrothed,*

The harsher punishment of stoning applies only if she has not yet undergone the second stage of the marital process, *nisuin* (see mishnah 5).

וְהִיא בְּבֵית אָבִיהָ. — *and still in her father's house.*

During betrothal, conjugal relations with her husband are still forbidden. Consequently, though she is legally a married woman, the betrothed continues to live with her parents. To be subject to the punishment of stoning, she cannot have even begun the process of completing her marriage. But if the father gave her over to messengers of the husband to bring her from her father's house to his home to complete their marriage, even though they have not yet entered the *chupah* she acquires the status of other married women whose adultery is punishable by strangulation, not stoning (*Rav*).

בָּאוּ עָלֶיהָ שְׁנַיִם, הָרִאשׁוֹן בִּסְקִילָה וְהַשֵּׁנִי בְּחֶנֶק. — *[If] two men cohabited with her, the first is stoned and the second is strangled.*

Once one man has cohabited with her, she is no longer a virgin and the punishment of stoning is therefore no longer applicable to any subsequent man who cohabits with her. The latter therefore is executed by strangulation, like anyone else who commits adultery (*Rambam Comm.; Yad Ramah*).

This explanation assumes the mishnah to refer only to cases of natural intercourse. If the first man performed an act of sodomy with the girl, so that the physical signs of her virginity were not impaired, she would still be legally classified a virgin and the second man would also be liable to stoning.

Rashi, however, explains the mishnah to be discussing a situation in

a virgin, betrothed, and still in her father's house. [If] two men cohabited with her, the first is stoned and the second is strangled.

which the first one performed an act of sodomy, so that she is still physically a virgin. Nevertheless, once she has had intimate relations with a man she can no longer be legally classified a virgin and stoning therefore no longer applies. This follows the view of R' Yehudah HaNasi, cited in the *Gemara* (66b). The Sages, however, contend that such relations do not legally remove her from the classification of virgin. Thus, even the second man would be liable to stoning.[1] The halachah follows this view of the Sages (*Meiri; Rambam, Hil. Isurei Biah* 3:6; see *Maggid Mishneh, Mishneh LaMelech* ad loc.).

10.

This mishnah takes up the subject of *Deuteronomy* Ch. 13 — the crime of influencing or attempting to influence others to worship other gods. The Torah divides its discussion of this crime into three categories — a person claiming a prophecy commanding people to worship a certain deity (vs. 1-6), a common person who attempts to convince his fellow Jews to serve another god [but without claiming any prophetic basis for this] (vs. 7-13), and an entire town which is led astray (vs. 13-19).

There are various distinctions between these categories. For example, although one who worships a false god is executed by stoning, the members of an entire town which went astray into foreign worship are executed by beheading. This and various other aspects of the punishment of a town gone astray are discussed in Ch. 10:4-6.

The subject of this mishnah is the punishment of those who lead others astray. In connection with this, the *Gemara* (67a) cites a *Baraisa* which records two disputes between R' Shimon and the Sages. The first dispute concerns the form of execution mandated for one who attempts to persuade another individual to serve a false god based on a prophecy he claims to have received. According to the Sages, a prophetic instigator to foreign worship is treated no differently than any other instigator and he is executed by stoning; R' Shimon, however, derives from a verse that he is executed by strangulation. Similarly, the Sages rule that those who lead astray an entire city are also subject to stoning, while R' Shimon considers them liable only to strangulation. The following mishnah deals with these matters and there are different opinions in the *Gemara* as to which of these views the anonymous *Tanna* of this mishnah follows. These will be explained in the commentary.

1. Regardless of whether sodomy removes her legal classification of virgin, it is considered an act of intercourse, despite its unnaturalness (*Gem.* 54a; see *Yevamos* 6:2). Thus, he is liable for stoning even for this unnatural act.

[י] **הַמֵּסִית** — זֶה הֶדְיוֹט הַמֵּסִית אֶת הַהֶדְיוֹט: אָמַר לוֹ: „יֵשׁ יִרְאָה בְמָקוֹם פְּלוֹנִי; כָּךְ אוֹכֶלֶת; כָּךְ שׁוֹתָה; כָּךְ מְטִיבָה; כָּךְ מְרִיעָה".

כָּל חַיָּבֵי מִיתוֹת שֶׁבַּתּוֹרָה אֵין מַכְמִינִין עֲלֵיהֶם חוּץ מִזּוֹ. אָמַר לִשְׁנַיִם, וְהֵן עֵדָיו, מְבִיאִין אוֹתוֹ לְבֵית דִּין וְסוֹקְלִין אוֹתוֹ.

ר' עובדיה מברטנורא

(י) **זה הדיוט המסית.** דוקא הדיוט שהסית. שנביא המסית מיתתו בחנק. והמסית את ההדיוט, לאו דוקא, שלא מצינו חילוק בין מסית את ההדיוט למסית את הנביא, אלא למעוטי מסית את הרבים, כגון מדיחי עיר מישראל, שמיתתן בחנק: **מכמינין.** לשון מארב:

יד אברהם

הַמֵּסִית — *An instigator [to idolatry]*

One who instigates another to serve a false god is punished by stoning, as stated explicitly in the Torah (*Deut.* 13:11,12).

זֶה הֶדְיוֹט — *is a common person*

I.e., the instigator speaks as a common person and does not claim to be a prophet speaking in the Name of God. In the view of this mishnah, only a commoner who incites others to idolatry is stoned; one who claims to have a prophecy from HASHEM to follow another god is executed by strangulation (*Rav* from *Gem.* 67a). Thus, this anonymous statement of the mishnah follows the view of R' Shimon (see preface).

The *Gemara,* however, cites a *Baraisa* in which the Sages dispute this. In the view of the Sages, even a prophet who instigates is stoned. The halachah follows the latter view (*Rambam, Hil. Avodas Kochavim* 5:1).

This applies only if the prophet claims a prophecy from HASHEM as the basis of his instigation. However, if he cites a prophecy he claims to have received from another god as the basis for his instigation, he is judged by the standard *of the prophet of a false god,* who is executed by strangulation (*Meiri;* see mishnah 11:6).

There is another view in the *Gemara* (ibid.), that the mishnah can be reconciled with the view of the Sages. In this view, the word הֶדְיוֹט is meant in the sense of a lowly person. Accordingly, the mishnah states that the instigator [regardless of his rank) is a lowly person — meaning, that he is not to be treated with the same legal safeguards as other suspected criminals. Rather, he may be entrapped into repeating his sin before witnesses so that he can be convicted [see below] (*Rashi*).

הַמֵּסִית אֶת הַהֶדְיוֹט: — *who instigates a common person:*

I.e., he attempts to persuade an individual to worship a false god. This is meant to exclude one who incites an entire town, who is executed by strangulation rather than stoning. Although the mishnah will

10. **A**n instigator [to idolatry] — is a common person who instigates a common person: He says to him: "There is a deity in such and such a place; thus it eats; thus it drinks; thus it benefits; thus it does harm."

We do not conceal witnesses [to entrap] anyone punishable by death according to Torah law except for this one. [If] he spoke to two, and they are his witnesses, they bring him to court and stone him.

YAD AVRAHAM

state below that such people are stoned, the *Tanna* of this statement of the mishnah disputes the view stated below, and follows the opinion of R' Shimon, that one who persuades an entire town to serve idols is strangled (*Gem.* 67a). [Although this entire mishnah is stated anonymously, we find occasionally that different parts of anonymous mishnayos reflect conflicting views.]

We do not interpret the mishnah to be excluding a prophet, as before, because there is no basis to differentiate between one who instigates a layman and one who instigates a prophet (*Rav; Rashi*).

The *Gemara,* however, cites another explanation that reconciles this phrase of the mishnah with the view of the Sages, that one who leads astray an entire town is stoned. According to this explanation the phrase *who instigates a common person* is not meant to exclude anything. Rather, the *Tanna* first states the law in regard to an individual and later [see below] in regard to a town.

The halachah follows the view of the Sages, that those who lead astray an entire town are also stoned (*Rambam, Avodas Kochavim* 4:1).

אָמַר לוֹ: „יֵשׁ יִרְאָה בְמָקוֹם פְּלוֹנִי; כָּךְ אוֹכֶלֶת; כָּךְ שׁוֹתָה; כָּךְ מְטִיבָה; כָּךְ מְרִיעָה". — *He says to him: "There is a deity in such and such a place; thus it eats; thus it drinks; thus it benefits; thus it does harm."*

One is considered to have instigated to idolatry if he comes with a description of the idol and the benefits to be gained from it as well as the harm to be avoided (*Meiri*).

כָּל חַיָּבֵי מִיתוֹת שֶׁבַּתּוֹרָה אֵין מַכְמִינִין עֲלֵיהֶם חוּץ מִזּוֹ. — *We do not conceal witnesses [to entrap] anyone punishable by death according to Torah law except for this one.*

In no other case involving a possible death sentence may a suspect be entrapped. On the contrary, witnesses must first warn the transgressor in order for him to be liable to the death penalty. One suspected of the crime of instigation to idolatry, however, may be entrapped (*Meleches Shlomo*).

אָמַר לִשְׁנַיִם, וְהֵן עֵדָיו, מְבִיאִין אוֹתוֹ לְבֵית דִּין וְסוֹקְלִין אוֹתוֹ. — *[If] he spoke to two, and they are his witnesses, they bring him to court and stone him.*

I.e., if he attempted to seduce to idol worship two people who are eligible

אָמַר לְאֶחָד, הוּא אוֹמֵר „יֵשׁ לִי חֲבֵרִים רוֹצִים בְּכָךְ". אִם הָיָה עָרוּם וְאֵינוֹ יָכוֹל לְדַבֵּר בִּפְנֵיהֶם, מַכְמִינִין לוֹ עֵדִים אֲחוֹרֵי הַגָּדֵר, וְהוּא אוֹמֵר לוֹ „אֱמֹר מַה שֶׁאָמַרְתָּ לִי, בְּיִחוּד". וְהַלָּה אוֹמֵר לוֹ, וְהוּא אוֹמֵר לוֹ „הֵיאָךְ נַנִּיחַ אֶת אֱלֹהֵינוּ שֶׁבַּשָּׁמַיִם וְנֵלֵךְ וְנַעֲבוֹד עֵצִים וַאֲבָנִים?" אִם חוֹזֵר בּוֹ, הֲרֵי זֶה מוּטָב. וְאִם אָמַר „כָּךְ הִיא חוֹבָתֵנוּ; וְכָךְ יָפֶה לָנוּ",

ר' עובדיה מברטנורא

אם היה המסית ערום ואינו יכול לדבר בפניהם. כלומר, אומר לניסת שאינו יכול לדבר בפניהם מפני יראת בית דין: **ביחוד.** כלומר, אין איש עמנו, ויכול אתה לומר עתה מה שאמרת לי כבר:

יד אברהם

אָמַר לְאֶחָד, הוּא אוֹמֵר „יֵשׁ לִי חֲבֵרִים רוֹצִים בְּכָךְ". — *[If] he spoke to one, he says, "I have friends who desire this."*

If he tries to instigate one man alone, that person cannot bring him to justice, since he is only one witness. Therefore, if he is a loyal Jew and wishes to see justice done, he should try to convince the instigator to repeat his instigation in front of others, so that they can testify against him in court (*Meiri*).

אִם הָיָה עָרוּם וְאֵינוֹ יָכוֹל לְדַבֵּר בִּפְנֵיהֶם, — *If he is clever and [says that] he is unable to speak before them,*

If the instigator is clever enough to avoid this too, and he refuses to speak in front of others for fear of leaving himself open to court charges (*Rav*).

מַכְמִינִין לוֹ עֵדִים אֲחוֹרֵי הַגָּדֵר, — *they conceal witnesses behind a partition,*

The instigator must be lured into a lighted room outside of which to be witnesses against him (*Yad Ramah*), they may come to court, testify against him, and have him convicted on their testimony. [Although they were themselves the object of his instigation they are not considered principals in this case, and they may therefore testify against him.][1] Not only are they eligible to serve as his witnesses, but they need not even warn him. They proceed immediately to court to have him tried and convicted. This is derived from the verse concerning the instigator (*Deut.* 13:9): *Do not have mercy on him* (*Rashi*).

It is clear from this that the instigator is executed even though those he instigated — in this case the witnesses who testify against him — did not accede to his instigation (*Rambam, Hil. Avodas Kochavim* 5:1; *Kesef Mishneh* ibid.).

1. The wording of the mishnah found in the *Gemara* deletes the *vav* from וְהֵן and thus reads: *If he said to two, they are his witnesses ...*

[If] he spoke to one, he says, "I have friends who desire this." If he is clever and [says that] he is unable to speak before them, they conceal witnesses behind a partition, and he says to him, "Say that which you said to me, in private." The other says [it] to him, to which he replies, "How can we abandon our God in heaven and go and worship wood and stones?" If he retracts, it is good. If he says, "This is our obligation; it is proper for us,"

YAD AVRAHAM

witnesses are concealed. Since the room is lighted while they are outside in shadow, they can see into the room without being detected by the instigator. The room must be so arranged so that they can also hear what is being said (*Gem.* 67a).

וְהוּא אוֹמֵר לוֹ „אֱמֹר מַה שֶּׁאָמַרְתָּ לִי, בְּיִחוּד״. — *and he says to him, "Say that which you said to me, in private."*

Having arranged the trap, the person previously instigated asks the instigator to repeat his words in this place, which is safe because it is private (*Rav*).

וְהַלָּה אוֹמֵר לוֹ, וְהוּא אוֹמֵר לוֹ „הֵיאָךְ נַנִּיחַ אֶת אֱלֹהֵינוּ שֶׁבַּשָּׁמַיִם וְנֵלֵךְ וְנַעֲבוֹד עֵצִים וַאֲבָנִים?״ — *The other says [it] to him, to which he replies, "How can we abandon our God in heaven and go and worship wood and stones?"*

If the instigator repeats his statement, the listener must argue that it is not proper to serve idols. Although such a protest was not required in the previous case in which the instigation took place before witnesses, it is required in this case. The difference is that one who instigates two people is forewarned that he is opening himself to a capital charge and that he can be testified against. However, when he instigates only one person and is unaware of the presence of the hidden witnesses and thus of his liability to prosecution, he must be given at least this minimal degree of warning. Furthermore, when he instigates an individual, so that the listener must prod him to repeat his instigation before two witnesses, the second instigation lacks the absolute quality of an instigation, as it does not come unprompted. Since his prosecution is based on this second instigation, it is therefore necessary for the listener to make clear his objection to it, so that the instigator's further cajoling can be considered a full instigation (*Yad Ramah*).

For this reason also, two witnesses aside from the listener are necessary, and he cannot be part of the group of witnesses. Since the normal rules of testimony are being bent to allow entrapment, this degree of strictness is called for (*Tos. Yom Tov;* see *Margoliyos Ha Yam*).

אִם חוֹזֵר בּוֹ, הֲרֵי זֶה מוּטָב. — *If he retracts, it is good.*

If he agrees to the argument of the listener, or he is silent and does not persist with his incitement, he is not punishable (*Meiri*).

הָעוֹמְדִין מֵאֲחוֹרֵי הַגָּדֵר מְבִיאִין אוֹתוֹ לְבֵית דִּין וְסוֹקְלִין אוֹתוֹ.

הָאוֹמֵר: אֶעֱבֹד, אֵלֵךְ וְאֶעֱבֹד, נֵלֵךְ וְנַעֲבֹד; אֲזַבֵּחַ, אֵלֵךְ וַאֲזַבֵּחַ, נֵלֵךְ וּנְזַבֵּחַ; אַקְטִיר, אֵלֵךְ וְאַקְטִיר, נֵלֵךְ וְנַקְטִיר; אֲנַסֵּךְ, אֵלֵךְ וַאֲנַסֵּךְ, נֵלֵךְ וּנְנַסֵּךְ; אֶשְׁתַּחֲוֶה, אֵלֵךְ וְאֶשְׁתַּחֲוֶה, נֵלֵךְ וְנִשְׁתַּחֲוֶה. הַמַּדִּיחַ — זֶה הָאוֹמֵר „נֵלֵךְ וְנַעֲבוֹד עֲבוֹדָה זָרָה".

—— ר' עובדיה מברטנורא ——

האומר אעבוד. באחד מכל הלשונות הללו, הוי מסית וחייב: **המדיח.** ואם מדיח את הרבים הוא, אינו חייב עד שיאמר בלשון רבים נלך ונעבוד:

יד אברהם

וְאִם אָמַר „כָּךְ הִיא חוֹבָתֵנוּ; וְכָךְ יָפֶה לָנוּ", הָעוֹמְדִין מֵאֲחוֹרֵי הַגָּדֵר מְבִיאִין אוֹתוֹ לְבֵית דִּין וְסוֹקְלִין אוֹתוֹ — *If he says, "This is our obligation; it is proper for us," those standing behind the partition bring him to court and stone him.*

[If he reiterates his instigation, he is brought to court and executed on the testimony of the hidden witnesses.]

Although he was not successful in instigating the listener to practice idolatry, he is nevertheless liable for the effort. The crime is the *instigation* to idolatry; the outcome of that instigation is irrelevant (*Rambam, Avodas Kochavim* 5:1).

הָאוֹמֵר: אֶעֱבֹד, — *[Included in this is] anyone who says: I shall serve,*

The following phrases are all considered statements of instigation for which the instigator is liable to stoning (*Rav; Rashi* 67a; *Meiri; Rambam,* loc. cit. 5:2). The first is if he says, "I shall serve this idol." Although the instigator does not explicitly advocate to the listener that he too worship the idol, since his intention was to persuade the listener to follow suit, he is liable for instigation to idolatry (*Meiri,* Maharam to 61a; see also *Kesef Mishneh, Hil. Avodas Kochavim* 5:2).

The *Gemara* (61a) deduces from this mishnah that if the listener responds to the instigation with this statement, he too is liable to stoning even though he has not yet worshiped. Although mishnah 6 stated liability only for one who actually worshiped, this mishnah teaches that in the case of one who is responding to an instigation, his mere declaration of acceptance is sufficient to render him liable to stoning (*Meiri* 61a, based on the resolutions of Abaye and Ravina in the *Gem.* 61b). This is derived by the *Gemara* (61b) from the Torah's warning to the person being instigated (*Deut.* 13:9): *Do not accede or listen to him,* implying that if he does accede to his suggestion — even verbally — he is liable.[1]

אֵלֵךְ וְאֶעֱבֹד, — *I shall go and serve,*

Although the idol is not present, and there is a possibility that he will change

1. *Tos. Yom Tov* here understands from the *Gemara* (61a) and *Rashi* (there) that this part of the mishnah — *"I shall serve"* — refers to the statement of the person being instigated, not the instigator. *Rashi* to this mishnah, however, explains it to refer to the instigator, as do *Rambam* and *Meiri* (followed by *Rav*). Our commentary has followed the view of *Maharam* (61a) who reconciles *Rashi's* statements there with his explanation of the mishnah here.

7
10 those standing behind the partition bring him to court and stone him.

[Included in this is] anyone who says: I shall serve, I shall go and serve, let us go and serve; I shall slaughter [an offering], I shall go and slaughter [an offering], let us go and slaughter [an offering]; I shall burn [an offering], I shall go and burn [an offering], let us go and burn [an offering]; I shall pour a libation, I shall go and pour a libation, let us go and pour a libation; I shall bow down, I shall go and bow down, let us go and bow down. One who leads astray is one who says, "Let us go and serve idols."

YAD AVRAHAM

his mind before serving it, he is nonetheless liable (*Rashi* to 61a).

נֵלֵךְ וְנַעֲבֹד; — *let us go and serve;*

Even in this case, in which he included himself in a group, and it is thus possible that if they refuse he will not go alone, he is liable for his instigation (*Meiri, Rashi* 61a as explained by *Maharam*).

אֲזַבֵּחַ, אֵלֵךְ וַאֲזַבֵּחַ, נֵלֵךְ וּנְזַבֵּחַ; אַקְטִיר, אֵלֵךְ וְאַקְטִיר, נֵלֵךְ וְנַקְטִיר; אֲנַסֵּךְ, אֵלֵךְ וַאֲנַסֵּךְ, נֵלֵךְ וּנְנַסֵּךְ; אֶשְׁתַּחֲוֶה, אֵלֵךְ וְאֶשְׁתַּחֲוֶה, נֵלֵךְ וְנִשְׁתַּחֲוֶה. — *I shall slaughter [an offering], I shall go and slaughter [an offering], let us go and slaughter [an offering]; I shall burn [an offering], I shall go and burn [an offering], let us go and burn [an offering]; I shall pour a libation, I shall go and pour a libation, let us go and pour a libation; I shall bow down, I shall go and bow down, let us go and bow down.*

Whether he instigates by committing himself to serve the idol in its normal manner, or to serve it in any of the four ways in which the Almighty is served in the Temple — slaughtering and burning animal offerings, wine libations, prostration — even if it is not the way in which this idol is ordinarily served (see mishnah 6), he is liable (*Meiri*).

- הַמַּדִּיחַ — *One who leads astray*

One who instigates an entire town to serve false gods, thereby causing the town to become an עִיר הַנִּדַּחַת, *apostate town* (*Gem.* 67a; see 1:5), is punished by stoning, as he is included in the general category of one who instigates to idolatry (*Meiri* to mishnah 4). [As noted in the preface to this mishnah, R' Shimon (*Gem.* 67a) is of the opinion that one who leads a town astray is *not* included in the category of the instigator and is subject to strangulation, not stoning.] Though the mishnah above adopted this view according to one explanation (see s.v. המסית את ההדיוט), this part of the mishnah [which includes the instigator of a large group of people in the list of those stoned (*Rashi*)] reflects the view of the Sages that even those who instigate an entire town are stoned (*Gem.* 67a).

זֶה הָאוֹמֵר ,,נֵלֵךְ וְנַעֲבֹד עֲבוֹדָה זָרָה". — *is one who says, "Let us go and serve idols."*

I.e., he is liable only if he expresses his instigation in plural form (*Rav*).

[יא] הַמְכַשֵּׁף — הָעוֹשֶׂה מַעֲשֶׂה חַיָּב, וְלֹא הָאוֹחֵז אֶת הָעֵינַיִם. רַבִּי עֲקִיבָא אוֹמֵר מִשּׁוּם רַבִּי יְהוֹשֻׁעַ: שְׁנַיִם לוֹקְטִין קִשּׁוּאִין — אֶחָד לוֹקֵט פָּטוּר וְאֶחָד לוֹקֵט חַיָּב. הָעוֹשֶׂה מַעֲשֶׂה חַיָּב; הָאוֹחֵז אֶת הָעֵינַיִם פָּטוּר.

ר׳ עובדיה מברטנורא

(יא) העושה מעשה. ממש, בסקילה: **ולא האוחז את העינים.** מראה לבריות כאילו עושה, ואינו עושה כלום: **שנים לוקטים קשואים.** במכשפות בפניו, אחד מהן ליקט וחייב מיתה, וחבירו ליקט ופטור מן המיתה, כילד, העושה מעשה שלקט ממש בכשפים, חייב, והאוחז את העינים, הראה לנו כאילו נתקבצו כולן למקום אחד והקשואים לא זזו ממקומן, פטור מן המיתה:

יד אברהם

11.

הַמְכַשֵּׁף — *A sorcerer*

The Torah (*Deut.* 18:10) prohibits sorcery and mandates the death sentence for its practice (*Ex.* 22:17). The *Gemara* (67a) derives exegetically that the punishment for this offense is stoning.

הָעוֹשֶׂה מַעֲשֶׂה חַיָּב, — *who performs a deed is liable,*

If he actually performs magic he is punishable by stoning (*Rav*).

וְלֹא הָאוֹחֵז אֶת הָעֵינַיִם. — *but not one who creates illusions* (lit., *seizes the eyes*).

[Someone who merely creates an illusion of magic is not punishable by death.] However, this too is forbidden, and one who does so is flogged by Rabbinic decree (*Meiri; Rambam, Hil. Avodas Kochavim* II:15).[1]

1. *Rambam* (ibid. 11: 16) concludes the chapter in which he discusses the prohibitions against the various types of sorcery discussed by the mishnah in this chapter by stating that all of them operate only through various methods of deception and not through any supernatural powers. A similar view concerning a practitioner of *Ov* (see mishnah 7) is cited by *Radak* (*I Samuel* 28:24) from *R' Shmuel bar Chofni Gaon* and *R' Hai Gaon.* [According to this view, the mishnah's distinction between one who performs a deed and one who creates an illusion must be that the former creates an actual physical result by legerdemain, whereas the latter — as explained by *Meiri* — creates only an optical illusion (see *Kesef Mishneh* ibid. 11:15). Ed.] However, this view is rejected by the majority of later authorities who understand the numerous Talmudic discussions concerning these matters to refer to genuine supernatural forces (*Beur HaGra, Yoreh Deah* 179:13).

11. **A** sorcerer who performs a deed is liable, but not one who creates illusions. R' Akiva says in the name of R' Yehoshua: Two [people may] gather cucumbers — one [of them] gathers [and] is exempt while [the other] one gathers [and] is liable. The one who performs a deed is liable; the one who creates an illusion is exempt.

YAD AVRAHAM

Rambam rules in *Hil. Avodas Kochavim* 11:9 that one who creates an illusion is flogged by Torah law for transgressing the prohibition against a מְעוֹנֵן, which is translated by the Sages (65b) to be an illusionist; yet, following the mishnah's statement here, he rules that an illusionist receives lashes only by Rabbinic decree. However, it is possible that *Rambam* means to say only that he cannot be flogged by Torah law for the prohibition of sorcery, as he explains, but only for that of מְעוֹנֵן. Alternatively, מְעוֹנֵן refers to one who creates an illusion of an unnatural act, whereas *Rambam* here is discussing the illusion of having accomplished a natural act through magical means, as in the example cited below in the mishnah (*Kesef Mishneh*, ibid. 11:15). See *Chochmas Adam* 89:6.

רַבִּי עֲקִיבָא אוֹמֵר מִשּׁוּם רַבִּי יְהוֹשֻׁעַ: שְׁנַיִם לוֹקְטִין קִשּׁוּאִין - אֶחָד לוֹקֵט פָּטוּר וְאֶחָד לוֹקֵט חַיָּב. — *R' Akiva says in the name of R' Yehoshua: Two [people may] gather cucumbers — one [of them] gathers [and] is exempt while [the other] one gathers [and] is liable.*

Two people standing in a field of cucumbers gather them together magically before others: one is stoned for sorcery and one is not (*Rav*).

הָעוֹשֶׂה מַעֲשֶׂה חַיָּב; — *The one who performs a deed is liable;*

The one who actually moved the cucumbers magically is stoned (*Rav*).

הָאוֹחֵז אֶת הָעֵינַיִם פָּטוּר. — *the one who creates an illusion is exempt.*

The one who did not actually move them, but only made it appear as if he had, is not liable (*Rav*).

R' Akiva's intention is not to dispute the statement of the first *Tanna*, but elaborates it with an illustration (*Tos. Yom Tov;* cf. *Meleches Shlomo; Margoliyos HaYam*).

פרק שמיני

Chapter Eight

This chapter deals primarily with the laws of the בֵּן סוֹרֵר וּמוֹרֶה, *ben sorer umoreh,* literally, a wayward and rebellious son. The Torah says conceming this (*Deut.* 21:18-21): כִּי־יִהְיֶה לְאִישׁ בֵּן סוֹרֵר וּמוֹרֶה אֵינֶנּוּ שֹׁמֵעַ בְּקוֹל אָבִיו וּבְקוֹל אִמּוֹ וְיִסְּרוּ אֹתוֹ וְלֹא יִשְׁמַע אֲלֵיהֶם. וְתָפְשׂוּ בוֹ אָבִיו וְאִמּוֹ וְהוֹצִיאוּ אֹתוֹ אֶל־זִקְנֵי עִירוֹ וְאֶל־שַׁעַר מְקֹמוֹ. וְאָמְרוּ אֶל־זִקְנֵי עִירוֹ בְּנֵנוּ זֶה סוֹרֵר וּמֹרֶה אֵינֶנּוּ שֹׁמֵעַ בְּקֹלֵנוּ זוֹלֵל וְסֹבֵא. וּרְגָמֻהוּ כָּל־אַנְשֵׁי עִירוֹ בָאֲבָנִים וָמֵת וּבִעַרְתָּ הָרָע מִקִּרְבֶּךָ — *If a man shall have a wayward and rebellious son who does not heed the voice of his father and the voice of his mother, and they chasten him and he does not heed them. His father and mother shall seize him and they shall take him out to the elders of his town and to the gate of his locale. And they shall say to the elders of his town, "This son of ours is wayward and rebellious, he does not heed our voice; he is a glutton and a drunkard." And all the citizens of his town shall stone him with stones and he shall die; and you will eradicate the evil from your midst.*

[א] **בֵּן** סוֹרֵר וּמוֹרֶה — מֵאֵימָתַי נַעֲשֶׂה בֵּן סוֹרֵר וּמוֹרֶה? מִשֶּׁיָּבִיא שְׁתֵּי שְׂעָרוֹת וְעַד שֶׁיַּקִּיף זָקָן — הַתַּחְתּוֹן, וְלֹא הָעֶלְיוֹן; אֶלָּא שֶׁדִּבְּרוּ חֲכָמִים בְּלָשׁוֹן נְקִיָּה — שֶׁנֶּאֱמַר: ,,כִּי־יִהְיֶה לְאִישׁ בֵּן" — בֵּן וְלֹא בַת; בֵּן וְלֹא אִישׁ. הַקָּטָן פָּטוּר שֶׁלֹּא בָא לִכְלַל מִצְוֹת.

ר' עובדיה מברטנורא

פרק שמיני – בן סורר ומורה. (א) בן סורר ומורה. משיביא שתי שערות. והוא בן שלשה עשרה שנה ויום אחד, דמקמי הכי אין השערות סימן אלא שומא: **עד שיקיף זקן התחתון.** האי זקן דאמור רבנן, התחתון אמרו, שיקיף השער סביבות הגיד: **ולא העליון.** זקן ממש: **שנאמר בן ולא איש.** משהקיף זקן התחתון, איש הוא, ואף על גב דמקטנותו הוא קרוי בן, לא מצינו לחייבו מקמי שיביא שתי שערות, דקטן פטור, שלא בא לכלל המצות, הלכך חיוביה בתר הכי הוא, והכי קאמר קרא, כי יהיה לאיש בן, בן הסמוך לגבורתו של איש, בתחלת אישותו חייביה קרא, ומשהקיף זקן התחתון, איש גמור הוא:

יד אברהם

1.

בֵּן סוֹרֵר וּמוֹרֶה – מֵאֵימָתַי נַעֲשֶׂה בֵּן סוֹרֵר וּמוֹרֶה? — *A ben sorer u'moreh — when does he become a ben sorer u'moreh?*

In mishnah 4 of the previous chapter, the *ben sorer u'moreh* was listed among those who are punished by stoning. The mishnah will now delineate the age at which he is eligible to be included in this category (*Meiri*).

מִשֶּׁיָּבִיא שְׁתֵּי שְׂעָרוֹת — *From when he produces two hairs*

[The earliest he can classify in this legal category is when he grows two pubic hairs. This is the mark of physical maturity required for classification as an adult.] This, however, must take place after he reaches the age of thirteen [the legal age of adulthood] (*Rav*). To be considered an adult in Torah law, a boy must be both thirteen and have physically matured to the extent of having produced at least two pubic hairs (*Rambam, Ishus* 2:10).

וְעַד שֶׁיַּקִּיף זָקָן – — *until his beard grows around* —

This was the text of the rule that had been handed down to the Sages of the mishnah from the Sages of earlier times. The mishnah now goes on to explain what was meant by this (*Tif. Yis.*).

הַתַּחְתּוֹן, וְלֹא הָעֶלְיוֹן; — *the lower, not the upper;*

The beard referred to here is a euphemism meaning the patch of pubic hair, not the beard of the face. Once pubic hairs have fully surrounded the penis, he can no longer be classified a *ben sorer u'moreh* (*Rav* from *Gem.* 68b). However, once three months have passed from the onset of adulthood, even if the pubic hair is not fully grown, he is also no longer eligible for this status. The mishnah's

8
1

1. **A** *ben sorer u'moreh* — when does he become a *ben sorer u'moreh?* From when he produces two hairs until his beard grows around — the lower, not the upper; but the Sages employed delicate terminology — as it is written: *If a man shall have a son* — a son and not a daughter; a son and not a man. A minor is exempt because he has not entered the realm of commandments.

YAD AVRAHAM

rule is meant as a limiting factor — if this occurs within the three months, he is immediately excluded from *ben sorer u'moreh* status (*Gem.* 69a). Indeed, if this were to occur on his thirteenth birthday, he would never be eligible (*Meiri*).

אֶלָּא שֶׁדִּבְּרוּ חֲכָמִים בְּלָשׁוֹן נְקִיָּה — *but the Sages employed delicate terminology* (lit., *spoke in clean language*) —

[The Sages who first formulated the language of the mishnah used the euphemism *beard* in reference to the pubic hairs because it was the custom of the Sages to avoid explicit references of these matters.]

שֶׁנֶּאֱמַר: ,,כִּי־יִהְיֶה לְאִישׁ בֵּן'' — *as it is written* (*Deut.* 21:18): *"If a man shall have a son"* —

[The source for the ruling that one can be judged a *ben sorer umoreh* only within this short period is from this verse, as will be explained.]

בֵּן וְלֹא בַת; — *a son and not a daughter;*

This is a Biblical decree restricting the law of the *ben sorer u'moreh* to sons and not daughters (*Gem.* 70a). However, a rationale can be given for this as well — viz., the Torah required this strict preventative measure only for men, who are more wont to become deeply involved in their lusts (*Meiri; Rambam, Hil. Mamrim* 7:11; see *Radbaz; Lechem Mishneh,* ad loc.).

בֵּן וְלֹא אִישׁ. — *a son and not a man.*

The Torah refers to him as a son, rather than as a man, despite the fact that this law applies only to one who is no longer a minor — as stated below. This indicates that this law is restricted to one who has barely entered the status of adulthood and does not yet have the full development of a man (*Rav* from *Gem.* 68b) [i.e., his pubic hairs are not fully grown].

הַקָּטָן פָּטוּר שֶׁלֹּא בָא לִכְלַל מִצְוֹת. — *A minor is exempt because he has not entered the realm of commandments.*

[The Torah cannot be understood to refer to an actual minor, because a minor is exempt from all the commandments of the Torah and could therefore not be subject to the punishment of stoning.]

The *Gemara* (70a) explains that this reason is not really applicable here, since, as stated later (mishnah 5), a *ben sorer u'moreh* is executed in order to prevent future depravity, not on the strength of his present misdeeds

[ב] **מֵאֵימָתַי** חַיָּב? מִשֶּׁיֹּאכַל טַרְטֵימַר בָּשָׂר וְיִשְׁתֶּה חֲצִי לֹג יַיִן הָאִיטַלְקִי. רַבִּי יוֹסֵי אוֹמֵר: מָנֶה בָּשָׂר וְלֹג יַיִן. אָכַל בַּחֲבוּרַת מִצְוָה, אָכַל בְּעִבּוּר הַחֹדֶשׁ;

ר׳ עובדיה מברטנורא

(ב) **טרטימר.** חלי מנה, והוא שיהיה הבשר בשיל ולא בשיל, כדרך שהלסטים אוכלים: **מן היין האיטלקי.** שהוא משובח וממשיך בתריה, והוא דשתי ליה מזיג ולא מזיג: **רבי יוסי אומר כו׳.** ואין הלכה כרבי יוסי: **אכל בחבורת מצוה.** בסעודה של מלוה: **אכל בעבור החדש.** אף על גב דאין עולין לאותה סעודה אלא בפת וקטנית בלבד, ואיהו אסיק בשר ויין, הואיל ובמלוה קעסיק, לא ממשיך:

יד אברהם

alone. Nevertheless, a minor is excluded by virtue of the words כִּי־יִהְיֶה לְאִישׁ בֵּן, *If a man shall have a son,* which is interpreted homiletically to mean a man who is a son — i.e., one who can still be referred to as a son despite having entered adulthood. This is one who has grown pubic hairs and reached the age of thirteen but whose hairs are not yet fully developed (ibid.). The point of the mishnah is that this period begins with the onset of adulthood, rather than earlier, since a minor is generally excluded from all commandments [and thus once it has been established that the Torah does not necessarily mean a minor, it is legitimate to assume that this case is no exception to the general rule] (*Tos.*).

2.

מֵאֵימָתַי חַיָּב? — *When is he liable?*

[What must he do to become classified as a *ben sorer u'moreh*?] All of the requisites cited in the mishnah were included in the Oral Law handed down to Moshe at Sinai and transmitted down through the generations (*Rambam, Mamrim* 7:2).

מִשֶּׁיֹּאכַל טַרְטֵימַר בָּשָׂר — *When he eats a tartemar of meat*

A *tartemar* is half a *maneh* (*Rav* from *Gem.* 70a), i.e., the weight of fifty *dinars* (see below). This large amount of meat must be eaten at one time (*Rambam, Mamrim* 7:2) [so that it be a gluttonous consumption (see ibid.:1)]. Furthermore, in order to be liable, he must eat it among people of low character, and it must be eaten כְּמַאֲכַל בֶּן דְּרוֹסָאִי — i.e., semi-cooked, in the manner that bandits [who are on the run] eat meat [Ben Derosai was a famous bandit] (*Rav* from *Gem.* 70a). It must also be purchased from money stolen from his father, as mishnah 3 will explain.

וְיִשְׁתֶּה חֲצִי לֹג יַיִן הָאִיטַלְקִי. — *and drinks a half-log of Italian wine.*

Italian wine was considered to be of superior quality, and he is therefore likely to be drawn to it more and more (*Rav*). The same would apply to any other superior wine (*Meiri*). Other wines, however, being less addictive, would need to be drunk in larger quantities to render him a *ben sorer*

8
2

2. **W**hen is he liable? When he eats a *tartemar* of meat and drinks a half-*log* of Italian wine. R' Yose says: A *maneh* of meat and a *log* of wine. [If] he ate at a gathering for a *mitzvah*, [or] he ate at the [meal for the] intercalation of the month;

u'moreh (*Rashi*). The wine must be drunk semidiluted (*Rav* from *Gem.* 70a) [i.e., partially diluted, but less diluted than standard wine].

Rambam (*Hil. Mamrim* 7:2) omits the Italian factor from the list of wine requirements necessary to convict him of being a *ben sorer u'moreh*. It is possible that *Rambam* understood the *Tanna's* choice of Italian wine to be merely illustrative of a fine wine in his area, but not to be a legally significant factor (*Kesef Mishneh*).

Others interpret the word *Italian* to refer to the half-*log*, as the Italian log was a greater quantity than a standard log (*Yad Ramah*).

.רַבִּי יוֹסֵי אוֹמֵר: מָנֶה בָשָׂר וְלֹג יַיִן — *R' Yose says: A maneh of meat and a log of wine.*

[He requires twice the quantity of meat and wine required by the first *Tanna*. A *maneh* is the weight of one hundred *dinar*.]

The halachah follows the first view (*Rav; Rambam, Mamrim* 7:2).

,אָכַל בַּחֲבוּרַת מִצְוָה — *[If] he ate at a gathering for a mitzvah,*

Even if he stole money, bought wine and meat, and ate these quantities at a meal which was in honor of a mitzvah celebration [e.g., a wedding] (*Rav*), he does not become a *ben sorer u'moreh* through this, because involvement in a *mitzvah* does not draw a person to continued indulgence (*Gem.* 70b).

This is true even if those participating in the meal are people of low character. One who partakes of a meal together with upright people does not become classified as a *ben sorer u'moreh* even if there was no *mitzvah* involved (*Gem.*, ibid.).

;אָכַל בְּעִבּוּר הַחֹדֶשׁ — *[or] he ate at the [meal for the] intercalation of the month;*

As explained in the first chapter (mishnah 2), a lunar month can be either twenty-nine or thirty days, and only in the former case is it necessary for the court to officially declare the following day to be the beginning of the new month. Even so, in the case of a thirty-day month, they gathered together ten or more people to convene a meal on the thirty-first day in order to publicize the advent of the New Moon (*Rashi, Meiri* from *Gem.* 70b). The custom was to prepare a meal of bread and beans. Nevertheless, if this boy ate large quantities of meat and wine in the midst of this meal, he does not become classified as a *ben sorer u'moreh*, since it is a meal convened for *mitzvah* purposes (*Rav* from *Gem.* 70b).

As stated above, the law of a *ben sorer u'moreh* applies only to one who eats among people of low character and it seems unlikely that the courts would delegate such people for the purpose of declaring the New Moon. Nevertheless, even if such people convened this meal on their own initiative, since its purpose is for a *mitzvah*, one who eats meat and drinks wine among them does not become a *ben sorer u'moreh* (*Yad Ramah;* cf. *Meiri*).

אָכַל מַעֲשֵׂר שֵׁנִי בִּירוּשָׁלַיִם; אָכַל נְבֵלוֹת וּטְרֵפוֹת, שְׁקָצִים וּרְמָשִׂים; [אָכַל טֶבֶל, וּמַעֲשֵׂר רִאשׁוֹן שֶׁלֹּא נִטְּלָה תְרוּמָתוֹ, וּמַעֲשֵׂר שֵׁנִי וְהֶקְדֵּשׁ שֶׁלֹּא נִפְדּוּ;] אָכַל דָּבָר שֶׁהוּא מִצְוָה

ר׳ עובדיה מברטנורא

אבל מעשר שני בירושלים. כיון דכדרך מלותו הוא, דכתיב במעשר שני (דברים יד, כו) בבקר ובלאן וביין ובשכר, לא ממשיך: **נבלות וטריפות שקצים ורמשים.** דכתיב (שם כא, יח) איננו שומע בקולנו, ולא זה, שאפילו בקולו של המקום אינו שומע: **דבר שהוא מצוה.** דרבנן, לאתויי תנחומי אבלים, דאי מרישא, הוה אמינא חבורת מלוה היינו כהנים שאוכלים קדשים או אכילת פסחים:

יד אברהם

אָכַל מַעֲשֵׂר שֵׁנִי בִּירוּשָׁלַיִם; — *[or] he ate maaser sheni in Jerusalem;*

[The produce of crops grown in Eretz Yisrael must be tithed (*maaser*). The first tithe (*maaser rishon*) is given to the *Leviim*. In addition, in the first, second, fourth, and fifth years of every seven-year *Shemittah* cycle, one must also take a second tithe — *maaser sheni* — from his crops and either bring it to Jerusalem and eat it there or else redeem it with money which is then spent on food in Jerusalem.]

The mishnah refers to a case in which he stole *maaser sheni* money and took it to Jerusalem, where he purchased with it meat and wine, which he ate there (*Rashi* 70b). Although he stole money and bought meat and wine with it, since he followed the procedure outlined by the Torah (*Deut.* 14:26) for the proper use of *maaser sheni* funds, he is not deemed involved in an activity which will draw him into further improper indulgence (*Rav* from *Gem.* ibid.).

אָכַל נְבֵלוֹת וּטְרֵפוֹת, — *[or] he ate neveilos or tereifos,*

[He ate the meat of animals which had not been slaughtered according to Torah law (*neveilos*) or from those which had been properly slaughtered but which were subsequently found to be defective in a major organ (*tereifos*) and thus unfit for kosher meat.]

שְׁקָצִים וּרְמָשִׂים; — *[or] abominable or creeping animals;*

Or he ate from nonkosher birds or small, scurrying creatures [such as rodents and lizards, etc.) (*Rashi* to 70b, s.v. סתם שקצים). Consumption of these forbidden meats does not bring him into the category of the *ben sorer u'moreh*, because the Torah (*Deut.* 21:18) specifies in its description of him that he is one who *does not heed the voice of his father ...*, which excludes one who ignores even the voice of God by eating that which is forbidden (*Rav* from *Gem.* 70b).

Even if he ate the meat of kosher birds he is not classified a *ben sorer u'moreh*, because fowl does not have the same desirability as meat and he will not be so strongly drawn to it. That which the mishnah specifies nonkosher birds is to indicate that even if he ate primarily meat, but one olive's bulk of the required *tartemar* was nonkosher fowl, he does not

[or] he ate *maaser sheni* in Jerusalem; [or] he ate *neveilos* or *tereifos*, [or] abominable or creeping animals; [(or) he ate *tevel*, (or) *maaser rishon* from which its *terumah* had not been taken, or *maaser sheni* or *hekdesh* which had not been redeemed;] [or] he ate something which is a *mitzvah*

become a *ben sorer u'moreh* (*Gem.* ibid.). Had he eaten meat with just a little bit of kosher poultry to complete the *tartemar*, however, he would be liable (*Rashi*).

[אָכַל טֶבֶל, וּמַעֲשֵׂר רִאשׁוֹן שֶׁלֹּא נִטְּלָה תְרוּמָתוֹ, — *[(or) he ate tevel, (or) maaser rishon from which its terumah had not been taken,*

[Before *maaser* (tithe) is separated from a crop to be given to a *Levi*, a portion of the produce of Eretz Yisrael must be separated to be given to a *Kohen*. This is known as *terumah*. Produce which has not had its *terumah* or *maasros* removed is called *tevel* and it is forbidden for consumption.

Additionally, the *maaser rishon* (first tithe) which is given to the *Levi* must in turn be tithed by him, with that tithe of the tithe given to a *Kohen*. This is known as *terumas maaser* — the *terumah* of the *maaser*. Before the *Kohen's* portion has been separated, the *Levi* too is forbidden to eat from his tithe.

וּמַעֲשֵׂר שֵׁנִי וְהֶקְדֵּשׁ שֶׁלֹּא נִפְדּוּ;] — *or maaser sheni or hekdesh which had not been redeemed;]*

[As explained above, *maaser sheni* food must be either transported to Jerusalem to be eaten there, or redeemed for money. It is forbidden, however, to eat unredeemed *maaser sheni* outside Jerusalem. Similarly, *hekdesh* (consecrated foods) which are not used sacrificially are nevertheless forbidden for consumption until they are redeemed.] If he ate any of these foods — *tevel, maaser rishon, sheni* or *hekdesh* — before they have been properly treated to render them permissible, he does not become classified a *ben sorer u'moreh* by their consumption.

Some authorities maintain that these last four cases do not belong in the mishnah since they apply only to produce, and only the eating of meat can cause one to be classified a *ben sorer u'moreh* (*Yad Ramah; Tos. Yom Tov*). Others explain those versions which include these cases to be referring to the drinking of wine, to which these laws do apply. The word *he ate* is meant in a general sense and actually refers to drinking (*Tif. Yis.; Rashash; Shinuyei Nuschaos*).

[Unredeemed *hekdesh* could refer to meat as well in the case of an animal set aside for certain types of sacrifices which developed a blemish that renders it unfit for use as an offering. Such an animal (שׁוֹר פְּסוּלֵי הַמּוּקְדָּשִׁין) is redeemed and then slaughtered and eaten with the money going to purchase a new sacrifice. Before redemption, however, it remains forbidden for slaughter and consumption.]

אָכַל דָּבָר שֶׁהוּא מִצְוָה — *[or] he ate something which is a mitzvah*

If he consumed the meat and wine during a meal designated for a

וְדָבָר שֶׁהוּא עֲבֵרָה; אָכַל כָּל מַאֲכָל וְלֹא אָכַל
בָּשָׂר; שָׁתָה כָל מַשְׁקֶה וְלֹא שָׁתָה יַיִן — אֵינוֹ
נַעֲשֶׂה בֶן סוֹרֵר וּמוֹרֶה, עַד שֶׁיֹּאכַל בָּשָׂר וְיִשְׁתֶּה
יַיִן, שֶׁנֶּאֱמַר: ,,זוֹלֵל וְסֹבֵא". וְאַף עַל פִּי שֶׁאֵין
רְאָיָה לַדָּבָר, זֵכֶר לַדָּבָר, שֶׁנֶּאֱמַר: ,,אַל־תְּהִי
בְסֹבְאֵי־יָיִן בְּזֹלֲלֵי בָשָׂר לָמוֹ".

[ג] **גָּנַב** מִשֶּׁל אָבִיו וְאָכַל בִּרְשׁוּת אָבִיו; מִשֶּׁל

ר' עובדיה מברטנורא

ודבר שהוא עבירה. לאתויי תענית צבור שאיסורו מדברי סופרים: **(ג) גנב: משל אביו
ואכל ברשות אביו.** אף על גב דסתיך ליה לגנוב משל אביו, הואיל ואכל ברשות אביו,
מתפחד ומתבעת מאביו שמא יראנו ולא ממשיך:

Rabbinic *mitzvah*, such as the one eaten upon comforting the bereaved, it does not render him a *ben sorer u'moreh* (*Rav* from *Gem.* ibid.).

It is necessary that this be stated, because the previously stated case of *mitzvah* could be referring only to those of Biblical origin, such as *Kohanim* who eat *kodashim* (*Rav; Rashi*).

Although the meal eaten for the intercalation of the month is also of Rabbinic origin (*Tos. Yom Tov*), the commandment with which it is involved — that of intercalation of the month — is of Biblical origin, while this case refers to a meal associated with a Rabbinic *mitzvah* (*Mahariach*).

וְדָבָר שֶׁהוּא עֲבֵרָה; — *or something which is a transgression;*

Although the mishnah has already stated that consumption of forbidden foods does not lead to classification as a *ben sorer u'moreh*, the mishnah repeats this to include consumption which violates only a Rabbinic prohibition, such as one of the fast days which are mandated by Rabbinic law (*Rav* from *Gem.* ibid.).

אָכַל כָּל מַאֲכָל וְלֹא אָכַל בָּשָׂר; — *[or] he ate any food but meat* (lit., he did not eat meat);

[As explained above, only the gluttonous consumption of meat and wine classified him as a *ben sorer u'moreh*.]

Some authorities maintain that the meat of an undomesticated animal (e.g., deer) has the same status as that of a domesticated animal regarding this issue, and its consumption can also render a *ben sorer u'moreh* (*Yad Ramah*). Others contend that since it is less available, it does not have the same power to draw one into gluttony and thus does not qualify for this law (*Meiri*).

שָׁתָה כָל מַשְׁקֶה וְלֹא שָׁתָה יַיִן — *or he drank any beverage other than wine* —

Even if he consumed other intoxicants, he does not become classified a *ben sorer umoreh* (*Gem.* 70b), because they are not as habit forming (*Rashi*; cf. *Meiri*).

אֵינוֹ נַעֲשֶׂה בֶן סוֹרֵר וּמוֹרֶה, עַד שֶׁיֹּאכַל בָּשָׂר וְיִשְׁתֶּה יַיִן, שֶׁנֶּאֱמַר: ,,זוֹלֵל וְסֹבֵא". — *he does not become a ben sorer u'moreh*

or something which is a transgression; [or] he ate any food but meat; or he drank any beverage other than wine — he does not become a *ben sorer u'moreh*, unless he eats meat and drinks wine, as it says: *He is a glutton and a drunkard.* Although there is no proof to the matter, [there is] an indication to the matter, as it says: *Be not among wine bibers and gluttonous eaters of meat.*

3. [If] he stole from his father and ate in his father's domain; [or] from

YAD AVRAHAM

unless he eats meat and drinks wine, as it says (Deut. 21:20): "He is a glutton and a drunkard."

The word זוֹלֵל, *glutton*, refers to one who eats meat gluttonously, and סֹבֵא, *drunkard*, applies to one who drinks wine to excess (*Rambam, Hil. Mamrim* 1:1).

וְאַף עַל פִּי שֶׁאֵין רְאָיָה לַדָּבָר, זֵכֶר לַדָּבָר, שֶׁנֶּאֱמַר: ,,אַל־תְּהִי בְסֹבְאֵי־יָיִן בְּזֹלְלֵי בָשָׂר לָמוֹ״. — *Although there is no proof to the matter, [there is] an indication to the matter, as it says* (*Proverbs* 23:20): *"Be not among wine bibers and gluttonous eaters of meat."*

Although it cannot be conclusively proven that the words זוֹלֵל וְסֹבֵא, *glutton and drunkard*, refer specifically to meat and wine, there is an indication to this to be found in the verse in *Proverbs* where these terms are used expressly in regard to meat and wine (*Rashi*).

3.

The excessive consumption of meat and wine does not suffice to have a boy classified a *ben sorer u'moreh.* The following mishnah adds requirements in regard to the source of the funds used to purchase these items and the site of their consumption. Underlying the mishnah's rulings is the law (not otherwise stated explicitly) that the money used to obtain the meat and wine must have been stolen from his father. The reason for this may be that, as will be seen in mishnah 5, the rationale given for the severe punishment of such a boy is because of the likelihood that such behavior will lead him to pursue a life of crime. Therefore, as long as he has not shown a willingness to steal to satisfy his desires, this assumption is not yet valid (*Yad Ramah;* see there for another reason).

גָּנַב מִשֶּׁל אָבִיו וְאָכַל בִּרְשׁוּת אָבִיו; — *[If] he stole from his father and ate in his father's domain;*

One becomes a *ben sorer u'moreh* only if he steals money from his father, uses that money to purchase meat and wine, and consumes it outside his father's domain (*Gem.* 71a). However, if he consumes it in his father's domain, he is likely to be

אֲחֵרִים וְאָכַל בִּרְשׁוּת אֲחֵרִים; מִשֶּׁל אֲחֵרִים וְאָכַל בִּרְשׁוּת אָבִיו — אֵינוֹ נַעֲשֶׂה בֵּן סוֹרֵר וּמוֹרֶה — עַד שֶׁיִּגְנֹב מִשֶּׁל אָבִיו וְיֹאכַל בִּרְשׁוּת אֲחֵרִים. רַבִּי יוֹסֵי בַּר רַבִּי יְהוּדָה אוֹמֵר: עַד שֶׁיִּגְנֹב מִשֶּׁל אָבִיו וּמִשֶּׁל אִמּוֹ.

[ד] **הָיָה** אָבִיו רוֹצֶה וְאִמּוֹ אֵינָהּ רוֹצָה, אָבִיו אֵינוֹ רוֹצֶה וְאִמּוֹ רוֹצָה — אֵינוֹ נַעֲשֶׂה בֵּן סוֹרֵר וּמוֹרֶה — עַד שֶׁיְּהוּ שְׁנֵיהֶם רוֹצִים.

ר׳ עובדיה מברטנורא

גנב משל אחרים. לא שכיח ליה שיוכל בכל עת לגנוב משל אחרים, ולא ממשיך: **עד שיגנוב משל אביו.** דשכיח ליה לגנוב בכל עת: **ויאכל ברשות אחרים.** שאינו מתבעת שם מאביו, דבכי האי גוונא ודאי ממשיך: **ומשל אמו.** מנכסים שיש לה, שאין לאביו רשות בהן, כגון שנתן לה אחר נכסים במתנה על מנת שאין לבעלה רשות בהן. ואין הלכה כרבי יוסי ברבי יהודה: (ד) **ראויה לאביו.** שוה ודומה לאביו בקול במראה וקומה, דכתיב (דברים כא,יח) איננו שומע בקולנו, מדלא כתיב בקולותינו, שמע מינה קול אחד לשניהם, ומדקול בעינן שוים, מראה וקומה נמי בעינן שוים. ואין הלכה כרבי יהודה:

יד אברהם

afraid of discovery and will therefore not pursue this course for long. Therefore, doing so does not qualify him as a *ben sorer u'moreh* (*Rav* from *Gem.* ibid.).

מִשֶּׁל אֲחֵרִים וְאָכַל בִּרְשׁוּת אֲחֵרִים; — *[or] from others and he ate in the domain of others;*

If he stole from others he does not become a *ben sorer u'moreh,* because the opportunity to do so is not readily available, and his wanton behavior is thus not necessarily likely to continue unchecked (ibid.).

מִשֶּׁל אֲחֵרִים וְאָכַל בִּרְשׁוּת אָבִיו – *[or] from others and he ate in his father's domain —*

In this case he certainly does not qualify, since his opportunities to continue stealing are less assured and he is also fearful of discovery by his father (*Gem.* ibid.). [The mishnah mentions this only to round out the series of cases cited.]

אֵינוֹ נַעֲשֶׂה בֵּן סוֹרֵר וּמוֹרֶה – עַד שֶׁיִּגְנֹב מִשֶּׁל אָבִיו וְיֹאכַל בִּרְשׁוּת אֲחֵרִים. — *he does not become a ben sorer u'moreh — unless he steals from his father and eats in the domain of others.*

In such a case, opportunities for theft abound and he is also not afraid of having his gluttony and drunkenness discovered. Therefore, he is likely to continue on this path, and his behavior is thus classified as that of a *ben sorer u'moreh* (*Rav* from *Gem.* ibid.).

Additionally, he must steal from his father the money used to purchase the meat and wine. If he steals the meat and wine themselves, he is not

others and he ate in the domain of others; [or] from others and he ate in his father's domain — he does not become a *ben sorer u'moreh* — unless he steals from his father and eats in the domain of others. R' Yose the son of R' Yehudah says: Unless he steals from his father and his mother.

4. [If] his father was willing and his mother was not, [or] his father was not willing and his mother was willing — he does not become a *ben sorer u'moreh* — unless they are both willing.

YAD AVRAHAM

rendered a *ben sorer u'moreh* (*Gem.* 71a, *Rashi*).

רַבִּי יוֹסֵי בַר רַבִּי יְהוּדָה אוֹמֵר: עַד שֶׁיִּגְנֹב מִשֶּׁל אָבִיו וּמִשֶּׁל אִמּוֹ. — *R' Yose the son of R' Yehudah says: Unless he steals from his father and his mother.*

[He must steal from his mother as well as his father to be classified a *ben sorer u'moreh.*]

This presents something of a problem, since the law is that a woman's possessions belong to her husband [and thus stealing even those possessions which she brought into the marriage would not constitute stealing from the mother]. However, if someone gives her something with the stipulation that her husband have no share in it, the law is that it remains hers. Thus, the mishnah may refer to such property (*Rav* from *Gem.* ibid.). Alternatively, if he stole money which had been set aside to be spent on both his mother and his father, that is considered tantamount to stealing from his mother as well (*Gem.* ibid.).

The halachah follows the view of the first *Tanna*, that it is sufficient to steal from just his father (*Rav; Rambam, Hil. Mamrim* 7:2).

4.

The previous mishnayos have delineated the personal requirements of the son and the nature and conditions of his crimes which must pertain in order to classify him a *ben sorer u'moreh.* The following mishnah details the conditions which must inhere in the parents before this classification can be made.

הָיָה אָבִיו רוֹצֶה וְאִמּוֹ אֵינָהּ רוֹצָה, אָבִיו אֵינוֹ רוֹצֶה וְאִמּוֹ רוֹצָה - — *[If] his father was willing and his mother was not, [or] his father was not willing and his mother was willing* —

[Someone fulfilled the prerequisites of a *ben sorer u'moreh,* but either his father or mother was unwilling to bring him to court to be judged.]

אֵינוֹ נַעֲשֶׂה בֵּן סוֹרֵר וּמוֹרֶה - עַד שֶׁיְּהוּ שְׁנֵיהֶם רוֹצִים. — *he does not become a ben sorer u'moreh — unless they are both willing.*

This is derived from the wording of the Torah (*Deut.* 21:19): *And his father and mother shall seize him* — which

רַבִּי יְהוּדָה אוֹמֵר: אִם לֹא הָיְתָה אִמּוֹ רְאוּיָה לְאָבִיו אֵינוֹ נַעֲשֶׂה בֵּן סוֹרֵר וּמוֹרֶה.

הָיָה אֶחָד מֵהֶם גִּדֵּם, אוֹ חִגֵּר, אוֹ אִלֵּם, אוֹ סוּמָא, אוֹ חֵרֵשׁ, אֵינוֹ נַעֲשֶׂה בֵּן סוֹרֵר וּמוֹרֶה, שֶׁנֶּאֱמַר: „וְתָפְשׂוּ בוֹ אָבִיו וְאִמּוֹ" — וְלֹא גִדְּמִין; „וְהוֹצִיאוּ אוֹתוֹ — וְלֹא חִגְּרִין; „וְאָמְרוּ" — וְלֹא אִלְּמִין; „בְּנֵנוּ זֶה" — וְלֹא סוּמִין; „אֵינֶנּוּ שֹׁמֵעַ בְּקֹלֵנוּ" — וְלֹא חֵרְשִׁין.

ר' עובדיה מברטנורא

גידם. ידו קטועה: **בננו זה.** משמע שמראין אותו: **חרשים.** אם אמר להם איני מקבל מכם, אינם שומעים אותו, ואף על פי שרואים אחר כך שאינו מקיים מצותן, מכל מקום התורה אמרה איננו שומע בקולנו, דמשמע דבשעת הקול קאמרי דלא שמע, ששמעוהו שאמר איני מקבל מכם:

יד אברהם

indicates that they must both be involved in bringing him to court (*Rambam, Hil. Mamrim* 7:2). The rationale for this can be understood to be that the Torah requires their combined judgment before initiating so severe a process (*Meiri*).

רַבִּי יְהוּדָה אוֹמֵר: אִם לֹא הָיְתָה אִמּוֹ רְאוּיָה לְאָבִיו אֵינוֹ נַעֲשֶׂה בֵּן סוֹרֵר וּמוֹרֶה. — *R' Yehudah says: [If] his mother did not correspond to his father he does not become a ben sorer u'moreh.*

In order for these laws to apply, the mother must be similar to the father in her voice, appearance, and height. This is derived from the verse (ibid.): *He does not heed our voice* — rather than voices — which indicates that they speak in one voice, because their voices are so similar. Since, in R' Yehudah's derivation, the Torah requires that their voices be alike, it stands to reason that the same applies to their appearance and height (*Rav* from *Gem.* 71a; *Rashi* ad loc.). We find a similar rule in the case of the two goats which are sacrificed on *Yom Kippur*, that the Torah requires that they must be similar in these respects (*Yoma* 6:1). This may be the precedent for the ruling here as well (*Tos. Yom Tov*).

In accordance with R' Yehudah's view, the *Gemara* cites the statement that there never was and never will be a *ben sorer u'moreh*, since the possibility of fulfilling all these prerequisites is remote in the extreme. Nevertheless, the Torah gave this law so that we may study it and be rewarded. The *Gemara*, however, also cites the opinion of R' Yonasan that the execution of a *ben sorer u'moreh* was something that had happened.

The halachah does not follow R' Yehudah's view (*Rav; Rambam Comm.*).

הָיָה אֶחָד מֵהֶם גִּדֵּם, אוֹ חִגֵּר, אוֹ אִלֵּם, אוֹ סוּמָא, אוֹ חֵרֵשׁ, אֵינוֹ נַעֲשֶׂה בֵּן סוֹרֵר וּמוֹרֶה, — *[If] one of them is missing a hand or was lame, mute, blind, or deaf, he does not become a ben sorer u'moreh,*

8
4

R′ Yehudah says: [If] his mother did not correspond to his father he does not become a *ben sorer u′moreh.*

[If] one of them is missing a hand or was lame, mute, blind, or deaf, he does not become a *ben sorer u′moreh,* as it says: *And his father and mother shall seize him* — which excludes those missing a hand; *and they shall take him out* — which excludes the lame; *and they shall say* — which excludes the mute; *this son of ours* — which excludes the blind; *does not heed our voice* — which excludes the deaf.

YAD AVRAHAM

[I.e., if either of the parents is afflicted with one of these handicaps, their son cannot become a *ben sorer u′moreh.*]

Although the mishnah derives this from the verse, this too has a logical rationale. People with these handicaps are often embittered, and it is therefore possible that their bitterness leads them to initiate this harsh action (*Meiri*).

שֶׁנֶּאֱמַר: ,,וְתָפְשׂוּ בוֹ אָבִיו וְאִמּוֹ" - וְלֹא גִדְּמִין; — *as it says* (*Deut.* 21:19,20): *"And his father and mother shall seize him" — which excludes those missing a hand;*

[The Torah describes both of them as seizing him and bringing him to court,] and one who is missing a hand would be unable to do this (*Yad Ramah*).

,,וְהוֹצִיאוּ אוֹתוֹ" - וְלֹא חִגְּרִין; — *"and they shall take him out" — which excludes the lame;*

The Torah stipulates that his father and mother shall take out their son to the judges of the city. Since one who is lame is barely capable of transporting himself, let alone others, they are excluded by this stipulation (ibid.).

,,וְאָמְרוּ" - וְלֹא אִלְּמִין; — *"and they shall say" — which excludes the mute;*

[Since the Torah dictates that they both make the prescribed statement, if either of them is mute these laws do not apply.]

,,בְּנֵנוּ זֶה" - וְלֹא סוּמִין; — *"this son of ours" — which excludes the blind;*

In order to be able to point him out in the manner portrayed by this phrase, it is necessary for them to be able to see him (*Rav*).

,,אֵינֶנּוּ שֹׁמֵעַ בְּקֹלֵנוּ" - וְלֹא חֵרְשִׁין. — *"does not heed our voice" — which excludes the deaf.*

Such a statement implies that they heard from him a refusal to heed their admonishment (*Rav; Rashi*). Alternatively, for both of them to say, "He does not heed our voice" — in the plural form — it is necessary for each to have heard the admonishment of the other, as well as being aware of their own (*Yad Ramah*).

סנהדרין
ח/ד

מַתְרִין בּוֹ בִּפְנֵי שְׁלֹשָׁה וּמַלְקִין אוֹתוֹ. חָזַר וְקִלְקֵל, נִדּוֹן בְּעֶשְׂרִים וּשְׁלֹשָׁה. וְאֵינוֹ נִסְקָל עַד שֶׁיְּהוּ שָׁם שְׁלֹשָׁה הָרִאשׁוֹנִים, שֶׁנֶּאֱמַר: „בְּנֵנוּ זֶה" — זֶהוּ שֶׁלָּקָה בִּפְנֵיכֶם.

בָּרַח עַד שֶׁלֹּא נִגְמַר דִּינוֹ וְאַחַר כָּךְ הִקִּיף זָקָן הַתַּחְתּוֹן, פָּטוּר. וְאִם מִשֶּׁנִּגְמַר דִּינוֹ בָּרַח, וְאַחַר כָּךְ הִקִּיף זָקָן הַתַּחְתּוֹן, חַיָּב.

ר׳ עובדיה מברטנורא

ומתרין בו בפני שלשה. הכי קאמר, ומתרין בו בפני שנים שלא ירגיל, ואם לא שמע, מלקין אותו בבית דין של שלשה, כדתנן בפרק קמא (משנה ב) מכות בשלשה, דויסרו אותו האמור בבן סורר ומורה, מלקות הוא, כתיב הכא (דברים כא,יח) בן סורר ומורה, וכתיב התם (שם כה,ב) והיה אם בן הכות הרשע: **זה הוא שלקה בפניכם.** ואף על גב דמיבעי ליה זה ולא סומין, אם איתא דלהך מלתא לחוד אתא, לזה הוא שלקה בפניכם, לכתוב בננו הוא, מאי בננו זה, שמעת מינה תרתי: **ואחר כך הקיף זקן התחתון פטור.** כיון דאילו עביד השתא, לאו בר קטלא הוא: **ואם משנגמר דינו ברח.** הוי כגברא קטילא וחייב אפילו לאחר כמה שנים:

יד אברהם

מַתְרִין בּוֹ בִּפְנֵי שְׁלֹשָׁה — *They warn him before three*

The *Gemara* (71b) emends the mishnah to read: *They warn him before two and flog him before three* — i.e., when the parents see their son indulging in hedonism to the degree described above (*Meiri*), they warn him before two witnesses that he must cease such activity (*Rav*).

This is not part of the general principle that a warning is required before the commission of a transgression in order for the penalty of lashes to be imposed. That warning must be made by the witnesses *immediately* prior to the misdeed (*Rashi*). This is simply a requirement that the parents admonish him and warn him of the consequences of his behavior before he can be punished (*Meiri*). Others contend that the warning described is the same as that required for the punishment of every transgression (*Rambam Comm.; Hil. Mamrim 7:7*). [Even those who understand otherwise would agree that the witnesses must also warn him at the time of his act (see *Meiri*).]

וּמַלְקִין אוֹתוֹ. — *and flog him.*

If he continues his behavior after their warning, they bring him to court and produce testimony of the warning they gave him and his continued transgressions. He is then flogged by the court (*Meiri*). This is derived by the *Gemara* (71b) from the words וְיִסְּרוּ, *and they chasten him,* which is interpreted exegetically to refer to lashes (*Rav*).

חָזַר וְקִלְקֵל, נִדּוֹן בְּעֶשְׂרִים וּשְׁלֹשָׁה. — *[If] he repeats his misdeed, he is judged by twenty-three.*

If he continues even after the flogging to pursue his evil ways, his

8
4
They warn him before three and flog him. [If] he repeats his misdeed, he is judged by twenty-three. He is not stoned unless the original three are present, as it says: *this son of ours* — this son, who was flogged in your presence.

[If] he fled before the sentence was pronounced and his lower beard then grew around, he is exempt. If he fled after the sentence was pronounced and his lower beard then grew around, he is liable.

YAD AVRAHAM

parents bring him to a court of twenty-three [the number needed for capital cases] with witnesses who testify to his degenerate behavior and their warning to him (*Meiri*).

וְאֵינוֹ נִסְקָל עַד שֶׁיְּהוּ שָׁם שְׁלֹשָׁה הָרִאשׁוֹנִים, שֶׁנֶּאֱמַר: „בְּנֵנוּ זֶה״ - זֶהוּ שֶׁלָּקָה בִּפְנֵיכֶם. — *He is not stoned unless the original three are present, as it says (ibid.): "this son of ours" — this son, who was flogged in your presence.*

[From the seemingly unnecessary word *this* in the cited phrase, we derive that the court of twenty-three must include the three judges who had previously ordered him flogged.]

בָּרַח עַד שֶׁלֹּא נִגְמַר דִּינוֹ וְאַחַר כָּךְ הִקִּיף זָקָן הַתַּחְתּוֹן, פָּטוּר. — *[If] he fled before the sentence was pronounced and his lower beard then grew around, he is exempt.*

[If he managed to escape before the court sentence was passed, and prior to being recaptured he reached the age at which one can no longer be judged a *ben sorer u'moreh* (see mishnah 1), he is no longer liable to being sentenced.] Since if he were to commit the offense at this time he would not be punishable, he is no longer susceptible to judgment for that offense (*Rav; Rashi* from *Gem.* 71b).

Alternatively, a person is not considered to be liable for a transgression until the legal process, culminating with his sentencing, has been completed; thus, in this case, his sentencing is considered the final stage of his designation as a *ben sorer u'moreh.* Accordingly, he cannot be sentenced if he is no longer of an age in which he can be so classified (*Yad Ramah* from *Gem.* ibid.).

וְאִם מִשֶּׁנִּגְמַר דִּינוֹ בָּרַח, וְאַחַר כָּךְ הִקִּיף זָקָן הַתַּחְתּוֹן, חַיָּב. — *If he fled after the sentence was pronounced and his lower beard then grew around, he is liable.*

The authority of the judiciary in Jewish law is such that once sentence has been passed on someone, his legal status is defined by that sentence. Thus one who has received a death sentence is considered tantamount to one who has already been executed in regard to all legal issues. Therefore, his punishment may be carried out even if he is no longer of an age of liability (*Rav, Rashi* from *Gem.* ibid.).

[ה] **בֵּן** סוֹרֵר וּמוֹרֶה נִדּוֹן עַל שֵׁם סוֹפוֹ: יָמוּת זַכַּאי, וְאַל יָמוּת חַיָּב. שֶׁמִּיתָתָן שֶׁל רְשָׁעִים הֲנָאָה לָהֶן וַהֲנָאָה לָעוֹלָם, וְלַצַּדִּיקִים, רַע לָהֶן וְרַע לָעוֹלָם. יַיִן וְשֵׁנָה לָרְשָׁעִים, הֲנָאָה לָהֶן וַהֲנָאָה לָעוֹלָם; וְלַצַּדִּיקִים, רַע לָהֶן וְרַע לָעוֹלָם. פִּזּוּר לָרְשָׁעִים, הֲנָאָה לָהֶן וַהֲנָאָה לָעוֹלָם; וְלַצַּדִּיקִים, רַע לָהֶן וְרַע לָעוֹלָם. כִּנּוּס

ר' עובדיה מברטנורא

(ה) **נדון על שם סופו.** סוף שמכלה ממון אביו, ומבקש מה שהורגל בו ואינו מוצא, ויושב בפרשת דרכים ומלסטס את הבריות, אמרה תורה ימות זכאי ואל ימות חייב: **הנאה להן.** שאינן מוסיפין לחטוא: **והנאה לעולם.** שקטה כל הארץ: **רע להן.** שהיו מוסיפים זכיות: **ורע לעולם.** שהיו מגינים על דורן ומוכיחין את הדור: **יין ושינה לרשעים.** כל זמן ששותים וישנים, אין חוטאין ואין מריעין לבריות: **לצדיקים רע להם.** שאינם עוסקין בתורה: **ורע לעולם.** שכשהן מתבטלים, פורענות באה לעולם:

יד אברהם

According to the second interpretation cited above, the *Gemara* means simply that once sentence has been passed his age is no longer an issue, since his designation as a *ben sorer u'moreh* has been finalized (*Yad Ramah*).

5.

The law of the *ben sorer u'moreh* seems on the face of it incomprehensible, since despite his wayward and rebellious behavior, he has done nothing which should incur the death penalty according to the general rules of the Torah. The punishment of death seems out of all proportion to the crimes actually committed. This mishnah explains the rationale behind the Torah's decree of such severe punishment.

בֵּן סוֹרֵר וּמוֹרֶה נִדּוֹן עַל שֵׁם סוֹפוֹ: — *A ben sorer u'moreh is judged according to his eventual outcome:*

[One who sets out on adult life by stealing from his father to gorge himself with meat and guzzle wine, and who has proven himself incorrigible by persisting in the face of warnings and even official lashes,] is destined eventually to exhaust his father's estate and go on to support his lifestyle by taking the property of others through robbery and murder (*Rav* from *Gem.* 72a).

יָמוּת זַכַּאי, וְאַל יָמוּת חַיָּב. — *let him die innocent, not guilty.*

Rather than waiting until he fulfills this destiny, the Torah dictates that he be put to death at this time, when his course has been clearly set but he is not yet guilty of such severe deeds. Since his lifestyle will also include the desecration of the Sabbath, which is punishable by stoning, his punish-

5. **A** *ben sorer u'moreh* is judged according to his eventual outcome: let him die innocent, not guilty. For the death of the wicked is beneficial to them and beneficial to the world, but that of the righteous is detrimental to them and detrimental to the world. Wine and sleep for the wicked are beneficial to them and beneficial to the world; but for the righteous, they are detrimental to them and detrimental to the world. Dispersal of the wicked is beneficial to them and beneficial to the world; but that of the righteous is detrimental to them and detrimental to the world. Assembly

YAD AVRAHAM

ment at this point is the same (*Yad Ramah;* see *Margoliyos HaYam*).

Although one who endeavors to desecrate the Sabbath may not be killed in order to prevent him from doing so (mishnah 7), the Torah prescribes this drastic preventive measure in this case because he will undoubtedly pursue others to kill them as well. The point about the Sabbath is pertinent only to explain why stoning is chosen as the manner of his execution (ibid.).

It is because he has not yet done anything that actually calls for the death penalty that he is given so many warnings (see mishnah 4), unlike those guilty of any other capital transgression who are punished by death after their first offense (*Toras Chaim*).

שֶׁמִּיתָתָן שֶׁל רְשָׁעִים הֲנָאָה לָהֶן וַהֲנָאָה לָעוֹלָם, — *For the death of the wicked is beneficial to them and beneficial to the world,*

[That this preventive course is worthwhile is part of the larger principle] that the death of all wicked people is actually a benefit to them. By dying when they do they are prevented from further sins [and are thus spared still greater punishments in the World to Come]. Their death also benefits society at large by sparing it their further depredations (*Rav; Rashi*).

וְלַצַּדִּיקִים, רַע לָהֶן וְרַע לָעוֹלָם. — *but that of the righteous is detrimental to them and detrimental to the world.*

When the righteous die, they lose their opportunity to acquire even greater merit and reward. In addition, they are no longer available to protect the world with their merit and to admonish them to act correctly (ibid.).

יַיִן וְשֵׁנָה לָרְשָׁעִים, הֲנָאָה לָהֶן וַהֲנָאָה לָעוֹלָם; וְלַצַּדִּיקִים, רַע לָהֶן וְרַע לָעוֹלָם. — *Wine and sleep for the wicked are beneficial to them and beneficial to the world; but for the righteous, they are detrimental to them and detrimental to the world.*

When the wicked are drunk and asleep, they are not pursuing their evil deeds and the world is thus protected from them; when the righteous are in a state of torpor, they and the world lose the merit of their Torah study (ibid.).

סנהדרין
ח/ו

לָרְשָׁעִים, רַע לָהֶן וְרַע לָעוֹלָם; וְלַצַּדִּיקִים, הֲנָאָה לָהֶן וַהֲנָאָה לָעוֹלָם. שֶׁקֶט לָרְשָׁעִים, רַע לָהֶן וְרַע לָעוֹלָם; וְלַצַּדִּיקִים, הֲנָאָה לָהֶן וַהֲנָאָה לָעוֹלָם.

[ו] **הַבָּא** בַמַּחְתֶּרֶת נִדּוֹן עַל שֵׁם סוֹפוֹ.

ר׳ עובדיה מברטנורא

פיזור. שהן נפרדים זה מזה, ואין יכולים להועץ ולסייע זה את זה: **(ו) הבא במחתרת.** שאמרה תורה יהרג: **נדון על שם סופו.** שסופו להרוג את בעל הבית אם יעמוד כנגדו להציל את שלו:

יד אברהם

פִּזּוּר לָרְשָׁעִים, הֲנָאָה לָהֶן וַהֲנָאָה לָעוֹלָם; וְלַצַּדִּיקִים, רַע לָהֶן וְרַע לָעוֹלָם. כִּנּוּס לָרְשָׁעִים, רַע לָהֶן וְרַע לָעוֹלָם; וְלַצַּדִּיקִים, הֲנָאָה לָהֶן וַהֲנָאָה לָעוֹלָם. — *Dispersal of the wicked is beneficial to them and beneficial to the world; but that of the righteous is detrimental to them and detrimental to the world. Assembly of the wicked is detrimental to them and detrimental to the world; but that of the righteous is beneficial to them and beneficial to the world.*

Certain large-scale activities can be undertaken only through the concerted action of large numbers of people. When the wicked are assembled, therefore, the level of harm they can cause is greatly increased. Thus their dispersal benefits the world by limiting them to the evil which can be perpetrated by an individual; it thereby spares them from being punished for the larger and graver crimes that their massed numbers would empower them to perform. The reverse holds true for the potential of the righteous to bring benefit to the world [and thus to themselves as well] (*Rav*).

שֶׁקֶט לָרְשָׁעִים, רַע לָהֶן וְרַע לָעוֹלָם; וְלַצַּדִּיקִים, הֲנָאָה לָהֶן וַהֲנָאָה לָעוֹלָם. — *Tranquility for the wicked is detrimental to them and detrimental to the world; but for the righteous, it is beneficial to them and beneficial to the world.*

Tranquility allows one time and peace of mind to pursue his chosen course of action. Therefore, it is beneficial when enjoyed by the righteous and detrimental when granted to the wicked (*Yad Ramah*).

6.

Having mentioned the fact that a *ben sorer u'moreh* is executed because of his anticipated future, the mishnah now discusses another Torah law in which death is meted out because of the anticipation of future action. This involves a thief who enters another's home through a tunnel (*Ran*). The Torah states (*Ex.* 22:1) that one who does this has no blood — i.e., his life is forfeit, and it is permitted to kill him (*Rashi*, ibid.). The mishnah now proceeds to explain the reasoning behind this ruling.

8
6

of the wicked is detrimental to them and detrimental to the world; but that of the righteous is beneficial to them and beneficial to the world. Tranquility for the wicked is detrimental to them and detrimental to the world; but for the righteous, it is beneficial to them and beneficial to the world.

6. One who enters through a tunnel is judged according to the eventual outcome.

YAD AVRAHAM

הַבָּא בַּמַּחְתֶּרֶת נִדּוֹן עַל שֵׁם סוֹפוֹ. — *One who enters through a tunnel is judged according to the eventual outcome.*

When a burglar breaks into a house, he is well aware that the owner of the house will stand and defend his belongings if he catches him. It is therefore assumed that his course of action includes a decision to kill the owner if that becomes necessary. Accordingly, the owner is permitted to kill the intruder, in accordance with the maxim: *One who comes to kill you, rise up and kill him first*[1] (*Gem.* 72a).

The *Gemara* (72b) states that not only the owner himself is authorized to kill the intruder, but so is any observer, and it may be done in any manner. Some say that he should be beheaded, if possible, since that is the punishment for one who murders (*Ran; Meiri*). *Rambam* (*Hil. Geneivah* 9:7), however, does not seem to agree with this (*Aruch LaNer*).

The *Gemara* (ibid.) states that this law actually applies to any intruder whether his attempt to break in is through a tunnel or any other entry. This raises the question of why the Torah specifies entering through a tunnel. One opinion is that the Torah simply chose a common example. Another view maintains that only if he takes such pains can it be assumed for certain that he will kill if necessary, and it is therefore permitted to kill him without any warning. In other circumstances, he must first be warned that if he does not desist he will be killed, after which he must state that he intends to continue his action nonetheless (*Rashi*). Others contend that although the warning is necessary, it is not required that he acknowledge it (*Meiri*).

There is another interpretation of this second view in the *Gemara*, that entering through a tunnel is an example of a situation in which it is clear that his intention is to steal; the same would apply if he climbed up a ladder and entered through a window. If he enters through an open door, however, his intentions may be legitimate, and he may not be attacked without being warned (*Yad Ramah*).

Rambam (*Hil. Geneivah* 9:8) rules in accordance with the first view in the

1. This principle is derived from the verse (*Num.* 21:17): *Oppress the Midianites and smite them because they are oppressing you*, etc. (*Tanchuma* 45:1, cited by *Meiri*).

הָיָה בָא בַמַּחְתֶּרֶת וְשָׁבַר אֶת הֶחָבִית, אִם יֶשׁ לוֹ דָמִים, חַיָּב; אִם אֵין לוֹ דָמִים, פָּטוּר.

[ז] **וְאֵלּוּ** הֵן שֶׁמַּצִּילִין אוֹתָן בְּנַפְשָׁן: הָרוֹדֵף אַחַר חֲבֵרוֹ לְהָרְגוֹ,

ר' עובדיה מברטנורא

אם יש לו דמים חייב. כגון האב הבא במחתרת על הבן, שבידוע שרחמי האב על הבן, לפיכך אין הבן רשאי להרגו, ואם שבר האב החבית, חייב לשלם: **אין לו דמים פטור.** ושאר כל אדם הבא במחתרת, שאם הרגו בעל הבית אין לו דמים, אם שבר את החבית, פטור מלשלם, שכיון שהוא מתחייב בנפשו, פטור מן התשלומין, שאין אדם מת ומשלם: **(ז) ואלו הן שמצילין אותן בנפשן.** שמצילין אותן מן העבירה בנפשן, שניתן רשות לכל אדם להרגם כדי להצילן מן העבירה: **הרודף אחר חבירו להרגו.** דכתיב אצל נערה המאורסה (דברים כב,כו) כי כאשר יקום איש על רעהו ורצחו נפש כן הדבר הזה, מקיש רוצח לנערה מאורסה, מה נערה מאורסה ניתן להצילה בנפשו אף רוצח ניתן להצילו בנפשו, ונערה מאורסה נפקא לן מקרא, דכתיב (שם פסוק כז) צעקה הנערה המאורשה ואין מושיע לה, הא יש מושיע לה, חייב להושיעה בכל דבר שיכול להצילה:

יד אברהם

Gemara, that there is no difference between entry through a tunnel or burglary by any other means. *Meiri* maintains that the latter opinion in the *Gemara* is to be followed.

הָיָה בָא בַמַּחְתֶּרֶת וְשָׁבַר אֶת הֶחָבִית, — *[If] he was coming through a tunnel and he broke a barrel,*

One who commits a crime which is punishable by death is exempted from any monetary obligations he may incur in the course of his action. This is known as the principle of קִים לֵיהּ בִּדְרַבָּה מִנֵּיהּ, *he suffers [only] the more severe punishment* (see *Kesubos* 3:2). According to this rule, if an intruder damages property during his break-in he is exempt from paying for it, since he was liable to being summarily killed during his intrusion.

אִם יֶשׁ לוֹ דָמִים, — *if his blood is accountable* (lit., *if he has blood*),

I.e., if he is an intruder whom it is forbidden to kill (*Rashi*), so that if the occupant of the house does kill him, he is held accountable for murdering the intruder (*Tif. Yis.*). This statement of the mishnah applies to one whose affection for the owner of the house is so clear as to preclude any possibility that he could have intentions of murdering him in the course of the break-in. The classic example of this is a father who burglarizes his son's house. It can be taken for granted that, even if caught, he would not kill his own son; therefore, he may not be stopped by killing him (*Rav* from *Gem.* 72b).

חַיָּב; — *he is liable;*

[Since this intruder is not subject to being killed by the owner of the house, he must pay for any damage.]

אִם אֵין לוֹ דָמִים, פָּטוּר. — *if his blood is not accountable* (lit., *he has no blood*), *he is exempt.*

If the intruder's life is forfeit (see preface; cf. *Yad Ramah*) because he is

8 [If] he was coming through a tunnel and he broke a
7 barrel, if his blood is accountable, he is liable; if his blood is not accountable, he is exempt.

7. **T**hese are those who are saved at the cost of their lives: one who pursues another to kill him,

YAD AVRAHAM

considered dangerous, and it is thus permissible to kill him, he is not liable for the damage he inflicts while breaking in, because one is not punished with death and monetary payment for the same deed (*Rav* from *Gem.* ad loc.; see *Bava Kamma* 3:10). Even if he escaped the episode unharmed [and he is thus no longer under the onus of a death penalty since he did not murder anyone], he is exempt from monetary obligations, because the *Gemara* (*Kesubos* 35a) concludes that one who causes damage while pursuing a course of action which carries the death penalty is free of pecuniary obligations even if he escapes the penalty on a technicality (*Rav*).

Rambam, in his commentary, offers a totally different interpretation of this section of the mishnah. If he broke a barrel while entering the home, at which time one who sees him may kill him, he is exempt from monetary obligation [as explained above]. However, if it occurs upon his exit, at which time there is no longer any reason to kill him, since if spotted he will now seek to escape rather than kill, he is obligated to reimburse the owner for the damage he caused. See further, *Hil. Geneivah* 9:11.

7.

Similar to the principle just stated, granting the right to kill an intruder to forestall his possible murder of the occupant of a house, is the obligation to prevent other foul deeds from occurring even if it means killing the perpetrator to prevent his intended crime (*Meiri*).

This principle is derived from the passage in the Torah concerning a betrothed *naarah* (see 7:4) who is raped. The Torah (*Deut.* 22:27) states that if the act occurred in a place where no one could hear her call for help, she is not culpable because אֵין מוֹשִׁיעַ לָהּ, *there was no one to save her*. From this the *Gemara* (73a) derives that if there was someone there who could save her, he may do so using whatever means necessary, even by killing the rapist if there is no other way. This principle is extended to saving a potential murder victim as well.

וְאֵלּוּ הֵן שֶׁמַּצִּילִין אוֹתָן בְּנַפְשָׁן: — *These are those who are saved at the cost of their lives* (lit., *souls*):

The following transgressions may be prevented even if it requires saving the perpetrator from committing them by killing him (*Rav; Rashi*). Others interpret this phrase to refer to the victim: *These are those who are saved* [from their pursuers] *even at the cost of their* [the pursuers'] *lives* (*Rambam Comm.; Meiri*).

הָרוֹדֵף אַחַר חֲבֵרוֹ לְהָרְגוֹ, — *One who pursues another to kill him,*

A person attempting to kill another may be killed to save the life of the

אַחַר הַזָּכוּר, וְאַחַר הַנַּעֲרָה הַמְאֹרָסָה. אֲבָל הָרוֹדֵף אַחַר הַבְּהֵמָה, וְהַמְחַלֵּל אֶת הַשַּׁבָּת, וְהָעוֹבֵד עֲבוֹדָה זָרָה אֵין מַצִּילִין אוֹתָן בְּנַפְשָׁן.

ר׳ עובדיה מברטנורא

ואחר הזכור. נפקא לן דאמר קרא (שם פסוק כו) ולנערה לא תעשה דבר, נער כתיב חסר ה"א, זה זכור, והוא הדין לכל חייבי כריתות ומיתות בית דין שבעריות, שמצילין אותן בנפשן, דכתיב (שם) חטא מות, חטא, אלו חייבי כריתות, מות, אלו חייבי מיתות בית דין: **אבל הרודף אחר הבהמה.** אף על פי שדומה לעריות: **והמחלל את השבת והעובד עבודה זרה.** אף על פי ששניהם כופרים בעיקר: **אין מצילין אותם בנפשן.** וכל שכן שאר חייבי כריתות ומיתות בית דין שאינן של עריות, שאין מצילין אותם בנפשם, ואין מותר להרגן כלל עד שיעברו עבירה בעדים ויהיו חייבים מיתה בבית דין:

יד אברהם

intended victim, if no other means of saving him is practical.[1] This is derived from that which the Torah (*Deut.* 22:26) explicitly compares the case of raping a betrothed *naarah* to an act of murder (*Rav* from *Gem.* 73a). The attacker may be killed either by his intended victim in self-defense or by anyone else who observes the incident (*Rav*). In fact, one is obligated to save someone in danger, even if it requires taking the life of the pursuer (*Rambam, Hil. Rotzeach* 1:6; see *Tos.* 73a s.v. אף רוצח). However, if the victim can be saved without killing the attacker — e.g., by wounding and disabling him — he may not be killed (*Gem.* 74a; *Rambam, Hil. Rotzeach* 1:13; *Choshen Mishpat* 425:1).

Even a child, who is generally not subject to punishment, is killed if he is in pursuit of another to kill him, in order to save the victim (*Rambam* ad loc.; *Choshen Mishpat* 425:1).

Furthermore, the general requirement in capital cases that one be warned of the consequences of his deed and acknowledge

1. This principle is applied to the issue of abortion: If the fetus endangers the life of the mother it may be aborted because it is viewed as a pursuer of the mother's life. However, if the head of the baby has already come out, it can no longer be killed, for the danger to the mother is a natural phenomena (*Rambam, Hil. Rotzeach* 1:9; *Choshen Mishpat* 425:2).

This ruling requires explanation, because the mishnah in *Ohalos* (7:6) gives a different reason for the permissibility of aborting the child to save the mother; viz. that her life takes precedence. As explained by *Rashi* (72b, s.v. יצא ראשו) this is because an unborn child is not yet considered a full-fledged human being. Accordingly, the principle of the pursuer would seem superfluous here (*Tos. R' Akiva* to *Ohalos* ad loc.; *Pischei Teshuvah* 425:1; see also *Teshuvos Chavos Yair* 31, *Chidushei Rabbeinu Chaim HaLevi* for resolutions to this problem).

8
7

[or who pursues] a male, or a betrothed *naarah*. However, one who pursues a beast, and one who desecrates the Sabbath, and one who engages in idolatry are not saved at the cost of their lives.

the warning does not apply in this case. It is sufficient merely to warn him without receiving any acknowledgment in return (*Rambam* ibid. 1:7; *Choshen Mishpat* loc. cit.) — i.e., to inform him that his intended victim is Jewish and killing him would render him liable for capital punishment. Even if he could not warn him thusly he may still kill him to protect the other (*Sma* ad loc.).

אַחַר הַזְּכוּר, — *[or who pursues] a male,*

[A man pursuing or attacking another man in order to sodomize him may also be stopped even at the cost of his life.] This is derived from the passage of the betrothed *naarah*, in which the word נַעֲרָה, *naarah*, is spelled נער, without the *hei*, thereby alluding to a male (*Rav* from *Gem.* ibid.).

וְאַחַר הַנַּעֲרָה הַמְאֹרָסָה. — *or a betrothed naarah.*

As explained above (preface).

The *Gemara* (loc. cit.) derives exegetically that the same applies to a man attacking any of the other *arayos* — women forbidden to him on pain of *kares* [Divinely imposed death] or execution (*Rav*).

אֲבָל הָרוֹדֵף אַחַר הַבְּהֵמָה, — *However, one who pursues a beast,*

I.e., a person attempting to commit an act of bestiality. Although this is similar to attempting to rape one of the *arayos*, in that it is an act punishable by death (see 7:4), the perpetrator may not be killed to prevent his doing this (*Rav*).

וְהַמְחַלֵּל אֶת הַשַּׁבָּת, — *and who desecrates the Sabbath,*

Although this is considered tantamount to rejecting the principle of creation, which is fundamental to all of Judaism, it is nonetheless not permitted to prevent someone from transgressing at the expense of his life (ibid.).

וְהָעוֹבֵד עֲבוֹדָה זָרָה — *and one who engages in idolatry*

This too, obviously, is a negation of the entire basis of our religion. Nevertheless, the person doing this may not be summarily killed to prevent his doing so (ibid.).

אֵין מַצִּילִין אוֹתָן בְּנַפְשָׁן. — *are not saved at the cost of their lives.*

Despite the grave nature of these offenses, one may not kill to prevent them from taking place, as the Torah only mandated such steps to prevent murder and acts of grave immorality, which include great humiliation and taintedness [along with the transgression itself] (*Rashi*). All other transgressors are warned and if they persist and follow through, they are brought to court for trial and execution (*Rav*).

פרק תשיעי
Chapter Nine

[א] **וְאֵלּוּ** הֵן הַנִּשְׂרָפִין: הַבָּא עַל אִשָּׁה וּבִתָּהּ, וּבַת כֹּהֵן שֶׁזִּנְּתָה. יֵשׁ בִּכְלָל אִשָּׁה וּבִתָּהּ בִּתּוֹ, וּבַת בִּתּוֹ, וּבַת בְּנוֹ; וּבַת אִשְׁתּוֹ, וּבַת בִּתָּהּ, וּבַת בְּנָהּ; חֲמוֹתוֹ, וְאֵם חֲמוֹתוֹ, וְאֵם חָמִיו.

ר׳ עובדיה מברטנורא

פרק תשיעי – ואלו הן הנשרפים. (א) אלו הן הנשרפים. הבא על אשה ובתה. על אשה שכבר נשא בתה, דהיינו חמותו: **ובת כהן.** וכן בת כהן שזנתה, היא בשריפה: **יש בכלל אשה ובתה.** כלומר באשה ובתה כתיבא שריפה בהדיא (ויקרא כ, יד) ואיש אשר יקח את האשה ואת אמה וגו׳ באש ישרפו, ומינה ילפינן כולהו הנך נמי דאיתנהו בשרפה: **בתו.** מאנוסתו, דלאו בת אשתו היא דלחייב עליה משום בת אשתו, דהא לאו בת אשתו היא: **בת בתו ובת בנו.** שהיו לו מאנוסתו: **בת אשתו.** בין שהיא בתו בין שהיא חורגתו: **וחמותו.** אף על גב דתנא לה רישא בהדיא, הבא על אשה שנשא בתה, ולא מדרשא אתיא, איידי דתני בהך כללא אם חמותו ואם חמיו דאתיא מדרשא, תנא נמי אגב ריהטא חמותו בהדייהו:

יד אברהם

1.

After concluding the discussion concerning those who are stoned with a delineation of the laws of the *ben sorer u'moreh* (8:5), the mishnah moves on [after a minor digression in the last two mishnahs of Ch. 8] to discuss the other forms of execution, beginning with burning — the next most severe form of execution (see 7:1).

וְאֵלּוּ הֵן הַנִּשְׂרָפִין: — *These are the ones who are burned:*

[These are the transgressors who are punished with execution by burning.]

הַבָּא עַל אִשָּׁה וּבִתָּהּ, — *One who cohabits with a woman and her daughter,*

One who cohabits with a woman to whose daughter he is wed — i.e., with his mother-in-law (*Rav* from *Gem.* 65a). The same is true if he is married to the mother and cohabits with the daughter, as the mishnah will state below. He must, however, first be married to one of them in order for his cohabitation with the other to be a capital offense. If he merely cohabited with both a woman and her daughter out of wedlock without ever having married either, the *woman and her daughter* prohibition does not apply (*Rashi* 75b from *Yevamos* 11:1, 97a). Similarly, if he first cohabited with one of them out of wedlock and then married the other, he has not violated a capital offense (*Yevamos* 11:1).

The punishment of burning for this act is mandated explicitly in the Torah (*Lev.* 20:14).

וּבַת כֹּהֵן שֶׁזִּנְּתָה. — *and the daughter of a Kohen who commits adultery.*

The Torah (*Leviticus* 21:9) specifies that if the daughter of a *Kohen* commits adultery she is burned [unlike any other adulteress who is

9
1

1. **T**hese are the ones who are burned: One who cohabits with a woman and her daughter, and the daughter of a *Kohen* who commits adultery. Included in the category of a woman and her daughter are his daughter, his daughter's daughter, and his son's daughter; his wife's daughter, her daughter's daughter, and her son's daughter; his mother-in-law, his mother-in-law's mother, and his father-in-law's mother.

YAD AVRAHAM

punished by strangulation (see 11:1)]. However, only the woman is burned; her partner in the adultery is killed by strangulation, as is any adulterer (*Rashi*), as derived from the Torah's emphasis on the word *she* (*Gem.* 5la).

יֵשׁ בִּכְלָל אִשָּׁה וּבִתָּהּ — *Included in the category of a woman and her daughter*

Although the verse states this punishment explicitly only concerning a mother-in-law, it is interpreted exegetically to include the following cases as well (*Rav*).

בִּתּוֹ, וּבַת בִּתּוֹ, וּבַת בְּנוֹ; — *are his daughter, his daughter's daughter, and his son's daughter;*

I.e., the prohibition on incest with one's daughter or granddaughter is included in the Torah's prohibition of intimacy with one's wife's daughter or granddaughter. The novelty of this ruling of the mishnah is not in respect to his daughter by his wife, since this would be included in the mishnah's next case of his wife's daughter and granddaughter — she is no less his wife's daughter for being his daughter as well. Rather, this case teaches that even a daughter who was born out of wedlock, or the daughter of such a daughter or son, is prohibited to him by this verse on punishment of burning (*Rav*). The *Gemara* (*Yevamos* 97a) derives from the verse that although she is not the daughter of a woman to whom he was married, since she is his daughter, he is prohibited to her.

וּבַת אִשְׁתּוֹ, וּבַת בְּנָהּ; — *his wife's daughter, her daughter's daughter, and her son's daughter;*

The prohibition on a woman and her daughter extends to intimacy with a woman and her granddaughter as well. It applies whether or not she is his daughter or granddaughter (ibid.).

חֲמוֹתוֹ, וְאֵם חֲמוֹתוֹ, וְאֵם חָמִיו. — *his mother-in-law, his mother-in-law's mother, and his father-in-law's mother.*

[The prohibition on a woman and her daughter also applies to a woman and her mother and grandmother. I.e., if he is married to the daughter, he may not subsequently have relations with her mother or grandmother.]

The latter two of this group are derived exegetically. The case of his mother-in-law is actually the one cited in the beginning of the mishnah; it is repeated here because it is part of

וְאֵלּוּ הֵן הַנֶּהֱרָגִים, הָרוֹצֵחַ וְאַנְשֵׁי עִיר הַנִּדַּחַת.
רוֹצֵחַ שֶׁהִכָּה אֶת רֵעֵהוּ בְּאֶבֶן אוֹ בְּבַרְזֶל, וְכָבַשׁ
עָלָיו לְתוֹךְ הַמַּיִם אוֹ לְתוֹךְ הָאוּר וְאֵינוֹ יָכוֹל
לַעֲלוֹת מִשָּׁם, וָמֵת, חַיָּב. דְּחָפוֹ לְתוֹךְ הַמַּיִם אוֹ
לְתוֹךְ הָאוּר וְיָכוֹל לַעֲלוֹת מִשָּׁם, וָמֵת, פָּטוּר.
שִׁסָּה בּוֹ אֶת הַכֶּלֶב, שִׁסָּה בּוֹ אֶת הַנָּחָשׁ, פָּטוּר.

───── ר' עובדיה מברטנורא ─────

כבש עליו. אחז ראשו של חברו ותקפו בתוך המים שלא יוכל להרים ראשו: **שיסה.** גירה:

יד אברהם

the category mentioned (*Rav* from *Gem.* 75a).

The *Gemara* (76b, according to the interpretation of *Rava*) cites a dispute between R' Yishmael and R' Akiva whether the prohibition on one's mother-in-law continues to apply with the same severity after his wife has died. According to R' Yishmael there is no difference; whether his wife is alive or dead, intimate relations with his mother-in-law are punishable by burning. R' Akiva, however, rules that after the wife has died, relations with his former mother-in-law — though prohibited — are no longer punishable by burning. They are, however, still subject to the penalty of *kares* (*Rambam, Isurei Biah* 2:8; *Ravad* cited by *Meiri; Tos.* to *Yevamos* 94b). However, *Rashi* here (76b) seems to understand R' Akiva to exclude her even from *kares* (see *Tos. R' Akiva* to *Yevamos* 1:1 4).

According to *Rambam* (ibid.) the exclusion applies not only to his mother-in-law but to his wife's grandmothers, daughters, and granddaughters as well. Once his wife has died, intimacy with them is subject only to *kares*, not burning. Others, however, dissent and rule that the exemption from burning applies only to his wife's mother and grandmother, not the others listed here (*Rambam, Rashba, Ritva* to *Yevamos* 99a).

There are thus a total of ten cases which are punishable by burning; the nine variations of the mother-and-

daughter prohibition and the daughter of a *Kohen* who commits adultery.

וְאֵלּוּ הֵן הַנֶּהֱרָגִים: — *These are the ones who are beheaded:*

After concluding the list of those subject to the punishment of burning, the mishnah lists those subject to death by beheading, the third method of execution listed in 7:1 (*Yad Ramah*).

הָרוֹצֵחַ — *A murderer*

The Torah states that one who kills another shall be put to death (*Ex.* 21:12). The method used is decapitation, as derived exegetically from the law concerning the murder of a Canaanite slave (*Gem.* 52b).

וְאַנְשֵׁי עִיר הַנִּדַּחַת. — *and the inhabitants of an apostate town.*

If an entire town, or the majority of it (10:4), was led astray to worship a false god, they are liable to execution by beheading (rather than the usual penalty for idol worship — stoning). Those who instigated them, however, are stoned (*Meiri*; see 7:4).

רוֹצֵחַ שֶׁהִכָּה אֶת רֵעֵהוּ בְּאֶבֶן אוֹ בְּבַרְזֶל, — *[If] a murderer struck another with a stone or with an iron,*

These are the examples used by the Torah to describe an act of murder

9
1

These are the ones who are beheaded: A murderer and the inhabitants of an apostate town. [If] a murderer struck another with a stone or with an iron, or he held him down in water or fire so that he could not escape, and he died, he is liable. [If] he pushed him into the water or into the fire and he was able to escape, but he died, he is exempt. [If] he incited a dog or a snake against him, he is exempt.

(*Num.* 35). In the case of a stone, the verse makes clear (v. 17) that the weapon used must be large enough to inflict death under the circumstances involved in order for the murderer to be liable. [But if death from this weapon must be considered a fluke, the murderer is not liable to execution. See *Rambam, Rotzeach* 3:2,3 for a list of the factors that must be weighed.] When speaking of iron, however, the Torah does not add this stipulation. From this the *Gemara* deduces that iron is considered capable of causing death no matter what its size (*Gem.* 76b). Some explain this to be because it can pierce a person in a vital organ and cause death (*Rashi; Meiri*). Others attribute this unique status to the fact that it can cause infection (*Tos.*). The unique liability for murder with a metal weapon of any size is only if it is used by its point to pierce. If it is used as a club, however, it is subject to the same provisions as every other weapon (*Gem.* 76b; *Rambam, Rotzeach* 3:4).

וְכָבַשׁ עָלָיו לְתוֹךְ הַמַּיִם אוֹ לְתוֹךְ הָאוּר וְאֵינוֹ יָכוֹל לַעֲלוֹת מִשָּׁם, וָמֵת, חַיָּב. — *or he held him down in water or fire so that he could not escape, and he died, he is liable.*

Even if he did not push him into the water or fire, but merely held him there until he died — or until he no longer had strength to escape (*Rambam, Rotzeach* 3:9) — he is guilty of murder and liable for execution (*Gem.* 76b).

The mishnah cites these examples because they parallel the four methods of execution used by the courts; stoning, beheading [with an iron sword], strangling [and thereby causing suffocation, similar to drowning], and burning. This is done in order to indicate that despite the fact that he employed these diverse methods of murder his punishment is nevertheless beheading (*Rashash*).

דְּחָפוֹ לְתוֹךְ הַמַּיִם אוֹ לְתוֹךְ הָאוּר וְיָכוֹל לַעֲלוֹת מִשָּׁם, וָמֵת, פָּטוּר. — *[If] he pushed him into the water or into the fire and he was able to escape, but he died, he is exempt.*

I.e., a person in his condition should have been able to escape, but something happened and he was unable to and died (*Rashi*). Despite the fact that he actually pushed him into the fire or water, he is not liable if the victim was capable of escaping under normal circumstances (*Gem.* ibid.).

שִׁסָּה בּוֹ אֶת הַכֶּלֶב, שִׁסָּה בּוֹ אֶת הַנָּחָשׁ, פָּטוּר. — *[If] he incited a dog or a snake against him, he is exempt.*

If he incited a dog or a snake to attack someone, and the animal killed

הִשִּׁיךְ בּוֹ אֶת הַנָּחָשׁ, רַבִּי יְהוּדָה מְחַיֵּב, וַחֲכָמִים פּוֹטְרִים.

הַמַּכֶּה אֶת חֲבֵרוֹ, בֵּין בְּאֶבֶן בֵּין בְּאֶגְרוֹף, וַאֲמָדוּהוּ לְמִיתָה, וְהוּקַל מִמַּה שֶּׁהָיָה וּלְאַחַר מִכָּאן הִכְבִּיד וָמֵת — חַיָּב. רַבִּי נְחֶמְיָה אוֹמֵר: פָּטוּר, שֶׁרַגְלַיִם לַדָּבָר.

ר' עובדיה מברטנורא

הִשִּׁיךְ. שֶׁאָחַז הַנָּחָשׁ בְּיָדוֹ וְהוֹלִיכוֹ וְהִגִּיעַ שִׁנֵּי הַנָּחָשׁ לְגוּף חֲבֵירוֹ: **רַבִּי יְהוּדָה מְחַיֵּב.** דְּסָבַר אֶרֶס נָחָשׁ בְּשִׁנָּיו עוֹמֵד, וּמִכֵּיוָן שֶׁהִגִּיעַ שִׁנֵּי הַנָּחָשׁ בִּבְשָׂרוֹ שֶׁל חֲבֵרוֹ, הֲוֵי כְּאִלּוּ הֲרָגוֹ וְחַיָּב: **וַחֲכָמִים פּוֹטְרִין.** דְּקָא סָבְרֵי אֶרֶס נָחָשׁ מֵעַצְמוֹ הוּא מֵקִיא, הִלְכָּךְ לָאו אִיהוּ קְטָלֵיהּ אֶלָּא גִּרְמָא בְּעָלְמָא הוּא וּפָטוּר. וְהִלְכָה כַּחֲכָמִים: **וַאֲמָדוּהוּ לְמִיתָה.** אֲבָל אֲמָדוּהוּ תְּחִלָּה לְחַיִּים, אֲפִילוּ לְרַבָּנָן פָּטוּר: **הֵיקַל מִמָּה שֶׁהָיָה.** וְחָזְרוּ וַאֲמָדוּהוּ לְחַיִּים: **שֶׁרַגְלַיִם לַדָּבָר.** שֶׁלֹּא מֵת מֵחֲמַת מַכָּה זוֹ:

יד אברהם

the person, the inciter is not liable to the death sentence [since he did not murder him directly] (*Rav*). However, he is considered guilty of murder by the rules of the Heavenly Court [since he caused it to happen] (*Meiri*), and He Who avenges innocent blood will see to this person's punishment (*Rambam, Rotzeach* 3:10). A human court, though, can only execute someone who murders by direct action.

הִשִּׁיךְ בּוֹ אֶת הַנָּחָשׁ, — *[If] he caused the snake to bite him,*

I.e., he took the snake in his hand and pierced the victim's flesh with its fangs (*Rav*).

רַבִּי יְהוּדָה מְחַיֵּב, — *R' Yehudah considers [him] liable,*

He maintains that the poison of a snake is present in its fangs and therefore, upon pressing the fangs into someone's flesh, he has directly injected him with poison

(*Rav* from *Gem.* 78a).

וַחֲכָמִים פּוֹטְרִים. — *but the Sages exempt [him].*

They contend that the snake injects the poison through his fangs after having pierced the flesh and the murderer is thus not directly responsible for the poisoning (ibid.).

[Although it is clear that the snake's poison is not stored in its fangs, R' Yehudah apparently maintains that when aroused, the poison flows from its sac to the fangs even prior to biting; thus the poison is already in its fangs when they pierce the victim's flesh (cf. *Tif. Yis.*).]

הַמַּכֶּה אֶת חֲבֵרוֹ, בֵּין בְּאֶבֶן בֵּין בְּאֶגְרוֹף, — *[If] one struck another, whether with a stone or his fist,*

These examples are cited because they are the ones mentioned in the Torah (*Ex.* 21:18) in its discussion of one who first partially recovers from a blow but subsequently dies (*Tos. Yom Tov*).

[If] he caused the snake to bite him, R' Yehudah considers [him] liable, but the Sages exempt [him].

[If] one struck another, whether with a stone or his fist, and they predicted that he would die, but his [condition] improved; subsequently he deteriorated [again] and died — he is liable. R' Nechemiah says: He is exempt because there is indication to that effect.

YAD AVRAHAM

וַאֲמָדוּהוּ לְמִיתָה, — *and they predicted that he would die,*

The court[1] evaluated that the blow was likely to prove fatal (*Rashi*). In such a case the assailant is imprisoned until the victim's fate is known (*Gem.* 78b). If he should die, the assailant is executed (*Rambam, Rotzeach* 4:3). If the initial prognosis was that he would survive the blow, however, the assailant is released and he is liable only to the monetary payments imposed on one who assaults another, even if the victim should subsequently die (*Rambam* ibid. from *Gem.* 78b).

וְהוּקַל מִמַּה שֶּׁהָיָה; וּלְאַחַר מִכָּאן הִכְבִּיד וָמֵת - חַיָּב. — *but his [condition] improved; subsequently he deteriorated [again] and died — he is liable.*

After hovering near death, the victim's condition improved unexpectedly to the point that it was assumed he would survive (*Rav*). He did not, however, recover entirely (*Meiri*). If the condition should subsequently deteriorate again and he dies, the attacker is executed. [Since the original prognosis was that he would die of his wounds, and he did in fact die without ever recovering entirely, it may be taken for granted that the attack was the cause of his demise.]

רַבִּי נְחֶמְיָה אוֹמֵר: פָּטוּר, שֶׁרַגְלַיִם לַדָּבָר. — *R' Nechemiah says: He is exempt because there is indication to that effect.*

The fact that he first improved indicates that it was not the effects of the blow which killed him (*Rav*).

Yerushalmi cites a different version to the mishnah ... *and he died, R' Nechemiah exempts [him] and the Sages render him liable, because there is indication to that effect* [i.e., the fact that it occurred at this time indicates that the death was due to the blow].

Rambam (*Hil. Rotzeach* 4:5) rules in accordance with the Sages (cf. *Meiri*).

1. The court's involvement is necessary since they must decide whether to free him or to incarcerate him and await the outcome of the victim's condition. Assumedly, the court appoints doctors to advise them concerning the prognosis (see *Rambam, Rotzeach* 4:3).

[ב] **נִתְכַּוֵּן** לַהֲרוֹג אֶת הַבְּהֵמָה וְהָרַג אֶת הָאָדָם, לַנָּכְרִי וְהָרַג אֶת יִשְׂרָאֵל, לַנְּפָלִים וְהָרַג אֶת בֶּן קַיָּמָא — פָּטוּר. נִתְכַּוֵּן לְהַכּוֹתוֹ עַל מָתְנָיו, וְלֹא הָיָה בָהּ כְּדֵי לְהָמִית עַל מָתְנָיו, וְהָלְכָה לָהּ עַל לִבּוֹ וְהָיָה בָהּ כְּדֵי לְהָמִית עַל לִבּוֹ, וָמֵת — פָּטוּר. נִתְכַּוֵּן לְהַכּוֹתוֹ עַל לִבּוֹ, וְהָיָה בָהּ כְּדֵי לְהָמִית עַל לִבּוֹ, וְהָלְכָה לָהּ עַל מָתְנָיו, וְלֹא הָיָה בָהּ כְּדֵי לְהָמִית עַל מָתְנָיו, וָמֵת — פָּטוּר.

ר׳ עובדיה מברטנורא

(ב) **והיה בה כדי להמית על לבו ומת פטור.** דתרתי בעינן, שיהא מתכוין למכת מיתה, וגם שיכנו מכת מיתה:

יד אברהם

2.

נִתְכַּוֵּן לַהֲרוֹג אֶת הַבְּהֵמָה וְהָרַג אֶת הָאָדָם, — *One who aimed to kill an animal but killed a human,*

Someone attempted to kill an animal [by throwing a rock at it, for example — see *Rashi* 79a, s.v. והיה], but his blow hit the person standing next to it instead, killing him (*Rashi*).

לַנָּכְרִי וְהָרַג אֶת יִשְׂרָאֵל, — *[or who aimed to kill] a gentile but killed a Jew,*

A Jew who kills a gentile is not punishable by death.

לַנְּפָלִים וְהָרַג אֶת בֶּן קַיָּמָא – — *[or who aimed to kill] a premature baby but killed a viable one —*

He endeavored to kill a baby who was born prematurely and was not expected to survive. The murder of such a newborn is not punishable by death because the baby is considered as if already dead (*Rashi*). Accidentally, however, he struck a normal baby instead.

פָּטוּר — *is exempt.*

In all three of these cases the killer is exempt from execution because he did not intend to commit a capital offense. Accordingly, the murder which he did in fact commit is considered tantamount to an inadvertent act, for which there is no death penalty (*Yad Ramah*).

Others explain the reason differently: Since it was not possible to know in advance that the killer's blow would hit the wrong person and render him guilty of a murder for which he is liable to execution, any warning the witnesses might have given him as to the possible consequences of his actions was uncertain, and the rule is that an uncertain warning is not sufficient enough a warning to render a person liable to punishment. Since a person cannot be convicted of a capital crime unless he has been properly warned (see above, 8:4), no death penalty can be imposed for this murder. Even if the witnesses warned him that his blow might hit the other party and

2. **O**ne who aimed to kill an animal but killed a human, [or who aimed to kill] a gentile but killed a Jew, [or who aimed to kill] a premature baby but killed a viable one — is exempt. [If] he aimed to strike him on his loins, and the force [of the blow] was not sufficient to kill at that spot, but it struck his chest where its force was sufficient to kill, and he died — he is exempt. [If] he aimed to strike him on his chest, and the blow contained sufficient force to kill at that spot, but it struck his loins where its force was insufficient to kill, and he died — he is exempt.

YAD AVRAHAM

kill him, and even if he acknowledged that he was prepared to assume the risk of being executed if he should strike or kill that other party, he is still exempt, since their warning to him contained an element of uncertainty (*Rashi;* see *Tif. Yis.*).

The principle that an uncertain warning by witnesses is not sufficient is actually the subject of a dispute between R' Yochanan and Reish Lakish (*Makkos* 15b). Since the halachah follows R' Yochanan (*Rambam, Hil. Sanhedrin* 16:4; see *Yevamos* 36a), it is difficult to understand why *Rashi* offers an explanation to the mishnah which is valid only according to Reish Lakish. However, it is possible that in a case such as this even R' Yochanan would agree that the warning is insufficient, because in this situation it is the outcome of the act which is uncertain, not merely the intent of the transgressor [as in the cases in which R' Yochanan and Reish Lakish disagree] (*Tos.*). See *Tiferes Yisrael* (*Boaz*) at length.

נִתְכַּוֵּן לְהַכּוֹתוֹ עַל מָתְנָיו, וְלֹא הָיָה בָהּ כְּדֵי לְהָמִית עַל מָתְנָיו, וְהָלְכָה לָהּ עַל לִבּוֹ וְהָיָה בָהּ כְּדֵי לְהָמִית עַל לִבּוֹ, וָמֵת – פָּטוּר. — *[If] he aimed to strike him on his loins, and the force [of the blow] was not sufficient to kill at that spot, but it struck his chest* (lit., *it went to his heart*) *where its force was sufficient to kill, and he died — he is exempt.*

For example, he threw a rock at him which was heavy enough to kill him if it hit near his heart but it was not heavy enough to do such damage if it struck his loins (*Rashi*). Since his intention was to strike his loins he cannot be considered as having intent to kill; therefore, no death sentence is warranted (*Rav*).

According to the second approach cited above, this ruling, too, is because of the lack of certainty in the warning of the witnesses (*Rashi*). Thus, even if he accepted the possibility that it might strike his chest and kill him, he cannot be executed for this act.]

נִתְכַּוֵּן לְהַכּוֹתוֹ עַל לִבּוֹ, וְהָיָה בָהּ כְּדֵי לְהָמִית עַל לִבּוֹ, וְהָלְכָה לָהּ עַל מָתְנָיו, וְלֹא הָיָה בָהּ כְּדֵי לְהָמִית עַל מָתְנָיו, וָמֵת – פָּטוּר. — *[If] he aimed to strike him on his chest, and the blow contained sufficient force to kill at that spot, but it struck his loins where its force was insufficient to kill, and he died — he is exempt.*

Although his intent was to commit

נִתְכַּוֵּן לְהַכּוֹת אֶת הַגָּדוֹל, וְלֹא הָיָה בָהּ כְּדֵי לְהָמִית הַגָּדוֹל, וְהָלְכָה לָהּ עַל הַקָּטָן, וְהָיָה בָהּ כְּדֵי לְהָמִית אֶת הַקָּטָן, וָמֵת — פָּטוּר. נִתְכַּוֵּן לְהַכּוֹת אֶת הַקָּטָן, וְהָיָה בָהּ כְּדֵי לְהָמִית אֶת הַקָּטָן, וְהָלְכָה לָהּ עַל הַגָּדוֹל, וְלֹא הָיָה בָהּ כְּדֵי לְהָמִית אֶת הַגָּדוֹל, וָמֵת — פָּטוּר. אֲבָל נִתְכַּוֵּן לְהַכּוֹת עַל מָתְנָיו, וְהָיָה בָהּ כְּדֵי לְהָמִית עַל מָתְנָיו, וְהָלְכָה לָהּ עַל לִבּוֹ, וָמֵת — חַיָּב. נִתְכַּוֵּן לְהַכּוֹת אֶת הַגָּדוֹל, וְהָיָה בָהּ כְּדֵי לְהָמִית אֶת הַגָּדוֹל, וְהָלְכָה לָהּ עַל הַקָּטָן, וָמֵת — חַיָּב. רַבִּי שִׁמְעוֹן אוֹמֵר: אֲפִלּוּ נִתְכַּוֵּן לַהֲרוֹג אֶת זֶה וְהָרַג אֶת זֶה — פָּטוּר.

ר' עובדיה מברטנורא

רבי שמעון אומר אפילו נתכוין להרוג את זה. לאו אסיפא דמלתא דתנא קמא קאי, אהא דקאמר תנא קמא נתכוין להכות את הגדול והיה בה כדי להמית את הגדול והלכה על הקטן ומת חייב, דאי אהא קאי, רבי שמעון פוטר מיבעי ליה, ולמה ליה למיהדר ולפרושי אפילו נתכוין להרוג את זה והרג את זה, הא בפירוש אמרו תנא קמא, ומאי אפילו, אלא רבי שמעון ארישא קאי, נתכוין להרוג את הבהמה והרג את האדם פטור, הא נתכוין להרוג את האדם והרג אדם אחר חייב, ועלה קאמר רבי שמעון אפילו נתכוין להרוג את זה והרג את זה פטור. והלכה כרבי שמעון:

יד אברהם

murder and the victim in fact died, he cannot be punished, because the actual blow was not capable of causing death. Although death did inexplicably occur, one can be punished only for a blow which under normal circumstances has the capacity to kill (ibid.).

נִתְכַּוֵּן לְהַכּוֹת אֶת הַגָּדוֹל, וְלֹא הָיָה בָהּ כְּדֵי לְהָמִית הַגָּדוֹל, וְהָלְכָה לָהּ עַל הַקָּטָן, וְהָיָה בָהּ כְּדֵי לְהָמִית הַקָּטָן, וָמֵת – פָּטוּר. — *[If] he aimed to strike an adult, and the force was not sufficient to kill an adult, but he struck a child, whom it was sufficient to kill, and he died — he is exempt.*

[The ruling stated above applies just the same to a situation in which

the accident was related to the identity of the victim rather than the location of the blow. If he intended to strike an adult, who would not be killed by such a weak blow, and instead struck a child, who could be killed by such a blow, and the child died, he is not liable for execution.)

נִתְכַּוֵּן לְהַכּוֹת אֶת הַקָּטָן, וְהָיָה בָהּ כְּדֵי לְהָמִית אֶת הַקָּטָן, וְהָלְכָה לָהּ עַל הַגָּדוֹל, וְלֹא הָיָה בָהּ כְּדֵי לְהָמִית אֶת הַגָּדוֹל, וָמֵת – פָּטוּר. — *[If] he aimed to strike a child, and the force was sufficient to kill a child, but he struck an adult, whom it was not sufficient to kill, and he died — he is exempt.*

[Although he intended to kill the

[If] he aimed to strike an adult, and the force was not sufficient to kill an adult, but he struck a child, whom it was sufficient to kill, and he died — he is exempt. [If] he aimed to strike a child, and the force was sufficient to kill a child, but he struck an adult, whom it was not sufficient to kill, and he died — he is exempt. However, [if] he aimed to strike him on his loins, and the force was sufficient to kill at that spot, but he struck his chest, and he died — he is liable. [If] he aimed to strike an adult, and the force was sufficient to kill an adult, but he struck a child, and he died — he is liable. R' Shimon says: Even [if] he aimed to kill this one and he killed that one he is exempt.

YAD AVRAHAM

child with this blow, since it struck and killed an adult who should not have died from its force, he is exempt from execution.)

אֲבָל נִתְכַּוֵּן לְהַכּוֹת עַל מָתְנָיו, וְהָיָה בָהּ כְּדֵי לְהָמִית עַל מָתְנָיו, וְהָלְכָה לָהּ עַל לִבּוֹ, וָמֵת – חַיָּב. נִתְכַּוֵּן לְהַכּוֹת אֶת הַגָּדוֹל, וְהָיָה בָהּ כְּדֵי לְהָמִית אֶת הַגָּדוֹל, וְהָלְכָה לָהּ עַל הַקָּטָן, וָמֵת – חַיָּב. — *However, [if] he aimed to strike him on his loins, and the force was sufficient to kill at that spot, but he struck his chest, and he died — he is liable. [If] he aimed to strike an adult, and the force was sufficient to kill an adult, but he struck a child, and he died — he is liable.*

As long as the intent to murder was present and the blow was one which had the capacity to kill, he is subject to the death penalty [despite the fact that his precise intent was not realized] (*Meiri*).

The mishnah cites the case of hitting the wrong part of the body to emphasize that if his aim was to strike a part of the body where it would not kill, he is exempt despite the fact that he killed the person he was aiming for by striking a more sensitive part of his body. The second case, of two separate people (adult and child), emphasizes that he is liable in a case in which there is intent to kill and a blow of sufficient strength to do so, despite that fact that he hit the wrong person (*Tif. Yis.*).

רַבִּי שִׁמְעוֹן אוֹמֵר: אֲפִלּוּ נִתְכַּוֵּן לַהֲרוֹג אֶת זֶה וְהָרַג אֶת זֶה – פָּטוּר. — *R' Shimon says: Even [if] he aimed to kill this one and he killed that one, he is exempt.*

This statement of R' Shimon's refers back to the first case of the mishnah, which states that if he aimed to kill an animal but he killed a person instead, he is exempt — thus implying that had he intended to kill a person and he hit another person and killed him, he is punishable. R' Shimon disputes that implication and contends that as long as one does not kill the person he intended to kill he is not subject to the death penalty (*Rav* from *Gem.* 79a).

סנהדרין [ג] **רוֹצֵחַ** שֶׁנִּתְעָרֵב בַּאֲחֵרִים, כֻּלָּן פְּטוּרִין. רַבִּי ט/ג יְהוּדָה אוֹמֵר: כּוֹנְסִין אוֹתָן לְכִפָּה. כָּל חַיָּבֵי מִיתוֹת שֶׁנִּתְעָרְבוּ זֶה בָּזֶה, נִדּוֹנִין בַּקַּלָּה.

ר' עובדיה מברטנורא

(ג) רוצח שנתערב באחרים. כגון שנים שהיו עומדים ויצא חן מביניהם והרג, שניהם פטורים, ואפילו אחד משניהם מוחזק בחסידות ובידוע שהוא לא זרק החן, אפילו הכי לא מחייבין ליה לאידך בחזקה זו: **רבי יהודה אומר כונסין אותן לכיפה.** מתניתין חסורי מחסרא והכי קתני, ושור שנגמר דינו שנתערב בשוורים אחרים, סוקלים אותם, דהא על כרחך כולהו אסורים בהנאה, ואפילו הן אלף, מפני זה המעורב בהן, הלכך סוקלין את כולם כדי שתתקיים מצות סקילה במחוייב בה, [רבי יהודה אומר] כונסין אותן לכיפה, ואין צריך לסקלן, אלא כונסין אותן לחדר והן מתים ברעב. ואין הלכה כרבי יהודה:

יד אברהם

R' Shimon could just as well have taken issue with the last ruling of the *Tanna Kamma*, that one who aims to kill an adult and kills a child is liable. However, from the length of his statement it is clear that the specific object of R' Shimon's contention is not this last ruling but an earlier one. Had he been referring to the previous ruling of the mishnah, the mishnah would simply have said *R' Shimon exempts* (*Gem.* ibid.). R' Shimon chose to express himself this way, rather than simply responding to the final words of the first *Tanna*, to avoid the possible misunderstanding that he refers even to the case of hitting someone on the chest instead of the loins (*Rashi*, ibid.).

R' Shimon derives his view from the verse (*Deut.* 19:11), *and he shall ambush him and come upon him,* which implies that intent for the actual victim is a prerequisite for the death penalty (*Gem.* ad loc.).

According to some authorities, the halachah follows the view of R' Shimon (*Rav; Rambam, Hil. Rotzeach* 4:1, as interpreted by *Maggid Mishneh* to *Hil. Chovel Umazik* 4:5,6; *Lechem Mishneh* ad loc.; *Tos. Yom Tov; cf. Kesef Mishneh, Hil. Rotzeach* loc. cit.). Others contend that the prevailing view is that of the first *Tanna* (*Ravad*, ad loc.).

3.

רוֹצֵחַ שֶׁנִּתְעָרֵב בַּאֲחֵרִים, — *[If] a murderer['s identity] was lost in a group* (lit., *a murderer who was mixed together with others*),

For example, two people were standing together and one shot an arrow which killed someone, and it cannot be determined which of them shot it (*Rav* from *Gem.* 80a).

כֻּלָּן פְּטוּרִין. — *they are all exempt.*

[Since it cannot be determined which is the murderer, they must

both be released.] Even if one of them is a man of such moral caliber that it is impossible to imagine that he performed such a deed, the other cannot be executed on that basis (ibid.).

רַבִּי יְהוּדָה אוֹמֵר: כּוֹנְסִין אוֹתָן לְכִפָּה. — *R' Yehudah says: We place them in a cell.*

Since it is obvious that R' Yehudah cannot be referring to the previous case and requiring that the innocent be imprisoned with the guilty, the

---

9
3

3. [If] a murderer['s identity] was lost in a group, they are all exempt. R' Yehudah says: We place them in a cell. Any [time] people sentenced to execution become confused with one another, they are subjected to the most lenient [one].

YAD AVRAHAM

Gemara (79b-80a) concludes that there is a clause missing from the mishnah to which R' Yehudah is responding. The mishnah must be emended in the following manner: *And [if] an ox which was sentenced [to death] became mixed together with other oxen, they are all stoned. R' Yehudah says: We place them [all] in a cell.* The meaning of this is as follows: An ox which has been sentenced to death [for killing someone, for example — see above, 1:4] is forbidden for use and benefit even before it is executed. Once it becomes mixed together with other oxen and it cannot be determined which is the condemned ox, all the oxen become forbidden since each of them may be the condemned animal.[1] Since they are all forbidden in any case, the *Tanna Kamma* rules that they should all be stoned in order to fulfill the *mitzvah* of stoning the guilty one. R' Yehudah, however, maintains that it is not necessary to go to the bother of stoning them. Rather, they may be placed in a cell (see mishnah 5) and allowed to die there by starvation (*Rav*).

If the ox was lost in a group prior to its sentencing, none of them may be killed. The court cannot pronounce its sentence and then follow the course prescribed above because sentence may not be passed in absentia (*Gem.* 79b; *Rambam, Nizkei Mamon* 11:10), and sentencing an unidentified offender is considered the equivalent of sentencing in absentia (*Rashi*).

כָּל חַיָּבֵי מִיתוֹת שֶׁנִּתְעָרְבוּ זֶה בָזֶה, נִדּוֹנִין בַּקַּלָּה. — *Any [time] people sentenced to execution become confused with one another, they are subjected to the most lenient [one].*

If several people who had been sentenced to death became mixed together, and it was forgotten who had been sentenced to which type of execution, they all receive the most lenient form of death to which any of them had been sentenced. They cannot all be executed by the harsher methods, because we may not inflict upon a person a worse death than he deserves. Consequently, they are all executed by the least harsh method.

The *Gemara* (80b) questions why they should be subjected to even the least harsh method of execution. As we have learned several times, in order for a person to become liable to the death penalty, he must not only commit the crime, but he must also first have been warned that his

1. There is a general rule that forbidden things which become mixed together with a larger number of similar permitted things lose their identity — and thus their prohibition — in the overall mixture. This is the rule of בִּטּוּל בְּרוֹב, *nullification in the majority.* This rule, however, does not apply here because living creatures are deemed too significant to lose their individual identity even in a group; see *Zevachim* 73a.

הַנִּסְקָלִין בַּנִּשְׂרָפִין — רַבִּי שִׁמְעוֹן אוֹמֵר: נִדּוֹנִין בִּסְקִילָה, שֶׁהַשְּׂרֵפָה חֲמוּרָה. וַחֲכָמִים אוֹמְרִים: נִדּוֹנִין בִּשְׂרֵפָה, שֶׁהַסְּקִילָה חֲמוּרָה. אָמַר לָהֶן רַבִּי שִׁמְעוֹן: אִלּוּ לֹא הָיְתָה שְׂרֵפָה חֲמוּרָה, לֹא נִתְּנָה לְבַת כֹּהֵן שֶׁזִּנְּתָה. אָמְרוּ לוֹ: אִלּוּ לֹא הָיְתָה סְקִילָה חֲמוּרָה, לֹא נִתְּנָה לַמְגַדֵּף וְלָעוֹבֵד עֲבוֹדָה זָרָה.

יד אברהם

actions are forbidden and subject to the death penalty, and he must have accepted the warning by declaring his willingness to proceed despite the penalty. Since the acceptance of the warning and penalty are necessary components of any death penalty, how can a less harsh form of execution be substituted for a more severe one, when the condemned was never warned concerning that penalty, nor did he ever accept such a penalty upon himself as the price of his crime?

The *Gemara* offers two solutions: One is that implicit in the acceptance of any harsh penalty is the acceptance of any less severe penalty as well. Thus, although the less severe form of execution was never mentioned in the witnesses' warning to him as a possible penalty for this act, their warning and his acceptance referred to it implicitly.

However, the validity of this principle is questioned by the *Gemara* here and elsewhere [*Kesubos* 33a] (*Tos.*). Accordingly, the *Gemara* offers another explanation, that the mishnah refers to a case in which the witnesses warned the condemned that his act would bring upon him a death penalty, but without specifying any method of execution. Accordingly, their warning and his acceptance are construed to refer to all methods. Therefore, though at his conviction he must be sentenced to the method appropriate to his transgression, there is no problem substituting an alternate method when this becomes necessary.

Although the validity of this type of nonspecific warning is subject to a Tannaitic dispute, our mishnah follows the view that the warning need only mention the death penalty but need not specify which one. This is indeed the view accepted as halachah (*Rambam, Hil. Sanhedrin* 12:2).

הַנִּסְקָלִין בַּנִּשְׂרָפִין — *[If] those sentenced to be stoned [became confused] with those sentenced to be burned —*

The mishnah now illustrates the rule stated above. For example, if people sentenced to stoning became mixed together with others who had been sentenced to burning and it is not known who had been sentenced to which type of execution (*Gem.* 80b).

רַבִּי שִׁמְעוֹן אוֹמֵר: נִדּוֹנִין בִּסְקִילָה, שֶׁהַשְּׂרֵפָה חֲמוּרָה. — *R' Shimon says: They are [all] executed by stoning, as burning is more severe.*

[In R' Shimon's view, burning is the harshest form of execution; consequently, they are executed by the less severe stoning.]

The novelty of this ruling is that it applies even in a case in which the

9 [If] those sentenced to be stoned [became
3 confused] with those sentenced to be burned — R′ Shimon says: They are [all] executed by stoning, as burning is more severe. But the Sages say: They are executed by burning, as stoning is more severe. Said R′ Shimon to them: If burning were not more severe, it would not have been meted out to the daughter of a *Kohen* who commits adultery. They said to him: If stoning were not more severe, it would not have been meted out to the blasphemer and idolater.

YAD AVRAHAM

majority of the convicts had been sentenced to burning. Although the principle of רוֹב, *following the majority,*[1] would dictate that they all be burned, we nevertheless cannot impose a harsher death than is absolutely certain. They are therefore all stoned since that — according to R′ Shimon — is the less severe method of execution (*Gem.* ibid.).

וַחֲכָמִים אוֹמְרִים: נִדּוֹנִין בִּשְׂרֵפָה, שֶׁהַסְּקִילָה חֲמוּרָה. — *But the Sages say: They are executed by burning, as stoning is more severe.*

The Sages dispute R′ Shimon's assertion that burning is more severe and rule that stoning is the harshest form of punishment (as noted above, 7:1). Thus, even if the majority had been sentenced to stoning they would be executed by burning, all the more so in this case in which the majority had been condemned to burning (ibid.).

אָמַר לָהֶן רַבִּי שִׁמְעוֹן: אִלּוּ לֹא הָיְתָה שְׂרֵפָה חֲמוּרָה, לֹא נִתְּנָה לְבַת כֹּהֵן שֶׁזִּנְּתָה. — *Said R′ Shimon to them: If burning were not more severe, it would not have been meted out to the daughter of a Kohen who commits adultery.*

The normal punishment for adultery is strangulation (see below, 1:1), unless the woman was a betrothed *naarah,* in which case the punishment is stoning (see above, 7:4). However, in the case of a *Kohen's* daughter who commits adultery, the Torah sentences her to burning, as we learned in mishnah 1. R′ Shimon understands the verse to mean that the Torah sentences her to burning under all circumstances — even if she is a betrothed *naarah.* This can only be because the Torah considers this a more severe penalty than stoning — the penalty imposed on a betrothed *naarah* who is not the daughter of a *Kohen* (*Gem.* 50a).

אָמְרוּ לוֹ: אִלּוּ לֹא הָיְתָה סְקִילָה חֲמוּרָה, לֹא נִתְּנָה לַמְגַדֵּף וְלָעוֹבֵד עֲבוֹדָה זָרָה. — *They said to him: If stoning were not more severe, it would not have been meted out to the blasphemer and idolater.*

[The fact that these particular evildoers are stoned is evidence that

1. This principle dictates that when a group of legally different things must be treated by one rule, they are all treated by the laws pertaining to the majority component of that group.

הַנֶּהֱרָגִין בַּנֶּחֱנָקִין — רַבִּי שִׁמְעוֹן אוֹמֵר: בְּסַיִף. וַחֲכָמִים אוֹמְרִים: בְּחֶנֶק.

[ד] **מִי** שֶׁנִּתְחַיֵּב בִּשְׁתֵּי מִיתוֹת בֵּית דִּין, נִדּוֹן בַּחֲמוּרָה. עָבַר עֲבֵרָה שֶׁיֵּשׁ בָּהּ שְׁתֵּי מִיתוֹת, נִדּוֹן בַּחֲמוּרָה. רַבִּי יוֹסֵי אוֹמֵר:

ר׳ עובדיה מברטנורא

רבי שמעון אומר בסייף. שהחנק חמור: **וחכמים אומרים בחנק.** שהסייף חמור: **(ד) מי שנתחייב שתי מיתות.** כגון שעבר עבירה קלה ונגמר דינו לעבירה קלה, וחזר ועבר עבירה חמורה, סלקא דעתך אמינא כיון דנגמר דינו לעבירה קלה, האי גברא קטילא הוא, קא משמע לן: **עבר עבירה שיש בה שתי מיתות.** כגון חמותו, והיא אשת איש: **נדון בחמורה.** בשריפה, מפני שהיא חמותו, ולא כאשת איש שהיא בחנק:

יד אברהם

If those who had been sentenced to be strangled became confused with those sentenced to be beheaded, they must all receive the lesser punishment. According to R' Shimon that is beheading, whereas the Sages opine that strangulation is the lesser of the two (*Rav;* see 7:1).

R' Shimon holds that those who lead astray an apostate town are punished with strangulation (see above, 7:10), and it is thus evident that this is a more severe form of punishment, since it is implemented for such a major crime. The Sages, however, contend that the instigators are stoned, and there is thus no basis for R' Shimon's assumption, since all agree that beheading and strangulation are less severe than stoning and burning (*Gem.* 50a).

this is the most severe punishment.] They do not consider their position to be refuted by R' Shimon's proof because they contend that the special punishment assigned to the adulterous daughter of a *Kohen* is only if she committed adultery after being fully married, not during her betrothal. Had she not been a *Kohen's* daughter, she would then have been subject to strangulation, a method of execution all agree is less severe than burning. A betrothed *naarah,* however, is executed by stoning for her adultery, even if she is the daughter of a *Kohen* [see next mishnah) (ibid.).

הַנֶּהֱרָגִין בַּנֶּחֱנָקִין – רַבִּי שִׁמְעוֹן אוֹמֵר: בְּסַיִף. וַחֲכָמִים אוֹמְרִים: בְּחֶנֶק. — *[If] those to be beheaded [became confused] with those to be strangled — R' Shimon says: [They are executed] by beheading. But the Sages say: By strangulation.*

4.

Having discussed how to treat a group of people sentenced to different forms of execution when it is no longer remembered who is liable to which form of execution, the *Tanna* goes on to discuss how to deal with a person who has incurred two different death penalties.

9
4

[If] those to be beheaded [became confused] with those to be strangled — R' Shimon says: [They are executed] by beheading. But the Sages say: By strangulation.

4. One who became liable to two forms of execution is subjected to the more severe [form]. [If] he committed a transgression which was punishable by two [forms] of execution, he is subjected to the more severe [one]. R' Yose says:

YAD AVRAHAM

מִי שֶׁנִּתְחַיֵּב בִּשְׁתֵּי מִיתוֹת בֵּית דִּין, נִדּוֹן בַּחֲמוּרָה. — *One who became liable to two forms of execution is subjected to the more severe [form].*

If someone transgressed a prohibition for which he was sentenced to one of the less severe forms of execution [e.g., strangulation), and he then performed an act for which he can be sentenced to an execution of greater severity [e.g., stoning], we do not say that having been sentenced to death he is legally considered dead and no new death sentence can be imposed upon him. Rather, he now becomes subject to the more severe method of execution (*Rav*).

This is derived from the verse (*Ezekiel* 18:10-13): *But he begat a violent son, who sheds blood ... and his neighbor's wife he defiled ... and he lifted his eyes to the idols ... he shall surely die; his blood will be upon himself.* Of the crimes listed in this verse, bloodshed is punishable by beheading, adultery by strangulating, and idol worship by stoning. Yet, the prophet uses the code phrase *his blood shall be upon him* to define his liability for his crimes, a phrase which is always used to indicate stoning. It is thus apparent that although he committed previous crimes which call for execution of a lesser severity, he is nevertheless liable for his later ones (*Gem.* 81a).

[In the previous mishnah, the form of execution due each convict was in question; consequently, only the less severe one could be imposed. In the cases of this mishnah, however, he is subject to two penalties; consequently, the more severe one is given.]

עָבַר עֲבֵרָה שֶׁיֵּשׁ בָּהּ שְׁתֵּי מִיתוֹת, נִדּוֹן בַּחֲמוּרָה. — *[If] he committed a transgression which was punishable by two [forms] of execution, he is subjected to the more severe [one].*

[One act may violate two prohibitions, each of which carries the death penalty. If this should happen, he is subjected to the harsher form of execution.] For example, if one had relations with his mother-in-law while she was married, he receives the penalty of burning for transgressing the sin of cohabiting with his mother-in-law rather than strangulation for adultery (*Rav*).

נִדּוֹן בְּזִקָּה הָרִאשׁוֹנָה שֶׁבָּאָה עָלָיו.

[ה] **מִי** שֶׁלָּקָה וְשָׁנָה, בֵּית דִּין מַכְנִיסִים אוֹתוֹ לְכִפָּה וּמַאֲכִילִין אוֹתוֹ שְׂעוֹרִין עַד שֶׁכְּרֵסוֹ מִתְבַּקַּעַת. הַהוֹרֵג נֶפֶשׁ שֶׁלֹּא בְעֵדִים,

ר' עובדיה מברטנורא

נדון בזיקה הראשונה. באותו איסור שהוזקק תחלה להזהר ולפרוש ממנו הוא נדון, אבל לא באיסור הבא עליו אחרון, ואף על פי שהוא חמור, דקסבר רבי יוסי אין איסור חל על איסור, ואפילו חמור על הקל, ואם נשא בת אלמנה, שהיתה תחלה חמותו כשהיתה פנויה ואחר כך נשאת, נדון בשריפה. ואם היתה אשת איש ואחר כך נעשית חמותו, נדון בחנק כמיתה של אשת איש שהיתה תחלה. ואין הלכה כרבי יוסי: (ה) **מי שלקה ושנה.** שלקה שני פעמים על עבירה שחייבים עליה כרת, שכל חייבי כריתות לוקים, כשיחזור ויעשה אותה עבירה עצמה פעם שלישית: **מכניסין אותו לכיפה.** מקום כשיעור קומת אדם ולא יותר, ומאכילין אותו תחלה לחם צר ומים לחץ עד שיוקטנו בני מעיו, והדר מאכילין אותו שעורים שנופחות במעיו עד שכריסו נבקעת: **שלא בעדים.** שלא בעדות שיהיה מחוייב עליה מיתה, ומכל מקום ידוע לבית דין שהדבר אמת שבודאי הרג, אלא שהוכחשו העדים בבדיקות או שלא היתה שם התראה מספקת:

יד אברהם

רַבִּי יוֹסֵי אוֹמֵר: נִדּוֹן בְּזִקָּה הָרִאשׁוֹנָה שֶׁבָּאָה עָלָיו. — *R' Yose says: He is subjected to the one by which he was first enjoined.*

R' Yose subscribes to the principle of אֵין אִסּוּר חָל עַל אִסּוּר, *a prohibition cannot take legal effect over another prohibition*, i.e., that once someone or something has become prohibited to a person by one prohibition, no new prohibition can take effect relative to him, not even one of greater severity. Accordingly, if she was married at the time he married her daughter, only the prohibition of adultery applies — since she was prohibited to him as a married woman even before he became her son-in-law — and he is therefore sentenced to strangulation rather than burning. The penalty of burning for transgressing the prohibition applies only if she was widowed or divorced when he married her daughter (*Rav*).

The *Gemara* (81a) states that R' Yose agrees that if the second prohibition is a more widespread one, prohibiting people not covered by the first one, that the second prohibition takes effect as well [אִסּוּר מוֹסִיף]. Since there is nothing to prevent its prohibiting these others, it takes effect in regard to them; having done so, it prohibits everyone affected by it even though they are already forbidden for some other reason (*Rashi*). Accordingly, if his mother-in-law was unmarried at the time he married his wife and she subsequently married, she would become forbidden to him as a married woman as well. Since before her marriage she was permitted to men other than her son-in-law, and her marriage caused her to become forbidden to them, it forbids her as a married woman to her son-in-law as well, even according to R' Yose. However, as regards capital punishment this is irrelevant, since the mother-in-law prohibition carries a more severe death penalty than the adultery prohibition, and he can only be executed once (*Gemara* 81b). The only relevance of this rule is in regard to sin-offerings for inadvertent transgression. Thus, if he cohabited with her thinking that she was his wife (for

He is subjected to the one by which he was first enjoined.

5. Someone who was flogged twice is placed by the court in a cell where he is fed barley until his stomach bursts. Someone who murders without witnesses [to that effect]

YAD AVRAHAM

example), R' Yose would agree that he must bring two sin-offerings, one for the sin of a mother-in-law, the other for adultery.[1]

The halachah follows the view of the first *Tanna* (*Rav; Rambam, Hil. Sanhedrin* 14:4).

5.

Following the discussion concerning one who was liable to two death sentences, the mishnah goes on to deal with one who had been twice sentenced to flogging (*Yad Ramah*).

מִי שֶׁלָּקָה וְשָׁנָה, — *Someone who was flogged twice* (lit., *was flogged and repeated*)

Someone was flogged for having committed a transgression whose penalty is *kares,* after which he repeated the transgression and was flogged a second time (*Rav* from *Gem.* 81b). However, if the floggings were for two different transgressions, the ruling stated in this mishnah does not apply (ibid.).

בֵּית דִּין מַכְנִיסִים אוֹתוֹ לְכִפָּה — *is placed by the court in a cell*

If he commits that transgression a third time, he is considered an incorrigible sinner. Accordingly, though the court cannot execute him outright, the court imprisons him and brings about his death (*Gem.*). To this end he is placed in a cramped cell, which allows him no room to stretch or lie down (*Rav* from *Gem.* 81b).

וּמַאֲכִילִין אוֹתוֹ שְׂעוֹרִין עַד שֶׁכְּרֵסוֹ מִתְבַּקַּעַת. — *where he is fed barley until his stomach bursts.*

They first place him on small rations of bread and water, thereby causing his stomach to shrink (see below). They then feed him barley, which causes it to rapidly expand and thereby burst (*Rav* from *Gem.* 81b). Having deliberately committed an act which is punishable by *kares* (Divinely imposed death), he is actually fit to die, only his time has not yet arrived. When he persists in his behavior, he forgoes the extension Heaven has granted him, and the courts therefore bring about his death. This is alluded to in the verse (*Psalms* 34:22): *The deathblow of the wicked is evil* (*Gem.* ibid.), but the actual law was handed down orally to Moshe at Sinai (*Rashi;* cf. *Yad Ramah, Margoliyos HaYam* 15).

הַהוֹרֵג נֶפֶשׁ שֶׁלֹּא בְעֵדִים, — *Someone who murders* (lit., *killed a soul*) *without witnesses [to that effect]*

I.e., the court was able to ascertain

1. Actually, this could be relevant to the capital issue as well, if the witnesses warned him against sinning with her because she was a married woman but failed to warn him in regard

מַכְנִיסִין אוֹתוֹ לְכִפָּה וּמַאֲכִילִין אוֹתוֹ לֶחֶם צַר וּמַיִם לַחַץ.

[ו] **הַגּוֹנֵב** אֶת הַקַּסְוָה, וְהַמְקַלֵּל בַּקּוֹסֵם, וְהַבּוֹעֵל אֲרַמִּית, קַנָּאִין פּוֹגְעִין בּוֹ.

ר׳ עובדיה מברטנורא

ומאכילין אותו לחם צר ומים לחץ. תחלה, ואחר כך מאכילין אותו שעורים עד שכריסו נבקעת, והיינו רישא, ומה שחיסר זה גלה זה: **(ו) הגונב את הקסוה.** אחד מכלי שרת, מלשון קשות הנסך (במדבר ד, ז): **והמקלל בקוסם.** המברך את השם בשם עבודה זרה: **והבועל ארמית.** עובדת כוכבים: **קנאים פוגעים בו.** המקנאים קנאתו של מקום היו

יד אברהם

from witnesses that this person had indeed murdered someone, but, for technical reasons, the testimony of these witnesses was insufficient to bring about a death sentence — e.g., they had not properly warned him [though it is clear that he knew what he was doing], or the accounts of the two witnesses differed in non-essential details [see above, 3:6] (*Rav* from *Gem.* 81b; see *Gem.* for other possibilities). The mishnah cannot, however, be referring to a case in which there were no witnesses at all, since in that case they cannot know that the accused is guilty (*Gem.*).

מַכְנִיסִין אוֹתוֹ לְכִפָּה וּמַאֲכִילִין אוֹתוֹ לֶחֶם צַר וּמַיִם לַחַץ. — *is placed in a cell where he is fed spare bread and scant water.*

As stated above, they place him on such a diet to shrink his stomach, after which they then feed him barley which bursts it (*Rav* from *Gem.*).

The mishnah mentions only half the procedure in each of the above cases because the half mentioned in each case is the more necessary information for that case. In the first case, in which no murder was committed, one might think that he is merely imprisoned but not caused to die; therefore that aspect is emphasized. In the latter case, the death penalty is understandable and it is the fact that he is fed at all during this time which must be noted (*Margaliyos HaYam* 23).

This punishment is given only to someone who murders and cannot be executed directly, as explained above; any of the other transgressions which warrant the death penalty are not dealt with in this manner. This is because the destructive effect an act of murder has on society is greater than that of any other transgression, even those which are intrinsically more severe (*Rambam, Hil. Rotzeach* 4:9).[1]

to the mother-in-law prohibition. Since without this warning he cannot be punished for it, he is punished for the adultery for which he was warned (*Tos. R' Akiva Eiger*).

1. It seems strange that one who murdered without a clear warning should be put to death in a more painful manner than one who was warned. However, one who acknowledges the warning of witnesses that he will be put to death for his deed and goes on to kill nonetheless is obviously motivated by some great passion. A crime committed in these circumstances is less abhorrent than a murder committed in a more deliberate state of mind and it is therefore dealt with less severely (*Margaliyos HaYam* 26).

9 is placed in a cell where he is fed spare bread and
6 scant water.

6. **O**ne who steals a service vessel, blasphemes by a supernatural force, or cohabits with a gentile woman, zealots may smite him.

YAD AVRAHAM

6.

Having initiated a discussion concerning those who cannot be executed directly by the courts but are nonetheless put to death indirectly, the mishnah continues with cases of extrajudicial execution (*Yad Ramah*). These do not involve court action, but are carried out in the first three cases by zealots and in the fourth by the *Kohanim* in the Temple.

הַגּוֹנֵב אֶת הַקַּסְוָה, — *One who steals a service vessel,*

The word קסוה is used by the Torah (*Ex.* 25:29; *Num.* 4:7) to refer to the hollow pipes which separated the layers of *Panim* bread in the Temple. The *Tanna* chose this as an example of a service vessel which was stolen because, being a small, simple utensil, it is more likely than other vessels to be taken (*Meiri*). The punishment for this is derived from the verse (*Num.* 4:20): *and they shall not come to see when the sanctified objects are covered, lest they die.* The word כְּבַלַּע, *when it is covered,* can also be interpreted to refer to theft, since the thief conceals that which he steals. However, that is not the primary interpretation of the verse, merely an allusion. The true basis for this principle was handed down orally from Sinai (*Rashi* to 81b; see below, s.v. ומפיעין).

וְהַמְקַלֵּל בַּקּוֹסֵם, — *blasphemes by a supernatural force,*

He blasphemes the Almighty in the name of an idol to whom he attributes supernatural powers (*Rav; Rambam Comm.*). Since it is so similar to one who blasphemes *Hashem* in the name of *Hashem* (see 7:4), it is fitting that one who does so be killed (*Gem.* 82b).

וְהַבּוֹעֵל אֲרַמִּית, — *or cohabits with a gentile* (lit., *Aramean*) *woman,*

The execution here may only be carried out if he is intimate with a gentile woman who is the daughter of an idolater, and only in a case in which the perpetrator consorts with her publicly — i.e., before ten or more Jews (*Rav;* see *Avodah Zarah* 36b; *Rambam, Isurei Biah* 12:4,5). The Biblical prototype of this principle is the case of Pinchas who killed Zimri, while the latter was cohabiting with a Midianite princess whom he had publicly brought to his tent (*Num.* 25:6-15).

There is discussion among the authorities as to whether the same ruling applies to a Jewish woman who has relations with a gentile man (see *Margaliyos HaYam* to 81b 29). A rationale offered for those who differentiate between a Jewish man cohabiting with a gentile woman and a Jewish woman cohabiting with a gentile man is that in the former case their intimacy can bring about the birth of a gentile child from a Jewish father, since the offspring follows the nationality of the mother in such a case (see *Rambam, Hil. Isurei Biah* 12:7). In the latter case, this does not apply, since any child will be Jewish (*Noda BiYehudah* vol.2, *Even HaEzer* 150).

קַנָּאִין פּוֹגְעִין בּוֹ. — *zealots may smite him.*

כֹּהֵן שֶׁשִּׁמֵּשׁ בְּטֻמְאָה, אֵין אֶחָיו הַכֹּהֲנִים מְבִיאִין אוֹתוֹ לְבֵית דִּין; אֶלָּא פִּרְחֵי כְהֻנָּה מוֹצִיאִין אוֹתוֹ חוּץ לָעֲזָרָה וּמַפְצִיעִין אֶת מוֹחוֹ בְּגִזִירִין. זָר שֶׁשִּׁמֵּשׁ בַּמִּקְדָּשׁ — רַבִּי עֲקִיבָא אוֹמֵר: בְּחֶנֶק. וַחֲכָמִים אוֹמְרִים: בִּידֵי שָׁמָיִם.

ר׳ עובדיה מברטנורא

הורגים אותו, והוא שתהיה הנכרית בת עובדי עבודה זרה, ובשעת מעשה, ובפני עשרה מישראל, ואם חסר אחד מן התנאים הללו, אסור להרגו, אבל ענשו מפורש על פי נביא, יכרת ה׳ לאיש אשר יעשנה (מלאכי ב, יב). ומלקין אותו ארבע מלקיות מדברי סופרים, משום נדה, משום שפחה, משום עובדת כוכבים, משום זונה: **פרחי כהונה.** בחורים שמתחיל שער זקנם לפרוח בהם: **בגזרין.** בקעיות של עצים: **רבי עקיבא אומר בחנק.** נאמר כאן (במדבר א, נא) והזר הקרב יומת, ונאמר להלן (דברים יג, ו) והנביא ההוא או חולם החלום ההוא יומת, מה להלן בחנק אף כאן בחנק: **וחכמים אומרים בידי שמים.** נאמר כאן יומת, ונאמר להלן (במדבר יז, כח) כל הקרב הקרב אל משכן ה׳ ימות, מה להלן בידי שמים אף כאן בידי שמים. והלכה כחכמים. ומיתה בידי שמים הוא פחות מן הכרת, שהכרת יש עליו עונש לאחר מיתה אם לא עשה תשובה כראוי, ומיתה בידי שמים אין לאחר מיתה עליו כלום. ורש״י כתב בפרק במה מדליקין (שבת כה, א) דמיתה בידי שמים ימיו נקצרים ואינו הולך ערירי, כרת אית ביה תרתי, ימיו נכרתים והולך ערירי. ומחוייבי מיתה בידי שמים שעל עסקי מקדש וקדשים הם אחד עשר, ואלו הן, האוכל טבל, וכהן טמא שאכל תרומה טהורה, וזר שאכל תרומה, וזר וטמא וטבול יום ששמשו, ומחוסר כפורים, ומחוסר בגדים, ושלא קדש ידים ורגלים, ושתויי יין, ופרועי ראש, קצת מהם נאמר מיתה בהם בפירוש, וקצתם למדום רבותינו מפי הקבלה בגזירה שוה ובהיקש:

יד אברהם

A worthy person who takes upon himself to avenge the honor of the Almighty may, at the time of the deed, kill one who commits such an act (*Rashi*). Once the deed has been completed, however, it is no longer permissible to do so. Rather, the transgressor is punishable by *kares* (*Rav* from *Gem.* 82a).

If someone comes to the court to inquire as to whether he should inflict such a punishment he is not advised to do so (*Gem.* ibid.), as this law applies only to one who is moved to do so on his own (*Rashi*). Some say that this principle applies to all of the cases mentioned (*Meiri*). *Rambam*, however, (followed by *Rav*) cites it only in regard to one who has relations with a gentile woman (*Isurei Biah* 12:4), but not when discussing the general principle of zealots killing one who performs these deeds (*Hil. Sanhedrin* 11:6).

[In the case of the blasphemer this seems impossible since before he completes the blasphemy he has not done anything, nor can we conclude that he will indeed blaspheme. However, the general principle of תּוֹךְ כְּדֵי דִבּוּר כְּדִבּוּר דָּמֵי — that the brief moment following a legal act is legally considered simultaneous with the act — could possibly be applied here to allow a zealot to kill the blasphemer within that moment.]

כֹּהֵן שֶׁשִּׁמֵּשׁ בְּטֻמְאָה, — *[If] a Kohen serves while tamei,*

9
6

[If] a *Kohen* serves while *tamei,* his brother *Kohanim* do not bring him to court; rather the young *Kohanim* remove him from the courtyard and split his skull with clubs. A non-*Kohen* who serves in the Temple — R' Akiva says: [He is executed] by strangulation. But the Sages say: By the hand of Heaven.

YAD AVRAHAM

It is prohibited by the Torah (*Lev.* 22:2) for a *Kohen* to perform the Temple service while in a state of *tumah,* and if done intentionally is punishable by heavenly imposed death (*Gem.* 82b). In common with all transgressions subject to this penalty, it is also subject to lashes (*Rambam, Bias Mikdash* 4:1).

אֵין אֶחָיו הַכֹּהֲנִים מְבִיאִין אוֹתוֹ לְבֵית דִּין; — *his brother Kohanim do not bring him to court;*

They are not required to bring him to court to be flogged for transgressing this prohibition (*Rambam, Bias Mikdash* 4:2).

אֶלָּא פִרְחֵי כְהֻנָּה מוֹצִיאִין אוֹתוֹ חוּץ לָעֲזָרָה וּמַפְצִיעִין אֶת מוֹחוֹ בִּגְזִירִין. — *rather the young Kohanim* (lit., *flowers of the Kehunah*) *remove him from the courtyard and split his skull with clubs.*

The term פִּרְחֵי, literally, *flowers,* refers to the fact that they are of an age when the hair of their beards has just begun to grow [from the root פרח, *sprout*] (*Rav*). The young *Kohanim* are designated to carry out this judgment because *Kohanim* under twenty are not permitted to perform the actual service; thus the risk of their becoming *tamei* through contact with the body of the one they kill is not of any consequence (*Margaliyos Hayam* 34). Furthermore, such an act is unworthy of punishment by the older and more distinguished *Kohanim* (*Tif. Yis.*).

All of the punishments cited here were handed down orally from Sinai (*Rav*).

There is another view, based on the words of *Rambam* (loc. cit.), that in all these cases, with the exception of one who has relations with a gentile woman, there is no law calling for his execution in this manner. The Rabbis merely declared that one who does so is within his rights, due to the gravity of the transgression, and he is not viewed as a murderer (*Teshuvos Radbaz,* vol.11 631).

זָר שֶׁשִּׁמֵּשׁ בַּמִּקְדָּשׁ - — *A non-Kohen who serves in the Temple —*

This is prohibited by the Torah (*Num.* 18:4) under penalty of death (v. 7).

רַבִּי עֲקִיבָא אוֹמֵר: בְּחֶנֶק. — *R' Akiva says: [He is executed] by strangulation.*

He maintains that the death penalty stated in this case is compared by exegetical process to that which is stated concerning a false prophet (*Deut.* 13:6) whose execution is by strangulation [11:1] (*Rav* from *Gem.* 84a).

וַחֲכָמִים אוֹמְרִים: בִּידֵי שָׁמַיִם. — *But the Sages say: By the hand of Heaven.*

The Sages contend that his death is not in the hands of a human court but

is left to Heaven, as derived from the death penalty stated (*Num.* 17:28) in regard to the congregation of Korach, who were killed by Divine intervention (*Rav* from *Gem.*).

The distinction between death at the hand of Heaven and *kares*, which is also Divinely executed, lies in that which one who is subject to *kares* receives further punishment in the World to Come if he has not repented properly, whereas one who is subject to death at the hand of Heaven has received his full penalty with his early death (*Rav*). Others explain that *kares* includes dying without leaving descendants, whereas this death does not include this additional penalty (*Rashi* to *Shabbos* 25a). A third view, cited from *Yerushalmi* (*Bikkurim* 2), is that *kares* brings death by the age of fifty while death at the hand of Heaven occurs by sixty. However, our *Gemara* (*Moed Katan* 28a) maintains that *kares* also allows one to live until sixty. According to this view, death at the hand of Heaven may even be past sixty (*Tos.* to *Yevamos* 2a, s.v. אשת אחיו).

The halachah follows the view of the Sages (*Rav; Rambam, Bias Mikdash* 9:1).

פרק עשירי

Chapter Ten

In the *Gemara,* this chapter is the last chapter of the tractate and it comes after the next one which details the laws of those who are executed by strangulation. According to that order, after completing its discussion of the four methods of execution, the Mishnah goes on to define those whose sins are so grave that they forfeit their share in the World to Come (*Rashi*).[1] In the Mishnayos, however, this chapter precedes the chapter on those who are executed by strangulation and is the tenth chapter; the same order exists in the *Talmud Yerushalmi.* This order is borne out by the fact that the chapter concludes with a delineation of the laws of an apostate town, whose inhabitants are executed by beheading, thus indicating that it follows the ninth chapter, which discusses those who are beheaded (*Yad Ramah; Tos. Yom Tov*). According to this order, the mishnah interjects a discussion about the World to Come by way of digression, as the Mishnah so often does. Having mentioned a case of Divine retribution in the previous chapter, the *Tanna* goes on to discuss reward and punishment in the World to Come (*Yad Ramah*).

According to most commentators, the World to Come refers to the eternal reward awaiting the righteous. After the ultimate redemption and a lengthy Messianic era, there will be a general resurrection, in which body and soul will be reunited in a union of a much more spiritual nature than that of the present. Those resurrected will then bask in the glory of the Almighty forever. According to this view, the reward allotted to one's soul after death prior to the resurrection is not under discussion here [although no one disputes its existence] (*Rav; Yad Ramah; Ramban, Shaar HaGemul; Derech Hashem* I:3).

Rambam (*Hil. Teshuvah* 8:1), however, contends that the World to Come refers to the reward allotted to the souls alone. According to most interpretations of *Rambam,* this alludes to the period between death and resurrection, as described above (*Ran; Kesef Mishneh* ad loc.). Others explain his view to be that after an extremely long life enjoyed by both body and soul following resurrection, death will eventually occur again and the souls will go on to their eternal reward (*Yad Ramah*).

As an introduction to this chapter which deals with the prerequisites to eternal reward, *Rambam* presents the thirteen fundamental principles of our faith.

1. According to *Rashi's* view, the first statement in mishnah 1 is not really part of the mishnah itself but a prefatory phrase which was added to begin the chapter on a positive note (*Maharshal*).

Although others dispute his approach and contend that only three principles can be considered primary principles (*Sefer HaIkarim; Bais Elokim*), *Rambam's* approach has been accepted by the Jewish nation as a whole and has even been incorporated into our liturgy. It is therefore appropriate to present these principles at this time.

(1) The first principle is the belief in the Almighty as the Ultimate Being. He is the cause of all other existence as well as the source of the continued existence of everything.

(2) The second principle is the absolute oneness of God. Unlike all His creations, He is not comprised of parts but is an entity of total and inseparable unity, beyond human comprehension.

(3) The third principle is that God has no physical body and that all physical concepts and occurrences have no application to Him. Any Scriptural reference to the contrary is meant merely in a metaphoric context.

(4) The fourth principle is that God must be recognized as preceding all other entities. Only He has existed from eternity; all other beings were created at some point in time.

(5) The fifth principle is that only the Almighty is fit to be worshipped, no other being, no matter how lofty.

(6) The sixth principle is that of prophecy; that it is possible for human beings to reach a level at which they can receive direct communication from the Almighty.

(7) The seventh principle is the fact that Moses was the greatest of all prophets and that his prophecy achieved a higher level of revelation than that granted to any other human being — past, present, and future. Furthermore, his prophecy differed qualitatively from that of all other prophets in four respects. First, God's communication with him was direct whereas to others He spoke only through a medium [i.e., an angel]. Secondly, Moses was able to receive prophecy while awake, while all others received their prophecies either in their sleep or in a trance. Thirdly, all others were completely overwhelmed by the experience whereas Moses retained his normal state. Finally, only Moses was capable of achieving prophecy any time he wished.

(8) The eighth principle is that every word of the entire Torah which we have was given to Moses by the Almighty Himself. Similarly, the transmitted interpretation of the laws of the written Torah [i.e., the Oral Law] — for example, the precise nature of *tefillin, succah, shofar*, etc. — is also exactly as received by Moses from God.

(9) The ninth principle is that no one may add to the Torah or detract from it.[1]

(10) The tenth principle is that God is aware of and notes all the deeds of all human beings.

(11) The eleventh principle is that the Almighty rewards those who follow the commandments of the Torah and punishes those who transgress them. The ultimate setting for this reward and punishment is the World to Come.

1. *R' Y. Kafich*, in his new translation of the original Arabic text of *Rambam's Commentary to the Mishnah* into Hebrew, states that the standard Hebrew text here was substantially shortened because of fear of the censors. The original principle prefaced the part stated in the standard texts with the statement: The Torah is eternal and its laws will never be revoked or altered in any way. This was deleted, however, because of its unacceptability to both Moslem and Christian censors.

(12) The twelfth principle is the belief in the coming of the Messiah who, in common with all the kings of Israel, will be a descendant of King David through his son Solomon.

(13) Finally, a Jew is obligated to believe in the ultimate resurrection of the souls.

סנהדרין
י/א

[א] **כָּל** יִשְׂרָאֵל יֵשׁ לָהֶם חֵלֶק לָעוֹלָם הַבָּא, שֶׁנֶּאֱמַר: ,,וְעַמֵּךְ כֻּלָּם צַדִּיקִים לְעוֹלָם יִירְשׁוּ אָרֶץ נֵצֶר מַטָּעַי מַעֲשֵׂה יָדַי לְהִתְפָּאֵר״.

וְאֵלּוּ שֶׁאֵין לָהֶם חֵלֶק לָעוֹלָם הַבָּא: הָאוֹמֵר אֵין תְּחִיַּת הַמֵּתִים מִן הַתּוֹרָה,

ר׳ עובדיה מברטנורא

פרק עשירי – כל ישראל. (א) כל ישראל יש להם חלק לעולם הבא. אפילו אלו שנתחייבו מיתה בבית דין מפני רשעתן, יש להם חלק לעולם הבא, ועולם הבא האמור כאן הוא העולם הבא אחר תחיית המתים, שעתידים לחיות ולעמוד בגופם ובנפשם חיים נצחיים, כחמה וכלבנה וככוכבים, כדמייתי בגמרא בהאי פרקא (צב, א), מתים שעתידים לחיות אין חוזרין לעפרן, והעולם הבא אין בו לא אכילה ולא שתיה, ואף על פי שיש בו גוף וגויה, אלא צדיקים יושבין ועטרותיהן בראשיהן ונהנין מזיו שכינה, ומפני שאין כל ישראל שוין בו, אלא הגדול לפי גדלו והקטן לפי קטנו, משום הכי קתני יש להם חלק: **האומר אין תחיית המתים מן התורה.** בגמרא (צ, א) קאמר, וכל כך למה, תנא, הוא כפר בתחיית המתים, לפיכך לא יהיה לו חלק בתחיית המתים, ומכאן אני מוכיח שעולם הבא האמור במשנה זו אינו העולם שהנשמות מונחות בו בזמן הזה, אלא העולם של תחיית המתים כדפרישית:

יד אברהם

1.

כָּל יִשְׂרָאֵל יֵשׁ לָהֶם חֵלֶק לָעוֹלָם הַבָּא, — *All Israel has a share in the World to Come,*

Even those evildoers who are executed for their sins retain their share [as long as they are not included in the categories listed below], but they must first undergo punishment for their transgressions (*Rav; Meiri*). The mishnah refers to this reward as a *share* because it is allocated in accordance with one's merit, and not all receive the same reward (*Rav*).[1]

Although Israel is specified here, all people can attain a share in the eternal reward, as evidenced by the mishnah's exclusion of Balaam [mishnah 2] (*Rambam, Hil. Teshuvah* 3:5 from *Gem.* 102b).

The precise translation of this phrase is *a share to the World to Come*. This is to indicate that a person works toward his eternal reward by means of his deeds. These create the spiritual benefits which constitute his reward, rather than merely earning reward unrelated intrinsically to the deeds themselves (*Ruach Chaim* to *Avos*). Alternatively, it refers to the spark within every Jew's soul which is fit for the World to Come (*Tif. Yis.*).

1. The description we find many times in the Talmud of a certain person being a בֶּן עוֹלָם הַבָּא, *son of the World to Come* (e.g., *Gem.* 88b), refers to a reward beyond the basic share allotted to every Jew (*Be'er Sheva;* cf. *Chofetz Chaim* on *Avos*). The statement in the *Gemara* (*Kesubos* 103b) that "anyone present at the burial of R' Yehudah HaNasi is destined to the World to Come" — implying some unique status — means that he attained his reward without undergoing prior judgment and suffering (*Tos.* ibid.).

1. **A**ll Israel has a share in the World to Come, as it is stated: *And your people are all righteous, they shall inherit the land forever; the branch of my plantings, the work of my hands to be glorified.*

These are the ones who have no share in the World to Come: One who says there is no [basis for] the resurrection in the Torah,

YAD AVRAHAM

שֶׁנֶּאֱמַר: ,,וְעַמֵּךְ כֻּלָּם צַדִּיקִים לְעוֹלָם יִרְשׁוּ אָרֶץ — *as it is stated* (Isaiah 60:21): *"And your people are all righteous, they shall inherit the land forever;*

All those who accept the basic premises of our faith, and are thus fit to be referred to by God as "My nation," are included in the World to Come despite their misdeeds (*Meiri*). Once they have been punished for their sins they *are all righteous* (*Maharsha*).

נֵצֶר מַטָּעַי מַעֲשֵׂה יָדַי לְהִתְפָּאֵר". — *the branch of my plantings, the work of my hands to be glorified."*

This refers to the World to Come, which is the handiwork of the Almighty alone and is therefore reserved for rewarding the righteous. This is in contrast to this world, limited in its scope and quality by the involvement of human endeavor, in which the truly wicked who have lost their share in the World to Come are paid off for their good deeds (*Maharsha*).

Others understand this phrase to refer to the Jewish people. Although there are many who sin, their souls are nonetheless *Hashem's* handiwork and pride and, as such, they are fit for ultimate inclusion in the World to Come (*Alshich* to Isaiah ad loc.; *Tif. Yis.*).

וְאֵלּוּ שֶׁאֵין לָהֶם חֵלֶק לָעוֹלָם הַבָּא: — *These are the ones who have no share in the World to Come:*

They have no share in the eternal spiritual reward (*Tif. Yis.*), but are subject to eternal punishment for their sins (*Meiri*). It is important to note, however, that even those who are so designated can regain their share through repentance in this world (*Rambam, Hil. Teshuvah* 3:14).

The Kabbalists teach that even those Jews cited as having no share in the World to Come will ultimately be included in the eternal bond between the Almighty and the Jewish people. However, they will have no share of their own but will stand among the masses [of such evildoers] and receive these benefits as part of the multitude (*Recanti* to *Ex.* 33:19; *Rabbeinu Bachya* to *Lev.* 18:29; see comm. to mishnah 2, s.v. וגחזי) who are granted this benefit in the merit of the truly righteous through that which *Hashem* linked the entire Jewish people together into one general "soul" (see *Derech Hashem* II 3:8).

הָאוֹמֵר אֵין תְּחִיַּת הַמֵּתִים מִן הַתּוֹרָה, — *One who says there is no [basis for] the resurrection in the Torah,*

I.e., either he denies belief in the resurrection entirely or, though accepting it, he denies that it has a Scriptural basis (*Rashi*).

The *Gemara* (9a) cites several

וְאֵין תּוֹרָה מִן הַשָּׁמַיִם, וְאַפִּיקוֹרוֹס. רַבִּי עֲקִיבָא אוֹמֵר: אַף הַקּוֹרֵא בִּסְפָרִים הַחִיצוֹנִים,

ר׳ עובדיה מברטנורא

אפיקורוס. שמבזה תלמידי חכמים, וכל שכן המבזה התורה עצמה: **בספרים החיצונים.** ספרי מינים, כגון ספרי אריסט"ו היוני וחביריו, ובכלל זה הקורא בספר דברי הימים של מלכי עובדי עבודה זרה ובשירים של עגבים ודברי חשק, שאין בהם חכמה ולא תועלת אלא אבוד זמן בלבד:

יד אברהם

Biblical allusions to resurrection. By way of example, one of these is the Torah's (*Num.* 18:28) command to the *Leviim* to give one-tenth of the tithe they receive to the *Kohanim.* This is expressed with the words: *And you shall give the terumah of* HASHEM *from it to Aaron the Kohen. Now in fact Aaron never received any terumah, since this obligation did not apply until the Jewish nation entered the Land of Israel, by which time Aaron had died. Since God is aware of the future, why did He phrase His command to give this tithe in terms of giving terumah to Aaron? Thus this phrase is seen to allude to the eventual resurrection of Aaron at which time it will indeed be possible to give him terumah.*

One who denies the validity of all these interpretations and thus maintains that resurrection has no Biblical basis is considered a heretic, since if it has no Biblical basis there is no reason to assume it to be true (*Rashi* as found in the standard texts).[1]

Meiri, however, interprets the phrase *there is no basis for resurrection in the Torah* to mean that he claims that resurrection was not a belief of the Prophets [i.e., Biblical Judaism did not subscribe to the belief in resurrection but that it was later adopted by the Rabbis — a fairly common misconception. According to *Meiri,* then, the mishnah makes no statement about the Scriptural sources of this belief].

Since he denies the truth of resurrection, he does not merit being included in it, in accordance with the concept that God deals with a person according to his own deeds and positions (*Rav* from *Gem.* 90a).[2]

Other texts of the mishnah do not include the words *in the Torah.* According to this, only one who actually denies the principle of resurrection is precluded from the World to Come (*Yad Ramah*). This is also the version cited in the text of *Rambam's Comm.* (see Kafich ed.),

1. Although each of the passages cited by the *Gemara* as proof for resurrection is open to alternate interpretations, the Oral Tradition which explains them in this manner is authoritative and supersedes any of our own theories (*Teshuvos HaRashba* 1:9).

2. The use of this principle to explain why one who denies resurrection has no share in the World to Come is proof that the World to Come discussed in the mishnah follows the resurrection rather than precedes it (*Rav; Ran;* see preface). However, there appears to be conflicting views among the Sages regarding this matter (*Ran*).

[one who says] that the Torah is not from Heaven, and an *apikorus.* R' Akiva says: Also one who reads external books,

YAD AVRAHAM

and in his code (*Hil. Teshuvah* 3:6). [In effect the view of *Meiri* cited above concurs with this approach except that he seeks to reconcile it with the standard text of the mishnah.]

וְאֵין תּוֹרָה מִן הַשָּׁמַיִם, — *[one who says] that Torah is not from Heaven,*

If someone maintains that the Torah, or any portion of it — even a single word — was written by Moses on his own, not by Divine command, he is considered a heretic (*Gem.* 99a). The same applies to one who denies the validity of the Oral Tradition which was handed down to Moses to explain the Torah (*Rambam, Hil. Teshuvah* 3:8). Since the medium which elevates a person from the limits of this physical world and connects him to the World to Come is the Torah, one who denies its heavenly source has effectively denied any possibility of elevating himself beyond the limits of this world. He is therefore not included in the reward of the World to Come (*Maharal Tiferes Yisrael* Ch. 15).

וְאַפִּיקוֹרוֹס. — *and an apikorus.*

This refers to one who disgraces the Torah itself or its scholars (*Rav* from *Gem.* 99b). Actually, this term applies to any attitude or deed which denigrates the ultimate value of the Torah — e.g., one who denies the existence of God or denies the validity of prophecy, or one who publicly transgresses the precepts of the Torah in a brazen manner (*Meiri;* cf. *Rosh Hashanah* 17a, *Rambam, Hil. Teshuvah* Ch. 3).

The term *apikorus* comes from the root הֶפְקֵר, *hefker*, something under no one's ownership. It is used to denote one who treats the Torah in a cavalier manner, as if it were ownerless property and thus subject to abuse (*Rambam Comm.*). Others connect it to Epicurus, a Greek philosopher who taught heretical views (*Sefer HaIkkarim* Ch. 1).

Rambam (*Hil. Teshuvah* 3:8) defines an *apikorus* as one who denies the validity of prophecy, or specifically the prophecy of Moshe, or denies God's awareness of the deeds of mankind. It is unclear why he ignores the definition of the *Gemara* and offers his own (*Kesef Mishneh*).

רַבִּי עֲקִיבָא אוֹמֵר: אַף הַקּוֹרֵא בִסְפָרִים הַחִיצוֹנִים, — *R' Akiva says: Also one who reads external books,*

This refers to heretical books such as the works of Aristotle (*Rav*). Others explain it to allude to works which interpret Scripture without being faithful to the interpretations of our Sages (*Rif; Rosh*).

Some authorities maintain that this applies only to one who reads such works for the sake of following their teachings (*Meiri*). Others contend that even simply reading them is prohibited because one may be influenced by them (*Teshuvos Rivash* 45; *Yad Ramah*).

Rav (from *Rambam Comm.*) adds that this precept also includes works which have no true value; study of them thus constitutes waste of time (cf. *Tif. Yis.*).

וְהַלּוֹחֵשׁ עַל הַמַּכָּה וְאוֹמֵר: „כָּל־הַמַּחֲלָה אֲשֶׁר־שַׂמְתִּי בְמִצְרַיִם לֹא־אָשִׂים עָלֶיךָ כִּי אֲנִי ה׳ רֹפְאֶךָ״. אַבָּא שָׁאוּל אוֹמֵר: אַף הַהוֹגֶה אֶת הַשֵּׁם בְּאוֹתִיּוֹתָיו.

[ב] **שְׁלשָׁה** מְלָכִים וְאַרְבָּעָה הֶדְיוֹטוֹת אֵין לָהֶם חֵלֶק לָעוֹלָם הַבָּא. שְׁלשָׁה מְלָכִים: יָרָבְעָם, אַחְאָב,

ר׳ עובדיה מברטנורא

והלוחש על המכה. וברוקק בלבד הוא דאין לו חלק לעולם הבא, לפי שאין מזכירין שם שמים על הרקיקה: **וההוגה את השם.** של ארבע אותיות כמו שהוא נכתב: **(ב) שלשה מלכים וארבעה הדיוטות.** אף על פי שגדולים וחכמים היו, אין להם חלק לעולם הבא: שלא היתה אמונתם שלימה. ואף על גב דבלעם מאומות העולם הוה, ואנן כל ישראל יש להם

יד אברהם

וְהַלּוֹחֵשׁ עַל הַמַּכָּה וְאוֹמֵר: „כָּל־הַמַּחֲלָה אֲשֶׁר־שַׂמְתִּי בְמִצְרַיִם לֹא־אָשִׂים עָלֶיךָ כִּי אֲנִי ה׳ רֹפְאֶךָ״. — *and one who whispers over a wound and says: "All the diseases which I have placed upon Egypt I shall not place upon you because I am HASHEM your healer"* (*Ex.* 15:26).

It is forbidden for one to use this verse as an incantation to whisper over a wound to heal it. This applies only to one who first expectorates and then whispers the Name of *Hashem* for the purpose of effecting a cure. It is prohibited to express the Name of *Hashem* over saliva (*Rav* from *Gem.* 101a; *Yoreh Deah* 179:8) because it shows disrespect [as if spitting at the name of *Hashem*] (*Turei Zahav*, ibid.).[1]

Others contend that this is prohibited even without expectoration because by so doing one implies that the words of the Torah are meant for worldly benefits rather than spiritual ones (*Rambam, Hil. Avodas Kochavim* 11:12 from *Yerushalmi Shabbos* 6:2). [By so doing, he loses the spiritual benefit of the Torah, which is the only medium available for reaching the World to Come (see above, s.v. ואין תורה מן השמים).]

The halachah follows the view of R' Akiva (*Yad Ramah; Yoreh Deah* 179:8) as stated in the *Gemara*, that one loses his share in the World to Come only with expectoration. However, to do so without expectoration is nonetheless prohibited. In a case of critical illness, this prohibition does not apply (*Rama* ibid.).[2]

אַבָּא שָׁאוּל אוֹמֵר: אַף הַהוֹגֶה אֶת הַשֵּׁם בְּאוֹתִיּוֹתָיו. — *Abba Shaul says: Also one who utters the Name according to its letters.*

One who utters the Divine Name of *Yud, Kei, Vav, Kei* the way it is written (and not the way it is normally pronounced) thereby profanes it, and

1. [The commentators are strangely silent on this point and offer no explanation as to why this particular show of disrespect — even when not done for that purpose — is considered to be of such great severity.]

2. [Apparently sustaining life itself is considered to be a benefit of a spiritual nature and thus doing this does not bear any degrading connotation.]

10 and one who whispers over a wound and says:
2 *"All the diseases which I have placed upon Egypt I shall not place upon you because I am HASHEM your healer"*. Abba Shaul says: Also one who utters the Name according to its letters.

2. **T**hree kings and four commoners have no share in the World to Come. The three kings [are]: Yarovam, Achav,

YAD AVRAHAM

he therefore loses his share in the World to Come (*Rav; Yad Ramah*). Others contend that this refers only to one who utters the Name of forty-two letters which was uttered in the Temple (*Rashi* to 101b).

The *Gemara* (ibid.) states that this applies to one who utters the Name outside the Temple and in a manner of עֲגָה. *Rashi* offers two possible interpretations of this word. One is that it means a foreign language; the degree of profanity required to exclude someone from eternal reward is present only if he uttered the Name of God in a language which is not imbued with the sanctity of Hebrew. Alternatively, it refers to a public utterance — only one who utters the Name publicly loses his share in the World to Come. [See further *Tosafos* to *Shevuos* 35a, s.v. באלף דלת; to *Succah* 5a, s.v. יו״ד ה״א; and to *Avodah Zorah* 18a, s.v. הוגה השם.]

2.

שְׁלֹשָׁה מְלָכִים וְאַרְבָּעָה הֶדְיוֹטוֹת אֵין לָהֶם חֵלֶק לָעוֹלָם הַבָּא. — *Three kings and four commoners have no share in the World to Come.*

[Although there were presumably many people excluded from the World to Come by the above-mentioned criteria,] the mishnah now lists seven individuals who were excluded despite their great wisdom (*Rav*) and eminence in Torah, because of their faulty beliefs in some of the fundamentals of Judaism (*Rambam Comm.*).

שְׁלֹשָׁה מְלָכִים: יָרָבְעָם, — *The three kings [are]: Yaravam,*

Yaravam (Jeroboam) revolted against the regime of Rechavam, the son of King Solomon, and led ten tribes in a break from the kingdom of the House of David. Fearing that if his subjects would go to the Temple in Jerusalem to offer sacrifices to God on the three festivals they would gradually resume their loyalty to the House of David, he established two golden calves within his kingdom for his people to serve and thus led them to idolatry (see *I Kings* 13). For this he lost his share in the World to Come, as derived from the verse (ibid. v. 34): *And this was a sin to the house of Yaravam, to cut it off and to destroy it from the face of the earth — to cut if off* from this world and *to destroy it* from the World to Come (*Gem.* 101b).

אַחְאָב, — *Achav,*

Achav (Ahab) was king of the ten tribes who, together with his wicked

סנהדרין
י/ב

וּמְנַשֶּׁה. רַבִּי יְהוּדָה אוֹמֵר: מְנַשֶּׁה יֵשׁ לוֹ חֵלֶק לָעוֹלָם הַבָּא, שֶׁנֶּאֱמַר: ,,וַיִּתְפַּלֵּל אֵלָיו וַיֵּעָתֶר לוֹ וַיִּשְׁמַע תְּחִנָּתוֹ וַיְשִׁיבֵהוּ יְרוּשָׁלַיִם לְמַלְכוּתוֹ״. אָמְרוּ לוֹ: לְמַלְכוּתוֹ הֱשִׁיבוֹ וְלֹא לְחַיֵּי הָעוֹלָם הַבָּא הֱשִׁיבוֹ. אַרְבָּעָה הֶדְיוֹטוֹת: בִּלְעָם, וְדוֹאֵג, וַאֲחִיתֹפֶל, וְגֵחֲזִי.

ר׳ עובדיה מברטנורא

חלק לעולם הבא תנן, משום דקיימא לן חסידי אומות העולם יש להם חלק לעולם הבא, אשמועינן דבלעם לאו מחסידי אומות העולם הוא:

יד אברהם

wife Izevel (Jezebel), introduced the worship of Baal into Israel. For his sins his fate was prophesied to be (*I Kings* 21:21): *And I will cut off from Achav ... he who is shut off and abandoned in Israel — shut off* in this world and *abandoned* in the World to Come (*Gem.* 102b).

וּמְנַשֶּׁה. — *and Menashe.*

Menashe (Manasseh), the son of the righteous Chizkiah (Hezekiah), king of Judah, was an idolatrous king who is compared by Scripture to Achav (*II Kings* 21:2,3), thereby indicating that he, too, lost his share in the World to Come (*Gem.* ibid.).

רַבִּי יְהוּדָה אוֹמֵר: מְנַשֶּׁה יֵשׁ לוֹ חֵלֶק לָעוֹלָם הַבָּא, שֶׁנֶּאֱמַר: ,,וַיִּתְפַּלֵּל אֵלָיו וַיֵּעָתֶר לוֹ וַיִּשְׁמַע תְּחִנָּתוֹ וַיְשִׁיבֵהוּ יְרוּשָׁלַיִם לְמַלְכוּתוֹ״. — *R' Yehudah says: Menashe has a share in the World to Come, as it is stated (II Chronicles 33:13): "And he prayed to Him, and He allowed Himself to be entreated and heard his plea, and He returned him to Jerusalem to his kingdom."*

After twenty-two years on the throne during which he spread idolatry throughout the land, God gave over Menashe into the hands of the Assyrians, who brought him in chains to Babylon. There, in his pain, Menashe called out to God and *became greatly humbled before the God of his fathers* (ibid. viz.). As the verse quoted here states, God accepted his prayer and returned him to his throne in Jerusalem where for the next thirty-three years (*Gem.* 103a) he attempted to repair the spiritual damage he had caused to his people in the first part of his reign (ibid. vs. 15-17). R' Yehudah maintains that Menashe's repentance was accepted even to the point that he recovered his share in the World to Come (*Gem.*).

אָמְרוּ לוֹ: לְמַלְכוּתוֹ הֱשִׁיבוֹ וְלֹא לְחַיֵּי הָעוֹלָם הַבָּא הֱשִׁיבוֹ. — *They said to him: He returned him to his kingdom but not to the World to Come.*

The Sages maintain that Menashe's repentance was not wholly sincere and was thus insufficient to reinstate him among those who share in the World to Come [after the great spiritual damage he had inflicted upon the Jewish people] (*Tif. Yis.*).

and Menasheh. R' Yehudah says: Menashe has a share in the World to Come, as it is stated: *And he prayed to Him, and He allowed Himself to be entreated and heard his plea, and He returned him to Jerusalem to his kingdom.* They said to him: He returned him to his kingdom but not to the World to Come. The four commoners [are]: Bilam, Doeg, Achitophel, and Gechazi.

YAD AVRAHAM

אַרְבָּעָה הֶדְיוֹטוֹת: בִּלְעָם, — *The four commoners [are]: Bilam,*

Bilam (Balaam) was the prophet hired by the king of Moab to curse the Israelites in the desert and thereby bring about their destruction (*Num.* Chs. 22-24). Although he was not Jewish, he was a prophet of God. God converted Bilam's attempts to curse the people into blessings of them. In one of these, Bilam prophesies about himself (*Num.* 23:10): *May my soul die the death of the straight and may my end be like theirs.* With this he intimated that only if he died a natural death would he have a share in the World to Come. Since he was killed in battle, it is evident that he has no such share (*Gem.* 105a).

וְדוֹאֵג, — *Doeg,*

Doeg was an adviser of King Saul who slandered David to him and thereby brought about the destruction of the city of Nov, the city of *Kohanim* (see *I Samuel* 22:9-22). Concerning him it is stated (*Psalms* 52:2,7): *Likewise, God will smash you for eternity, shall cut you off ... and uproot you from the land of life* (*Gem.* 106b).

וַאֲחִיתֹפֶל, — *Achitophel,*

Achitophel was the adviser of King David whose sage advice was so highly regarded that it was considered as accurate as consulting the word of God [through the *Urim VeTumim*]. Yet Achitophel deserted David and assisted the rebellion of Avshalom (Absalom) (see *II Samuel* 17). King David groups him together with Doeg (*Psalms* 55), thereby indicating that he too lost his share in the World to Come (*Tos. Yom Tov*).

וְגֵחֲזִי. — *and Gechazi.*

Gechazi was the servant of the prophet Elisha but he disgraced Torah scholars and led others to sin (*Gem.* 17b).

The *Gemara* (104b) cites the "interpreters of impressions" who derive exegetically that even these individuals — with the exception of Balaam — retained a share in the World to Come. Some explain that the term *interpreters of impressions* refers to the fact that they perceived the faint impression of sanctity enjoyed by even the most sinful Jew and concluded that even such people are ultimately included in the World to Come (*Machsheves Charutz,* p. 45 col. 1; see commentary to mishnah 1, s.v. ואלו).

[ג] **דּוֹר** הַמַּבּוּל אֵין לָהֶם חֵלֶק לָעוֹלָם הַבָּא, וְאֵין עוֹמְדִין בַּדִּין, שֶׁנֶּאֱמַר: ,,לֹא־יָדוֹן רוּחִי בָאָדָם לְעֹלָם" — לֹא דִין וְלֹא רוּחַ.

דּוֹר הַפְּלָגָה אֵין לָהֶם חֵלֶק לָעוֹלָם הַבָּא, שֶׁנֶּאֱמַר: ,,וַיָּפֶץ ה׳ אֹתָם מִשָּׁם עַל־פְּנֵי כָל־הָאָרֶץ" — ,,וַיָּפֶץ ה׳ אֹתָם" בָּעוֹלָם הַזֶּה; ,,וּמִשָּׁם הֱפִיצָם ה׳ " לָעוֹלָם הַבָּא.

אַנְשֵׁי סְדוֹם אֵין לָהֶם חֵלֶק לָעוֹלָם הַבָּא, שֶׁנֶּאֱמַר: ,,וְאַנְשֵׁי סְדֹם רָעִים וְחַטָּאִים לַה׳ מְאֹד" — ,,רָעִים" בָּעוֹלָם הַזֶּה, ,,וְחַטָּאִים" לָעוֹלָם הַבָּא. אֲבָל עוֹמְדִין בַּדִּין.

ר׳ עובדיה מברטנורא

(ג) **שנאמר לא ידון רוחי באדם לא דין ולא רוח.** שאין עומדים בדין ואין להם רוח לחיות עם הצדיקים שיש להם חלק:

יד אברהם

3.

דּוֹר הַמַּבּוּל אֵין לָהֶם חֵלֶק לָעוֹלָם הַבָּא, וְאֵין עוֹמְדִין בַּדִּין, — *The generation of the Flood has no share in the World to Come, nor will they stand for judgment,*

They have no share in the World to Come, but, on the other hand, they will not be punished for their sins on the final day of judgment which precedes the World to Come because they already received their punishment with the Flood (*Yad Ramah*).

Others interpret: Their souls have no share in the World to Come after their death (see preface to mishnah 1) and they will not participate in the judgment after resurrection (*Meiri*).

שֶׁנֶּאֱמַר: ,,לֹא־יָדוֹן רוּחִי בָאָדָם לְעֹלָם" – לֹא דִין וְלֹא רוּחַ. — *as it is stated* (*Gen.* 6:3): *"My spirit shall not contend evermore concerning man" — neither judgment nor spirit.*

[The *Tanna* interprets the word יָדוֹן, *contend*, as a derivative of the word דִין, *judgment*, thereby inferring that neither the judgment at the time of resurrection nor the spirit — i.e., the soul — which allows for inclusion in the World to Come is allotted to them.]

דּוֹר הַפְּלָגָה אֵין לָהֶם חֵלֶק לָעוֹלָם הַבָּא, שֶׁנֶּאֱמַר: ,,וַיָּפֶץ ה׳ אֹתָם מִשָּׁם עַל־פְּנֵי כָל־הָאָרֶץ" – ,,וַיָּפֶץ ה׳ אֹתָם" בָּעוֹלָם הַזֶּה; ,,וּמִשָּׁם הֱפִיצָם ה׳ " לָעוֹלָם הַבָּא. — *The generation of the Dispersal has no share in the World to Come, as it is stated* (ibid. 11:8): *"And* HASHEM *dispersed them from there across the face of the whole earth —" "*HASHEM *dispersed them" in this world; "and*

10
3

3. **T**he generation of the Flood has no share in the World to Come, nor will they stand for judgment, as it is stated: *My spirit shall not contend evermore concerning man* — neither judgment nor spirit.

The generation of the Dispersal has no share in the World to Come, as it is stated: *And HASHEM dispersed them from across the face of the whole earth — Hashem dispersed them* in this world; *and from there HASHEM scattered them* from the World to Come.

The people of Sodom have no share in the World to Come, as it is stated: *Now the people of Sodom were wicked and sinful toward HASHEM exceedingly — wicked* in this world, and *sinful* in the World to Come. However, they will stand for judgment.

YAD AVRAHAM

from there HASHEM scattered them" (ibid. v. 9) *from the World to Come.*

[The generation which constructed the tower of Bavel in an attempt to rebel against God (*Genesis* 11; see *Gem.* 109a) lost its share in the World to Come.] However, they will stand for judgment, since there is no indication to the contrary (*Tos. Yom Tov*).

[Unlike the generation of the Flood, these people will stand for judgment despite having lost their share in the World to Come, because their punishment in this world was not so severe.]

אֲנְשֵׁי סְדוֹם אֵין לָהֶם חֵלֶק לָעוֹלָם הַבָּא, שֶׁנֶּאֱמַר: „וְאַנְשֵׁי סְדֹם רָעִים וְחַטָּאִים לַה׳ מְאֹד״ – „רָעִים״ בָּעוֹלָם הַזֶּה, „וְחַטָּאִים״ לָעוֹלָם הַבָּא. — *The people of Sodom have no share in the World to Come, as it is stated* (ibid. 13:13): *"Now the people of Sodom were wicked and sinful toward HASHEM exceedingly" — "wicked" in this world, and "sinful" in the World to Come.*

[Although the terms רַע and חֵטְא generally refer to character of one's deeds,] they are also used in reference to punishment (*Tif. Yis.*). [Thus, their wickedness eradicated them from this world and their sinfulness erased them from the World to Come.]

אֲבָל עוֹמְדִין בַּדִּין. — *However, they will stand for judgment.*

Although they were punished in this world, the great magnitude of their sins requires further judgment in the Next World as well (*Yad Ramah*).

According to *Meiri* (see above, s.v. דור המבול), although their souls have no heavenly reward, they will nevertheless participate in the resurrection to be punished again both in body and soul (see also *Rashi* 108a).

רַבִּי נְחֶמְיָה אוֹמֵר: אֵלּוּ וָאֵלּוּ אֵין עוֹמְדִין בַּדִּין, שֶׁנֶּאֱמַר: ,,עַל־כֵּן לֹא־יָקֻמוּ רְשָׁעִים בַּמִּשְׁפָּט וְחַטָּאִים בַּעֲדַת צַדִּיקִים" — ,,עַל־כֵּן לֹא־יָקֻמוּ רְשָׁעִים בַּמִּשְׁפָּט": זֶה דּוֹר הַמַּבּוּל; ,,וְחַטָּאִים בַּעֲדַת צַדִּיקִים": אֵלּוּ אַנְשֵׁי סְדוֹם. אָמְרוּ לוֹ: אֵינָם עוֹמְדִים בַּעֲדַת צַדִּיקִים אֲבָל עוֹמְדִין בַּעֲדַת רְשָׁעִים.

מְרַגְּלִים אֵין לָהֶם חֵלֶק לָעוֹלָם הַבָּא, שֶׁנֶּאֱמַר: ,,וַיָּמֻתוּ הָאֲנָשִׁים מוֹצִאֵי דִבַּת הָאָרֶץ רָעָה בַּמַּגֵּפָה לִפְנֵי ה'" — ,,וַיָּמֻתוּ" בָּעוֹלָם הַזֶּה; ,,בַּמַּגֵּפָה" בָּעוֹלָם הַבָּא.

דּוֹר הַמִּדְבָּר אֵין לָהֶם חֵלֶק לָעוֹלָם הַבָּא, וְאֵין עוֹמְדִין בַּדִּין, שֶׁנֶּאֱמַר: ,,בַּמִּדְבָּר הַזֶּה

יד אברהם

רַבִּי נְחֶמְיָה אוֹמֵר: אֵלּוּ וָאֵלּוּ אֵין עוֹמְדִין בַּדִּין, שֶׁנֶּאֱמַר ,,עַל־כֵּן לֹא־יָקֻמוּ רְשָׁעִים בַּמִּשְׁפָּט וְחַטָּאִים בַּעֲדַת צַדִּיקִים" – ,,עַל־כֵּן לֹא־יָקֻמוּ רְשָׁעִים בַּמִּשְׁפָּט": זֶה דּוֹר הַמַּבּוּל; ,,וְחַטָּאִים בַּעֲדַת צַדִּיקִים": אֵלּוּ אַנְשֵׁי סְדוֹם. — *R' Nechemiah says: Neither these nor those will stand for judgment, as it is stated* (Psalms 1:5): *"Therefore the wicked shall not stand for judgment nor the sinful in the congregation of the righteous" — "Therefore the wicked shall not stand for judgment": this is the generation of the Flood; "nor the sinful in the congregation of the righteous": these are the people of Sodom.*

Although R' Nechemiah cites a verse concerning both the generation of the Flood and the people of Sodom, his dispute with the Sages concerns only the people of Sodom, since all agree that the generation of the Flood will not stand for judgment (*Rashi; Tos. Yom Tov*).

אָמְרוּ לוֹ: אֵינָם עוֹמְדִים בַּעֲדַת צַדִּיקִים אֲבָל עוֹמְדִין בַּעֲדַת רְשָׁעִים. — *They said to him: They shall not stand in the congregation of the righteous but they shall stand in the congregation of the sinful.*

[The verse clearly implies that they are excluded only from participation in the judgment of the righteous, not from the entire judgment.] However, R' Nechemiah understands the phrase *of the righteous* to refer to the righteous people in Sodom such as Lot. The wicked of Sodom were sinners in the congregation of the righteous [i.e., their guilt is even greater because they did not emulate the righteous among them] (*Tif. Yis.*).

מְרַגְּלִים אֵין לָהֶם חֵלֶק לָעוֹלָם הַבָּא, שֶׁנֶּאֱמַר: ,,וַיָּמֻתוּ הָאֲנָשִׁים מוֹצִאֵי דִבַּת הָאָרֶץ רָעָה בַּמַּגֵּפָה לִפְנֵי ה'" – ,,וַיָּמֻתוּ" בָּעוֹלָם הַזֶּה; ,,בַּמַּגֵּפָה" בָּעוֹלָם הַבָּא. — *The spies have no share in the World to Come, as it is*

R′ Nechemiah says: Neither these nor those will stand for judgment, as it is stated: *Therefore the wicked shall not stand for judgment nor the sinful in the congregation of the righteous — Therefore the wicked shall not stand for judgment:* this is the generation of the Flood; *nor the sinful in the congregation of the righteous:* these are the people of Sodom. They said to him: They shall not stand in the congregation of the righteous but they shall stand in the congregation of the sinful.

The spies have no share in the World to Come, as it is stated: *And the men who brought out an evil report about the land died in a plague before HASHEM. They died* — in this world; *in a plague* — in the World to Come.

The generation of the wilderness has no share in the World to Come, and they will not stand for judgment, as it is stated: *In this wilderness*

YAD AVRAHAM

stated (*Num.* 14:37): *"And the men who brought out an evil report about the land died in a plague before HASHEM." "They died" — in this world; "in a plague" — in the World to Come.*

[When the children of Israel first prepared to enter the Land of Israel, Moses sent twelve spies, one from each tribe, to explore the Land and bring back a report. When they returned, ten of them disparaged the Land and convinced the people that it was unconquerable. Only Calev and Joshua defended faithfully God's promise to conquer the Land for Israel. When the people were swayed by the negative report of the ten spies and despaired of taking the Land, God killed those ten in a plague and sentenced the rest of the nation to wander the wilderness for forty years until that entire generation died out. Only then could the next generation enter the Land under Joshua. The mishnah teaches that no only were these ten spies stricken from this world, but they also lost their share in the World to Come.] The reference to the plague as being *before HASHEM* implies that it refers to the World to Come (*Torah Temimah*, ad loc.).

דּוֹר הַמִּדְבָּר אֵין לָהֶם חֵלֶק לָעוֹלָם הַבָּא, וְאֵין עוֹמְדִין בַּדִּין, — *The generation of the wilderness has no share in the World to Come, and they will not stand for judgment,*

[The generation that died during the forty years in the desert because of the sin of the spies — those between

סנהדרין
י/ג

יִתַּמּוּ וְשָׁם יָמֻתוּ״; דִּבְרֵי רַבִּי עֲקִיבָא. רַבִּי אֱלִיעֶזֶר אוֹמֵר: עֲלֵיהֶם הוּא אוֹמֵר: ,,אִסְפוּ־לִי חֲסִידָי כֹּרְתֵי בְרִיתִי עֲלֵי זָבַח״.

עֲדַת קֹרַח אֵינָהּ עֲתִידָה לַעֲלוֹת, שֶׁנֶּאֱמַר: ,,וַתְּכַס עֲלֵיהֶם הָאָרֶץ״ — בָּעוֹלָם הַזֶּה; ,,וַיֹּאבְדוּ מִתּוֹךְ הַקָּהָל״ — לָעוֹלָם הַבָּא; דִּבְרֵי רַבִּי עֲקִיבָא. רַבִּי אֱלִיעֶזֶר אוֹמֵר: עֲלֵיהֶם הוּא אוֹמֵר: ,,ה׳ מֵמִית וּמְחַיֶּה מוֹרִיד שְׁאוֹל וַיָּעַל״.

עֲשֶׂרֶת הַשְּׁבָטִים אֵינָן עֲתִידִין לַחֲזוֹר,

ר׳ עובדיה מברטנורא

כורתי בריתי עלי זבח. שכרתו ברית עם המקום עלי זבחים ושלמים, דכתיב (שמות כד, ה) ויזבחו זבחים שלמים, וכתיב (שם שם, ח) ויזרוק על העם ויאמר הנה דם הברית: **אין עתידים לחזור.** ממקום שגלו, והא דאמרינן (ערכין לג, א) שירמיה החזירן ויאשיהו בן אמון מלך עליהם, לא כולן חזרו אלא מקצתן:

יד אברהם

the ages of twenty and sixty at the time of the sin — are excluded from the World to Come as well, according to this opinion.]

It seems inconceivable that the entire generation, which included many righteous people, were excluded from a share in the World to Come. Possibly, this refers only to those who rebelled against God in one form or another [which apparently included the bulk of the masses]. Those who were steadfast in their loyalty could certainly not be punished in the next world for the sins of the others (*Margaliyos HaYam* to 108a).

שֶׁנֶּאֱמַר: ,,בַּמִּדְבָּר הַזֶּה יִתַּמּוּ וְשָׁם יָמֻתוּ״; דִּבְרֵי רַבִּי עֲקִיבָא. — *as it is stated* (*Num.* 14:35): *"In this wilderness they shall be consumed and there they shall die"; [these are] the words of R' Akiva.*

The redundant wording of the verse indicates death in both worlds (*Tif. Yis.* see ibid.).

רַבִּי אֱלִיעֶזֶר אוֹמֵר: עֲלֵיהֶם הוּא אוֹמֵר: ,,אִסְפוּ־לִי חֲסִידָי כֹּרְתֵי בְרִיתִי עֲלֵי־זָבַח״. — *R' Eliezer says: Concerning them it is stated* (*Psalms* 50:5): *"Gather to Me My devout ones; those who sealed a covenant with Me by sacrifice."*

The generation of the desert, which brought sacrifices at Mt. Sinai to consummate a bond with the Almighty, are guaranteed a share in the World to Come (*Rav*) because of the repentance they did for their sins (*Meiri*). The *Gemara* (110b) cites the conclusion of R' Yochanan, that R' Eliezer's view is the correct one. He derives this from the words of *Jeremiah* (2:2) declaring that the loyalty the Jewish people showed in following God blindly into the

they shall be consumed and there they shall die; [these are] the words of R' Akiva. R' Eliezer says: Concerning them it is stated: *Gather to Me My devout ones; those who sealed a covenant with Me by sacrifice.*

The congregation of Korach is not destined to arise, as it is stated: *And the land covered them over* — in this world; *and they were lost from amidst the congregation* — in the World to Come; [these are] the words of R' Akiva. R' Eliezer says: Concerning them it is stated: *HASHEM kills and brings to life; he lowers into the grave and brings up.*

The Ten Tribes are not destined to return,

YAD AVRAHAM

wilderness stands as a source of merit for subsequent generations. If their merit is great enough to benefit others, contends R' Yochanan, it certainly sufficed to save them.

עֲדַת קֹרַח אֵינָהּ עֲתִידָה לַעֲלוֹת, שֶׁנֶּאֱמַר: ,,וַתְּכַס עֲלֵיהֶם הָאָרֶץ" – בָּעוֹלָם הַזֶּה; ,,וַיֹּאבְדוּ מִתּוֹךְ הַקָּהָל" – לָעוֹלָם הַבָּא; דִּבְרֵי רַבִּי עֲקִיבָא. רַבִּי אֱלִיעֶזֶר אוֹמֵר: עֲלֵיהֶם הוּא אוֹמֵר: ,,ה' מֵמִית וּמְחַיֶּה מוֹרִיד שְׁאוֹל וַיָּעַל". — *The congregation of Korach is not destined to arise, as it is stated* (*Num.* 16:33): *"And the land covered them over" — in this world; "and they were lost from amidst the congregation" — in the World to Come; [these are] the words of R' Akiva. R' Eliezer says: Concerning them it is stated* (*I Samuel* 2:6): *"HASHEM kills and brings to life; he lowers into the grave and brings up."*

[This verse is from the thanksgiving prayer of Channah, which the mishnah takes as a reference to the congregation of Korach, who were swallowed up alive beneath the earth.] R' Eliezer derives from here that they repented [as they fell into the abyss] and thereby recovered their eternal reward (*Meiri*).

עֲשֶׂרֶת הַשְּׁבָטִים אֵינָן עֲתִידִין לַחֲזוֹר, — *The Ten Tribes are not destined to return,*

[The ten tribes who broke with the House of David under Yaravam and formed their own kingdom (commonly known as the Northern Kingdom) were exiled from Israel by the Assyrian king, Sancheriv (Sennacherib), some one hundred years before the destruction of the First Temple.] In the opinion of R' Akiva, they will not return to the land from their exile in the times of the Messiah (*Meiri*), nor will they share in the World to Come (*Rabbeinu Dovid;* see *Gem.* 110b). This refers only to the generation actually exiled; their descendants, however, retain their share in the World to Come (*Rashi; Rabbeinu Dovid*).

שֶׁנֶּאֱמַר: „וַיַּשְׁלִכֵם אֶל־אֶרֶץ אַחֶרֶת כַּיּוֹם הַזֶּה״ — מָה הַיּוֹם הַזֶּה הוֹלֵךְ וְאֵינוֹ חוֹזֵר, אַף הֵם הוֹלְכִים וְאֵינָם חוֹזְרִים; דִּבְרֵי רַבִּי עֲקִיבָא. רַבִּי אֱלִיעֶזֶר אוֹמֵר: מָה הַיּוֹם מַאֲפִיל וּמֵאִיר, אַף עֲשֶׂרֶת הַשְּׁבָטִים שֶׁאָפַל לָהֶן, כָּךְ עָתִיד לְהָאִיר לָהֶן.

[ד] **אַנְשֵׁי** עִיר הַנִּדַּחַת אֵין לָהֶן חֵלֶק לָעוֹלָם הַבָּא, שֶׁנֶּאֱמַר: „יָצְאוּ אֲנָשִׁים בְּנֵי־בְלִיַּעַל מִקִּרְבֶּךָ וַיַּדִּיחוּ אֶת־יֹשְׁבֵי עִירָם״.

וְאֵינָן נֶהֱרָגִים עַד שֶׁיִּהְיוּ מַדִּיחֶיהָ מֵאוֹתָהּ הָעִיר

ר׳ עובדיה מברטנורא

(ד) **יצאו אנשים בני בליעל.** בניס שאינס עולים בתחיית המתים, ונדחין כמדיחין: **עד שיהיו מדיחיה מאותה העיר.** דכתיב (דברים יג,יד) וידיחו את יושבי עירם, ולא יושבי עיר אחרת:

יד אברהם

שֶׁנֶּאֱמַר: „וַיַּשְׁלִכֵם אֶל־אֶרֶץ אַחֶרֶת כַּיּוֹם הַזֶּה״ – מָה הַיּוֹם הַזֶּה הוֹלֵךְ וְאֵינוֹ חוֹזֵר, אַף הֵם הוֹלְכִים וְאֵינָם חוֹזְרִים; דִּבְרֵי רַבִּי עֲקִיבָא — *as it is stated* (*Deut.* 29:27): *"And he sent them to another land as of this day" — just as this day goes never to return, so they go never to return; [these are] the words of R' Akiva.*

The implication of this verse is that it refers to an exile in which all are exiled together to one land [and remain there throughout their exile]. Accordingly, it refers only to the Ten Tribes, as the two tribes of Judah and Benjamin, who were exiled later, were dispersed across many lands (*Rashi*).

רַבִּי אֱלִיעֶזֶר אוֹמֵר: מָה הַיּוֹם מַאֲפִיל וּמֵאִיר, אַף עֲשֶׂרֶת הַשְּׁבָטִים שֶׁאָפַל לָהֶן, כָּךְ עָתִיד לְהָאִיר לָהֶן — *R' Eliezer says: Just as the day darkens and [then] becomes light, so the Ten Tribes, for whom it became dark, shall have a future that becomes light for them.*

R' Eliezer explains the verse's comparison of the exile of the Ten Tribes to the quality of day differently. Just as the darkness of night eventually gives way to the light of day, so too, the darkness of their exile will eventually turn to light (*Rashi*).

4.

אַנְשֵׁי עִיר הַנִּדַּחַת אֵין לָהֶם חֵלֶק לָעוֹלָם הַבָּא — *The people of an apostate town have no share in the World to Come.*

This is the final example cited by the mishnah of those who have no share in the next world (*Rashi; Meiri*).

Others delete this phrase from the text of the mishnah. The apostate town is cited

as it is stated: *And he sent them to another land as of this day* — just as this day goes never to return, so they go never to return; [these are] the words of R' Akiva. R' Eliezer says: Just as the day darkens and [then] becomes light, so the Ten Tribes, for whom it became dark, shall have a future that becomes light for them.

4. **T**he people of an apostate town have no share in the World to Come, as it is stated: *There went out wicked men from your midst and they led astray the inhabitants of their town.*

They are not beheaded unless those that led them astray are from that town

YAD AVRAHAM

here in continuation of the discussion in Chapter 9 concerning those who are beheaded; it is not included in the topic of the World to Come (*Yad Ramah; Ran;* see preface to mishnah 1).

Although one who has been executed by the courts thereby receives atonement for his sin (see 6:2), the mishnah is discussing a case in which they escaped punishment by the court (*Tos.* to 47a, s.v. ואמאי). Alternatively, the mishnah refers to those who led the town astray to idolatry; since they were responsible for the defection and destruction of an entire town, they cannot achieve atonement and enter the World to Come (*Hagahos Yaavetz,* cited by *Margaliyos HaYam*).

שֶׁנֶּאֱמַר: ,,יָצְאוּ אֲנָשִׁים בְּנֵי־בְלִיַּעַל מִקִּרְבֶּךָ וַיַּדִּיחוּ אֶת־יֹשְׁבֵי עִירָם״. — *as it is stated* (*Deut.* 13:14): *"There went out wicked men from your midst and they led astray the inhabitants of their town."*

The term בְלִיַּעַל refers to those who have no share in the World to Come (*Rav*).

Alternatively, the phrase *they went out of your midst* intimates that they lost the share which they had together with the rest of Israel in the World to Come (*Rashi; Yad Ramah*).

וְאֵינָן נֶהֱרָגִים — *They are not beheaded*

[The mishnah now delineates the laws of the apostate town left undiscussed in Ch. 9 (see mishnah 1).] The inhabitants of an apostate town are executed according to the special laws of an apostate town only if the following conditions are met. If not, they are treated as individuals who served false gods — who are executed by stoning (*Yad Ramah;* see below).

עַד שֶׁיִּהְיוּ מַדִּיחֶיהָ מֵאוֹתָהּ הָעִיר — *unless those that led them astray are from that town*

The first condition is that those who lead the town to idolatry must be members of the town they led astray. This is derived from the verse (*Deut.* ibid.): *and they incited the inhabitants of their town* (*Rav* from *Gem.* 111b).

וּמֵאוֹתוֹ הַשֵּׁבֶט, וְעַד שֶׁיֻּדַּח רֻבָּהּ, וְעַד שֶׁיַּדִּיחוּם אֲנָשִׁים. הִדִּיחוּהָ נָשִׁים וּקְטַנִּים, אוֹ שֶׁהֻדַּח מִעוּטָהּ, אוֹ שֶׁהָיוּ מַדִּיחֶיהָ חוּצָה לָהּ, הֲרֵי אֵלּוּ כַּיְחִידִים. וּצְרִיכִין שְׁנֵי עֵדִים וְהַתְרָאָה לְכָל אֶחָד וְאֶחָד. זֶה חֹמֶר בַּיְחִידִים מִבַּמְרֻבִּים: שֶׁהַיְחִידִים בִּסְקִילָה; לְפִיכָךְ מָמוֹנָם פָּלֵט. וְהַמְרֻבִּים בְּסַיִף; לְפִיכָךְ מָמוֹנָם אָבֵד.

ר׳ עובדיה מברטנורא

ומאותו השבט. דכתיב (שם) מקרבך, מקרב השבט עצמו: **ועד שיודח רובה.** של עיר, דכתיב (שם) יושבי עירם, דמשמע ישובה של עיר דהיינו רובה: **הרי אלו כיחידים.** שעבדו עבודה זרה, וידונו בסקילה וממונן פלט: **וצריכים.** אנשי עיר הנדחת, שני עדים והתראה לכל אחד ואחד, שהיו מרבים להם בתי דינין, וכל מי שנמצא שעבד עבודה זרה בעדים והתראה, מפרישים אותן עד שיראו אם הם רובה של עיר מביאין אותן לבית דין הגדול וגומרין דינן שם והורגים אותם בסייף וממונן אבד, ואם לא נמצאו רובה של עיר, דנין אותן בסקילה וממונן פלט:

יד אברהם

וּמֵאוֹתוֹ הַשֵּׁבֶט, — *and that tribe,*

They must be members of the tribe within whose borders the town was (*Meiri*). This is derived from the words: *from your midst* — i.e., from within your tribe (*Rav*).

וְעַד שֶׁיֻּדַּח רֻבָּהּ, — *unless the majority [of the town] has been led astray,*

The majority of the town must succumb to the instigation to worship the idol in order for the town to be classified an apostate town. This is derived from the words (ibid.): *the inhabitants of their town* — implying the bulk of its inhabitants (*Rav*).

וְעַד שֶׁיַּדִּיחוּם אֲנָשִׁים. — *and unless they have been led astray by men.*

To be classified an apostate town they must have been led astray by men, not women or children, as specified in the verse by the word *men* (*Gem.* 111b).

הִדִּיחוּהָ נָשִׁים וּקְטַנִּים, אוֹ שֶׁהֻדַּח מִעוּטָהּ, אוֹ שֶׁהָיוּ מַדִּיחֶיהָ חוּצָה לָהּ, הֲרֵי אֵלּוּ כַּיְחִידִים. — *[If] they were led astray by women or children, or [only] a minority was led astray, or if those leading them astray were from outside the town, they are treated as individuals.*

If any of the above-mentioned conditions are lacking, the town cannot be classified an apostate town. Accordingly, all who served idolatry are judged like individuals who commit idolatry; their punishment is stoning, but their possessions are not destroyed [see below] (*Rav*).

וּצְרִיכִין שְׁנֵי עֵדִים וְהַתְרָאָה לְכָל אֶחָד וְאֶחָד. — *They require two witnesses and a warning for each one.*

[In accordance with the general rules pertaining to capital crimes,] each of the inhabitants of the town must have two witnesses to his transgression and he must have been warned of the

and that tribe, unless the majority [of the town] has been led astray, and unless they have been led astray by men. [If] they were led astray by women or children, or [only] a minority was led astray, or if those leading them astray were from outside the town, they are treated as individuals.

They require two witnesses and a warning for each one. This is the stringency of individuals over a multitude: individuals are stoned; therefore their property is spared. The multitude are beheaded; therefore their property is forfeit.

consequences of his act. Otherwise, the law of an apostate town does not apply [nor can they be judged as individuals] (*Rav; Yad Ramah*).

The process of assigning an apostate town was as follows: When the situation was such that its existence was deemed possible, they gathered many courts and began judging the inhabitants one by one. Those who were found guilty of idolatry were held, and if they turned out to be the majority of the town, the law of an apostate town was implemented. If they formed only a minority of the town's population, they were judged as individual idolaters (*Rav* from *Gem.* 112a; *Rambam, Hil. Avodas Kochavim* 4:6).

There is another view in the *Gemara* (ibid.), that one court of twenty-three is sufficient for this situation. They judge each individual separately and stone those who are found guilty. If a majority of the town turns out to have participated in the crime, all those subsequently found guilty are dealt with in accordance with the laws of an apostate town. Some authorities maintain that the halachah follows this view (*Yad Ramah*, cited by *Kesef Mishneh* to *Hil. Avodas Kochavim* loc. cit.; see ibid.).

זֶה חֹמֶר בַּיְחִידִים מִבַּמְרֻבִּים: שֶׁהַיְחִידִים בִּסְקִילָה; לְפִיכָךְ מָמוֹנָם פָּלֵט. וְהַמְרֻבִּים בְּסַיִף; לְפִיכָךְ מָמוֹנָם אָבֵד. — *This is the stringency of individuals over a multitude: individuals are stoned; therefore their property is spared. The multitude are beheaded; therefore their property is forfeit.*

The Torah (*Deut.* 13:17) imposes an additional penalty on the apostate town, that all its property be gathered into the street and, together with the entire town, be destroyed by fire. The property of individuals executed for idolatry, however, is not destroyed, but passes to their heirs. The mishnah states the rationale for this — since the Torah deals more strictly with individuals in regard to their punishment, it is more lenient with regard to their property (*Yad Ramah*).

Another explanation is that a member of a group which engages in idolatry shows less individual initiative for evil than one who does so on his own. On the other hand, the primary incentive which causes one to live among wicked people is the acquisition of money. Accordingly, the individual himself is punished more severely but an inhabitant of an apostate town is punished monetarily (*Margaliyos HaYam*).

[ה] ,,הַכֵּה תַכֶּה אֶת וגו׳ " — הַחַמֶּרֶת וְהַגַּמֶּלֶת הָעוֹבֶרֶת מִמָּקוֹם לְמָקוֹם, הֲרֵי אֵלּוּ מַצִּילִין אוֹתָהּ. ,,הַחֲרֵם אֹתָהּ וְאֶת־כָּל־אֲשֶׁר־בָּהּ וגו׳ — מִכָּאן אָמְרוּ: נִכְסֵי צַדִּיקִים שֶׁבְּתוֹכָהּ אוֹבְדִין, שֶׁבְּחוּצָה לָהּ פְּלֵטִין; וְשֶׁל רְשָׁעִים, בֵּין שֶׁבְּתוֹכָהּ בֵּין שֶׁבְּחוּצָה לָהּ, הֲרֵי אֵלּוּ אוֹבְדִין.

[ו] שֶׁנֶּאֱמַר: ,,וְאֶת־כָּל־שְׁלָלָהּ תִּקְבֹּץ אֶל־תּוֹךְ רְחֹבָהּ וגו׳ " — אִם אֵין לָהּ רְחוֹב, עוֹשִׂין לָהּ רְחוֹב. הָיָה רְחוֹבָהּ

ר׳ עובדיה מברטנורא

(ה) **החמרת והגמלת.** שיירא של חמרים ושל גמלים שנשתהו בעיר שלשים יום, הוי להו בכלל יושבי עירם: **הרי אלו מצילין.** אם רוב אנשי העיר הודחו ומיעוט לא הודחו, וחמרים וגמלים שלא הודחו משלימין את המועט לעשות רוב, הרי אלו מצילין, שאין ממונן אבד אלא נדונין כיחידים, והוא הדין דגורמין נמי לעשות עיר הנדחת, אם הודחו עמם לעשותם רוב, אלא דתנא אזכותא קא מהדר, ועוד דהא פסיקא ליה טפי, דסתם חמרת וגמלת אין דעתן מעורבת עם בני העיר שיהיו נדחין עמהן:

יד אברהם

5.

,,הַכֵּה תַכֶּה אֶת וגו׳ " — *"You shall surely smite, etc."* (*Deut.* 13:16) —

The full text of the first part of this verse is: *You shall surely smite the inhabitants of that town by the edge of the sword.*

הַחַמֶּרֶת וְהַגַּמֶּלֶת הָעוֹבֶרֶת מִמָּקוֹם לְמָקוֹם, הֲרֵי אֵלּוּ מַצִּילִין אוֹתָהּ. — *A donkey train or camel caravan which passes from place to place saves it.*

If the members of a camel caravan or donkey train were staying in the town when it went astray, and they did not serve the false god, they may tilt the scale to render the majority of the town innocent and thereby save the town from being judged as an apostate town (*Rav; Rashi*). However, in order to be considered part of the town in regard to this issue they must have resided there for at least thirty days (*Gem.* 112a).

Others interpret the *Gemara* that if they do not stay for thirty days, even if they worshiped falsely, they are saved from being included in the judgment of the town because they are not considered inhabitants of it (*Yad Ramah*).

,,הַחֲרֵם אֹתָהּ וְאֶת־כָּל־אֲשֶׁר־בָּהּ וגו׳ " — *"Destroy it and all that is in it, etc."* (ibid.) —

This is the concluding half of the verse. It reads, in full: *Destroy it and all that is in it and all its beasts by the edge of the sword.*

5. **Y**ou shall surely smite, etc. — A donkey train or camel caravan which passes from place to place saves it. *Destroy it and all that is in it, etc.* — From here they derived [that] the possessions of the righteous which are in it are forfeit, [while] those which are outside it are saved; those of the wicked, whether within or without, are forfeit.

6. **A**s it is stated: *And all its spoils you shall gather into its plaza, etc.* — If it has no plaza, they make one. [If] its plaza

YAD AVRAHAM

מִכָּאן אָמְרוּ: נִכְסֵי צַדִּיקִים שֶׁבְּתוֹכָהּ אוֹבְדִין, שֶׁבְּחוּצָה לָהּ פְּלֵטִין; — *From here they derived [that] the possessions of the righteous which are in it are forfeit, [while] those which are outside it are saved;*

When an apostate town is executed, only those who are actually found guilty of idolatry are executed. However, the destruction of the town and all its property includes the possessions of the inhabitants of the town who were not found guilty of idolatry. Only those possessions found within the town are included in the destruction of the town; their possessions outside the town are saved (*Meiri*). This is derived from the verse stated above; the stipulation *all that is in it* excludes the possessions from without; the word *all* comes to include the possessions found within even if they belong to those who are innocent (*Gem.* 112a).

וְשֶׁל רְשָׁעִים, בֵּין שֶׁבְּתוֹכָהּ בֵּין שֶׁבְּחוּצָה לָהּ, הֲרֵי אֵלּוּ אוֹבְדִין. — *those of the wicked, whether within or without, are forfeit.*

And all its spoils (v. 17) comes to include even the possessions of the guilty inhabitants which are not to be found within the town (*Gem.* ibid.). The *Gemara* (ibid.) states that this applies only to those possessions which "are gathered within it." According to *Rashi*, this means those which are to be found close enough to a town that they can be brought inside within a day. Others interpret this to refer to anything which at one time had been kept inside the town (*Yad Ramah*).

6.

שֶׁנֶּאֱמַר: „וְאֶת־כָּל־שְׁלָלָהּ תִּקְבֹּץ אֶל־תּוֹךְ רְחֹבָהּ וגו׳" – — *As it is stated* (*Deut.* 13:17): *"And all its spoils you shall gather into its plaza, etc"* —

I.e., the public square where the masses gather (*Rav*).

Some maintain that the words *as is stated* are out of place here and should be deleted (*Hagahos HaGra*).

אִם אֵין לָהּ רְחוֹב, עוֹשִׂין לָהּ רְחוֹב. — *If it has no plaza, they make one.*

The implication of the verse

חוּצָה לָהּ, כּוֹנְסִין אוֹתוֹ לְתוֹכָהּ. „וְשָׂרַפְתָּ בָאֵשׁ אֶת־הָעִיר וְאֶת כָּל שְׁלָלָהּ כָּלִיל לַה׳ אֱלֹהֶיךָ״ — „שְׁלָלָהּ״, וְלֹא שְׁלַל שָׁמַיִם. מִכָּאן אָמְרוּ: הַהֶקְדֵּשׁוֹת שֶׁבָּהּ יִפָּדוּ, וּתְרוּמוֹת יֵרָקְבוּ, מַעֲשֵׂר שֵׁנִי

ר׳ עובדיה מברטנורא

(ו) **היתה רחובה חוצה לה.** אם מקום קבוץ בני העיר היה חוצה לה, כונסים אותה לתוך העיר, שצריך לעשות לה רחוב בתוכה: **רחוב.** פלטיא גדולה: **הקדשות שבתוכה יפדו.** כלומר אין נשרפים אלא צריכים פדייה כשאר כל ההקדשות: **ותרומות ירקבו.** בגמרא (קיב, ב) מוקמינן לה בתרומה ביד כהן, דממון כהן הוא וחל עליה איסור דעיר הנדחת, ומיהו לא היו התרומות נשרפים כשאר שללה, דלא מזלזלינן בה כולי האי, לפיכך ירקבו, ואם תרומה ביד ישראל היא, שלל גבוה הוא ותנתן לכהן שבעיר אחרת: **ומעשר שני.** אף על גב דממון ישראל הוא, שהרי הוא נאכל לישראל, הואיל וקדש אקרי, לא ישרף אלא וגנז:

יד אברהם

includes not only a public square which existed at the time of the transgression but even one which was so designated at the time of judgment (*Gem.* 112a). [Thus, since the property must be gathered into the town square to be destroyed, if the town lacks such a square, one is constructed for this purpose.]

הָיָה רְחוֹבָהּ חוּצָה לָהּ, כּוֹנְסִין אוֹתוֹ לְתוֹכָהּ. — *[If] its plaza is outside it, they bring it in.*

If the public square was outside the confines of the town, they extend the wall of the town to include it (*Rambam, Hil. Avodas Kochavim* 4:6). Some maintain that they must also dismantle the section of wall which divides the town and the plaza (*Yad Ramah*).

„וְשָׂרַפְתָּ בָאֵשׁ אֶת־הָעִיר וְאֶת־כָּל־שְׁלָלָהּ כָּלִיל לַה׳ אֱלֹהֶיךָ״ – „שְׁלָלָהּ״, וְלֹא שְׁלַל שָׁמַיִם. — *"And you shall burn the town and its spoils completely to Hashem your God"* (ibid.) — *"its spoils," not the spoils of Heaven.*

[The phrase *its spoils* indicates that only property belonging to the inhabitants of the town is destroyed. Property which had been consecrated by the inhabitants is excluded from destruction since it is no longer theirs but "the spoils of Heaven."]

מִכָּאן אָמְרוּ: הַהֶקְדֵּשׁוֹת שֶׁבָּהּ יִפָּדוּ, — *From here they derived [that] the hekdesh objects in it are redeemed,*

Hekdesh objects are objects consecrated for Temple use. In this case, however, this refers specifically to those consecrated to the Temple treasury and not to those designated as sacrifices. The latter cannot be redeemed but must be killed, in accordance with the verse (*Proverbs* 21:27): *The sacrifice of the wicked is an abomination* (*Gem.* 112b). However, those which have been designated for use in meeting the Temple's non-sacrificial needs are the property of the Temple treasury and they are redeemed for money like any other object consecrated to the Temple treasury (*Rav; Yad Ramah; Ravad, Hil. Avodas Kochavim* 4:13).

is outside it, they bring it in. *And you shall burn the town and its spoils completely to Hashem your God* — its *spoils,* not the spoils of Heaven. From here they derived [that] the *hekdesh* objects in it are redeemed, the *terumos* are [left] to rot, [and the] *maaser sheni*

YAD AVRAHAM

Rambam (ibid.), however, contends that after they are redeemed and thereby removed from the category of consecrated property, they must be burned as part of the apostate town (see *Kesef Mishneh* ad loc.).

וּתְרוּמוֹת יֵרָקְבוּ, — *the terumos are [left] to rot,*

[The foodstuffs which have been sanctified as *terumah* (the portion of the crop which must be removed and given to a *Kohen*) are also not burned but are left to rot.]

This pertains to *terumah* which has already been given to a *Kohen* and is thus wholly in the property of its present owner, who is an inhabitant of the apostate town. Although it is classified as property of an apostate town and thus prohibited, due to its sanctity it is not demeaned by being burned but is rather left to rot. However, if the *terumah* is still in the hands of a non-*Kohen,* who may not keep it for himself in any event, it is considered the "spoils of Heaven" and it is given to a *Kohen* from a different town (*Rav* from *Gem.* 112b; *Rashi* ibid.). [Until *terumah* is given to a *Kohen* it is sanctified property which does not belong to anyone. It does not belong to the farmer, since he is under obligation to give it away and forbidden to use it; nor can it be said to belong to any specific *Kohen.* Once it has been given to a *Kohen,* it becomes his personal property (no other *Kohen* may take it from him), though its use is subject to certain restrictions arising from its sanctity.] In contrast to that which was designated for Temple use, the *terumah* need not be redeemed, because it is sanctified for its essence rather than for its value [i.e., its sanctification is for the purpose of being used in its state of holiness, not for selling in order to generate revenue] (*Rambam,* loc. cit. 14).

מַעֲשֵׂר שֵׁנִי — *[and the] maaser sheni*

Maaser sheni is the second tithe, the portion separated from the crop during the first, second, fourth, and fifth years of every seven-year *Shemittah* cycle. This tithe is taken to Jerusalem where it is eaten or redeemed for money, with the money being spent on food in Jerusalem. *Maaser sheni* produce and any money used to redeem *maaser sheni* are not burned with the town but are buried (*Ramba,* loc. cit. 15 from *Gem.* 112b). This is because *maaser sheni* is considered sanctified (and thus not fit for burning), even though it may be eaten in Jerusalem by anyone, even a non-*Kohen.* However, it is considered the possession of the tither and thus subject to prohibition if he was an inhabitant of an apostate town (*Rav; Rashi*).

סנהדרין
י/ו

וְכִתְבֵי הַקֹּדֶשׁ יִגָּנְזוּ. ,,כָּלִיל לַה׳ אֱלֹהֶיךָ״ — אָמַר רַבִּי שִׁמְעוֹן: אָמַר הַקָּדוֹשׁ בָּרוּךְ הוּא: אִם אַתֶּם עוֹשִׂים דִּין בְּעִיר הַנִּדַּחַת, מַעֲלֶה אֲנִי עֲלֵיכֶם כְּאִלּוּ אַתֶּם מַעֲלִין עוֹלָה כָלִיל לְפָנָי. ,,וְהָיְתָה תֵּל עוֹלָם; לֹא תִבָּנֶה עוֹד״ — לֹא תֵעָשֶׂה אֲפִלּוּ גַּנּוֹת וּפַרְדֵּסִים; דִּבְרֵי רַבִּי יוֹסֵי הַגְּלִילִי. רַבִּי עֲקִיבָא אוֹמֵר: ,,לֹא תִבָּנֶה עוֹד״ — לִכְמוֹ שֶׁהָיְתָה אֵינָהּ נִבְנֵית אֲבָל נַעֲשֵׂית הִיא גַּנּוֹת וּפַרְדֵּסִים. ,,וְלֹא־יִדְבַּק בְּיָדְךָ מְאוּמָה מִן־הַחֵרֶם״ — שֶׁכָּל זְמַן שֶׁהָרְשָׁעִים בָּעוֹלָם, חֲרוֹן אַף בָּעוֹלָם; אָבְדוּ רְשָׁעִים מִן הָעוֹלָם, נִסְתַּלֵּק חֲרוֹן אַף מִן הָעוֹלָם.

ר׳ עובדיה מברטנורא

כליל לה׳ אלהיך. אמר רבי שמעון וכו׳ גרסינן, ולא גרסינן שנאמר כליל לה׳ אלהיך: **לא תעשה גנות ופרדסים.** דעוד, לגמרי משמע: **כמו שהיתה.** בישוב בתים: **אבל נעשית היא גנות ופרדסים.** והלכה כרבי עקיבא:

יד אברהם

וְכִתְבֵי הַקֹּדֶשׁ — *and Holy Scriptures*

Although books of the Scripture are the property of their owner they may not be burned, since it is forbidden to burn something which contains the Name of God (*Yad Ramah*).

יִגָּנְזוּ. — *must be buried.*

[Since these are forbidden for use like all property of an apostate town, they must be removed so that they not be subject to misappropriation.]

Although *terumah* of an apostate town is allowed to rot, *maaser sheni* must be buried immediately. This is due to the superior sanctity of *terumah*, which is forbidden to a non-*Kohen* (*Yad Ramah*). In addition, ordinary people are accustomed to avoiding *terumah*, since it is permitted for consumption only to a *Kohen*. *Kohanim*, in turn, are especially careful in their observance of the Torah. Consequently, there is no fear that anyone will partake of the forbidden *terumah* before it rots. Tithes and Holy Scriptures, however, remain in the hands of everyone, and the Sages were thus concerned that they might be used inadvertently, which would be forbidden. Therefore, they required that they be buried (*Tos. Yom Tov; see Margaliyos HaYam*).

,,כָּלִיל לַה׳ אֱלֹהֶיךָ״ - אָמַר רַבִּי שִׁמְעוֹן: אָמַר הַקָּדוֹשׁ בָּרוּךְ הוּא: אִם אַתֶּם עוֹשִׂים דִּין בְּעִיר הַנִּדַּחַת, מַעֲלֶה אֲנִי עֲלֵיכֶם כְּאִלּוּ אַתֶּם מַעֲלִין עוֹלָה כָלִיל לְפָנָי. — *"Completely to Hashem your God"* (ibid.) — *said R' Shimon: The Holy One, Blessed is He, said: If you will carry out the judgment of an apostate town, it is as if* (lit., *I consider it for you as if*) *you bring a burnt-offering before Me.*

10
6 and Holy Scriptures must be buried. *Completely to Hashem your God* — said R' Shimon: The Holy One, Blessed is He, said: If you will carry out the judgment of an apostate town, it is as if you bring a burnt-offering before Me. *And it shall be a mound forever; it may not be rebuilt at all* — it may not even be made into gardens or orchards; [these are] the words of R' Yose HaGlili. R' Akiva says: *It may never again be rebuilt* — it may not be rebuilt to what it was but it may be made into gardens and orchards. And nothing of the banned matter shall stick to your hand — For as long as the wicked are in the world, there is anger in the world; [when] the wicked perish from the world, anger disappears from the world.

YAD AVRAHAM

A burnt-offering is specified because its owner receives no material benefit from it, similar to the apostate town from which it is forbidden to benefit (*Ein Yaakov*).

„וְהָיְתָה תֵּל עוֹלָם; לֹא תִבָּנֶה עוֹד" – לֹא תֵעָשֶׂה אֲפִלּוּ גַּנּוֹת וּפַרְדֵּסִים; דִּבְרֵי רַבִּי יוֹסֵי הַגְּלִילִי. — *"And it shall be a mound forever; it may not be rebuilt at all"* (ibid.) — *it may not even be made into gardens or orchards; [these are] the words of R' Yose HaGlili.*

Although the verse explicitly prohibits rebuilding the town, R' Yose understands the word עוֹד to mean *at all*, to teach that the site may never again be reconstructed in any form whatsoever (*Rav* from *Gem.* 113a; *Rashi* ibid.).

רַבִּי עֲקִיבָא אוֹמֵר: „לֹא תִבָּנֶה עוֹד" – לִכְמוֹ שֶׁהָיְתָה אֵינָהּ נִבְנֵית אֲבָל נַעֲשֵׂית הִיא גַּנּוֹת וּפַרְדֵּסִים. — *R' Akiva says: "It may never again be rebuilt" — it may not be rebuilt to what it was but it may be made into gardens and orchards.*

He interprets the word עוֹד to mean *again;* thus, it teaches only that it may not be restored to what it formerly was (*Gem.* ibid.). The halachah follows the view of R' Akiva (*Rav; Rambam,* loc. cit. 8).

Whoever rebuilds an apostate town receives lashes (*Rambam, Avodas Kochavim* 4:8). However, the number of houses which must be rebuilt for the town as a whole to be considered rebuilt is not clear (*Minchas Chinuch* 465).

„וְלֹא־יִדְבַּק בְּיָדְךָ מְאוּמָה מִן־הַחֵרֶם" – שֶׁכָּל זְמַן שֶׁהָרְשָׁעִים בָּעוֹלָם, חֲרוֹן אַף בָּעוֹלָם; אָבְדוּ רְשָׁעִים מִן הָעוֹלָם, נִסְתַּלֵּק חֲרוֹן אַף מִן הָעוֹלָם. — *"And nothing of the banned matter shall stick to your hand"* (ibid. v. 18) — *For as long as the wicked are in the world, there is anger in the world; [when] the wicked perish from the world, anger disappears from the world.*

The wicked mentioned here are not

those of the apostate town itself, as this is stated in reference to the verse discussing the prohibition against partaking of the spoils of the town (*Yad Ramah* to 113b). Rather it pertains to those who steal (*Gem.* ibid.) or otherwise take from that which is not theirs (*Yad Ramah*).

פרק אחד עשר
Chapter Eleven

[א] **אֵלּוּ** הֵן הַנֶּחֱנָקִין: הַמַּכֶּה אָבִיו וְאִמּוֹ, וְגוֹנֵב נֶפֶשׁ מִיִּשְׂרָאֵל, וְזָקֵן מַמְרֵא עַל פִּי בֵית דִּין, וּנְבִיא הַשֶּׁקֶר, וְהַמִּתְנַבֵּא בְּשֵׁם עֲבוֹדָה זָרָה, וְהַבָּא עַל אֵשֶׁת אִישׁ, וְזוֹמְמֵי בַת כֹּהֵן, וּבוֹעֲלָהּ.

הַמַּכֶּה אָבִיו וְאִמּוֹ אֵינוֹ חַיָּב עַד שֶׁיַּעֲשֶׂה בָהֶן חַבּוּרָה. זֶה חֹמֶר בַּמְקַלֵּל מִבַּמַּכֶּה —

ר׳ עובדיה מברטנורא

פרק אחד עשר – אלו הן הנחנקין. (א) אלו הן הנחנקין. ממרא על פי בית דין. שמסרב על דברי בית דין הגדול שבלשכת הגזית: **וזוממי בת כהן.** אף על פי שהם באים לחייבה שריפה, אין כדונים אלא במיתה שהיו מחייבים את בועלה שהוא בחנק, כשאר הבא על אשת איש, דכתיב (ויקרא כא, ט) היא באש תשרף, היא ולא בועלה, וזוממיה ילפינן מכאשר זמם לעשות לאחיו (דברים יט, יט), ולא לאחותו: **ובועלה.** לבת כהן כשהיא נשואה, אבל ארוסה, היא ובועלה בסקילה:

יד אברהם

1.

Having delineated in previous chapters the transgressions which incur the other three methods of execution, the *Tanna* now deals with those that earn strangulation. As a general rule, the *Gemara* (84b) states that whenever the Torah mandates execution without indicating which method, the intended method is strangulation.

אֵלּוּ הֵן הַנֶּחֱנָקִין: — *These are the ones who are strangled:*

[The mishnah first specifies the transgressions which call for strangulation and then discusses each one separately.]

הַמַּכֶּה אָבִיו וְאִמּוֹ, — *One who strikes his father or mother,*

Such an act incurs the death penalty, as stated in the Torah (*Ex.* 21:15).

וְגוֹנֵב נֶפֶשׁ מִיִּשְׂרָאֵל, — *one who kidnaps a Jew,*

One who kidnaps another Jew and sells him receives the death penalty (ibid. v. 16).

וְזָקֵן מַמְרֵא עַל פִּי בֵית דִּין, — *an elder who rebels against the word of the court,*

This refers to a sage who has received *semichah* (see 1:3) (*Rambam Comm.*), who refuses to accept a ruling of the High Court and continues to rule according to his own dissenting view (*Rav*). The Torah accorded honor to the High Court and declared their rulings to be binding; once they issue a ruling, it must be followed by all judges. The penalty for willful refusal on the part of a judge to follow their ruling in subsequent judicial decisions is death (see mishnayos 2-4). Even if the High Court is willing to waive its honor, the penalty applies, so as to limit disagreement in Torah practice (*Rambam Comm., Hil. Mamrim* 3:4). His penalty is specified by the Torah (*Deut.* 17:12).

וּנְבִיא הַשֶּׁקֶר, — *a false prophet,*

I.e., one who claims a prophecy from

11
1

1. These are the ones who are strangled: one who strikes his father or mother, one who kidnaps a Jew, an elder who rebels against the word of the court, a false prophet, one who prophesies in the name of a false god, one who commits adultery, the *zomemim* [witnesses] of the daughter of a *Kohen*, and the man who cohabited with her.

One who strikes his father or mother is not liable unless he makes a bruise. This is the stringency of one who curses over one who strikes —

YAD AVRAHAM

Hashem which he in fact never received; see mishnah 5.

וְהַמִּתְנַבֵּא בְּשֵׁם עֲבוֹדָה זָרָה, — *one who prophesies in the name of a false god,*

I.e., he claims to have received a prophecy not from *Hashem* but from one of the false gods; see mishnah 6.

וְהַבָּא עַל אֵשֶׁת אִישׁ, — *one who commits adultery,*

The death penalty for adultery is specified in *Leviticus* (20:10) for both the adulterer and the adulteress.

וְזוֹמְמֵי בַת כֹּהֵן, — *the zomemim [witnesses] of the daughter of a Kohen,*

As explained above (preface to Chapter 5), the Torah dictates that if false witnesses succeeded in having a person convicted on the basis of their false testimony and they are proven false [by the process of *hazamah;* see ibid.] before the sentence is carried out, the witnesses suffer the very same punishment they sought to impose on their victim (*Deut.* 19:19). Accordingly, if they testified falsely that a woman committed adultery, they are executed. Seemingly, if they testified falsely about the adultery of the daughter of a *Kohen*, their execution should be burning, since that is the form of execution their false testimony would have imposed upon her (see 9:1). Nevertheless, their execution is by strangulation, the same as that of the adulterer (*Rav;* see mishnah 6 for the reason).

וּבוֹעֲלָהּ. — *and the man who cohabited with her.*

[Although the daughter of a *Kohen* is executed for her adultery by burning, the man with whom she committed adultery is executed by strangulation; see mishnah 6.]

This concludes the list of those whose execution is by strangulation. The mishnah now goes back to discuss the details of these crimes.

הַמַּכֶּה אָבִיו וְאִמּוֹ אֵינוֹ חַיָּב עַד שֶׁיַּעֲשֶׂה בָהֶן חַבּוּרָה. — *One who strikes his father or mother is not liable unless he makes a bruise.*

I.e., unless he makes blood come out, whether it breaks through the skin or not (*Meiri*). If he strikes his parents without wounding them, he does not transgress the special prohibition but is guilty of the general prohibition of striking any Jew (*Bava Kamma* 8:3; *Rambam, Mamrim* 5:5).

זֶה חֹמֶר בַּמְקַלֵּל מִבַּמַּכֶּה - — *This is the stringency of one who curses over who one strikes —*

[As we learned above (7:1,8), cursing

סנהדרין
יא/א

שֶׁהַמְקַלֵּל לְאַחַר מִיתָה חַיָּב, וְהַמַּכֶּה לְאַחַר מִיתָה פָּטוּר.

הַגּוֹנֵב נֶפֶשׁ מִיִּשְׂרָאֵל אֵינוֹ חַיָּב עַד שֶׁיַּכְנִיסֶנּוּ לִרְשׁוּתוֹ. רַבִּי יְהוּדָה אוֹמֵר: עַד שֶׁיַּכְנִיסֶנּוּ לִרְשׁוּתוֹ וְיִשְׁתַּמֵּשׁ בּוֹ, שֶׁנֶּאֱמַר: „וְהִתְעַמֶּר בּוֹ וּמְכָרוֹ". הַגּוֹנֵב אֶת בְּנוֹ, רַבִּי יִשְׁמָעֵאל בְּנוֹ שֶׁל רַבִּי יוֹחָנָן בֶּן בְּרוֹקָה מְחַיֵּב, וַחֲכָמִים פּוֹטְרִין.

ר' עובדיה מברטנורא

שהמקלל לאחר מיתה חייב. דכתיב (ויקרא כ, ט) אביו ואמו קלל, וקרא יתירא הוא לרבות לאחר מיתה: **והמכה לאחר מיתה פטור.** דהא לא מחייב עד שיעשה בו חבורה, ואין חבורה לאחר מיתה: **עד שיכניסנו לרשותו.** דכתיב (שמות כא, טז) ונמצא בידו, ואין ידו אלא רשותו, וכן הוא אומר (במדבר כא, כו) ויקח את כל ארצו מידו: **וישתמש בו.** תשמיש שיש בו שוה פרוטה, ותנא קמא מחייב אפילו בתשמיש שהוא פחות משוה פרוטה. והלכה כתנא קמא: **הגונב את בנו.** טעמייהו דרבנן דפטרי, דכתיב (שמות כא, טז) ונמצא בידו, וקרא יתירא הוא, דהא כתיב (דברים כד, ז) כי ימצא איש, אלא למדרש מינה פרט לזה שהוא מצוי. והלכה כחכמים:

יד אברהם

one's parents is also a capital offense, punishable by stoning. Aside from its more severe punishment, cursing one's parents carries with it an inherent stringency over hitting them.]

שֶׁהַמְקַלֵּל לְאַחַר מִיתָה חַיָּב, — *one who curses [his parents] after [their] death is liable,*

[Although they are no longer alive to be shamed by his curse, he is still liable for cursing them.]

This is derived from the otherwise redundant verse (*Lev.* 20:9): *His father and mother he has cursed* (*Rav* from *Gem.* 85b).

וְהַמַּכֶּה לְאַחַר מִיתָה פָּטוּר. — *whereas one who strikes [them] after [their] death is exempt.*

One incurs the death penalty for striking his parent only if he inflicts a bruise, and after death there can be no bruising (*Rav; Rambam Comm.*).

Even if he punctures the skin of the cadaver and thereby causes the blood to come out he is still not liable. The difference between striking and cursing would seem to be that after death the body is merely clay [and therefore the indignities inflicted upon it do not relate to the parent]. A curse, however, is directed toward the soul of a person [the essence of a person] and the soul lives on after death (*Meiri;* cf. *Sefer Chassidim* 576).

הַגּוֹנֵב נֶפֶשׁ מִיִּשְׂרָאֵל אֵינוֹ חַיָּב עַד שֶׁיַּכְנִיסֶנּוּ לִרְשׁוּתוֹ. — *One who kidnaps a Jew is not liable unless he takes him into his possession.*

This is derived from the verse (*Ex.* 21:16): *One who steals a person and sells him, and he was found in his hand, he shall be put to death.* The

11 one who curses [his parents] after [their] death is
1 liable, whereas one who strikes [them] after [their] death is exempt.

One who kidnaps a Jew is not liable unless he takes him into his possession. R' Yehudah says: Unless he brings him into his possession and makes use of him, as it is stated: *And he made use of him and sold him.* [If] one kidnaps his son, R' Yishmael the son of R' Yochanan ben Berokah renders [him] liable, but the Sages exempt [him].

YAD AVRAHAM

halachic sense of the phrase *in his hand* implies in his legal possession [by the standards which generally apply to property] (*Rav* from *Mechilta* ibid.).

Therefore, he is not liable for kidnapping unless he removes the victim from his property and takes him into his own (*Gem.* 85b; *Rambam, Geneivah* 9:2).[1]

רַבִּי יְהוּדָה אוֹמֵר: עַד שֶׁיַּכְנִיסֶנּוּ לִרְשׁוּתוֹ וְיִשְׁתַּמֵּשׁ בּוֹ, שֶׁנֶּאֱמַר: ,,וְהִתְעַמֶּר בּוֹ וּמְכָרוֹ״. — *R' Yehudah says: Unless he brings him into his possession and makes use of him, as it is stated* (*Deut.* 24:7): *"And he made use of him and sold him."*

[Thus, in order to incur the death penalty, he must kidnap him, take him into his possession, put him to work, and then sell him.]

The *Gemara* (85b) explains that the anonymous first *Tanna* also agrees that he must put him to work. The subject of their dispute is one who uses him for work which does not equal the value of a *perutah;* the first *Tanna* maintains that he is nevertheless liable whereas R' Yehudah exempts him (*Rav*). The halachah follows the view of the first *Tanna* (*Rav; Rambam, Hil. Geneivah* 9:2).

הַגּוֹנֵב אֶת בְּנוֹ, רַבִּי יִשְׁמָעֵאל בְּנוֹ שֶׁל רַבִּי יוֹחָנָן בֶּן בְּרוֹקָה מְחַיֵּב, וַחֲכָמִים פּוֹטְרִין. — *[If] one kidnaps his son, R' Yishmael the son of R' Yochanan ben Berokah renders [him] liable, but the Sages exempt [him].*

The Sages maintain that the phrase cited above, *and he is found in his hand,* is superfluous, since this law is also stated elsewhere (*Deut.* 24:7). Therefore, they interpret the verse to indicate that only a person who is to be found in his hand (possession) through kidnapping renders him liable to the penalty, but not one such as a son who may be expected to be found in the

1. The *Gemara* in *Kesubos* 31b presents a dispute between R' Acha and Ravina whether one who steals movable property from another's possession becomes liable for it by removing it from the owner's property into a public domain, or whether the thief must remove it into an area under his control in order to be liable for the theft (see also *Tos.* ibid. s.v. ברשות הרבים נמי קנה). *Minchas Chinuch* 36 discusses whether the dispute applies to liability for kidnapping as well.

גָּנַב מִי שֶׁחֶצְיוֹ עֶבֶד וְחֶצְיוֹ בֶּן חוֹרִין, רַבִּי יְהוּדָה מְחַיֵּב, וַחֲכָמִים פּוֹטְרִין.

[ב] **זָקֵן** מַמְרֵא עַל פִּי בֵית דִּין, שֶׁנֶּאֱמַר: „כִּי יִפָּלֵא מִמְּךָ דָבָר לַמִּשְׁפָּט וגו׳". שְׁלֹשָׁה בָתֵּי דִינִין הָיוּ שָׁם: אֶחָד יוֹשֵׁב

ר׳ עובדיה מברטנורא

רבי יהודה מחייב. דכתיב (שם) מאחיו מבני ישראל, מאחיו למעוטי עבדים, מבני ישראל, אי כתב בני ישראל הוה ממעטינן מי שחציו עבד וחציו בן חורין, השתא דכתיב מבני ישראל, מיעוטא אחרינא, ואין מיעוט אחר מיעוט אלא לרבות, ורבנן סברי, מאחיו לאו למעוטי עבדים, דהא אחים הם במצות, אלא, בני ישראל למעוטי עבדים, מבני ישראל, למעוטי מי שחציו עבד וחציו בן חורין. והלכה כחכמים: (ב) **שלשה בתי דינין היו שם.** בירושלים דמשתעי בה קרא (דברים יז, ח) וקמת ועלית:

יד אברהם

kidnappers's domain at any time (*Rav* from *Gem.* 86a).

The halachah follows the view of the Sages (*Rav; Rambam, Geneivah* 9:2). The same applies to one who kidnaps his younger brother, or anyone who is part of his household (*Rambam, Geneivah* 9:5).

גָּנַב מִי שֶׁחֶצְיוֹ עֶבֶד וְחֶצְיוֹ בֶּן חוֹרִין, — *[If] he kidnapped someone who was half slave and half free,*

[This situation comes to pass when a slave was owned by two partners and one of them emancipated his share, leaving the slave part free and part slave. The death penalty for kidnapping does not apply to kidnapping a slave. However, this person is part freeman — which may render his kidnapper liable.]

רַבִּי יְהוּדָה מְחַיֵּב, וַחֲכָמִים פּוֹטְרִין. — *R' Yehudah renders [him] liable, but the Sages exempt [him].*

The Torah specifies the victim of the kidnapping as being *from among his brothers from the Children of Israel* (*Deut.* ibid.). According to R' Yehudah, the term *his brothers* excludes a slave, and the additional phrase *the Children of Israel* would thus be sufficient to exclude a half-slave. Therefore, the extra "from" is an unnecessary exclusion, which, according to the rules of exegesis, is understood to add rather than exclude. The Sages, however, contend that a slave would not be excluded from the phrase *his brothers.* Therefore, the words *the Children of Israel* exclude a full slave and the extra "from" excludes a half-slave.

The halachah follows the view of the Sages (*Rav; Rambam, Geneivah* 9:6).

2.

The mishnah now considers the details of the third of the transgressions punishable by strangulation — the sage who rebels against the ruling of the High Court.

[If] he kidnapped someone who was half slave and half free, R' Yehudah renders [him] liable, but the Sages exempt [him].

2. **A** sage who rebels against the word of the court, as it is stated: *If there shall arise a matter too difficult for you to judge, etc.* There were three courts there: one sat

YAD AVRAHAM

זָקֵן מַמְרֵא עַל פִּי בֵית דִּין, שֶׁנֶּאֱמַר (שם יז): ,,כִּי יִפָּלֵא מִמְּךָ דָבָר לַמִּשְׁפָּט וְגוֹ׳״. — *A sage who rebels against the word of the court, as it is stated (Deut. 17:8): "If there shall arise a matter too difficult for you to judge, etc."*

This is the introductory verse of the passage dealing with the rebellious sage.

The full text of the passage reads: כִּי יִפָּלֵא מִמְּךָ דָבָר לַמִּשְׁפָּט בֵּין־דָּם לְדָם בֵּין־דִּין לְדִין וּבֵין נֶגַע לָנֶגַע דִּבְרֵי רִיבֹת בִּשְׁעָרֶיךָ וְקַמְתָּ וְעָלִיתָ אֶל־הַמָּקוֹם אֲשֶׁר יִבְחַר ה׳ אֱלֹקֶיךָ בּוֹ: וּבָאתָ אֶל־הַכֹּהֲנִים הַלְוִיִּם וְאֶל־הַשֹּׁפֵט אֲשֶׁר יִהְיֶה בַּיָּמִים הָהֵם וְדָרַשְׁתָּ וְהִגִּידוּ לְךָ אֵת דְּבַר הַמִּשְׁפָּט: וְעָשִׂיתָ עַל־פִּי הַדָּבָר אֲשֶׁר יַגִּידוּ לְךָ מִן־הַמָּקוֹם הַהוּא אֲשֶׁר יִבְחַר ה׳ וְשָׁמַרְתָּ לַעֲשׂוֹת כְּכֹל אֲשֶׁר יוֹרוּךָ: עַל־פִּי הַתּוֹרָה אֲשֶׁר יוֹרוּךָ וְעַל־הַמִּשְׁפָּט אֲשֶׁר־יֹאמְרוּ לְךָ תַּעֲשֶׂה לֹא תָסוּר מִן־הַדָּבָר אֲשֶׁר־יַגִּידוּ לְךָ יָמִין וּשְׂמֹאל: וְהָאִישׁ אֲשֶׁר־יַעֲשֶׂה בְזָדוֹן לְבִלְתִּי שְׁמֹעַ אֶל־הַכֹּהֵן הָעֹמֵד לְשָׁרֶת שָׁם אֶת־ה׳ אֱלֹקֶיךָ אוֹ אֶל־הַשֹּׁפֵט וּמֵת הָאִישׁ הַהוּא וּבִעַרְתָּ הָרָע מִיִּשְׂרָאֵל: וְכָל־הָעָם יִשְׁמְעוּ וְיִרָאוּ וְלֹא יְזִידוּן עוֹד: — *(8) If there shall arise a matter too difficult for you to judge, between blood and blood, between verdict and verdict, or between plague and plague, matters of dispute within your gates; you shall rise up and ascend to the place that HASHEM your God shall choose. (9) And you shall come to the Kohanim, the Leviim, and to the judge who will be in those days; and you shall inquire and they shall tell you the word of the judgment. (10) And you shall do according to the word which they tell you from that place that HASHEM shall choose; and you shall be careful to do according to everything that they will teach you. (11) According to the Torah that they will teach you and by the judgment that they will tell you, you shall do; you shall not deviate from the word that they will tell you, right or left. (12) But the man who shall act willfully, refusing to listen to the Kohen who stands there to serve HASHEM your God, or to the judge; that man shall die and you shall destroy the evil from Israel. (13) And the entire people shall hear and fear, and not act willfully anymore.*

[As the entire passage makes clear, the liability is for rebelling against an explicit ruling of the High Court. As the mishnah will now explain, the passage refers to a sage who submits a difficult matter of law to the High Court for a ruling and then refuses to accept that ruling.]

שְׁלֹשָׁה בָתֵּי דִינִין הָיוּ שָׁם: — *There were three courts there:*

[There was a hierarchy of three courts] in Jerusalem, the chosen place referred to in the verse (*Rav*). [When a question of law was brought to Jerusalem for a definitive ruling, it had

סנהדרין
יא/ב

עַל פֶּתַח הַר הַבַּיִת; וְאֶחָד יוֹשֵׁב עַל פֶּתַח הָעֲזָרָה; וְאֶחָד יוֹשֵׁב בְּלִשְׁכַּת הַגָּזִית. בָּאִים לָזֶה שֶׁעַל פֶּתַח הַר הַבַּיִת, וְאוֹמֵר, „כָּךְ דָּרַשְׁתִּי וְכָךְ דָּרְשׁוּ חֲבֵרַי, כָּךְ לִמַּדְתִּי וְכָךְ לִמְּדוּ חֲבֵרַי". אִם שָׁמְעוּ, אוֹמְרִים לָהֶם. וְאִם לָאו, בָּאִין לָהֶן לְאוֹתָן שֶׁעַל פֶּתַח הָעֲזָרָה, וְאוֹמֵר, „כָּךְ דָּרַשְׁתִּי וְכָךְ דָּרְשׁוּ חֲבֵרַי; כָּךְ לִמַּדְתִּי וְכָךְ לִמְּדוּ חֲבֵרַי". אִם שָׁמְעוּ, אוֹמְרִים לָהֶם. וְאִם לָאו, אֵלּוּ וָאֵלּוּ בָּאִים לְבֵית דִּין הַגָּדוֹל שֶׁבְּלִשְׁכַּת הַגָּזִית,

ר׳ עובדיה מברטנורא

אחד יושב על פתח הר הבית. הוא שער מזרחי שלפנים מן החיל, לפני עזרת נשים: **ואחד יושב.** למעלה הימנו, כשעברו עזרת נשים ובאים לפתח עזרת ישראל: **ואחד יושב בלשכת הגזית.** שהיא בנויה בתוך העזרה, חציה בקדש וחציה בחול: **באים לזה שעל פתח הר הבית.** זקן זה שהורה בעירו ונחלקו בית דין שבעירו עליו והזקיקן הכתוב לעלות לירושלים, באים הוא ובית דין שבעירו לזה בית דין שעל פתח הר הבית, שהרי בו פוגעים תחלה:

יד אברהם

to proceed through these courts to arrive before the High Court (the third of the three courts).]

אֶחָד יוֹשֵׁב עַל פֶּתַח הַר הַבַּיִת — *one sat at the entrance to the Temple Mount;*

This refers not to the entrances at the foot of the Temple Mount but to the eastern gate of the Women's Courtyard (*Rav; Rashi*), the gate by which one entered and exited the actual Temple structure. It may be referred to as the entrance to the Temple Mount because it is through this gate that one entered the Temple Mount area on exiting the actual Temple structure. Thus, it was the interior entrance to the Temple Mount (*Tos. Yom Tov*). *Rambam,* however, nowhere makes this distinction (see *Hil. Mamrim* 1:4, 3:8, *Hil. Sanhedrin* 1:3) but refers to the location of this court simply as at the entrance of the Temple Mount [indicating that in his view it met at the foot of the Temple Mount] (*Tos. Yom Tov; see Tif. Yis.*).

וְאֶחָד יוֹשֵׁב עַל פֶּתַח הָעֲזָרָה; — *one sat at the entrance to the Courtyard;*

I.e., by the gate between the Women's Courtyard and the main Temple Courtyard (*Rav; Rashi*). Both of these courts consisted of twenty-three judges (*Meiri*).

וְאֶחָד יוֹשֵׁב בְּלִשְׁכַּת הַגָּזִית. — *and one sat in the Chamber of Hewn Stone.*

This was a room built into the wall of the main courtyard to the right (when entering) of the gate. It was half within the sanctified area and half outside of it (*Rav*). Here sat the Great Sanhedrin of seventy-one judges (*Meiri*).

בָּאִים לָזֶה שֶׁעַל פֶּתַח הַר הַבַּיִת, — *They come to the one at the entrance to the Temple Mount,*

If a sage of a local sanhedrin of

at the entrance to the Temple Mount; one sat at the entrance to the Courtyard; and one sat in the Chamber of Hewn Stone. They come to the one at the entrance to the Temple Mount, where he says, "Thus I have expounded and thus my colleagues have expounded; thus I have taught and thus my colleagues have taught." If they have heard, they tell them. If not, they come to those at the entrance to the Courtyard, where he says, "Thus I have expounded and thus my colleagues have taught." If they have heard, they tell them. If not, they all come to the High Court in the Chamber of the Hewn Stone,

YAD AVRAHAM

twenty-three ruled on a point of Torah law, and his ruling was disputed by the other members of the court of that town, they all come together to Jerusalem to resolve the matter (*Rav; Rashi*).

וְאוֹמֵר, כָּךְ דָּרַשְׁתִּי וְכָךְ דָּרְשׁוּ חֲבֵרַי, כָּךְ לִמַּדְתִּי וְכָךְ לִמְּדוּ חֲבֵרָי. — *where he says, "Thus I have expounded and thus my colleagues have expounded; thus I have taught and thus my colleagues have taught."*

[He relates the dispute between himself and his colleagues, and the reasons for their respective positions,] whether these had been first propounded in public lectures or private study with disciples (*Tos. Yom Tov*).

אִם שָׁמְעוּ, אוֹמְרִים לָהֶם. — *if they have heard, they tell them.*

If the judges know the correct ruling for this matter, they repeat it to the disputants. However, if they have no tradition on the matter their own view is not binding on the sages who come to ask (*Rambam Comm.*; see *Tos. Yom Tov*).

Another interpretation is as follows: *If they* [the disputants] *agree to hear* [i.e., abide by] *the ruling of this court, they* [the court] *tell them* their view; otherwise they need not bother ruling (*Meiri; Rambam, Hil. Mamrim* 3:8 as explained by *Kesef Mishneh; Tos. Yom Tov*).

וְאִם לָאו, בָּאִין לָהֶן לְאוֹתָן שֶׁעַל פֶּתַח הָעֲזָרָה, וְאוֹמֵר, כָּךְ דָּרַשְׁתִּי וְכָךְ דָּרְשׁוּ חֲבֵרַי; כָּךְ לִמַּדְתִּי וְכָךְ לִמְּדוּ חֲבֵרָי. — *If not, they come to those at the entrance to the Courtyard, where he says, "Thus I have expounded and thus my colleagues have expounded; thus I have taught and thus my colleagues have taught."*

If the first court does not know, or their view is not accepted, they go on to the second court and repeat the procedure (*Meiri*; see above).

אִם שָׁמְעוּ, אוֹמְרִים לָהֶם. וְאִם לָאו, אֵלּוּ וָאֵלּוּ בָּאִים לְבֵית דִּין הַגָּדוֹל שֶׁבְּלִשְׁכַּת הַגָּזִית, — *If they have heard, they tell them. If not, they all come to the High Court in the Chamber of Hewn Stone,*

Both the disputing sages and the members of the courts to which the issue was brought come before the

שֶׁמִּמֶּנּוּ יוֹצֵאת תּוֹרָה לְכָל יִשְׂרָאֵל, שֶׁנֶּאֱמַר: ,,מִן הַמָּקוֹם הַהוּא אֲשֶׁר יִבְחַר ה׳״. חָזַר לְעִירוֹ וְשָׁנָה וְלִמֵּד כְּדֶרֶךְ שֶׁהָיָה לָמֵד, פָּטוּר; וְאִם הוֹרָה לַעֲשׂוֹת, חַיָּב; שֶׁנֶּאֱמַר: ,,וְהָאִישׁ אֲשֶׁר יַעֲשֶׂה בְזָדוֹן״ — אֵינוֹ חַיָּב עַד שֶׁיּוֹרֶה לַעֲשׂוֹת. תַּלְמִיד שֶׁהוֹרָה לַעֲשׂוֹת פָּטוּר; נִמְצָא חֻמְרוֹ קֻלּוֹ.

ר׳ עובדיה מברטנורא

תלמיד שהורה לעשות. תלמיד שלא הגיע להוראה ונחלק על בית דין שבעירו ובאו לבית דין הגדול ושאלו וחזר לעירו והורה כבתחלה, פטור, שאין להם לסמוך על הוראתו, והתורה לא חייבה אלא מופלא ומומחה לבית דין, כדילפינן מכי יפלא ממך, במופלא שבבית דין הכתוב מדבר: **נמצא חומרו קולו.** חומר העבירה שעבר והורה אף על פי שלא הגיע להוראה מוסף על ההמראה שהמרה על פי בית דין, היא נעשית לו קולא לפוטרו מן המיתה, שאם היה זקן שהגיע להוראה והמרה על פי בית דין היה חייב מיתה:

יד אברהם

High Court to receive a final ruling on the matter (*Tos. Yom Tov*).

They do not bring the matter to them immediately, because the High court would be overloaded (*Tif. Yis.*).

שֶׁמִּמֶּנּוּ יוֹצֵאת תּוֹרָה לְכָל יִשְׂרָאֵל, — *from where Torah goes forth to all Israel,*

This court is the final authority in interpreting the law, and if they have no tradition on the matter, they decide it by process of derivation and comparison (*Rambam Comm.*).

שֶׁנֶּאֱמַר (שם): ״מִן הַמָּקוֹם הַהוּא אֲשֶׁר יִבְחַר ה׳״. — *as it is stated* (*Deut.* 17:10): *"From that place that Hashem shall choose."*

[The verse makes clear that the court empowered to render final decisions on matters of Torah law should meet in the place specially chosen by *Hashem* — i.e., the Temple.]

חָזַר לְעִירוֹ וְשָׁנָה וְלִמֵּד כְּדֶרֶךְ שֶׁהָיָה לָמֵד, פָּטוּר; וְאִם הוֹרָה לַעֲשׂוֹת, חַיָּב; שֶׁנֶּאֱמַר (שם): ,,וְהָאִישׁ אֲשֶׁר יַעֲשֶׂה בְזָדוֹן - אֵינוֹ חַיָּב עַד שֶׁיּוֹרֶה לַעֲשׂוֹת. — *[If] he returned to his town and continued to teach* (lit., *repeated and taught*) *in the same manner as before, he is exempt; but if he ruled that it be done* (lit., *to act*), *he is liable; as it is stated* (ibid. v. 12): *"But the man who will act willfully" — he is not liable until he rules that it be done.*

I.e., if he continued teaching that the law follows his previously held position, he is exempt from punishment as a rebellious sage, as long as he does not issue a ruling to this effect in regard to some proposed action. If he explicitly ruled to others to act in accordance with his views, he is put to death (*Meiri*).

Since the verse states that the penalty is for one who *acts willfully*, it is clear that it refers to the judge who willfully ignores the ruling he received from the High Court, not to the person who acts on the rebel judge's ruling — since the latter is not acting willfully, but faithfully following the judge whose opinion he

from where Torah goes forth to all Israel, as it is stated: *From that place that HASHEM shall choose.* [If] he returned to his town and continued to teach in the same manner as before, he is exempt; but if he ruled that it be done, he is liable; as it is stated: *But the man who will act willfully* — he is not liable until he rules that it be done. A disciple who ruled that it be done is exempt; thus his stringency is his leniency.

YAD AVRAHAM

sought. Accordingly, the verse's reference to *acting* willfully (rather than *ruling* willfully) is understood to teach that the ruling must be in regard to a course of action, not merely an abstract teaching (*Sifrei* ibid. as explained by *Malbim*).

The *Gemara* (88b) states that he is liable only if he ruled that others act according to his view and they acted. However, *Rambam* (*Hil. Mamrim* 3:8) cites the mishnah as stated, that the ruling alone is sufficient for punishment. This is based on *Yerushalmi*, where a dispute to this effect is cited (*Margaliyos HaYam*).

The same applies if he himself acted according to his rejected opinion (*Rambam, Mamrim* 3:8 from *Gem.* 88b). Even if he was not warned by witnesses of the consequences of his act he is nonetheless put to death (ibid.) since he has already been forewarned by the High Court (*Rashi* ibid.). Rather, he is treated in the same fashion as one who instigates others to idolatry [see above, 7:10] (*Meiri*).

תַּלְמִיד שֶׁהוֹרָה לַעֲשׂוֹת, פָּטוּר, — *A disciple who ruled that it be done is exempt;*

If a disciple who has not yet been granted the authority to rule disputes the ruling of the court of his town and brings the case to the High Court, he does not achieve the status of a rebellious sage even if he later rules against their decision, because his ruling has no official status in any case and is therefore not included in the laws of this passage (*Rav*). This is derived from the words כִּי יִפָּלֵא מִמְּךָ, *If there shall arise* [a matter] *too difficult for you,* which the *Gemara* (87a) interprets to indicate that the passage is discussing a מוּפְלָא שֶׁבְּבֵית דִין, *an expert judge* (*Rav*). This is inferred by the emphasis on the difficulty of the case — implying that the judge in question is confused only because it is a truly difficult issue, and not because he has not yet completed his education and therefore lacks full knowledge of the law in general (*Rambam Comm.*).

נִמְצָא חֻמְרוֹ קֻלּוֹ. — *thus his stringency is his leniency.*

The same factor that makes his misdeed in ruling in halachic matters so severe — viz., his lack of proper qualification to render such rulings — is the factor that saves him from punishment as a rebellious sage (*Rav; Rambam Comm.*).

[ג] **חֹמֶר** בְּדִבְרֵי סוֹפְרִים מִדִּבְרֵי תוֹרָה. הָאוֹמֵר אֵין תְּפִלִּין — כְּדֵי לַעֲבוֹר עַל דִּבְרֵי תוֹרָה — פָּטוּר. חָמֵשׁ טוֹטָפוֹת — לְהוֹסִיף עַל דִּבְרֵי סוֹפְרִים — חַיָּב.

[ד] **אֵין** מְמִיתִין אוֹתוֹ לֹא בְּבֵית דִּין שֶׁבְּעִירוֹ וְלֹא בְּבֵית דִּין שֶׁבְּיַבְנֶה.

ר׳ עובדיה מברטנורא

(ג) **האומר אין תפילין.** פטור, שאין זו הוראה, דזיל קרי בי רב הוא: **חמש טוטפות.** יש הוראה, ואף על פי שאין דבר זה אלא להוסיף על דברי סופרים, חייב, שבמדרש סופרים, [לטטפת לטטפת] לטוטפת כתיב, הרי כאן ארבע פרשיות: (ד) **ולא בבית דין שביבנה.** שאלו לבית דין שבלשכת הגזית, ואמרו לו, וחזר לעירו ושהה שם ימים רבים עד שגלתה סנהדרי גדולה ליבנה, ואחר כך הורה כבתחלה, אין ממיתין אותו ביבנה, אף על פי שסנהדרי גדולה שם, ואף על פי שעדיין הבית קיים, כיון שסנהדרי גדולה אינה יושבת במקומה בלשכת הגזית:

יד אברהם

3.

חֹמֶר בְּדִבְרֵי סוֹפְרִים מִדִּבְרֵי תוֹרָה. — *There is a greater stringency attached to the words of the scribes than to the words of the Torah.*

The laws of the Torah which require the interpretation of the Sages in order to be properly understood are — in the sense described below — treated with greater stringency than those which are stated explicitly (*Tos. Yom Tov*).

הָאוֹמֵר אֵין תְּפִלִּין - כְּדֵי לַעֲבוֹר עַל דִּבְרֵי תוֹרָה - — *[If] one says there is no [mitzvah of] tefillin — in order to transgress the words of the Torah —*

I.e., he did not deny the Torah's obligation of the *mitzvah* of *tefillin*, but rather ruled that one should not comply with it (*Rambam Comm.*).

פָּטוּר. — *he is exempt.*

He is exempt from the punishment as a rebellious sage because this is such an obvious distortion that it cannot be viewed as a ruling of Torah law whatsoever (*Rav; Rashi;* cf. *Rambam Comm.*). If he denies the validity of the *mitzvah* itself he is a heretic who denies the Torah and he is put to death (*Rambam Comm.*) in accordance with the dictum (*Avodah Zarah* 26b) that a heretic may be thrown into a pit [to die] and may not be rescued [if he should fall on his own] (*Tos. Yom Tov*).

חָמֵשׁ טוֹטָפוֹת - לְהוֹסִיף עַל דִּבְרֵי סוֹפְרִים - חַיָּב. — *[If he says] there are five compartments [to tefillin] — to add to the words of the scribes — he is liable.*

The number of compartments in the *tefillin* box is not stated explicitly in the Torah (*Tos. Yom Tov*) — thus a ruling by a sage that there should be five instead of four is considered a legal (albeit incorrect) ruling (*Rav*). Nevertheless, since the tradition has been handed from the scribes, who received it from earlier generations [going back to Moses], that the intent of the verses is that *tefillin* are

3. There is a greater stringency attached to the words of the scribes than to the words of the Torah. [If] one says there is no [*mitzvah* of] *tefillin* — in order to transgress the words of the Torah — he is exempt. [If he says] there are five compartments [to *tefillin*] — to add to the words of the scribes — he is liable.

4. They do not execute him in the court of his town nor in the court at Yavneh.

YAD AVRAHAM

composed of four compartments (*Tos. Yom Tov*), and indeed they showed that this may be derived from Scripture (*Rav*), one who instructs against this ruling is considered a rebellious sage (*Rav; Rashi*).

The *Gemara* (88b) quotes a statement of R' Oshaya that one is liable as a rebellious sage only if he ruled concerning something which has its roots in Biblical law and is interpreted by the Rabbis, and it is possible to add to it but when adding one detracts. The *Gemara* interprets this to refer to *tefillin*, which require four compartments, and if one adds a fifth compartment afterward he invalidates them.

The basic requisite that the matter be something rooted in Biblical law and interpreted by the Sages is actually the view of R' Yehudah in a *Baraisa* cited earlier (87a). He is quoted there in opposition to R' Meir, who states that one becomes classified as a rebellious elder only if he rules on a matter which, when transgressed intentionally, carries a punishment of *kares*. There is discussion among the commentators as to whether R' Yehudah means to limit the scope of this law — i.e., even among matters calling for *kares*, only those which are rooted in Biblical law and explained by the Sages are pertinent to the laws of a rebellious sage — or to broaden its scope to include these matters in addition to those bearing a penalty of *kares* (see *Chidushei HaRan*).

Rambam (*Hil. Mamrim* 4:2) rules that one becomes a rebellious sage if he rules against the High Court in a matter which carries the penalty of *kares* or is capable of bringing one to a transgression which does — e.g., he contested the intercalation of the year (see 1:2) thereby affecting the time for the prohibition against eating *chametz* on *Pesach*, whose penalty is *kares*. In addition, he states (3) that a law was handed down from Sinai that one who rules to add a fifth compartment to *tefillin* is also judged as a rebellious elder (cf. *Ravad; Kesef Mishneh; Lechem Mishneh* ad loc.).

4.

אֵין מְמִיתִין אוֹתוֹ לֹא בְּבֵית דִּין שֶׁבְּעִירוֹ — *They do not execute him in the court of his town*

A sage who continues to rule in accordance with his view even after the High Court has ruled otherwise is tried and sentenced in the court of his own town. However, they are not permitted to carry out that death sentence themselves (*Meiri*).

וְלֹא בְּבֵית דִּין שֶׁבְּיַבְנֶה. — *nor in the court at Yavneh.*

If he received the ruling of the High Court when it was still in Jerusalem,

אֶלָּא מַעֲלִין אוֹתוֹ לְבֵית דִּין הַגָּדוֹל שֶׁבִּירוּשָׁלַיִם, וּמְשַׁמְּרִין אוֹתוֹ עַד הָרֶגֶל, וּמְמִיתִין אוֹתוֹ בָּרֶגֶל, שֶׁנֶּאֱמַר: „וְכָל הָעָם יִשְׁמְעוּ וְיִרָאוּ וְלֹא יְזִידוּן עוֹד״; דִּבְרֵי רַבִּי עֲקִיבָא. רַבִּי יְהוּדָה אוֹמֵר: אֵין מְעַנִּין אֶת דִּינוֹ שֶׁל זֶה. אֶלָּא מְמִיתִין אוֹתוֹ מִיָּד וְכוֹתְבִין וְשׁוֹלְחִין שְׁלוּחִים בְּכָל הַמְּקוֹמוֹת „אִישׁ פְּלוֹנִי בֶּן אִישׁ פְּלוֹנִי נִתְחַיֵּב מִיתָה בְּבֵית דִּין״.

[ה] **נְבִיא** הַשֶּׁקֶר — הַמִּתְנַבֵּא עַל מַה שֶּׁלֹּא

ר׳ עובדיה מברטנורא

(ה) מה שלא שמע. מה שלא נאמר בנבואה לשום נביא בעולם, ומה שנאמר לחברו ולא לו, ושמעה מפי חבירו ובא ואמר שנאמרה לו, שני אלו נביאי השקר הם, ומיתתן בחנק, דכתיב

יד אברהם

but did not defy their ruling until after they were exiled to Yavneh [i.e., by the Romans, at the destruction of the Second Temple], he can no longer be put to death, because the authority to execute a rebellious sage is restricted to a High Court sitting in Jerusalem (*Rav; Rashi*).

Tosafos reject this interpretation because the *Gemara* (41a) states that from the time the Sanhedrin left its place in the Temple forty years before the destruction, capital cases ceased to be tried. Thus, he could not be executed even in Jerusalem during that era. They maintain therefore that the mishnah refers to one who actually defied the ruling of the High Court and was convicted of this crime while they were still in Jerusalem, but they were exiled before he could be executed. [Thus, as long as they were in Jerusalem, he could be executed even though new capital cases were no longer being tried.]

According to *Rashi,* that which the mishnah states below — that he is brought to Jerusalem and executed during the festival — refers back to the first case of one who was tried by the court of his town. In the second case of the mishnah, once the Sanhedrin was exiled to Yavneh there was no longer a court in the *Lishkas HaGazis* to which to be brought (*Tos. Yom Tov*).

אֶלָּא מַעֲלִין אוֹתוֹ לְבֵית דִּין הַגָּדוֹל שֶׁבִּירוּשָׁלַיִם, — *Rather, they bring him up to the High Court in Jerusalem*

He may only be executed by the High Court sitting in the *Lishkas HaGazis* [*Chamber of Hewn Stone*] in the Temple (*Meiri*).

וּמְשַׁמְּרִין אוֹתוֹ עַד הָרֶגֶל, וּמְמִיתִין אוֹתוֹ בָּרֶגֶל, — *and guard him until the festival and execute him during the festival,*

[The rebellious sage was not executed immediately upon his conviction as all other convicts were executed, but he was incarcerated and held until the next festival, at which time he was executed.] The execution was carried out during the intermediate days of the festival. During the primary days [i.e., the first and last days of *Pesach* and *Succos,* as well as the festival of *Shavuos*] executions may not be carried out (*Tif. Yis.*).

שֶׁנֶּאֱמַר: „וְכָל הָעָם יִשְׁמְעוּ וְיִרָאוּ וְלֹא יְזִידוּן עוֹד״; דִּבְרֵי רַבִּי עֲקִיבָא. — *as it is stated*

Rather, they bring him up to the High Court in Jerusalem and guard him until the festival and execute him during the festival, as it is stated: *And the entire nation shall hear and shall fear, and they shall no longer sin willfully;* [these are] the words of R' Akiva. R' Yehudah says: They do not delay this person's judgment. Rather, they execute him immediately and write and send messengers to all places [saying], "So-and-so was sentenced to death by the court."

5. **A** false prophet — [is] one who prophesies concerning that which he did not hear

YAD AVRAHAM

(*Deut.* 17:13): *"And the entire nation shall hear and shall fear, and they shall no longer sin willfully"; [these are] the words of R' Akiva.*

Since the Torah specifies that the entire populace must hear about the execution to instill in them a fear of repeating this transgression, it is necessary to carry out the execution at a time when it will be publicized so that it will serve as a deterrent (*Meleches Shlomo*). Consequently, they postponed the execution until the people gathered in Jerusalem for one of the festivals, and when carrying it out, they proclaimed that "so-and-so is being put to death for such and such a deed" (*Meiri*).

רַבִּי יְהוּדָה אוֹמֵר: אֵין מְעַנִּין אֶת דִּינוֹ שֶׁל זֶה. — *R' Yehudah says: They do not delay this person's judgment.*

Since the Torah specifies only that the masses hear of his execution, not that they should see it, there is no basis for prolonging his agony by delaying his punishment (*Gem.* 89a). [This is the reason why all executions are conducted immediately after the conviction; see above, 6:1.]

אֶלָּא מְמִיתִין אוֹתוֹ מִיָּד וְכוֹתְבִין וְשׁוֹלְחִין שְׁלוּחִים בְּכָל הַמְּקוֹמוֹת „אִישׁ פְּלוֹנִי בֶּן אִישׁ פְּלוֹנִי נִתְחַיֵּב מִיתָה בְּבֵית דִּין". — *Rather, they execute him immediately and write and send messengers to all places [saying], "So-and-so was sentenced to death by the court."*

[It is sufficient for the court to publicize the event in this manner to create the desired effect, and a public proclamation at the time the masses are gathered together is not necessary.] The messengers must also specify the nature of his crime (*Tif. Yis.*; see 6:2).

The halachah follows the view of R' Akiva (*Rambam, Hil. Mamrim* 3:8).

5.

נְבִיא הַשֶּׁקֶר — *A false prophet —*

I.e., one who presents himself falsely as a prophet (*Meiri*).

הַמִּתְנַבֵּא עַל מַה שֶּׁלֹּא שָׁמַע — *[is] one who prophesies concerning that which he did not hear*

שָׁמַע וּמַה שֶּׁלֹּא נֶאֱמַר לוֹ; מִיתָתוֹ בִּידֵי אָדָם.
אֲבָל הַכּוֹבֵשׁ אֶת נְבוּאָתוֹ, וְהַמְוַתֵּר עַל דִּבְרֵי
הַנָּבִיא, וְנָבִיא שֶׁעָבַר עַל דִּבְרֵי עַצְמוֹ — מִיתָתָן
בִּידֵי שָׁמַיִם, שֶׁנֶּאֱמַר: ,,אָנֹכִי אֶדְרֹשׁ מֵעִמּוֹ".

ר' עובדיה מברטנורא

(דברים יח, כ) אַךְ הַנָּבִיא אֲשֶׁר יָזִיד לְדַבֵּר דָּבָר בִּשְׁמִי, זֶה הַמִּתְנַבֵּא מַה שֶּׁלֹּא שָׁמַע מִעוֹלָם, אֲשֶׁר
לֹא צִוִּיתִיו, הָא לְחַבֵרוֹ צִוִּיתִי, זֶה הַמִּתְנַבֵּא מַה שֶּׁלֹּא נֶאֱמַר לוֹ וְנֶאֱמַר לַחֲבֵרוֹ, וּכְתִיב וּמֵת הַנָּבִיא
הַהוּא, וְכָל מִיתָה הָאֲמוּרָה בַּתּוֹרָה סְתָם אֵינָה אֶלָּא חֶנֶק: מִיתָתָן בִּידֵי שָׁמַיִם. דִּכְתִיב (שָׁם שָׁם,
יט) וְהָיָה הָאִישׁ אֲשֶׁר לֹא יִשְׁמַע אֶל דְּבָרַי, קְרֵי בֵיהּ לֹא יִשְׁמַע, וּקְרֵי בֵיהּ לֹא יַשְׁמִיעַ, וּקְרֵי בֵיהּ לֹא
יִשְׁמַע הוּא עַצְמוֹ אֶל דְּבָרַי, הֲרֵי שָׁלָשְׁתָּן בַּכְּלָל, וּכְתִיב (שָׁם) אָנֹכִי אֶדְרֹשׁ מֵעִמּוֹ, בִּידֵי שָׁמַיִם:

יד אברהם

I.e., he proclaims a prophecy which was never given to any prophet (*Rav* from *Gem.* 89a). This assumption may be made if either he predicts the future in his prophecy and it does not come to pass [see *Deut.* 18:21,22],[1] or he declares in the name of God that it is necessary to transgress one of the laws of the Torah (*Margaliyos HaYam* 14).

However, someone who is already accepted as a true prophet may dictate a temporary exception to the commandment of the Toras as long as he does not call for its permanent negation. The classic example of this was Elijah's instruction during his public confrontation with the prophets of Baal at Mt. Carmel (*I Kings* Ch. 13) to build an altar and offer a sacrifice on it, in violation of the prohibition against offering sacrifices outside the Temple in Jerusalem [see *Zevachim* 13:1, 14:8] (*Rambam, Hil. Yesodei HaTorah* 9:3 from *Gem.* 89b, *Yevamos* 90b).

וּמַה שֶּׁלֹּא נֶאֱמַר לוֹ; — *or that which was not said to him;*

He presents as his own a prophecy that was given to another prophet (*Rav* from *Gem.* 89a).

מִיתָתוֹ בִּידֵי אָדָם. — *he is executed at the hands of man.*

[These are the cases cited above for which the punishment is strangulation for the crime of false prophecy.] This is derived from the verse (*Deut.* 18:20): *But the prophet who shall act willfully to speak a matter in My Name which I did not command him to say ...* The phrase *who shall act willfully* refers to one who claims a prophecy which was never stated at all; *which I did not command him* pertains to claiming a prophecy given to another, not to him (ibid.).

אֲבָל הַכּוֹבֵשׁ אֶת נְבוּאָתוֹ, — *But one who suppresses his prophecy,*

He was commanded by God to announce his prophecy and he refused (*Tif. Yis.*).

Although he is not executed by the courts for this, he is nevertheless flogged (*Gem.* 89b). This does not refer to the thirty-nine lashes meted out to one who transgresses a Torah prohibition, since there is no explicit prohibition for this matter. Rather it alludes to the authority of the court to force compliance with the Torah's laws by

1. This is only true of a prophecy concerning something positive. Such a prophecy, once given, is never retracted by God. A prophecy predicting a calamity, however, may be retracted by God if the people repent; see *Jeremiah* 28:7 and *Rashi* ibid.

or that which was not said to him; he is executed at the hands of man. But one who suppresses his prophecy, and one who disregards the words of a prophet, and a prophet who transgresses his own words — are executed at the hand of Heaven, as it is stated: *I shall demand it from him.*

YAD AVRAHAM

flogging someone who refuses to fulfill his obligations until he consents (*Tos.* 89a; cf. *Margaliyos HaYam* to 89b, 3). He is prosecuted on the testimony of fellow prophets who are aware of his prophecy and his suppression of it (*Gem.* 89b).

וְהַמְוַתֵּר עַל דִּבְרֵי הַנָּבִיא, — *and one who disregards the words of a prophet,*

I.e., he was commanded by a prophet to do something but he ignores the command completely (*Rashi*) or does not carry it out meticulously (*Rambam Comm.*).[1]

Not everyone who claims to be a prophet, even if he performs miraculous deeds, is accepted as such. Only one who is known to be wise in Torah and of saintly character and who shows some sign of the gift of prophecy — e.g., he predicts the future and it is borne out — is accepted as a legitimate prophet who must be heeded (*Meiri* to 89b; *Rambam, Hil. Yesodei HaTorah* 7:1,6).

וְנָבִיא שֶׁעָבַר עַל דִּבְרֵי עַצְמוֹ – — *and a prophet who transgresses his own words —*

[A prophet who transgresses a prophecy which was given to him personally also receives the penalty stated below.] As an example of this, the *Gemara* (89b) cites the story of Ado the prophet, as related [without mention of his name] in *I Kings* 13. Ado was commanded by God to go to the temple in Bethel where Yaravam was sacrificing on the altar he had erected there, and to warn Yaravam of the downfall of his royal house. In conjunction with this, he was commanded to refrain from eating or drinking in Bethel. When a person claiming to be a prophet told him to eat there he did so, thus transgressing his own prophecy, and he was killed by a lion shortly thereafter.

[It is possible that this episode is cited to emphasize the unique nature of this prohibition as opposed to the general obligation to heed any prophet. Even if a prophet believes that he was informed of a prophecy which negates his own, that which is transmitted directly to him takes precedence, and if he acts otherwise he is subject to death at the hand of Heaven.]

מִיתָתָן בִּידֵי שָׁמַיִם, שֶׁנֶּאֱמַר: ,,אָנֹכִי אֶדְרֹשׁ מֵעִמּוֹ.״ — *are executed at the hand of Heaven, as it is stated* (*Deut.* 18:19): *"I shall demand it from him."*

All three of these transgressions warrant execution at the hand of

1. *Minchas Chinuch* (516) contends that only one who ridicules the prophecy and transgresses it is included in this category. Otherwise, any transgression of Torah law would carry this penalty since the Torah was transmitted through the prophecy of Moshe. Others explain that only those who are commanded directly by the prophet incur this punishment (*Avodas HaMelech* to *Hil. Yesodei HaTorah* Ch. 9, cited by *Margoliyos HaYam*).

[ו] הַמִּתְנַבֵּא בְּשֵׁם עֲבוֹדָה זָרָה — וְאוֹמֵר ,,כָּךְ אָמְרָה עֲבוֹדָה זָרָה", אֲפִלּוּ כִּוֵּן אֶת הַהֲלָכָה לְטַמֵּא אֶת הַטָּמֵא וּלְטַהֵר אֶת הַטָּהוֹר.

הַבָּא עַל אֵשֶׁת אִישׁ — כֵּיוָן שֶׁנִּכְנְסָה לִרְשׁוּת הַבַּעַל לְנִשּׂוּאִין, אַף עַל פִּי שֶׁלֹּא נִבְעֲלָה, הַבָּא עָלֶיהָ הֲרֵי זֶה בְּחֶנֶק.

ר׳ עובדיה מברטנורא

(ו) **לרשות הבעל.** כגון שמסר האב לשלוחי הבעל ועדיין היא בדרך, תו לא קרינא בה בית אביה:

יד אברהם

also exegetically be interpreted to mean לֹא יַשְׁמִע, *who shall not make heard,* thus referring to one who suppresses his prophecy. It can also be exegetically interpreted as לֹא יִשָּׁמַע, *who shall not be heard,* referring to one who ignores a prophecy commanded to him (*Rav* from *Gem.* 89a).

Heaven, as derived from this verse, which is stated in reference to the previous words: *And the man who will not heed My words, which he* [i.e., the prophet] *shall speak in My Name, I shall demand it from him.* The words לֹא יִשְׁמַע, *who will not heed,* meaning follow the words of the prophet, can

6.

This mishnah concludes the list of those executed by strangulation by defining the legal parameters of the prophet of a strange god, adultery, and the *zomeimim* (false) witnesses of a *Kohen's* daughter and her adulterer.

הַמִּתְנַבֵּא בְּשֵׁם עֲבוֹדָה זָרָה - וְאוֹמֵר ,,כָּךְ אָמְרָה עֲבוֹדָה זָרָה", — *One who prophesies in the name of a strange god — and says, "Thus said the strange god,"*

[One who announces a prophecy in the name of any deity other than the true God — *Hashem* — incurs the death penalty,] as it is stated (*Deut.* 18:20): *and who shall speak in the name of other gods, that prophet shall die* (*Gem.* 89a).

אֲפִלּוּ כִּוֵּן אֶת הַהֲלָכָה לְטַמֵּא אֶת הַטָּמֵא וּלְטַהֵר אֶת הַטָּהוֹר. — *[is liable] even though he conformed with the law to render tamei that which is tamei or to render tahor that which is tahor.*

[Even if the point of the prophecy is in line with the laws of the Torah — for example, prophetically advocating the observance of something as *tamei* which is indeed *tamei* according to Torah law, or the observance of something as *tahor* which is indeed *tahor* — he is liable for proclaiming this as a prophecy from a false god.]

The implication of the mishnah is that a prophecy which conforms with the law should be valid, but is nevertheless punish-

6. One who prophesies in the name of a strange god — and says, "Thus said the strange god," [is liable] even though he conformed with the law to render *tamei* that which is *tamei* or to render *tahor* that which is *tahor*.

One who commits adultery — once she has entered the domain of the husband for marriage, even if she has not [yet] had conjugal relations, one who cohabits with her is strangled.

YAD AVRAHAM

able due to its illegitimate source. It follows that such a prophecy stated in the Name of God is valid. This would seem to contradict the view of *Rambam* (*Yesodei HaTorah* 9:4), who states that one who claims that God commanded him to decide a halachic question in a specific manner is executed as a false prophet, because once the Torah was given to Moses in its entirety, decisions in halachic matters are to be made here on earth and they are not dictated from Heaven through prophecy (*Rashash*). [However, *Rambam's* statement assumedly applies only to one who claims by prophecy to rule on a hitherto undecided issue, whereas the ruling of this mishnah would apply even if he reiterated a ruling already accepted, but did so in the name of a false god.]

הַבָּא עַל אֵשֶׁת אִישׁ - — *One who commits adultery* (lit., *comes upon a man's wife*) —

[As stated previously (7:9), adulterous relations with a betrothed *naarah* (one who has undergone only the *erusin* step in the marital process) are punishable by stoning. This mishnah teaches that once she is a fully married *nesuah* — even if she is still a *naarah* — the punishment is strangulation.]

כֵּיוָן שֶׁנִּכְנְסָה לִרְשׁוּת הַבַּעַל לְנִשּׂוּאִין, אַף עַל פִּי שֶׁלֹּא נִבְעֲלָה, הַבָּא עָלֶיהָ הֲרֵי זֶה בְּחֶנֶק. — *once she has entered the domain of the husband for marriage, even if she has not [yet] had conjugal relations, one who cohabits with her is strangled.*

[The state of betrothal ends, and the state of full marriage begins, as soon as she leaves her father's house and enters her husband's domain for the purpose of marriage. (This is in effect the equivalent of the *chuppah* ceremony performed today — see ArtScroll *Kiddushin*, General Introduction.) Conjugal relations with her husband are not a necessary component in the transition from *erusin* (betrothal) to *nisuin* (full marriage), and she may have the status of a *nesuah* even though she is still a virgin. Having become a *nesuah* (fully married woman), her adultery is punished by strangulation, not stoning.]

Even if she has not yet arrived at the home of her husband, but her father gave her over to his agents who come to escort her, she is considered out of the domain of her father and within that of her husband. Consequently, the punishment for one who commits adultery with her is strangling (*Rav*).

וְזוֹמְמֵי בַת כֹּהֵן וּבוֹעֲלָהּ — שֶׁכָּל הַזּוֹמְמִין מַקְדִּימִין לְאוֹתָהּ מִיתָה חוּץ מִזּוֹמְמֵי בַת כֹּהֵן וּבוֹעֲלָהּ.

ר׳ עובדיה מברטנורא

לאותה מיתה. שהיו מחייבין את הנדון: **ובועלה.** כלומר, וכל הבועלים נדונים כמיתת הנבעלת, חוץ מבועל בת כהן שהיא בשרפה והוא בחנק: נשלמה מסכת סנהדרין

יד אברהם

וְזוֹמְמֵי בַת כֹּהֵן וּבוֹעֲלָהּ — *The zomemim [witnesses] of the daughter of a Kohen and the one who cohabited with her —*

[As explained above (mishnah 1), although she is punished with burning for her adultery (see 9:1), the man with whom she committed adultery is executed by strangulation as would be any other adulterer.[1] Similarly, if witnesses should testify about her adultery and then be proven false by the process of *hazamah,* they are executed by strangulation, not burning.]

שֶׁכָּל הַזּוֹמְמִין מַקְדִּימִין לְאוֹתָהּ מִיתָה — *for all zomemim [witnesses] advance* (lit., *precede*) *to that death*

All witnesses discredited by the process of *hazamah* are sentenced to the same penalty they sought to impose on the subject of their testimony (*Rashi* to 90a from *Deut.* 19:19).

The mishnah uses the term מַקְדִּימִין, literally, *precede,* in order to indicate that although the preferred method of execution is that which they sought to impose, if for some reason that cannot be done, they are executed in any way possible (*Tos.* to *Makkos* 2a).

חוּץ מִזּוֹמְמֵי בַת כֹּהֵן — *except for the zomemim [witnesses] of the daughter of a Kohen*

[The exception to the above rule are the witnesses who testify falsely about the adultery of a *Kohen's* daughter, who are executed by strangulation despite the fact that she would have been burned had the witnesses not been discredited.]

וּבוֹעֲלָהּ. — *and the man who cohabited with her.*

Similarly, the punishment of the man who committed adultery with a *Kohen's* daughter is an exception to the general rule for punishing illicit cohabitation. In all other cases of

1. The mishnah refers to adultery by a fully married *Kohen's* daughter (or a betrothed one who is no longer a *naarah*). As noted above (9:3, s.v. אמרו לו), if she sinned while a betrothed *naarah* she is executed by stoning the same as any other betrothed *naarah,* according to the halachically accepted view that stoning is more severe than burning (the view of the Sages). In such a case her partner in the adultery is also executed by stoning.

The *zomemim* [witnesses] of the daughter of a *Kohen* and the one who cohabited with her — for all *zomeimim* [witnesses] advance to that death except for the *zomemim* [witnesses] of the daughter of a *Kohen* and the man who cohabited with her.

YAD AVRAHAM

forbidden cohabitation, the man and woman are subject to the same punishment. However, if a *Kohen's* daughter commits adultery, she is executed by burning while he is strangled [see above, 9:1] (*Rav; Rashi*).

These two statements are actually interrelated. The reason an exception to the general rule for punishing false witnesses is made in the case of the *zomemim* of a *Kohen's* daughter is because they receive the punishment they would have inflicted on the man rather than that of the woman. This is derived from the verse (*Deut.* 19:19): *And you shall do to him as he plotted to do to his brother* — and not his sister (*Gem.* 90a). [I.e., where their testimony would have affected both a man and a woman, their punishment follows the man's, not the woman's.]

The mishnah mentions the *zomemim* prior to the adulterer, despite the fact that the law of the former is based upon that of the latter, in order to indicate that even in a case in which he is not put to death — e.g., his identity is unknown — the witnesses are strangled rather than burned (*Margaliyos HaYam* to 84b 4).

Others interpret the word וּבוֹעֲלָהּ, *and the one who cohabited with her*, as referring back to the *zomemim* — i.e., the witnesses whose testimony falsely convicted a *Kohen's* daughter and a man for committing adultery together. In this view, only if both the man and the woman were sentenced to death because of false testimony are the witnesses strangled. However, if she only was sentenced, and thus the requirement to do to them as they wished to do their brother is not applicable, they receive her punishment of burning (*Tos. Yom Tov* based on *Rambam, Hil. Eidus* 20:10).[1]

סליק מסכת סנהדרין

1. *Tosafos Yom Tov* also cites *Rashi* as a source for this view. *Rashi* (90a) explains the rule to be that whenever their testimony convicts both a man and a woman of a capital offense, and their punishments differ, they receive that of the man. According to this, the mishnah's mention of the witnesses prior to the adulterer is easily understood, since we are not discussing the punishment of the adulterer himself but only that of the witnesses who testified falsely against him. However, *Rashi* explains the mishnah in the same manner as does *Rav*, that the adulterer is cited as a separate case. Accordingly, it is necessary to explain the order of the mishnah to be due to the need to emphasize the unusual ruling concerning the witnesses, since they receive a lesser punishment than that which they sought to impose [as strangling is less severe than burning] (see *Maharich* to mishnah 1). However, it remains unclear why *Rashi*, who clearly agrees with the *Rambam's* position, did not interpret the mishnah in the same manner as did *Tosafos Yom Tov*.

Glossary

baraisa: statement of a **Tanna** not included in any mishnah but recorded in the **Gemara.**

betrothal: see **erusin.**

betrothed naarah: see **naarah.**

chalitzah: legal process for releasing the widow of a childless man from her *yibum*-bond to her husband's surviving brothers, if they all refuse to marry her (see **yibum**). The formal act involves the widow's taking off the shoe of one of the brothers in the presence of a court (see mishnah 1:3).

Eretz Yisrael: the Land of Israel.

erusin: (1) the first stage of marriage, during which the couple is considered married in most respects, although they may not yet live together as man and wife. During this stage, the adultery prohibition is in effect and, if the couple should decide to break off their relationship, a regular divorce is required. [The commentary has used the word *betrothal* as a synonym for *erusin,* though the legal status of the latter is much greater than that generally associated with betrothal.] The marriage is completed with **nisuin;** see below. (2) the formal act by which the *erusin* stage of marriage is brought into existence [also known as *kiddushin*]. See *Kiddushin* 1:1.

ervah [pl. **arayos**]: any of the twenty-one women Biblically prohibited in marriage to a man by reason of kinship, either through blood or through marriage (see *Leviticus* 18).

Gemara: the section of the Talmud that explains the Mishnah.

halachah: (1) a Torah law; (2) in cases of dispute, the position accepted as definitive by the later authorities and followed in practice; (3) the body of Jewish law.

hazamah: the process by which witnesses are proven false and subject to punishment for testifying falsely. This occurs when other witnesses place the location of the first witnesses someplace other than where they claim to have been in order to have witnessed the event to which they testified. This suffices to discredit the first witnesses entirely and they are punished by being subjected to whatever penalty they sought to impose upon their intended victim. [If the second witnesses merely contradict the first ones, both testimonies are rejected, since the court does not know whom to believe.]

hekdesh: things consecrated to the Temple; such items are considered sanctified and are governed by a set of special laws.

kares: Divinely imposed premature death; the penalty decreed by the Torah for certain classes of transgression.

kesubah: (1) the marriage contract; the agreements made between a man and woman upon their marriage, whose foremost feature is the dower awarded her in the event of their divorce or his death [see General Introduction to ArtScroll *Kesubos*]; (2) the document in which this agreement is recorded.

kinyan [pl. **kinyanim**]: a formal, legal act by which property and certain types of legal rights are acquired. Different types of *kinyanim* are mandated for different kinds of property and rights — see General Introduction to ArtScroll *Bava Basra.*

Kohen [pl. **Kohanim**]: a member of the priestly family descended in the male line from Aaron. The *Kohen* is bound by special laws of sanctity decreed by the Torah, as well as accorded the special priestly duties and privileges associated with the Temple.

Kohen Gadol: High Priest.

Lishkas HaGazis: Chamber of Hewn Stone; the chamber in the Temple in which the Great Sanhedrin convened.

maaser [pl. **maasros**]: tithe; a ten-percent levy on the produce of Eretz Yisrael. Each year the farmer is required to separate two tithes from his crop — *maaser rishon* and either *maaser sheni* or *maaser ani.* **Maaser,** when it appears without any modifier, generally refers to *maaser rishon.*

— **maaser rishon:** [first tithe] is given to a Levite.

— **maaser sheni:** [second tithe] is taken in the first, second, fourth, and fifth years of each seven-year **Shemittah** cycle. It must be brought to Jerusalem and eaten there, or else redeemed for money which is then taken to

Jerusalem and used to buy food to eat there.

— **maaser ani:** [the tithe of the poor] replaces *maaser sheni* in the third and sixth years of the *Shemittah* cycle. [*Shemittah* crops are free of tithes.]

mitzvah: a Biblical or Rabbinic precept.

naarah: a girl of at least twelve years of age on whom two pubic hairs have grown. This marks her coming of age as an adult.

naarus: the state of being a *naarah*. The period of *naarus* lasts six months during which she is treated differently in certain respects by Torah law than other adult women [e.g., in regard to adultery during her betrothal; see 7:1,9].

nisuin: (1) the second and completed stage of marriage; (2) the formal act by which this stage of marriage is brought about; the *chupah* ceremony. Although the modern custom is to perform both parts of the marriage together at the wedding [the giving of the ring corresponds to *erusin*], the custom of earlier days was to separate the two, often by as much as a year. [See General Introduction to ArtScroll *Kiddushin*.]

Rosh Chodesh: the first day of the Jewish month.

Sanhedrin: [cap.] the High Court of Israel; the supreme court consisting of seventy-one judges whose decisions on questions of Torah law were definitive and binding on all courts.

sanhedrin: [l.c.] the courts of twenty-three judges in each city empowered to try capital cases.

semichah: (1) rabbinical ordination empowering one to serve as a judge (see preface to 1:1, comm. 1:3); (2) leaning of hands on the head of a sacrifice prior to its slaughter.

Shemittah/sheviis: the Sabbatical Year, occurring every seventh year, during which the land of Eretz Yisrael may not be cultivated. Various restrictions also apply to any produce which grows wild; see tractate *Sheviis*.

taharah: the state of ritual purity, the absence of **tumah** contamination.

tahor: a person or object which is in a state of *taharah*.

terumah: portion of the crop which must be separated and given to a *Kohen*. Upon separation it attains a state of sanctity which prohibits its being eaten by a non-*Kohen* or a *Kohen* in a state of *tumah*.

tamei: a person or object in a state of *tumah* contamination.

tumah: a legally defined state of contamination [or impurity] inherent in certain people (e.g., a *niddah* [menstruant]) or objects (e.g., a corpse) that under specific conditions can be transmitted to other people or objects. Those in a state of *tumah* are restricted from contact and certain other forms of interactions with sanctified or holy things by a series of intricate and complex laws.

Tanna [pl. Tannaim]: a Sage quoted in the mishnah or in other works of that period (e.g., **baraisa**).

Tanna Kamma: the anonymous first opinion of a mishnah.

yibum: levirate marriage; the marriage prescribed by the Torah between the widow of a childless man and one of his brothers. The widow in this context is known as a *yevamah* and the brother as a *yavam*. See tractate *Yevamos*.

Yovel: Jubilee Year; the year following the completion of seven *shemittah* cycles — thus the fiftieth year.

zomemim: witnesses proven false by the process of *hazamah*.